Speak with Confidence

Speak
with
Confidence

A PRACTICAL GUIDE

NINTH EDITION

Albert J. Vasile
Bunker Hill Community College

PEARSON

Boston | New York | San Francisco
Mexico City | Montreal | Toronto | London | Madrid | Munich | Paris
Hong Kong | Singapore | Tokyo | Cape Town | Sydney

Executive Editor: Karon Bowers
Editorial Assistant: Jennifer Trebby
Marketing Manager: Mandee Eckersley
Production Administrator: Michael Granger
Editorial-Production Service: Omegatype Typography, Inc.
Composition and Prepress Buyer: Linda Cox
Manufacturing Buyer: JoAnne Sweeney
Cover Administrator: Joel Gendron
Interior Design: Carol Somberg
Electronic Composition: Omegatype Typography, Inc.

For related titles and support materials, visit our online catalog at www.ablongman.com.

Between the time Website information is gathered and then published, it is not unusual for some sites to have closed. Also, the transcription of URLs can result in typographical errors. The publisher would appreciate notification where these errors occur so that they may be corrected in subsequent editions.

Library of Congress Cataloging-in-Publication Data

Vasile, Albert J.
   Speak with confidence : a practical guide / Albert J. Vasile. —9th ed.
     p. cm.
   Includes index.
   ISBN 0-205-37800-5
   1. Public speaking. 2. Oral communication. 3. Interpersonal communication.
    I. Title.

PN4129.15.V37 2004
808.5'1—dc21

2003041903

Printed in the United States of America
10 9 8 7 6 5 4 3 2 1 RRD-IN 08   07   06   05   04   03

To the eight most important and most beautiful people in my life—
My wife,
Evelyn
My two kids,
Albie and Wally
And their wives,
Barbara and Patty
And my three grandchildren,
Kaitlyn, Brian, and Kevin

"Uppa"

contents

3   You Don't Have to Say It to Convey It   48

4   You Can Overhear, but You Can't Overlisten   73

5   Make It Clear, Concise, Correct, . . . and Cohesive   91

6   Know Your Listeners and Speak Their Language

111

7   Selecting a Speech Topic and Doing Research

142

8 Putting It All Together 168

9 Delivering Your Speech 196

10 Let's Be Informative 217

chapter 11 Let's Be Persuasive   **239**

chapter 12 Show and Tell . . . Adding Sight to Sound   **275**

13 Saying a Few Words . . . Very Few!   300

14 Let's Meet and Discuss It   322

15 What Do You Say after You Say "Hello"?   **344**

Appendix A: *Speeches to Study*   *368*

Appendix B: *Suggested Speech Topics*   *394*

A Message to You, the Professor, and the Student

It has been almost thirty years since *Speak with Confidence* was first introduced to the publishing world and academia, pioneering a new philosophy and writing style for a basic one-semester speech book. It has evolved, developed, and matured into this Ninth Edition, which incorporates the best of previous editions and also a multitude of new improvements. Through the years, however, the basic philosophy has remained the same:

- Pragmatic information usable immediately
- Anecdotes, cartoons, and historical references that teach valuable speech lessons
- Easy-to-understand language
- A conversational style that speaks *to* students, not *at* students
- Concern for the student by way of encouragement, praise, and support
- Photographs of prominent people and students speaking/communicating

For almost thirty years, *Speak with Confidence* has been adopted by community colleges, business colleges, and four-year colleges and universities all across the United States, and has even been used in several countries in Europe and Asia. Its acceptance is, indeed, heartwarming.

Some Major Improvements and Additions to the Ninth Edition

In every chapter of this Ninth Edition, the language, style, and content have been sharpened in terms of clarity, conciseness, and relevance to student needs. Responding to the ever-increasing number of students from other countries and cultures, including those whose primary language is not English, who take speech courses, the feature, In Other Words (which first appeared in the Seventh Edition) has been greatly expanded. This vocabulary aid, which appears in the margins of many pages throughout the book, includes the meanings of commonly used American idioms, phrases, and expressions. And new to this Ninth Edition, appearing at the end of every chapter, is a feature called Quick Clicks where students may enhance their research or harvest more information about material studied in the chapter simply by visiting various addresses on the Internet.

This edition expands coverage of intercultural/multicultural communication.

New photographs of outstanding communicators are included, and many of the cartoons have been updated or replaced with new ones. As one of the book's trademarks, every chapter contains the most current events that deadlines allow, as well as many classic examples.

This Ninth Edition represents the most ambitious revision effort ever undertaken in the life of this book. I hope that you find it not only educationally enjoyable, but also fun to read.

Specifically, here are some of the major new additions and improvements, by chapter:

Chapter 1: I Just Can't Wait to Start This Course

- A new Vitalize Your Vocabulary section includes foreign words and phrases. There's also new information on shyness, assertiveness, and talk radio.

Chapter 2: Your First Talk: I'd Like to Introduce Myself

- New sections are titled, Be Sure to Use Correct English Grammar and Platform Etiquette. There's also an expanded section on alleviating nervousness.

Chapter 3: You Don't Have to Say It to Convey It

- A new section on color has been added, and the section on touching has been expanded.

Chapter 4: You Can Overhear, but You Can't Overlisten

- This chapter contains new information directed to international students on the importance of listening and eye contact. There is also new material on To Better Understand and Speak a New Language.

Chapter 6: Know Your Listeners and Speak Their Language

- New sections on ethnocentrism, cultural respect, and political correctness have been added. There are more examples of concrete and abstract words, and the section on nonsexist language has been expanded.

Chapter 7: Selecting a Speech Topic and Doing Research

- This chapter has been extensively updated to reflect computer and Internet use. It features new websites and significant new technological updating on researching and citing sources.

Chapter 8: Putting It All Together

- Expanded information is provided on outlining.

Chapter 9: Delivering Your Speech

- Expanded material is provided on using note cards, and the chapter covers cultures where memorization is an accepted mode of delivery.

Chapter 10: Let's Be Informative

- There are new updated examples of facts in the statistics section, and an expanded section for making talks more understandable. Also included is a new list of suggested topics for informative talks and a new Vitalize Your Vocabulary section featuring a listing of some of the more popular government agencies and their initials.

Chapter 11: Let's Be Persuasive

- New to this chapter are some media websites, more current historical examples, and a list of suggested topics for persuasive talks. Also new is "Forming and Use of Roman Numerals," in the Vitalize Your Vocabulary section.

Chapter 12: Show and Tell . . . Adding Sight to Sound

- There is significant updating of audiovisual technology throughout the chapter and expanded material on PowerPoint™.

Chapter 14: Let's Meet and Discuss It

- There is new material on how to address a person chairing a meeting in the section "The Correct Form of Address" and an expanded section on panel discussion.

Chapter 15: What Do You Say after You Say "Hello"?

- New to this chapter is a list of international conversational taboos—where certain subjects are recommended not to be discussed when conversing with individuals from various cultures . . . and the section on interrupting has been expanded.

Thank You

No one book—or any worthwhile endeavor, for that matter—can be completed, let alone be successful, without the assistance of many talented individuals. This Ninth Edition of *Speak with Confidence* is no exception. A number of people contributed their ideas, suggestions, and recommendations to bring this Ninth Edition home.

I am very pleased with the final product and would like to thank the following persons for sharing their unique talents and efforts, resulting in this, the finest and most comprehensive edition yet of *Speak with Confidence*.

First and foremost, very special thanks go to my ever-understanding and patient wife, Evelyn, who constantly strived to keep my sense of sanity somewhat intact (although I am sure, that, at times, she found it quite challenging) during the very trying and tedious stages of completing the final manuscript preparation.

I would like to thank executive editor Karon Bowers for making this Ninth Edition possible, and her very able assistant, Jennifer Trebby, who was always there to address my many inquiries. And, once again, special thanks go to my developmental editor, Nancy Crochiere, whose many suggestions and ideas, not only regarding the copy but also the cartoons, have contributed greatly to this final product. Since the Seventh Edition, Nancy's guidance and wise counsel have been indispensable. And to Steve Miles, my cartoonist, who has been around since the First Edition . . . what can I say . . . but thank you, thank you. Another great job, Steve.

Two of my colleagues at Bunker Hill Community College deserve high praise: Diane Smith, library director (acting), who, once again, provided outstanding contributions to Chapters 7 and 12; and Professor Gloria Aluise for her excellent work in Chapter 11 and for her very creative efforts in producing the book's new feature, Quick Clicks, which appears at the end of every chapter. I would also like to thank a very patient Professor Tim McLaughlin, chairman of our English Department, who endured and responded to my many interruptions whenever I solicited his wise counsel and comments. Thanks, Tim.

Responsible reviewers are extremely important to new development and revisions. For their much appreciated critical analysis and significant contributions, I would like to express my gratitude to: Barbara Cole, Sandhills Community College; Herbert Sennett, Southeastern College; Simon Waltzer, Ventura College; and Thomas Wylie, York County Technical College.

And, finally, I would like to thank everyone who has directly or indirectly contributed their talent and effort in making possible this very fine final product, *Speak with Confidence*, Ninth Edition.

—Albert J. Vasile

Speak with Confidence

I Just Can't Wait to Start This Course

More men have talked their way up the ladder of success than have climbed it in any other way.
—Bruce Barton, best-selling author, advertising pioneer, and lecturer

After reading and understanding this chapter, you should know:

- The importance of this course in enriching your personal life and your career

- The benefits you will get from working at this course

- Ways to conquer shyness, if you're shy

- The difference between being assertive and being aggressive

- The importance of making business and social contacts

- The importance and application of ethics

- The ethical responsibilities of the speaker and listener

- The meaning of plagiarism and how to avoid it

Assuming that you do the assigned work, you will gain substantial benefits from this course: more self-confidence; an increased ability to communicate one to one within a group, and to a group; help in conquering shyness; understanding the importance of ethics from the standpoint of the speaker and listener and the seriousness of plagiarism; a keen sense of personal accomplishment; and a heightened ability to listen. These benefits can help you attain your full potential in the career and lifestyle you seek. In other words, as many former students have said, this course may well turn out to be the most important one of your college years.

Appearing in this (and every) chapter is a feature called In Other Words, which will greatly benefit foreign and ESL (English as a Second Language) students. To aid in their understanding of common American idioms and phrases, these expressions will be defined in the margin of the page on which they are introduced.

Sounding Off

It is difficult to recall any era in our history more saturated with controversial issues than today—issues such as terrorism here in the United States; the threat of chemical, biological, or nuclear warfare on our homeland; airport security; racial profiling; crime and violence in our neighborhoods; abused children and battered women; gay marriages; the continuing AIDS problem, to cite a few. Such areas of concern have motivated thousands of otherwise inactive Americans to become activated, from writing to their local newspapers to joining and, in some cases, organizing groups and movements to express their views and exert their influence.

In recent elections, voters in several states publicly shouted their anger at government by adopting "initiative petitions": citizen-sponsored petitions that, if approved by the voters, become law. The petitions sought to limit the number of terms an elected official can serve; roll back taxes, fees, and fines; and restructure state and local government.

More and more citizens are calling radio talk programs nationwide to express their opinions and, in many cases, their anger about some of the continued major concerns as we embark on this new millennium: a sex scandal in the White House, the number of politicians and government officials who either were forced to leave office, resigned, were indicted or convicted and even went to prison for unethical, questionable, or criminal behavior. In 1995 alone, 825 politicians and government officials were indicted, as opposed to 45 in 1970.[1]

And how about these sobering statistics directly involving the Clinton administration:

> Number of individuals and businesses associated with the Clinton machine who have been convicted of or pleaded guilty to crimes: 47. Number of these convictions during Clinton's presidency: 33. Number of indictments/misdemeanor charges: 61. Number of congressional witnesses who have pleaded the Fifth Amendment, fled the country to avoid testifying, or, in the case of foreign witnesses, refused to be interviewed: 122.[2]

Other concerns persist—such as the poor quality of public education and parents' demands for vouchers; elimination of bilingual education; the growing power and influence of insurance companies over doctors, hospitals, and patients; young children shooting and killing their schoolmates and teachers; and more and more teenagers drinking, driving, and smashing their cars, killing themselves and other teens. Some other concerns include the questionable state of our Social Security system and lack of job security due to the large

---

[1]Ronald Brownstein, "Life in the Time of Scandal," *U.S. News & World Report,* 27 April 1998, 13.

[2]John Leo, "Bill's Long Goodbye," *U.S. News & World Report,* 29 January 2001, 9.

number of mega mergers by large corporations, causing many layoffs. More and more Americans are taking to the airwaves as their forum for sounding off.

Talk radio is so popular throughout the United States that many politicians tune in regularly or direct members of their staff to do so to monitor the frustrations and concerns of their constituents. And, quite frequently, a legislator may personally call a talk program to respond to a particular issue.

It has never been easier for Americans to express their views on talk radio stations or to listen to TV news and commentaries. According to the Federal Communication Commission, as of September 30, 2000, there are:

Radio stations

AM	4,685
FM	5,892
FM educational	2,140
Total	12,717

TV stations

UHF Commercial	721
VHF Commercial	567
UHF Educational	250
VHF Educational	125
Total	1,663

And we haven't even mentioned cable networks and cable-accessed community stations. The ability to ventilate your views of the news on a talk radio or TV station is as a close as your telephone.

As easy as it is to "air" your views, it's just as easy to find programs on regular TV, cable, and even on the Internet, that expose other people's opinions. Some of the more common sources include ABC News; BBC News; CBS News; CNN News; C-Span; Fox News; MSNBC; PBS; and World newspaper.com.

Also available for viewing are such opinion-oriented news and discussion shows as *CNN Transcripts* and *Crossfire,* also on CNN; *EqualTime* and *Hardball* on MSNBC; *Fox News Sunday, Hannity & Colmes, The O'Reilly Factor,* and *Special Report with Brit Hume,* all on Fox. Then, of course, we have two of the longest-running programs on TV: *Face the Nation* on CBS and *Meet the Press* on NBC.

If you're online, and you probably are, you might wish to check out some of the following credible newspapers:

The *Los Angeles Times*	http://latimes.com
The *New York Times*	www.nyt.com
NewsHound (The *San Jose Mercury News*)	www.newshound.com/main.htm

The *Sacramento Bee*	www.sacbee.com
The *San Francisco Chronicle*	www.sfgate.com
USA Today	www.usatoday.com
The *Wall Street Journal*	www.wsj.com
The *Washington Post*	www.washingtonpost.com

And don't forget to visit one or more of the Web addresses in the Quick Clicks box at the end of this chapter.

If you feel you need more self-confidence and assertiveness to express yourself—by calling a radio talk show, speaking before a group, or just conversing one on one—then taking this course is a positive beginning.

Let's face it, you're taking this basic course in speech for one of two reasons:

1. You *want* to.
2. You *have* to.

If you *want* to take the course, you have nothing to worry about. Apparently, you appreciate the importance of oral communication and the boost that this course can contribute to the career and lifestyle you want. If you simply exert the effort, you will develop into a more self-confident communicator whom people will listen to and respect.

If you've been "drafted" into the speech course, this is a ***different ballgame.*** To most Americans, the idea of compulsion is self-defeating, destructive, and, in many instances, antilearning. Yet, during college or after college, we sometimes have to do things that we don't want to do.

For example, if we decided to obey traffic lights and speed limits only at our own convenience, what would happen? If pilots decided not to abide by their preestablished flight patterns and procedures from takeoff to landing, what would happen?

If this course is required and you're not really ecstatic about taking it, try to control your enthusiasm by accepting this experience with an ***open mind.*** Who knows, you may enjoy the course. You may find yourself warming up to the challenge and even thriving on the zestful ***give-and-take*** of verbal jousting in class. ***Take the plunge*** on a positive note. Remember, you'll never know what you're capable of doing until you try.

How Important Is This Course to You?

Every day you communicate orally without giving it a thought. You greet people. You express opinions and desires. You ask questions, and you answer them. You agree with people, and you disagree. Sometimes you try to influence them.

Have you ever envied someone else's ability to express thoughts and opinions authoritatively? Have you ever experienced a situation in which you wished you had had the confidence and ability to communicate ideas and opinions? Do you have problems meeting people and making new friends? Have you ever wished you were a better conversationalist? If you answered "yes" to all or some of these questions, then get set for one of the most important courses of your life.

Talking, listening, writing, and reading are acts of communication that you perform throughout your life. Of these four acts, there's no question that talking and listening predominate in business, social, personal, and political relationships. For every word you write, you may speak thousands of words to carry you through a typical day. Consider the following circumstances in which effective oral communication may be crucial to you:

- Voicing your opinions at home, in classes, in politics, at the office, and at weekend orientations.
- Evaluating and selecting courses with your faculty adviser. In order to receive maximum benefit from the consultation, you must be able to express your course selections in the light of your long- or short-range goals.
- Interviewing for a job or seeking a raise or promotion. Unless you express yourself knowledgeably and confidently, what would your chances be?
- Disagreeing with your boss or immediate supervisor without being disagreeable.
- Wanting some time off from your job without having to call in sick.
- Handling a delicate situation such as sexual harassment on the job (male or female).
- Expressing your views at a school committee meeting on the subject of sex education being taught at your child's school.
- Testifying as a witness in court or at a hearing.
- Participating in community, business, or political action groups. PTAs and consumer, taxpayer, environmental, and labor organizations, for example, need people who have ideas and the ability to communicate them as well as to execute them. How many of us shy away because we lack confidence in our ability to champion our beliefs?

An ability to communicate orally will be crucial in your chosen career, whether you're interacting with a doctor or patient as a nurse, explaining a design or decision in engineering, asking for specific instructions in electronics or accounting, preparing and giving a report to your superiors or peers in the business world, or explaining a process in computer technology. No matter what your vocation—sales, education, marketing, advertising, administration—being able to *speak with confidence* will be an invaluable asset to your personal development.

These experiences will confront you throughout life, so you should prepare yourself to cope with them to your advantage. No matter who you are, the keys to achieving your lifetime goals are your competence on the job and your ability to communicate effectively with your fellow humans.

Some of the specific skills that you can learn from taking this course include analyzing an audience; selecting an appropriate topic; researching and orga-

Like being sexually harassed on the job . . .

nizing your material; outlining your talk; methods of delivering your talk; expanding your vocabulary; understanding the importance of nonverbal communication; using audiovisual aids; and giving informative and persuasive talks.

We thought that you might be interested in the opinions of some of your peers who have completed this course. Here are some representative quotations:

- "I liked the course very much, even though I was going to drop it because I didn't have confidence in myself to get up in front of people. I have that confidence now and I think it's great."
- "My initial reaction to this course, at the beginning, was utter panic. Needless to say, however, by the end of the semester this course turned out to be the best I ever had."
- "The course was terrific. I received confidence, warmth, and a real feeling of belonging."
- "This course has helped me tremendously, not only to be able to better communicate in my other classes but also on the job when communicating with my peers and superiors. Thank you."
- "Not only has this course taught me a great deal about myself, but I learned a lot from and about my classmates."
- "Because of the number of foreign students in the class, I've developed a much better understanding not only of their culture, which was tremendously interesting, but also of their personal concerns regarding their country."

● "This course gave me the courage and confidence that I needed to be able to stand and give a talk in front of an audience. The book helped me to learn and understand the proper ways to address a group of people. I never thought that a textbook could be so much fun to read."

Although this course can do much for you, you should understand that it is a basic course, only a beginning. One semester won't transform you into a scintillating and dynamic speaker/communicator, but it certainly can help. The speaking skills that you learn will develop and improve through practice over a period of time.

Don't Be Shy

I remember, when I was quite a young child, the number of times that my parents would refer to me as "being shy" whenever we went visiting or entertained visitors. Perhaps you, too, have similar recollections. To this day, I have to classify myself, to some degree, as a shy person as opposed to an extroverted one.

The important thing to remember is that shyness is a fairly universal human trait, and that everyone, at one time or another, has experienced it. The overwhelming majority of people who experience a certain degree of shyness function normally in their day-to-day activities. It's when your shyness reaches an uncomfortable level, when it seriously affects your daily personal, social, or occupational behavior, that professional help should be sought.

Shyness doesn't have to have a negative impact on your life—if you're willing to do something about it. Some well-known people who have done quite well despite being shy include Johnny Carson, Barbara Walters, Dana Carvey, David Letterman, Robert Frost, Eleanor Roosevelt, and Albert Einstein, to name a few. If they could overcome their shyness, you can, too.

There's nothing wrong with being shy—if that is what you want. Please read the preceding sentence again, especially the last six words. These words—"if that is what you want"—say it all. If you're shy and you feel comfortable with your shyness, it's because you *choose* to be that way, but you don't *have* to be. Although you weren't born shy, there may be a multitude of reasons, especially during your adolescent years, for your development in that direction. One valid reason might be that you were never encouraged to participate in conversation or in other activities involving social exchanges. Another reason might be that you allowed people to make you feel inferior or inadequate. Allowing people to make you feel inferior, inadequate, and/or embarrassed could be a direct result of your not being assertive—and we'll **take up** that important quality very soon.

I think it's interesting to note that, according to Stanford University psychologist Philip Zimbardo, Ph.D., a shyness authority and author of *The Shy Child*, approximately 40 percent of U.S. college students admit being shy, another 40 percent say they used to be shy, and around 15 percent confess to

in other words:
take up—to discuss

being shy in certain situations. Professor Zimbardo also points out quite interestingly, that more than 80 percent of all Americans have reported feeling shy at some time in their lives. So you see, if you're just a little bit shy, you're not alone. What you should strive to do is to control your shyness, so you'll comfortably be able to function socially, rather than have your shyness control you.

Many women suffer from shyness because they were brought up to equate being bashful with being feminine. This is particularly prevalent in some Asian, Middle Eastern, and Latin American cultures, but it also happens in American culture.

Whatever the reason for your shyness, the vital point is that if you don't want to be shy, you don't have to be. You must decide, and it could be one of the most crucial decisions you'll make during your lifetime. Overcoming shyness will allow you to:

- Greet and meet people comfortably
- Participate in conversations
- Express (instead of repress) your opinions
- Socialize more
- Cultivate new friendships and renew old ones
- Become more assertive (say "no" or disagree without being aggressive or feeling guilty)

You must constantly strive to think about yourself in a positive manner. You can reinforce this principle by first deciding that you're going to change, and then by repeating to yourself dozens of times daily such positive thoughts as:

"I am going to be more outgoing."

"I am an attractive person."

"I am going to be more friendly to people."

"People are going to like me."

"I can contribute to a conversation as well as any of my friends can."

"I am a good person and I have a lot to offer."

By reiterating such statements, you will help raise your levels of self-esteem and self-confidence. Author Diane Baroni, in her article on self-esteem, put it rather nicely when she stated that "In truth, this precious gift [self-esteem] can be had once you learn to parent *yourself*. Be lavish with love, praise, respect, and you'll feel a soaring sense of worth!"[3] At the same time, your degree of shyness should gradually diminish. You should already start to feel positive about yourself because you've made an important decision—independently. You must constantly remind yourself that you're no longer going to accept

---

[3]Diane Baroni, "Esteem—Why Is It So Hard to Get?" *Cosmopolitan*, September 1996, 238.

"I'm no longer going to be shy. . . . I'm no longer going to be shy. . . . I'm no longer. . . ."

your shyness, and you must constantly visualize yourself as being more gregarious. It's a very important beginning.

This course will present you with many opportunities to develop ways to overcome your diffidence, and your class environment will provide you with the necessary encouragement. Your most important mentor at this stage will be your speech instructor who will, most likely, be supportive, understanding, and sympathetic. Make an appointment to see your instructor as soon as possible and explain your decision and goal. As your speech course progresses, listen carefully to your classmates and ask questions after their talks.

In addition, before and after class, make an effort to talk to a classmate, even if you start with a simple greeting such as "Good morning," "Hi, *how are you doing?*" or "I enjoyed your talk today. You know what I'd like to ask you?" Every day, try to start a conversation with a different classmate, and always try to remember names. It will be difficult at first, but will become easier as the days pass.

When you begin to feel more self-confident and relaxed, expand this new approach to people in your other classes, at home, at work, and at social gatherings. If you notice someone at a social occasion whom you would like to meet or who appears alone, *go out of your way* to *strike up* a conversation. Take a deep breath, smile, and confidently approach that person. Extend your hand and introduce yourself. Often you'll be pleasantly surprised with the results. That person may be grateful to meet and talk with someone who is friendly.

in other words:

how are you doing?—how are you? (a cordial greeting)

go out of your way—make an effort

strike up—to start or begin

People listen to and respect a self-confident talker.

Remember, being friendly and outgoing could open new vistas for a more meaningful, interesting, and exciting personal, as well as professional, life for you. It's *your choice.* Good luck!

Here's something else to think about. According to some psychologists, because of the increased use of computers, e-mail, and particularly the Internet, there is growing concern that some shy people could easily become more shy as they immerse themselves into this cyberspace phenomenon. I know that you are up to the challenge and you'll be able to **handle it.**

in other words:
handle it—to understand and be able to address the situation

Be More Assertive

Earlier, we mentioned that among the benefits of overcoming shyness is becoming more assertive. That is, confidently being able to express your thoughts and feelings as well as to disagree and be able to say "no" without feeling guilty or being aggressive. Being aggressive means forcing your feelings and views on others. Aggressive people usually are not too popular, whereas an assertive individual is a responsible person who not only has empathy for others, but also feels secure and comfortable presenting an opposing view.

An assertive person usually earns the accolade, "You certainly know where she stands," or "You can always count on him to tell it like it is." Assertive men and women generally are well liked and respected because of their honest, responsible, and empathic manner. In other words, they can honestly express themselves without *turning people off.*

You might also like to know that being assertive can have some positive health ramifications. Many health care providers agree that it's much healthier to be vocal and express your views rather than to be silent and suppress them.

Making Business and Social Contacts

Almost everyone would agree that making contacts and knowing the *right people* are invaluable aids in moving ahead. Making contacts can help you move ahead in your career and in many other ways. Perhaps you are looking for summer or part-time work; perhaps you want a favor from a politician—a letter of recommendation or introduction—perhaps you are seeking college admission or membership in a prestigious organization. Your chances of achieving these goals will be immensely improved if you know people in a position to help you.

You should realize that it's no shame to ask for a favor. What is a shame is to need something and not get it because you don't know anyone who could possibly *open some doors* for you. (This topic is discussed further in Chapters 15 and 16.)

Knowing the right people can have a significant effect on your life, so you should strive to meet and interact with as many people as possible. You never know when they may be able to *come through* for you. *By the same token,* you should be helpful to others whenever you can, because helping is *a two-way street.*

Your sincere desire and ability to meet people should become an integral part of your daily life. The way to include them in your life is to communicate orally—speak, listen, question, answer, and get involved.

What This Course Can Do for You

Provided that you expend the effort—and it is vital that you do—this course will help you to:

● Develop more self-confidence when interacting with people, one to one, within a group, and to a group
● Be more **assertive,** as opposed to being aggressive
● Improve your ability to listen
● Learn how to present your ideas more clearly, logically, and forcefully
● Acquire a sense of accomplishment
● Learn the secrets of meeting and being accepted by people
● Be more convincing

- Develop a more positive self-image
- ***Sell yourself*** to an employer, a group, or friends

You can start to develop these abilities and reap the advantages by exerting yourself in the following ways:

1. By giving many talks on various topics. In this way, you'll communicate your views, experiences, and feelings to your colleagues.

2. By responding to questions from the audience after your talk. The key to performing well in a question-and-answer period is to know your subject thoroughly. If you've done your homework, you will, like most people, be exhilarated by your effort. The adrenaline racing through your veins could produce ***a new "high"*** for you. As a result, you will speak more forcefully and fluently than ever before.

3. By asking questions after others have spoken. Listening intently and having some knowledge of the subject under discussion will enable you to ask interesting and penetrating questions. Perhaps you will disagree with the speaker or perhaps you can shed light on a questionable point; in that case, think first and then speak your mind. Your self-confidence will grow once you notice that others listen to you. Remember, the more often you speak, the more self-confident you'll become.

4. By talking or debating with fellow students. The question-and-answer session after a talk often triggers discussion among class members, sometimes

"And then I shoulda said. . . ."

in other words:

keep in mind—to remember

without involving the original speaker. Someone may ask a question or present an opinion that incites others to reply. This exchange may result in a sizzling, crackling demonstration of the power of the spoken word to move people.

5. By meeting, greeting, and conversing with students from other cultures and countries. Not only will they appreciate your friendliness, but this experience could also prove to be interesting and culturally rewarding to you.

6. If English is not your first language, take this great opportunity to listen intently to the English-speaking students in your class and your instructor so that you can become more proficient in the English language. And please ***keep in mind,*** if a speaker or your professor is talking too fast, raise your hand and ask her or him to please slow down.

After each talk, you'll feel a sense of accomplishment, and rightfully so. Even after your first effort, you'll admit not only to great relief (which you've earned) but, far more important, to a feeling of tremendous satisfaction. With each talk you give, you can only become more confident, and that glow of achievement will intensify.

Keep in mind that this course will not only teach you how to research, prepare, and deliver an effective speech in public or private, but will also help you develop your self-confidence whether you are interacting one to one, participating in a small group, or speaking before a large gathering. Remember, once you achieve self-confidence, you will be able to do almost anything you want, provided, of course, that you prepare properly.

Building self-confidence will enable you to stand up for yourself when someone treats you condescendingly or discriminates against you. Teresa Fischette, a Continental Airlines ticket agent, did just that when she was fired in May 1991 for not wearing make-up. Some weeks earlier the company had issued a new appearance code for customer-contact personnel, and the code required women to use cosmetics.

Teresa, who had always disliked make-up, refused to comply and was discharged. "Make-up should be a personal choice," she said. "It's not fair to ask women to adorn themselves with make-up when it's not part of the job. . . . I think this is a women's-choice issue."[4]

Not one to be pushed around, Teresa fought back with attorneys and rallied public support when she appeared on twenty radio talk shows, the *CBS Nightly News,* and the *Oprah Winfrey Show.* Because Teresa stood up for her rights and used her speaking skills and because the negative publicity tarnished the reputation of Continental Airlines, its chairman apologized to her face to face. He even restored her job, with back pay.

Now you see that one person can make a difference, especially if that person can *speak with confidence.* And that's what this book is all about.

---

[4]*Boston Globe,* 11 May 1991, 1.

What's This about Ethics?

Among the most sincere qualities that you, a speaker, can enjoy is credibility and trust (further discussed in Chapter 3)—that is, the degree of believability your audience has in you and your message. Another trait equally as significant and one that enhances your credibility is the hallmark—**ethics.**

As a competent public speaker you should always strive for excellence, which includes high ethical standards. (As a matter of fact, you should always strive for excellence in everything you do every day of your life.) But, ***getting back*** to the subject of ethics, it is one that has been discussed, debated, and dissected for ages by such philosophers as Aristotle, Plato, and Quintilian and is currently discussed on campuses throughout most parts of the world.

Instead of becoming involved in an ambitious, multisided, verbose, and pedantic discussion on the subject of ethics, let's simply state that being ethical is being honest, truthful, fair, decent, and considerate, and having high morals. To be sure, our early developing years were inundated with lectures, admonitions, and discussions about right and wrong. It is hoped that these lessons, whether at home or at school, were not only well learned but are still inculcated and should certainly apply when communicating to an audience.

in other words:
getting back— to return

"... and as I have said many times ... ask not what your country can do for you ... ask what you can do for your country!

Therefore, in an effort to minimize the theoretical and maximize the pragmatic, let's focus on the following three facets of ethical behavior with which you'll mostly be concerned:

- Ethical responsibilities of the speaker
- Ethical responsibilities of the listener
- Plagiarism and how to avoid it

Ethical Responsibilities of the Speaker

As an ethical speaker, you should:

1. Fully understand the objectives and ramifications that your message may have on your audience. If your topic is controversial or even explosive, you want to be sure not to direct your comments to specific individuals or groups. You can get your points across without getting personal.
2. Be very much aware of the audience's **make-up.** Are different age groups, political groups, or ethnic groups represented? (See Chapter 6.)
3. Be fully prepared. While researching your topic, gather the most current and complete documented data and sources (see Chapter 7) and transform them into easily understandable language (see Chapter 5) for *all* members of your audience. If nonnative speakers are present, it will be considerate and surely appreciated to slow your delivery.
4. Avoid excluding information, even though it may be contrary to your primary message. Presenting both sides is not only fair, but emphasizing and defending your position can earn you respect and credibility.
5. Know the difference between fact and opinion (see Chapter 11) and be sure that your listeners are aware when you are employing them. When using facts, state the source. When stating your opinion or editorializing, simply state, "In my opinion . . . " or simply, "I feel. . . ." Audiences resent being manipulated, as you would.
6. Always credit and cite your sources. Taking someone else's ideas, or words as if they were your own is wrong. It is plagiarism. Plagiarism is not only unethical, it is **out-and-out** stealing and could result in some serious consequences. I'll have more to say on this subject a little later in this chapter.
7. Try to answer every question during your question-and-answer period (if there is one) as honestly and **straightforwardly** as possible. If you don't know an answer to a question, say so. Simply stating, "I don't know the answer but I can **look it up** and have it for you at the next class or meeting," will be satisfying and appreciated.

Ethical Responsibilities of the Listener

Just as a speaker has ethical responsibilities to his or her audience, you as a listener have ethical responsibilities to the speaker. Remember, a completed oral communication cycle includes a speaker who has something to say and a listener to assimilate that message and provide vital feedback to the speaker (discussed further in Chapters 3 and 4).

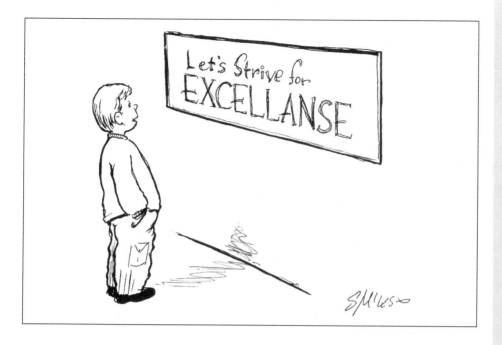

As an ethical listener, you should:

1. Prepare yourself thoroughly for a learning experience. If possible, try to find out something about the speaker and her topic. What's her background? Is she a recognized authority in her field? Has she authored any articles or books on the subject? What is the speaker's motivation for her viewpoints? The more you can ascertain beforehand, the better you'll be able to evaluate the message and the messenger.

2. Keep an open mind (discussed further in Chapter 4). Even if you think what the speaker has to say may, even in part, be contrary to your viewpoint, you have a responsibility and an obligation to yourself and the speaker to absorb the complete message. Possibly your original views may be strengthened; but there's also the chance that the speech may be so compelling and persuasive as to soften or even change your opinion completely. Whatever happens, you should, at least, come away a better-informed person. And no matter how much you may disagree with the message, the speaker is entitled to freedom of speech as much as you are.

3. Concentrate on the message. As discussed further in Chapter 4, your mind is capable of assimilating many more words per minute than any speaker can deliver, leaving a significant gap to entertain distractions. Discipline yourself to concentrate totally on the message. One effective way to do this is to take notes during the speech. Another is to write down questions to ask during the question-and-answer period. Don't permit your ***mind to wander.*** Don't think about things to be done at home, problems at work, what you did last weekend, or what you plan to do next weekend. Don't be distracted by

in other words:
mind to wander—to be distracted

people coughing, chairs moving, or students coming in late. Always *think* the message and the messenger—what is being said and how it's being said.

4. Provide feedback. As a responsible speaker, you are making constant eye contact with your audience—you are looking for feedback. As a responsible listener your eyes should be riveted on the speaker so that you can provide that critical feedback. If your eyes are wandering around the room, looking at your watch, sneaking a peek at your homework, or if you are yawning or whispering to a classmate, you're communicating negative messages to the speaker. But if you're sitting upright in your chair, looking alert, looking at the speaker and his or her every move, smiling and occasionally nodding approval, you're telling the speaker that you not only understand what is being said, but that you're interested in it.

5. Compensate for speaker flaws (discussed further in Chapter 4). Some speakers may display certain characteristics that detract from their message. Perhaps the speaker has a nervous cough, constantly pauses, has a monotonous delivery, or speaks too fast. Maybe she remains rigid in one position, doesn't move or gesture, or appears fidgety and is constantly moving. The speaker's clothes may not coordinate, jewelry may fly about with every gesture, or long hair may be stubbornly falling over one eye. Such flaws can, at times, provide more fascination than the speaker's message. Try to overlook such distractions and immerse yourself in the message.

Plagiarism and How to Avoid It

in other words:

pass them off—pretend

Without becoming excessively didactic, **plagiarism** is not ethical, is not right, and is not being honest. It is stealing. Whenever you take someone else's ideas and or words and ***pass them off*** as though they are your own, you are plagiarizing, which can lead to serious consequences. Presidential candidate Senator Joseph R. Biden, Jr., was forced to withdraw from the 1988 campaign after members of the press discovered that two of his speeches were the works of others. A dean of communication at a large university lost his prestigious position when it was discovered that a speech he had given was written by someone else and was delivered practically verbatim. Students found guilty of plagiarism either receive failing grades, are suspended or expelled, or put their academic degrees in jeopardy. There is no excuse for plagiarism because it is so easy to avoid—*just give credit where credit is due.* Simple statements such as:

"From an article I recently read in [name the publication, date, and author] it clearly states. . . ."

"The solutions that I just presented come, in part, from a three-part series written by [name author, publication, and date]."

Or a simple, "According to [name author and publication]. . . ."

Remember, when you're quoting, summarizing, or paraphrasing someone else's work, just *cite the source* and avoid some unpleasant situations.

To Avoid Plagiarizing

1. Be sure to research a variety of sources; don't restrict yourself to only one.
2. During your research, keep an accurate listing or bibliography of all your sources and save them.
3. List all of your sources on 3-by-5 cards for convenience and accessibility. Write on one side only and be sure to number them.
4. Study and critically analyze all the information so that you'll be able to form your own conclusions. This should enable you to present your thoughts in your own words and in your own style of speaking.
5. When you're preparing your speech, be sure to include the sources. Don't wait until you've finished your preparation.
6. In your final draft, check to be sure that all the sources are properly cited.
7. And finally, it might not be a bad idea to have your sources prepared as a handout for those who request one.

Again, I want to emphasize that developing all the skills explained in this book to a high level of proficiency is not a realistic goal to accomplish in one or two semesters. However, this course can be a terrific beginning.

Nothing is more frustrating than having something to contribute to a discussion at school, at home, at work, or at a social affair—but not doing so for lack of self-confidence. "To sin by silence," said Abraham Lincoln, "when they should protest makes cowards of men." This course will help you make your contribution.

Quick Clicks

Welcome to a "surprise search." To further enhance your research or simply to harvest more information about some of the things you studied in this chapter, just drop in at any of the following addresses. What you'll discover may be serious, educational, bibliographical, surprising, factual, or even downright humorous, but it will definitely be informative.

So go ahead and give a "Quick Click."

www.shyness.com
www.ukans.edu/cwis/units/coms2/vpa/vpa.htm
www.public-speaking.org
www.iss.stthomas.edu/studyguides/Genius.htm
www.ethics.ubc.ca/resources
www.sja.ucdavis.edu/avoid.htm
www.presentersuniversity.com/courses/deskills.cfm?RecordID=131

Things to Discuss in Class

1. List a few topics that you can talk about for at least three minutes.
2. How would speech training help you in your current career or in one that you plan to enter?
3. Name a few benefits that you hope to gain from this course.
4. Which public figure do you consider an excellent speaker? Why?
5. Which public figure do you consider a poor speaker? Why?
6. Can you recall any times when you wanted to express your viewpoints and didn't? Why?
7. Do you ever envy friends because they express themselves better than you do?
8. Have you ever started to express yourself, then suddenly stopped for some reason?
9. Do you feel more confident when speaking to one person than when speaking to a group?
10. Do you have more (less) difficulty speaking to people of the opposite sex?
11. Bring to class three or four political ads from the newspaper and discuss their contents relative to what you've just learned about ethics.
12. You decide to base your next speech on a paper that your friend submitted in another class last semester. Is this ethical or not? Explain.

Vitalize Your Vocabulary

Sprinkled throughout our rich language are many commonly used foreign words and phrases. Here are some of the more popular ones that you're apt to hear or see, along with their birthplace (F = French; G = Greek; I = Italian; L = Latin; S = Spanish; Y = Yiddish).

ad hoc (L; ad-HOK) Formed to function with one specific purpose.

ad infinitum (L; ad in-fun-EYE-tum) To drag on and on, never ending.

afficionado (S; uh-FISH-ya-nah-doh) An ardent devotee or enthusiast.

apropos (F; ap-ruh-POH) At the appropriate time.

bon appetit (F; BOH nap-uh-teet) Enjoy your meal.

bona fide (L; BOH-na-fide) Made or carried out in good faith.

bon vivant (F; bon vee-VAHNT) One who enjoys good food, drink, and life in general.

carte blanche (F; kart-BLONSH) The power to act at one's own discretion. Unconditional authority.

cause célèbre (F; koz suh-LEB-ruh) A very popular controversial issue or case.

caveat emptor (L; KAV-ee-ot EMP-tor) Let the buyer beware.

chutzpah (Y; KHOOT-spuh) Having a lot of nerve/arrogance.

comme ci, comme ça (F; kom SEE kom SAH) so-so, noncommital.

coup d'état (F; koo day-TAH) The overthrow of a government by a small group.

déjà vu (F; DAY-zhah VOOH) The feeling that something happening has happened before.

détente (F; day-TAHNT) A lessening of strained relations.

dolce vita (I; DOLE-chay VEE-tuh) Enjoying the good and sweet life.

en masse (F; ahn MAHS) In one large group together.

ex post facto (L; EX post FAK-toh) To become effective retroactively.

fait accompli (F; fate ah-kom-PLEE) An accomplished, irreversible fact.

faux pas (F; foh PAH) A social blunder.

in loco parentis (L; in LOH-koh pa-REN-tiss) In the place of a parent.

in memoriam (L; in muh-MAWR-ee-uhm) In memory of.

ipso facto (L; IP-soh FAK-toh) By the very fact itself.

joie de vivre (F; zhwah duh VEEV-ruh) Hearty or carefree enjoyment of life.

modus operandi (L; MOH-duhs op-uh-RAN-dee) A method of operating.

nom de plume (F; nom duh PLOOM) A pseudonym or pen name.

nouveau riche (F; nooh-voh REESH) One who has recently come into wealth and who enjoys flaunting it.

persona non grata (L; per-SOH-nah non GRAH-tah) An individual who is fully unacceptable or unwelcome.

prima donna (I; pree-muh DAH-nuh) A leading female opera singer. Also, refers to a temperamental person.

pro bono (L; pro BOH-noh) Performing without compensation.

pro tempore (L; proh TEM-puh-ree) For the time being; temporarily.

que sera sera (I; keh sair-AH sair-AH) What will be will be.

quid pro quo (L; kwid proh KWOH) An equal exchange; something for something.

quorum (L: KWO-rum) The minimum number of group members required to be present in order to conduct business.

savoir faire (F; sav-wahr FAIR) The ability to say or do the correct thing.

schlemiel (Y; shleh-MEEL) A person who can't seem to do anything right.

status quo (L; STAY-tus QWOH) The existing condition.

veni, vidi, vici (L; VEN-ee VEE-dee VEE-chee) I came, I saw, I conquered.

verbatim (L; ver-BAY-tuhm) Word for word.

vis-à-vis (F; vee-ZUH-VEE) Compared with; in relation to.

2

Your First Talk

I'd Like to Introduce Myself

The first time I attempted to make a public talk . . . I was in a state of misery . . . my tongue clove to the roof of my mouth, and, at first, I could hardly get out a word.

—David Lloyd George, prime minister of England from 1916 to 1922 and one of the most eloquent speakers of this century

After reading and understanding this chapter, you should be able to:

- Appreciate the importance of knowing your subject well

- Prepare a short, interesting talk about yourself

- Deliver the talk about yourself

- Grasp the importance of eye contact and gestures

- Realize the importance of good posture, some movement, and the limited use of notes

- Understand that nervousness strikes everybody

- Realize the importance of using correct English grammar when speaking

chapter
preview

This chapter will introduce you to some of the ways of giving a good, stimulating talk. Since it's easier to talk with people you know, the sooner you get to know each other, the better. That's why your first talk will probably be an autobiographical sketch from four to six minutes long.

Thorough knowledge of a subject gives speakers more self-confidence than does anything else. Since you know yourself best, you should be able to talk for at least four to six minutes about yourself.

All of us like attention and respect. When you're "front and center," you're the focus of attention. If you follow the suggestions in this chapter and those in later chapters, you will earn the respect of your peers and other listeners.

Everybody, including professional speakers and actors, gets nervous before a performance. It's a normal reaction that usually diminishes soon after you get involved in your message. Since it's almost impossible to eliminate all nervousness, you should strive to control it. Suggestions are offered for that purpose.

Eye contact with your listeners is vital, so look them right in the eye. This arouses them initially and gives you the momentum to keep them interested. Eye contact also provides you with feedback on how you're doing.

Gestures support and dramatize your ideas. As long as your gestures are spontaneous and vigorous, use them. In addition, they're an excellent outlet for your nervous energy. Other nonverbal elements touched on briefly are movement, posture, facial expression, and appearance.

If using note cards will give you confidence, use them; professional speakers often do. Just don't read so much from the cards that you disrupt eye contact with your listeners.

This first talk will probably be the toughest one of all. Remember that giving good talks requires that you do your homework beforehand. Homework includes rehearsing, preferably with at least one listener.

In the Spotlight

Well, what do you know? You're about to give your first talk in front of the class. You're about to perform before a real live audience. If that isn't a guarantee to raise your blood pressure 15 or 20 points! Right? Actually, if you've never addressed a group before, this will be an exciting and memorable experience. Although your talk will probably be short, it could provide you with enough challenge and motivation to exert a positive influence on your life. Your instructor may ask you either to talk about yourself or to interview a classmate and then give a talk about him or her. No matter which talk you give, this chapter will guide you in how to plan and present it.

Since most of you are more relaxed when communicating with people you know, your instructor may feel that it's a good idea for everyone to give a brief autobiographical sketch. In this way you'll learn to know each other sooner and **get the feel** of giving a prepared talk before a group.

This short autobiographical talk will afford you an opportunity to listen to all members of the class introduce themselves. What an excellent chance to find out which classmates have the same interests as yours! Perhaps, while listening to someone interesting, you'll look forward to the class break or a chance to meet at the cafeteria to develop a more personal relationship on a one-to-one basis.

What an excellent opportunity to listen to other students from different countries and cultures describe their homeland experiences and way of life; their family responsibilities, schooling, and traditional celebrations; their reactions to coming to the United States. Listen to what their impressions are now and of their hopes for the future.

So prepare yourself to absorb what your classmates have to say and listen carefully for possible clues of mutual interest or concern. This talk is an important first step in developing new friends. In addition, this will be your introduction to a critical aspect of speech communication—audience analysis. (See Chapters 6 and 11.)

in other words:
get the feel—to experience or learn the way something feels

24

The distance from your seat to the speaker's stand may be only 15 feet, but it may seem like a mile to you when it's your turn to speak. This is understandable because of your anxiety about what's to come. Many things will **zip through** your mind, such as "I wonder if I'll be able to move when I'm called. I'll just play dead—on second thought, who'll be playing?" or "What am I doing here?" Believe it or not, you're here to give your first talk.

You shouldn't let this talk upset you because, in all probability, you won't be graded or critiqued. Your professor may wish only to introduce you to how it feels to stand up and speak before a group—and to convince you that there's nothing mysterious or life-threatening about doing so.

in other words:
zip through—
rapidly go
through

Know Your Subject

There seems to be some disagreement among speech professors as to the relative importance of knowing your topic versus your delivery when it comes to presenting an effective talk. Some say that *knowing your subject* counts for about 75 percent and *your delivery* for about 25 percent. Others believe that it's

"What am I doing here?"

about equal, fifty–fifty. But the one thing that is indisputable is the fact that the more you know about your subject, the better your chances of being an effective communicator. No one knows you better than you do, and no other topic should interest you more or provide you with more material, so your own life is an excellent topic for your first talk.

Preparing your first talk should be a simple exercise. With paper and pencil in hand, conduct a self-inventory and make notes. Think about your childhood, parents, and relatives. Where were you born and raised? Which schools did you attend? What made you decide to go to college? Why this one? Has any one person had a strong influence on you? Why did you select your major area of study?

Were you in the service? If so, what branch and what rank did you hold? How was basic training and where did you take it? What type of work did you do in the military and where were you stationed? Did you have any spine-tingling encounters? Tell us about it.

Maybe your parents were in the military and you moved from one military installation to another, from state to state or country to country. Perhaps you or one of your parents was involved in the Persian Gulf War or the war on terrorism in Afghanistan or elsewhere. Tell us about it.

Maybe you're working. Do you like your job—why or why not? How long have you worked there?

Do you ever travel? Where have you been and with whom? How long were you there? Would you like to return—why or why not?

Don't overlook your hobbies or other interests. Do you play a musical instrument? Perhaps you play for a group. If so, where and how often? Maybe you're **into** karate, automobile repair, ceramics, exercising, or gourmet cooking. Share your experiences with us.

Are you married or single? Do you have children? If so, how many and how old are they? Maybe you're a grandparent. What made you decide to return to school? How much of a challenge is it? Are you a full-time or part-time student? What is your major? What are your plans when you graduate?

Have you met any unusually interesting people or celebrities? Tell us about them. When and where did you meet them and under what circumstances? What were your impressions of them? If you've never met a celebrity but want to, who would it be and why?

You should now have some ideas on how to prepare for your first talk. Go over the preceding questions again and use them as a guide. I'm sure you can expand on them.

If your first talk in class doesn't appear serious—that is, if you're smiling, laughing and joking, making faces during your speech—you could very well damage your credibility in any future talks that may be of a serious nature. That's not to say that you can't give an effective persuasive talk later in the semester, and it's not to say that you can't be a little humorous in your first talk. But remember, if the first impression you give your listeners is that you're a comedian and you're not taking this assignment seriously, you just may find it very difficult, and frustrating, to transform your image from a *lightweight* to a *serious contender.*

---

in other words:

into— interested in

lightweight— someone not to be taken seriously

serious contender— someone to be taken seriously

If you're new to our country/culture, you can **count on** the fact that what you have to say should be of great interest to your classmates and your professor. Where did you come from? When did you arrive in the United States? Who came here with you? Why did you or your family decide to leave your country? Was it difficult to get a passport or a visa? Where did you first arrive in this country and what was your first impression? These answers along with your hopes and dreams are only a few observations that you could weave into a very interesting talk. You can also anticipate many questions during your question-and-answer session following your talk, as your listeners hope to learn more about you and your country/culture.

Remember, you can be an interesting person. You have something to say: you do things; you have likes and dislikes; you have opinions, dreams, and ambitions. Here is your chance to express them. Good luck.

Before we present a sample introductory talk, here are a format and outline that you may want to consider.

My name is _____.

My friends call me _____.

I live at _____

and my family consists of _____.

I attended the following schools: _____.

My favorite subject(s) were _____.

My extracurricular activities consisted of _____.

I am presently employed at _____

and my responsibilities are _____.

The days and hours I work are _____.

What I like best about my job is _____.

What I don't like about my job is _____.

I've decided to come to this college because _____.

My major is _____.

My plans after I graduate are _____.

I participate in the following college activities: _____.

I am a full-time/part-time student and I'm taking courses in _____.

My biggest obstacle in coming to college is _____.

As far as what my family thinks about my coming to college, _____.

I decided to return to college because _____.

My major is _____.

in other words:
count on—to be sure of

I enjoy traveling and have visited _____.

Of all the places I visited, I enjoyed _____

the most because _____.

I was a member of the Armed Forces (mention branch, length of service, duty stations, and occupational specialty): _____.

My short-term goal is _____.

My long-term goal is _____.

Some of the things I enjoy doing are _____.

Some of the things I don't enjoy are _____.

My biggest gripe is _____.

The one thing that gives me great pleasure is _____.

I think the biggest problem facing our society is _____.

in other
words:

a handle—
some idea

How you complete these statements should give your classmates *a handle* on who you are and where you come from and could lead to some stimulating relationships.

Your instructor may ask for an **outline** before you speak (see Chapter 8). If so, the outline for your talk may look something like this:

Title: Autobiographical Talk

  I. Personal information

    A. Name, age, hometown

    B. Family members

      1. Parents

      2. Brother(s)/sister(s)

      3. Spouse and children

      4. Pet(s)

  II. Schools attended

    A. Middle school

    B. High school

      1. Type of program enrolled in

      2. Favorite course(s)

      3. Most memorable teacher/coach

      4. Extracurricular activities

 III. Post–high school education

    A. Schools attended prior to this one

    B. Why I selected this school

    C. What I am majoring in

    D. Long-term and short-term goals

    E. Extracurricular activities

IV. Occupational experience
   A. Past job(s)
      1. Description and duties
      2. Likes and dislikes
   B. Present job(s)
      1. Description and duties
      2. Likes and dislikes
V. Military service
   A. Branch and location of basic training
   B. Military schools attended
   C. Rank and job description
   D. Duty station(s)   ·
   E. Other travel opportunities
VI. Hobbies/Interests
   A. Outdoor activities
   B. Indoor activities
   C. Collections
VII. Future career goals

Here's a sample introductory talk.

Sam Adams

1 Hi. My name is Sam Adams and my friends call me Sam. I live in Quincy with my mother, father, and two younger sisters; Kaitlyn who's 18, and Christine who's 16. I'm 21 years old. As a matter of fact, I turned 21 last month and, yes, I am now legally able to enjoy that famous, refreshing beverage that bears my name.

2 My family has lived in Quincy for over fifty years and I attended public schools in the city. Quincy is known as the City of Presidents because it's the birthplace of John Adams, the second President of the United States and his son, John Quincy Adams, who was our sixth President. They are both buried here in Quincy Center in the Church of the Presidents . . . because they're dead . . . and that's our history lesson for today.

3 I'm a graduate of Quincy High and did fairly well there. My average for the four years was a B– and, actually, I think I could have done better but I enjoyed playing sports a little more than studying. I played basketball and soccer. In fact, for the past two years I've been coaching soccer for a youth soccer league. It's fun working with the younger kids and teaching them the game.

4 My favorite subjects in high school were math and computers. English and history didn't rank very high on my list of favorite courses. Along with playing basketball and soccer, I also belonged to the computer club, which I enjoyed very much because not only did we have the chance to listen to guest speakers from the computer industry but, on occasion, we visited various companies in the area.

5   When I graduated from high school, I took a job with a small computer company in Cambridge right near Harvard. The work was very interesting, at first, and the money was really good. After a couple of years with the company I realized that I could go only so far with just a high school diploma and, frankly, I was getting bored with what I was doing.

6   Working in a small company, I got to know people in other departments, which gave me a good chance of looking at the bigger picture of the computer industry. I decided to return to school. In fact one of the girls, with whom I became friendly—very friendly—suggested I give some thought to going to Harvard. Right. Harvard. To go to Harvard my mother and father would have to mortgage the house, then I would have to mortgage my mother and father.

7   Anyway, when I went to give my notice; my supervisor asked me if I would be interested in working part-time, if he could arrange it, while I returned to school. To make a long story short, I was offered a part-time position and I took it. It's working out very well because not only am I able to pay my tuition, but I'm also able to save some money.

8   I selected this two-year college because it has a great computer program and the tuition is reasonable. I will be graduating this year with an Associate in Arts degree with my concentration in Computer Information Systems. My average, so far, is a 3.8 and I am a member of the Honor Society. In the fall, I hope to attend Boston College, where I plan to continue my studies in the computer field.

9   I've enjoyed my two years here at Boston Community College very much . . . especially because of the professors, who seem to be interested and communicate well with the students. If you want to sit and talk with them, or if you need extra help, they're there. For the past three semesters I volunteered to serve as a tutor in the Computer Lab. I really enjoy helping other students and wish I had more time to do it.

10   As far as what my family thinks about my coming to college, they were very pleased. I think that they would have been more pleased if I had come to college right after high school, but I wanted to go to work and make some money. But to get anywhere in the business world, especially in computers, you have to have a four-year college degree. I know it's early yet, but there's a pretty good chance that I'll go on to graduate school.

11   Traveling? I enjoy traveling and have been to England, Ireland, and Disney World in Florida with my family. During the summers, a group of us rent a cottage on Cape Cod, where on weekends we party, sail, party, golf, party, and, sometimes, swim. The one standard rule that we have is that anyone who comes to our parties must hand over the car keys, which are locked up until the next day. No one is allowed to drive once they enter the cottage and start partying. We've had many parties, lots of fun, but never a problem.

12   My biggest gripe is something that I think most of us with cars can relate to . . . and that's the ridiculously high cost of automobile insurance if you're under 25. My automobile insurance costs almost as much as my car is worth. That really **bugs** me.

13   I think the biggest problem facing our society today is the violence in the public schools, especially by kids carrying guns and other weapons. This is not a local problem but one that is nationwide . . . and very little, if anything, seems to be done about it. I just don't understand why troublemakers are permitted to stay in school; even if they're expelled, they're eventually reinstated.

14   The one thing that gives me great pleasure is . . . weekends; when I can really relax.

15   In conclusion, I would like to say that I enjoyed giving this "first" talk. But, if I said that, I would be lying. No, I'm only kidding. It really wasn't so bad, but I'm glad it's over. Are there any questions?

After you've finished your talk, you might answer questions from the class. This question-and-answer session (discussed further at the end of this chapter), more than any other exercise, will help you develop self-confidence because you'll have completed your formal talk, and you should be able to relax and answer questions on a subject that you thoroughly know—you.

Question-and-answer sessions have uncovered some unusual experiences, including the following:

- A young woman in the class appeared on TV programs several times a week and communicated to deaf viewers in sign language.
- A mother and her son and daughter attended this school at the same time. Each was enrolled in a separate section of speech classes.
- A young man enrolled in the course because he wanted to enter politics. He did, and won his campaign.
- A student told the class she signed up for this course to meet a prospective husband. You guessed it—a year later she was married.
- During semester breaks and summer vacations, a student works at Walt Disney World in Florida.
- A student told the class of her two hobbies—sky diving and hang gliding.
- A mother of two children worked one summer driving a cab. She was robbed twice and shot at once. She no longer drives a cab.

Here are some topics you might consider if your professor chooses not to assign an autobiographical talk. Remember, your first talk, if you have a choice, should be on a topic that you know very well.

1. Why I decided to come (return) to college
2. Tuitions are going right *out of sight*
3. Trying to juggle a job and classes
4. My most memorable teacher
5. The need for a longer school year
6. Daycare centers on campus
7. Being a single parent
8. How to select a reliable babysitter
9. Parent(s) should be more selective about what television programs their children watch

in other words:
out of sight—
very expensive

10. Some problems of being a parent today
11. Latchkey kids
12. Living at home versus living on your own
13. Searching for your first apartment
14. What is safe sex?
15. How to prevent date rape
16. My most embarrassing experience
17. An unforgettable vacation
18. How to buy a good used car
19. Why I own a foreign car
20. A person who has greatly influenced me
21. My biggest gripe

Of course, the kind of topic that you know well depends on your background. In recent years, there has been a significant increase in the number of foreign students enrolled in my speech classes. Here are some titles of talks that they shared with us:

1. Some Basic Differences of Buddhism, Shintoism, and Islam
2. The Day the North Vietnamese Arrested My Entire Family
3. The After-Effects of Chernobyl
4. Comparing the Cities of Moscow and Stalingrad
5. How I Escaped from a North Vietnamese Prison Camp with My Young Family
6. The Chinese Calendar and the Celebration of Holidays
7. I Was a Prisoner in a Nazi Concentration Camp
8. I Was a Participant at Tiananmen Square[1]
9. Trying to Leave Russia
10. Why My Family Left Cuba
11. Living in Haiti
12. The Woman's Role in Japan
13. American Statehood for Puerto Rico
14. Life as a Palestinian
15. Living at a Kibbutz
16. I Was a Northern Alliance Soldier Fighting in Afghanistan
17. My First Incident of Being Racially Profiled Following the Attack in New York on 9/11/01
18. Japan Is Now Taking a Second Look at Our Educational System
19. I Was an Officer in the South Vietnamese Army
20. Living with Terrorism Every Day in Israel

---

[1]A prodemocracy demonstration attended mostly by students, many of whom were massacred at Tiananmen Square in Beijing, China, in 1989.

Ice Cubes in the Stomach

Suddenly the professor calls your name—it's now your turn to address the class. Your heart pounds with such force that you think it can be heard across the room, your forehead breaks out with beads of perspiration, your mouth goes dry, and your stomach quivers.

You're experiencing an attack of nerves—**stage fright**—that is not unique to you. Most people get it, whether they admit it or not. This sensation, in varying degrees, occurs thousands of times daily: on an individual's first day on a new job, on a first date, and on a student's first day at a new school. It happens to actors and actresses just before the curtain goes up or the camera starts to roll, to students in other speech classes throughout the country ready to give their first talks, and to your own classmates who have spoken before you and to those who will follow you. Even instructors aren't immune.

For example, the week before each semester begins, the thought of facing four classes, each of approximately thirty strangers, *rattles* me. The thought of walking alone into each classroom, with students staring and trying to assess their "prof," and knowing that this first encounter is crucial in establishing respect and rapport for the entire semester, leads to many anxious moments. But once I start two-way communication and ***break the ice,*** the problems melt away. Then, when the first class ends, I enjoy a tremendous feeling of relief and accomplishment.

Speaking of the entertainment field, one of the greatest actors of the twentieth century, Sir Laurence Olivier, admitted to being so frightened just before he made his appearance on stage that he would flee to the bathroom and vomit before every performance. Look at the last four words of the preceding sentence: "vomit before every performance." Would you say that Mr. Olivier had a problem with stage fright? Yes, but it didn't stop him nor hinder his spectacular career.

Another classic example of stage fright concerns another legendary performer, the great opera tenor Enrico Caruso. Once, when a young tenor approached the "great Caruso" and asked why he nervously paced in the stage wings while awaiting his entrance, the famous tenor replied, "Young man, you can go out there and sing and all will be fine, but, night after night, I have to go out there and sound like Caruso." So, even if you experience only the slightest pangs of anxiety . . . remember, you're in good company.

Nervousness can be a form of positive energy that will keep you ***on your toes.*** If you accept it as normal, which it is, it will help you do your best. In a new environment, there is no stigma to feeling nervous or even frightened before speaking. It is a normal reaction, and its intensity will lessen the more you speak.

Even the great and the powerful suffer from nervous attacks. In a talk before London journalists years ago, a famous British cartoonist, David Low, said that every time he had to make a speech he felt as if he had a block of ice, nine inches by nine inches, in the pit of his stomach. Later he was approached by a member of the audience, Winston Churchill, one of the greatest speakers of the twentieth century. "Mr. Low," asked Churchill, "how large did you say that block of ice is?"

"Nine inches by nine inches," replied Low.

"What an amazing coincidence," said Churchill, "exactly the same size as mine."

There's no cure for nervousness, but to help control it, you should admit that you're nervous, a bit *uptight,* queasy, even petrified; some textbooks call it **speaking apprehension** or **speech tension.** You should be greatly relieved to learn how many of your peers share your feelings, and things don't seem quite that bad if you're able to talk freely about them. Discuss them at home, at school, at work, with other members of your class, and certainly with your instructor.

Yet another example of stage fright involves a person who decided to make government work her chosen career. She soon realized that her shyness and lack of self-confidence were impeding her deserved recognition and advancement. This young woman recalls: "While attending White House meetings in the 1970s, I would think of something and not say it . . . then some man would say what I had been thinking, and it would be hailed."[2] Can you imagine the level of frustration this person endured? But then this individual decided that if she was going to advance in her profession, she would have to work hard to overcome her shortcomings. And work hard she did. Over twenty years later President Bill Clinton selected Madeleine Albright to be his Secretary of State. Two more examples of people who didn't allow their nervousness and lack of self-confidence to rule their lives. You shouldn't allow them to rule yours.

Being nervous, being shy, and lacking self-confidence are traits that are very common. One of the most respected and admired individuals across the political and social spectrum, the late publisher of the *Washington Post* newspaper, Katharine Graham, was quoted by a friend, "as showing that a woman could be successful even while struggling with a severe lack of self-confidence."[3]

Here are two more examples of stage fright sufferers—this time two megasuperstars of show business. Since 1976, when Barbra Streisand was stricken with stage fright, she refused to perform before a live audience. And it wasn't until New Year's Eve 1994, over twenty years later, that she struggled with the decision and agreed to perform live in Las Vegas. You might be interested to know that for her two sell-out shows she earned more than $20 million.[4] Who says it doesn't pay to have confidence? In the other incident, the late Frank Sinatra confessed to a national TV interviewer that after decades of performing,

---

[2]*Newsweek,* 10 February 1999, 27.
[3]*Newsweek,* 20 August 2001, 12.
[4]Walter Scott, "Personality Parade," *Parade,* 30 January 1994, 2.

he still trembled with stage fright. He continued, ". . . the first four or five seconds I tremble every time I take a step and walk out of the wing onto the stage."[5]

Robert L. Montgomery put it quite nicely when he said, "The human voice is an amazing thing; it starts working the moment you're born and doesn't stop until you stand up to speak in public."

There's no simple antidote for nervousness, but you can take steps to help control this unwanted, involuntary behavior. Here are some suggestions:

1. Be totally prepared.
   a. Plan your presentation.
   b. Research and outline your topic.
   c. Cite your sources, if applicable.
2. Practice your talk several times out loud.
3. Take deep breaths before you're called to speak.
4. Don't hesitate to admit and discuss your apprehension with classmates and your instructor before the speech.
5. While waiting to be called, think only positive thoughts.
6. Realize that everyone in the audience is pulling for you, they want you to succeed just as much as they want to succeed when it's their turn.
7. Constantly remind yourself that there is no other person anywhere in the world like you and that your audience is looking forward to getting to know you.

For those of you who are overly concerned about speaker apprehension/ nervousness, I offer the following exercise that I have recommended to a multitude of students in the past with very positive results . . . they have told me. Not a cure, mind you, but very helpful. Before class, after class—actually, any time—find an empty classroom. Sit down. After a couple of minutes, imagine that someone has just introduced you. Take a deep breath, get up and walk to the front of the room and stand behind the lectern, if there's one in class, and look around the class imagining an audience. After a few minutes, walk back to your seat and sit there awhile. Then, repeat the activity several times.

When you feel comfortable and a bit more confident—perhaps while you're in front of the empty classrooms—visualize an audience and briefly introduce yourself. Over the years, many students have told me that this exercise was extremely helpful in lessening their degree of nervousness when facing an audience. Good luck.

No single action is more important in helping you develop self-confidence and in allaying that uptight feeling than ***knowing your subject cold.*** Chapter 9 contains further suggestions on what you can do, both before and during your talk, to help relieve tension and to diminish your nervousness.

And speaking of nervousness, you might enjoy the speech in Appendix A given by Mark Twain entitled, "Mark Twain's First Appearance," in which he discusses his experience with "stage fright."

<u>in other</u>
<u>words:</u>
knowing your subject cold— being very familiar with your subject

---

[5]"Celebrity," *Boston Herald,* 16 May 1988, 11.

Keep your cool.

Front and Center

When the initial shock of hearing your name has subsided, slowly draw a few deep breaths. This should help ease that uptight feeling. Walk to the front of the classroom with purpose and confidence. Don't shuffle your feet, don't look at the floor, and don't make any remarks to class members. Once you begin your talk, all their attention will be riveted on you.

Before starting to speak, you may find it reassuring to look around the classroom. You may sense encouragement from familiar faces. You may also observe a look of genuine understanding from those who appreciate your feelings because it will soon be their turn. You now realize that you're not alone. The preceding speakers sweated through the same experience, and the following speakers will do the same. The more quickly you appreciate this, the more relaxed you'll become.

As soon as you get wrapped up in what you're saying, perhaps twenty to thirty seconds into your talk, your nervousness should diminish. This is why we emphasize knowing your subject thoroughly. (In this regard, it may be helpful to memorize the first few sentences, and perhaps even the closing one, to avoid the hesitant, awkward, "Well, I guess that's just about it.")

Be Sure to Use Correct English Grammar

I think you'll agree that very few things are more impressive than listening to a person who speaks well. By speaking well, I refer to an individual who has a pleasant voice and who speaks clearly, distinctly, and with inflection, at an understandable rate of delivery. I'm talking about a person who articulates well and pronounces all the syllables within a word as well as word endings.

Although a speaker may possess all of these positive attributes, she or he can easily convey a negative impression by using poor English grammar when speaking. Unfortunately, poor English usage is much too common. You hear it in and out of class, at work, at socials, at meetings, and even, occasionally, on radio and TV during the play-by-play of sporting events. Just as a person who has a very good vocabulary usually creates the impression that he or she is an educated individual, the person who uses poor grammar usually gives the impression that he or she lacks a good education.

So, before you give your first talk in class, I'd like you to give some thought to your use of the English language. And here's something else to keep in mind. If you have classmates from another country or culture who are trying to improve their English, "they learn by listening." They endeavor to absorb not only what you say, but how you say it. So, in essence, as far as they are concerned, you are like a teacher. Remember, they learn by listening.

One more thing to ***keep in mind*** is the fact that using poor grammar stands out glaringly—particularly during job interviews and promotion considerations. Here are some of the more common English grammar mistakes heard daily:

in other words:
keep in mind— remember

Instead of saying . . .	You should say . . .
They don't know nothing	They don't know anything
They don't do that no more	They don't do that anymore
I've already did that	I've already done that
I done it	I did it
He/she don't	He/she doesn't
Ain't got or don't got	Don't have
She/he could of went	She/he could have gone
Should have saw	Should have seen
Could of did	Could have done
I seen him/her	I had seen him/her or I saw him/her
I go	I said
All ah yous	All of you
I don't want no	I don't want any
Me and my friends	My friends and I
You was	You were
I've already took	I've already taken

For more information on using proper English, head for the library or, on the Internet, search for "grammar" or "correct English" and see what happens. You'll find more on this subject in Chapter 5.

Say It without Words

First impressions are crucial to communicators, and all of you are communicators. Every day you see people, you greet people, and you meet people—at work, at school, and at social or business functions. Before you even say a word, you transmit impressions, favorable or not, through **nonverbal communication,** the conscious or subconscious transmission and reception of unspoken messages. (You are being introduced to this topic because it will be an integral part of your autobiographical talk. Chapter 3 is devoted entirely to this subject.) Some features of nonverbal communication include:

- *Your walk:* Is it slow, fast, listless, jerky, confident, or hesitant? Do you march, saunter, strut, shuffle, or stalk?
- *Your posture:* Are you straight as a drill sergeant? Do you slump, shift from one leg to the other, droop, or lean on the **lectern** (speaker's stand)?
- *Your facial expressions:* Do you smile, frown, or smirk? Do you look condescending, absorbed, disappointed, or troubled?
- *Your eyes:* Are they expressive, twinkling, shifty, piercing, friendly, cold, or penetrating?
- *Your dress:* Are you neat or sloppy? Is your hair combed? Are your colors coordinated or clashing?
- *Your cosmetics:* How much aftershave lotion, cologne, perfume, hairspray, or antiperspirant did you apply? Too much or not enough? Is your make-up caked on? Do you look like someone from Mars?
- *Your gestures:* What do you do with your hands, head, and shoulders? Are you constantly touching your face, ears, hair, or jewelry? Are your hands clasped in front of or behind you? Are they in your pockets? Are your head and shoulders constantly moving or immobile?

All the above nonverbal characteristics transmit messages that can have an important effect on the success of your oral presentation.

First impressions are usually long-lasting. How many times have you prejudged a person by any of the above criteria, only to change your assessment after you've become better acquainted? How many times have you reached a negative opinion about a person before he or she has had the opportunity to communicate orally?

Indeed, nonverbal communication can often influence your opinions more forcefully than the spoken word. The old aphorism that actions speak louder than words is more than mere rhetoric.

In all communication, you don't always have to say it to convey it, and in nonverbal communication you may often transmit messages entirely different from what you think you're transmitting. Call it what you like—**body language, silent language, soundless speech,** or nonverbal communication—it is an eloquent form of message transmission and reception. (For more on nonverbal communication, refer to Chapter 3.)

Importance of Eye Contact

Perhaps you know the feeling of approaching several of your friends who are involved in a discussion. When you join the group, you notice that the speaker doesn't look at you but continues looking at the others. Your presence isn't acknowledged, and you feel left out.

Eye contact with your audience is extremely important. Without it you will have immense difficulty conveying interest and sincerity. What is your reaction when you listen to someone who doesn't look you in the eye, at least occasionally? The speaker's believability is seriously impaired. When you appear before a group, you should remember that the people are not only listening *to* you, they are also *looking at you.*

As tempting as it is, don't gaze out windows, at notes, or at the floor or walls. Some speakers, by looking at people in the last row of a large audience, can give the impression that they're looking at everyone in front of them. In a smaller group, however, look at the students to your left, then to your right, then in between. Make eye contact. Don't make the mistake of some beginning

Eye contact with your audience is extremely important.

speakers, who focus their eyes solely on the professor. Just remember, people like to be talked to and looked at simultaneously.

Making eye contact means that you, the sender, are making a connection with your audience, the receiver. You're transmitting a message, and without eye contact the transmission is broken and communication is disrupted.

By maintaining eye contact with your audience you can receive visual feedback. Your listeners' eyes can tell you if they're getting your message. Do they look confused, bored, doubting, satisfied, or interested? Do they seem to enjoy and understand what you're saying? Do they look drowsy? As long as you're aware of *telltale* signals from your audience, the communication cycle can be complete. You have a message to communicate with your mind, your voice, your body, and your eyes—you maintain eye contact with your audience and you receive messages in response to your spoken thoughts. If you fail to look at your audience, you can't receive any reaction from them. (For more on eye contact, see Chapter 3.)

in other words:
telltale—
obvious

What about Gestures?

Many people **gesture** as naturally as they breathe. Perhaps you know people who would be speechless if their hands were tied behind their backs. If you find it natural to move your hands and arms while communicating, continue to do so. If, however, you tend to be carried away by gestures, don't be too concerned about them now because you'll learn to control them as the course progresses.

Your instructor will make suggestions as to the degree and effectiveness of your gestures. One practical exercise is to speak before a mirror and watch your body movements. Being videotaped is the best way to see yourself exactly as you appear to others.

Try to become more aware of how people gesture (nonverbal communication is also discussed in Chapters 3, 5, and 15) when they talk—for example, groups of students, your teacher, friends, family members, your boss, and performers on TV. Are their gestures meaningful and expressive, or do they look awkward and meaningless?

Hands always seem to be a problem for inexperienced speakers, but they don't have to be. We've already mentioned gesturing. You may use one or both hands simultaneously, but not constantly. On occasion you may clasp your hands behind your back. If there's no lectern, which is a speaker's stand resting on a table or desk to hold papers and notes (not to be confused with **podium,** an elevated platform or stage), you may hold notes in your hands.

Moving Around

As far as movement is concerned, many speakers feel that they must stay in one place and remain completely motionless. Not so. You should feel free to move

Many people gesture as naturally as they breathe.

around. Taking a few steps in either direction from the stand is desirable as long as you move smoothly, not jerkily, like a puppet.

However, avoid perpetual motion, for example, swaying back and forth or from side to side, crossing and uncrossing your feet, or fidgeting with your hands and fingers. Movement can be effective when done in moderation, with purpose and naturalness. It helps you develop poise and confidence, and it constructively channels your nervous energy.

Platform Etiquette

Good posture—standing straight and squarely on both feet—conveys an impression of confidence and alertness. Your posture communicates attitude, just as your face and voice do. Don't slouch, lean against a table, or drape yourself over the speaker's stand. These actions detract from your overall appearance and create a negative effect on your audience.

Perhaps the best way to improve your posture is to observe yourself on videotape or in a full-length mirror. There you can see if you're standing tall or hunched over, if your head is held high or drooping, and if your weight is equally distributed on both feet.

There's no question about it—erect posture helps you look sharper, feel more alert, and is a sign of good health.

It's okay to relax, but . . . .

Also as part of your "platform etiquette" while speaking before an audience, remember *not* to:

● Play with your hair (keep it from covering one or both of your eyes)
● Constantly touch your face, neck, ears, and nose
● Keep your hands in your pocket or in your belt/waist
● Play with necklaces, chains, rings, pendants, earrings, or bracelets
● Wear long sweatshirt sleeves that cover your hands

Just as you don't want any distractions from your audience, you don't want to do anything to distract them from your message.

Take Note

Using notes is recommended, because notes can give you a feeling of confidence and security. In fact, many professional speakers use them. Just be careful not to rely on them to the point that you read the entire talk without looking at your audience.

If there is no lectern, 3-by-5 cards can fit comfortably in the palm of your hand without annoying the audience. If your classroom is equipped with a lectern, 4-by-6 cards (or even standard-sized 8½-by-11 inch paper) may rest on it without being noticed. Try to keep your cards lying flat so they won't distract your audience, and, as you finish with one, simply slide it to the side unobtrusively. If you have more than two cards, number them in case you drop or misplace them (these things do happen).

Question-and-Answer Session

As you conclude your talk, don't lower your voice so that it becomes almost inaudible. Keep it strong and confident until you finally ask, "Are there any questions?" Some of your classmates and even your professor may have a few. If they do, you should feel complimented and, by this time, relaxed enough to answer them easily and naturally.

While you're answering questions, try not to focus your attention solely on the questioner. If the answer is long, you may glance around the class, but when you're concluding your reply, look again at the questioner. Pause a second or two as if to ask, "Did I answer you satisfactorily?" Then *field* the next inquiry.

in other words:
field—ask for

During the question-and-answer session, if you feel that a questioner's voice is too low or soft for everyone in the class to hear, then repeat the question. Nothing is more aggravating than sitting in the middle or near the rear during a lecture and hearing answers to inaudible or partly audible questions. If you don't understand a question, there's a pretty good chance that others don't either. In this case, ask that the question be repeated. Then, repeat it yourself so that the questioner will know that you understand it and so will your audience.

When you've *handled* all the questions, breathe deeply and return to your seat confidently. Don't rush. Don't crumple your notes and stuff them into your pocket, and don't collapse into your chair. Just sit down quietly.

handled—answered, dealt with

Knowing your subject and responding knowledgeably during the **question-and-answer period** will do more than anything else to bolster your self-confidence.

After a talk, many students feel that their nervousness was vividly displayed when, in most cases, just the opposite is true. In reality—and we wouldn't kid you—you don't look even half as nervous as you feel inside. Just ask your classmates.

There's no doubt that the question-and-answer session is extremely beneficial to the speaker as well as to members of the audience. And, since there's a welcome increase of students from other countries and cultures to our classrooms, I thought that I would offer some questions that you may wish to ask them, if they weren't already addressed during their talk:

Why did you decide to come to this school? What is your major or area of concentration? Why did you or your parents decide to leave your country? Was there a problem leaving? Do you plan to return to your country after you've completed your education? Could you compare the education system in your country to that here in the United States? What was your first impression of the United States? Was it what you expected?

What did you do in your country (work, study)? Did you study English in your country? Do you still have relatives in your country? Have you been back to your country since coming to the United States? What do you like the most about this country? What do you like the least? What is the most difficult culture adjustment you have had to make since being here? Are you a U.S. citizen? Do you plan on becoming one? Welcome to America . . . the true land of opportunity where it's no coincidence that *American* ends with "I can."

Congratulations! You've given your first talk. Was it as difficult as you thought it would be? Was it as traumatic an experience as you envisioned? It probably was. But you did it, and this was the most difficult talk you'll ever make—your toughest obstacle course. Your other talks should be easier and more enjoyable.

Quick Clicks

Welcome to a "surprise search." To further enhance your research or simply to harvest more information about some of the things you studied in this chapter, just drop in at any of the following addresses. What you'll discover may be serious, educational, bibliographical, surprising, factual, or even downright humorous. But it will definitely be informative.

So, go ahead and give a "Quick Click."

www.bartleby.com/124/index.html
www.comedy-zone.net/guide/quotes.htm
www.toastmasters.org/tips.htm
www.soyouwanna.com/site/syws/speaking/speaking.html
http://jlasc.com/educ/idea.htm
www.public-speaking.org

Things to Discuss in Class

1. Be aware of eye contact among your friends, colleagues, speakers, and TV performers. When you are personally involved, observe the importance and effect of eye contact among your associates.

2. Using the format presented in this chapter as an aid, prepare and rehearse a four- to five-minute autobiographical talk.

3. Notice how people gesture when they speak. Do the gestures of anyone in particular impress you? Why or why not?

4. Watch speakers on TV, especially religious personalities, and observe their physical movements while speaking. Do they move at all? Do their movements coincide with their message? Are their movements distracting? Prepare to discuss your answers in class.

5. When you meet an individual for the first time, what determines your first impression of that person?

6. What are your personal feelings about judging an individual solely on the basis of physical appearance?

7. Do you have friends who never look directly at you when they talk with you? How do you feel about this behavior?

2. Is getting nervous before speaking uncommon? Explain.

3. Why is eye contact so vitally important?

4. When you speak before a group, why is it important to look around constantly at individuals in the audience rather than to focus on a limited area?

5. Do gestures enhance your ability to communicate? Why or why not?

6. What must you be aware of when you use notes?

7. What are two things you can do to help control nervousness?

8. Explain why good posture is important to a public speaker.

What Do You Remember from This Chapter?

1. What two elements in speaking do more than anything else to help you acquire self-confidence?

Vitalize Your Vocabulary

You can have a clear, musical voice, an attractive appearance, good eye contact, and a solid knowledge of your subject; but if your vocabulary is weak and vague, your presentation will also be weak and vague. Whether you're communicating with one or two people or a group of thirty, an extensive vocabulary is a major asset. That is why, starting in Chapter 1 and continuing with each succeeding chapter, we include a list of words (and their most basic meanings) that educated people should not only understand, but be able to use.

The lists of words vary considerably. Some lists contain families of words that relate to the same subject, for example, government and politics, health care and phobias, business and finance, computers and data processing. Other lists consist of synonyms and antonyms, words based on Latin and Greek roots, words from Native American languages, and words from Japan that have entered our language. In response to requests from students and professors who have

used this book, the number of words has been expanded.

We hope that these brief glimpses into the intriguing world of words will galvanize you into exploring more deeply into that world.

English words derive from countless languages, principally from Latin and Greek, and from other sources such as literature, art, and science. Among the most fascinating words are "eponyms"—words based on the names of real or mythical people who have accomplished something unusual.

Eponyms

blanket (n.) A large covering of wool or synthetic cloth material on a bed to provide warmth. The credit goes to Thomas Blanket, an Englishman, who around 1380 first made these bed coverings.

bogus (adj.) Something that is counterfeit or fake, not genuine. Attributed to a Mr. Borghese who, in the 1830s, did a fantastic business in flooding the American West with counterfeit bank notes.

booze (n.) An alcoholic drink. Attributed to Mr. E. Booze, who was a distiller in Kentucky around 1840. He sold his booze using his own name in bottles shaped like log cabins. The *Oxford English Dictionary*, however, states that the term was in use in 1529.

boycott (v.) To join together in refusing to buy, sell, use, or deal with; (n.) the act of boycotting. Derived from Captain Charles C. Boycott (1832–1897), a landlord's agent, whose job was to collect high rents from impoverished Irish tenant farmers.

Braille (n.) A system of printing and writing, using-raised dots, to enable blind people to communicate. Devised by the French teacher Louis Braille (1809–1852).

Broccoli (n.) The green flowery vegetable dates back to 1699 but was brought to America from Naples, Italy, in 1928 by Albert Broccoli.

cardigan (n.) A sweater or jacket that opens full length down the front, usually long-sleeved and collarless. Named after the seventh Earl of Cardigan (1799–1868), an English general.

casanova (n.) A man who has a reputation for being a promiscuous lover, with many female conquests. After Giovanni Casanova, an Italian adventurer and writer of the eighteenth century.

Celsius (adj.) A system for measuring temperature in which 0 stands for freezing and 100 is the boiling point of water. This system was invented by Anders Celsius, a Swedish astromer and professor, around 1700.

chauvinist (n.) An extremist in any cause, often militaristic or patriotic. Derived from Nicolas Chauvin, one of Napoleon's most fanatical followers.

Chesterfield (n.) A man's overcoat with concealed buttons and a velvet collar. Named after an Earl of Chesterfield in the nineteenth century after he gave explicit instructions to his tailor on how he wanted it made.

condom (n.) A sheath made of rubber or latex and used by men during sexual relations to avoid pregnancy or sexually transmitted disease. Supposedly first introduced in England around 1700 by a Dr. Condom.

crapper (n.) A flush toilet which was invented by Thomas Crapper (1837–1910), a Victorian English engineer.

derrick (n.) A large crane for lifting and moving heavy objects, especially during construction projects. Named after Thomas Derrick, a well-known hangman during the reigns of Elizabeth and James I around 1600.

derringer (n.) A short-barreled pistol, which is quite small and could easily fit into a woman's small purse. Invented by American Henry Deringer, a gunsmith, in the 1840s.

Doberman pinscher (n.) A breed of large dogs with smooth dark hair, tan markings, and erect ears, developed by German dog breeder Ludwig Dobermann around 1890.

dunce (n.) A stupid or lazy student. Named after John Duns Scotus (1265–1309), a Scottish philosopher and theologian.

epicure (n.) A person with refined and discriminating taste in fine foods and drinks, named after Epicurus, a Greek philosopher (342–270 B.C.), who advocated sensuous pleasure as the highest good.

Fahrenheit (adj.) A temperature scale invented by German physicist Daniel Gabriel Fahrenheit (1686–1736), in which 32 degrees is the freezing point of water and 212 degrees is its boiling point.

Ferris wheel (n.) A large upright wheel with seats hanging from the frame. Very popular at fairs and expositions, this amusement attraction was named after its inventor, George W. G. Ferris, in 1895–1896.

gerrymander (v.) To rearrange a voting district so as to favor the party in power. After Massachusetts Governor Elbridge Gerry, who in 1812 carved out a district whose shape resembled a salamander.

hooker (n.) A prostitute. During the Civil War, General Joseph Hooker's troops were encamped for a time in Washington. Prostitutes who "serviced" them became known as "Hooker's Division." After the troops moved out, the women were called "hookers."

Jacuzzi (n.) Underwater jets of water in a tub that massage the body is named after its creator, Italian-born Candido Jacuzzi (1903–1986).

leotard (n.) A one-piece, tight-fitting garment that covers the torso and is now worn by dancers and acrobats. Named for Jules Leotard, a nineteenth-century French trapeze artist.

Levi's® (trademark) Blue jeans. Named after Levi Strauss, a Texas merchant who popularized them in the 1800s.

Listerine® (trademark) The popular antiseptic mouthwash. From Joseph Lister, first Baron of Lyme Regis (1827–1912), the founder of antiseptic surgery.

machiavellian (adj.) Deceitful, unscrupulous, crafty. In accordance with the political ideas explained in *The Prince*, a classic book written by Niccolò Machiavelli (1469–1527), Italian statesman, political philosopher, and author.

masochist (n.) A person who receives sexual pleasure from being physically abused. Named after the Austrian novelist Leopold von Sacher-Masoch (1836–1895), whose writings and bizarre lifestyle reflected this obsession.

maverick (n.) An independent-minded person who usually goes against popular opinion. Named after the American pioneer Samuel A. Maverick (1803–1870), who was known for shady business practices as a rancher.

mentor (n.) A wise and trusted advisor. In Greek mythology, Mentor was the loyal friend and advisor of Odysseus (and instructor of his son Telemachus), from Homer's *Odyssey*.

mesmerize (v.) To hypnotize or be held spellbound. Derives from the name of the Austrian physician and hypnotist Franz Anton Mesmer (1734–1815), who was known for hypnotizing his patients.

Murphy's law (n.) A facetious or satirical proposition stating that if there is a possibility for something to go wrong, it will. This humorous canon is attributed to E. A. Murphy, Jr., a U.S. engineer who formulated the original version in 1949.

nicotine (n.) A poisonous substance that is the chief active ingredient in tobacco. From Jean Nicot, a seventeenth-century French diplomat who introduced Turkish tobacco into France.

pasteurize (v.) To destroy disease-producing bacteria and to stop fermentation in milk, beer, cider, and wine by heating the liquid to high temperatures. From Louis Pasteur (1822–1895), French chemist and bacteriologist.

ritzy (adj.) Meaning anything luxurious, elegant, or fashionable, derived from the founder of the elegant Ritz hotels, Swiss hotelier César Ritz (1850–1918).

sadist (n.) A person who enjoys inflicting pain on another. Named after the Marquis de Sade (1740–1814), French soldier and novelist, who conducted experiments on pain and wrote about them.

sandwich (n.) Two or more slices of bread with a filling of cheese, meat, jam, or fish between them; (v.) to squeeze between two persons, places, things, etc. After John Montague (1718–1792), the fourth Earl of Sandwich, who ate this way so as not to leave the gambling table for meals.

saxophone (n.) A woodwind instrument with a curved metal body. Invented by Antoine Sax (1814–1894), a Belgian maker of musical instruments.

solon (n.) A lawmaker or legislator, from the Athenian statesman and lawgiver Solon, who framed the democratic laws of Athens (640–559? B.C.).

stonewall (v.) To refuse to answer in the face of questioning. This behavior, very common in recent times, is attributed to General Thomas J. "Stonewall" Jackson, who fought for the South in the U.S. Civil War. He earned this title when he and his troops "stood like a stone wall" against the enemy during the Battle of Bull Run.

vandal (n.) Someone who deliberately destroys or damages another's property. The word derives from the Vandals, a Germanic people, who traveled southward from Scandinavia in the first four centuries A.D., causing tremendous devastation in Gaul, Spain, and North Africa.

3

You Don't Have to Say It to Convey It

He that has eyes to see and ears to hear may convince himself that no mortal can keep a secret. If his lips are silent, he chatters with his fingertips; betrayal oozes out of him at every pore.
—Sigmund Freud (1856–1939), founder of psychoanalysis

After reading and understanding this chapter, you should be able to:

- Define nonverbal communication

- Explain the vital roles that personal and nonpersonal nonverbal communication perform in the messages we transmit and receive daily

- Observe and explain the various personal modes that communicate nonverbal messages

- Explain the roles of non-personal factors such as time, space, clothes, artifacts, and color in nonverbal communication

- Understand more fully how some other cultures communicate nonverbal messages through eye contact, gestures, time, space, and color

chapter
preview

This chapter deals with nonverbal language—the "language without words" that we use, consciously or subconsciously, to convey and receive messages. This language is often termed body language, face language, silent language, and silent messages. You may, in fact, depend more on this wordless language than you do on words.

Some personal elements of nonverbal language include posture, eye contact, facial expressions, vocalics, body movement and gestures, clothes, smell, taste, and touch. Some impersonal elements are objects (artifacts), space, time, and color.

Also discussed is intercultural/multicultural communication, and how various cultures throughout the world communicate certain nonverbal messages.

Your appearance creates powerful first impressions, even before you utter a word. How often have you misjudged someone initially because he wore a beard or she exuded a perfume that you couldn't stomach? On the job and in your social life, your appearance can help you or hurt you—tremendously.

Impersonal aspects of nonverbal communication also create impressions about you. Time, and how you use it in relation to others, tells something about you. If you're a high-ranking manager, for instance, you can keep your employees waiting. Space, or "turf" as it is sometimes called, is another impersonal element that denotes your status and authority. As a manager, you probably have an office with a large desk, windows, a rug, extra furniture, air conditioning, recessed lighting, plants, and paintings on the walls. All these artifacts represent power, prestige, and prosperity.

You'll realize that another significant mode of nonverbal communication is the role that color plays in our daily lives, and in other cultures as well.

Our personal lives are influenced by our use of nonverbal language. Depending on how we control it, career decisions may be positively or negatively affected.

What Is Nonverbal Communication?

We have all heard any number of sayings and phrases that clearly demonstrate the importance and messages of **nonverbal communication**, such as:

● "Actions speak louder than words." Perhaps you can recall, as a child, the number of times you were told (verbal) not to do something, but you persisted to the point that the only "language" you really understood was a slap (nonverbal) on the hand or rear.
● "It wasn't so much *what* he said, but *how* he said it." Try to recall a number of situations to which this statement applies.
● "She had a look that could kill." If your mate discovers you where you shouldn't be, with someone you shouldn't be with, and doing something you shouldn't be doing, you'll understand this remark.

I'm sure that you'll have no difficulty understanding the implications of the following colorful sentences:

● Following the police exam, Erik was feeling rather blue, really down in the dumps.
● When Michelina found out that her roommate was going out with her former boyfriend, she saw red.

The nonverbal elements of communication are extremely important, in some instances more so than the spoken words. In fact, when a person's actions and words appear contradictory, the actions often communicate the true feelings. Indeed, it is estimated that when communicating one on one, as much as 90 percent of the message is communicated nonverbally.[1]

---

[1]Albert Mehrabian, *Silent Messages* (Belmont, CA: Wadsworth, 1981), 76.

As you learned in Chapter 2, nonverbal communication is the conscious or subconscious transmission and reception of unspoken messages. Authorities differ about the exact impact, but they all agree that the meaning of nonverbal messages is much more significant than verbal messages.

Nonverbal communication is often referred to by other terms, such as **silent language, body language,** *face language, silent messages,* and "beyond words." No matter what it is called, it means the conscious or subconscious transmission and reception of messages other than spoken words.

Nonverbal communication is a vast and ever-growing field of study and research. Some of its elements include facial expressions, eye contact, gestures, other body movements, and **paralanguage**—laughing, coughing, throat clearing, **vocal pitch,** and **pauses.** Other elements include space, time, sight, taste, smell, touch, clothes, color, sound, environment, weather, lighting, and objects. This is just a partial list of nonverbal elements. We will discuss only those over which you may have some control and which you may find important and common in your daily life.

How We Communicate without Words

We cannot *not* communicate. We communicate simply by being alive. Messages are transmitted to others via our sex; body frame; scars, birthmarks, and other visible features; hair color and style; skin and eye color; as well as the quality of our complexions. How many of us have made initial judgments of people from a superficial first glance—and been wrong?

Our **self-image** is crucial not only to us personally, but to how others perceive us. More and more people, regardless of age or sex, are spending thousands of dollars for cosmetic surgery, simply to look and feel more appealing or to change their image.

Would you like some interesting statistics on this topic? In the year 2001, there were 5.7 million cosmetic procedures performed on women in the United States, a whopping 25 percent increase over the preceding year. And, not to be left out, there was almost a 25 percent increase in cosmetic procedures performed on men. Alan Gaynor, a leading practioner, states, "Thanks to the aging baby boomers and medical advances, cosmetic surgery is now an $80 billion industry.[2] Vive la sex appeal!

Our very presence or absence "says something." If, for example, you registered for a certain course and then cut several classes, what messages might your absence transmit to the instructor? He might think you were ill, or that you were still vacationing, or that you had changed your mind and signed up for another course. In fact, maybe you had changed jobs and your new hours

---

[2]Sue Scheible, "The Kindest Cuts," *The Patriot Ledger,* Saturday/Sunday 5–6 May 2001, 1.

prevented you from going to that first class, or perhaps you had to stay home with an ill child. The instructor, though, might interpret your absence as apathy.

If you signed up for a course and attend from day one, your presence alone would transmit some of the following messages to your instructor: He would know your sex, approximate height and weight, and probably your taste in clothes or make-up. He might even know your socioeconomic background and your general health or, from the way you dress, whether you're conservative or liberal. Your facial expressions might announce that you're happy, sad, nervous, friendly, shy, frightened, or restless. Where you sit in class (front row, back row, near the door) and how you sit (straight up, slouched, feet resting on the chair in front of you) are other nonverbal signs that communicate messages to your instructor. Such messages are transmitted by your presence—even before you speak a word.

We communicate nonverbally by who we are; our appearance; the way we walk and stand; our facial expressions and eye contact; the way we move, gesture, and touch; and our **vocalics,** or paralanguage.

Our Appearance

Before we even open our mouths, we make an impression, favorable or unfavorable. The clothes we wear often communicate our status in life and our degree of self-confidence. Just from observing a person's apparel, you may have said that the person "has class" or "has no class."

What you wear to work can be as important as your job performance. According to a survey of over one hundred top executives of major corporations:

- 96 percent said that their employees had a better chance of getting ahead if they knew how to dress.
- 72 percent said they would stall the promotion of a person who didn't dress properly.
- 84 percent turned down people who dressed improperly for job interviews.[3]

An authority on apparel writes, "When you step into a room, even though no one in that room knows you or has seen you before, they will make ten decisions about you based solely on your appearance." He further states: "To be successful in almost any endeavor, you must be sure that these decisions about you are favorable, because in that first impression you make—*you are what you wear.*"[4]

For example, what impression would you make if you appeared before a group impeccably dressed but with messy hair and dirty fingernails? Your perfume, cosmetics, aftershave lotion, and deodorant (or lack of it) convey messages. Is your breath always fresh and your body clean? If not, it will be no secret.

---

[3]John T. Molloy, *Dress for Success* (New York: Warner Books, 1975), 36.

[4]William Thourlby, *You Are What You Wear* (New York: New American Library, 1978), 1.

A dental appointment? Root canal, perhaps?

Posture often reflects your attitude, pride, confidence, and general health. If your instructor observes—and she's adept at this—that you're sitting erect and looking at her, she'll probably conclude that you're alert and interested in her lecture. If, on the other hand, you're drooping in your chair, she'll conclude that you're tired, bored, or daydreaming.

A classic example of how posture can reflect your image took place in our nation's capitol. A slouched-over and shuffling secretary of defense was accompanied to a very important press conference by the ramrod-straight presence of the chairman of the Joint Chiefs of Staff. This prompted another high-ranking officer to complain of the secretary, "Why can't he stand up straight?"[5]

At the next chance, notice the way people walk. You can almost tell their mission by their posture and stride: Are they fast-paced, slow-paced, skipping, ambling, hunched over, or walking tall? Is one in a hurry? Perhaps he's late for a date. Is another slouching along? Maybe she's dreading a dental appointment. Good posture projects a positive image.

Our Facial Expressions

Perhaps no nonverbal code can be so easily misread as facial expressions, because so many people control them so well. Controlling these expressions can

[5]*U.S. News & World Report,* 12 July 1993, 32.

camouflage true feelings. We are better prepared to lie with our face than with any other nonverbal cue. Perhaps you can recall a situation when you were eating something you really didn't like, but, so as not to offend the cook, you said it was "delicious," and your remark was reinforced by your feigned smile and nod. You've heard the saying, "She lied through her teeth." When you consider that facial muscles can create thousands of different expressions, this saying makes sense.

To ensure **credibility** when speaking, we should strive to have our facial expression and verbal message coincide. Imagine the reaction if you smiled while talking about a tragedy such as the homeless or babies born with AIDS, or if you flashed an expression of indifference while congratulating someone on a happy occasion. Conversely, crying at a wedding is acceptable because, presumably, these are tears of joy.

Research tells us that facial expressions can communicate the following meanings: surprise, fear, happiness, contempt, disgust, anger, interest, determination, and sadness.[6] The following quote from Ralph Waldo Emerson is appropriate: "A man finds room in the few square inches of his face for the traits of all his ancestors, for the expression of all his history, and his wants."[7]

Our Eyes

Eye contact is necessary to establish and maintain a beam of communication between you and your listeners. If you're listening to a lecture and suddenly the speaker starts reading a long passage verbatim, the chances are that this strong line of communication has been disrupted and your attention may wander.

Eye contact also makes it possible for you to receive that all-important visual **feedback** from your listeners, which, in turn, permits you to respond to their behavior and reactions. If you're speaking too fast or too softly, if your listeners appear perplexed or bored, or if they seem to be pleased or sympathetic to your message, you should be able to "read" these nonverbal messages by looking directly at the members of your audience. Constant eye contact greatly enhances your credibility and makes your message more personal.

Along with your facial muscles, eyes can convey approval or disapproval; they can include or exclude a person during a conversation; they transmit happiness, sadness, confusion, and even terror. Eyes tell us if someone is interested or not. Eyes can communicate at a glance. If you've ever visited a singles bar, you've probably experienced the dynamics of communication via glances, winks, and stares.

Our culture teaches us that it's impolite to stare. The next time you're on a bus or a train, single out a person and stare at him or her. See how long it takes

----

[6]Paul Ekman, W. V. Friesen, and P. Ellsworth, *Emotion in the Human Face* (New York: Pergamon Press, 1972), 57–65.

[7]Ralph Waldo Emerson, "Behavior," *The Conduct of Life* (1860).

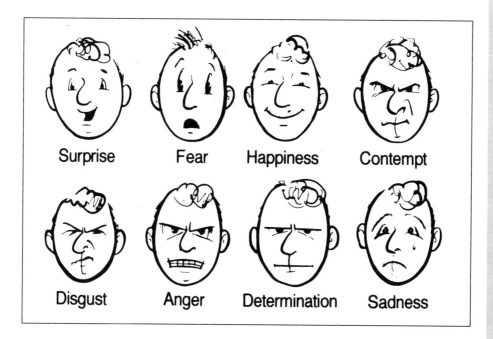

before the situation becomes awkward. When children are being scolded, they try to avoid eye contact but are ordered to "Look at me when I talk to you."

The next time you're in an elevator, notice how little eye contact takes place because of the occupants' proximity to each other. They will stare at the flashing floor numbers, the floor, or the ceiling, but seldom at each other unless, of course, they're seeking contact. Most people tend to increase eye contact with those from whom they seek approval or recognition. Eye contact greatly enhances your verbal message because you're looking directly at the people you wish to inform, persuade, inspire, or actuate.

Over the years, I've found that some of my foreign students—particularly many Japanese, Vietnamese, Chinese, Russian, and some Middle Eastern students—resist maintaining eye contact with their audience. Instead, they'll look at notes, the lectern, the floor, ceiling, and walls. In part, this is due to their culture: many of them have been raised to find prolonged eye contact embarrassing, or taught that it's rude or a sign of disrespect. (Yet, although they shy away from looking at and around the class, some of these students will look almost exclusively at their professor because, as many have said, "It gives me a sense of security.") While many American students also have difficulty making eye contact, this is less from cultural teachings and more often just a bad habit.

Our Body Movement

To appreciate the almost total power of nonverbal communication, watch a professional pantomimist perform—it is sheer artistry. Some of the classic characterizations in show business belong to such superstars as Jerry Lewis, the team of Penn and Teller, and the late Jackie Gleason, Lucille Ball, Charlie Chaplin, Red Skelton, and, of course, the unforgettable pauses and expressions of Jack Benny. (Fortunately, and thanks to the multitude of cable channels, many of these memorable stars can still be seen and appreciated on "reruns." It would be worthwhile to seek out some of these classics.) Their artful use of apparel, movement, eye contact, gestures, and facial expressions brings laughter and tears to millions of all ages. The ways in which they move their arms, hands and fingers, head and eyes and the ways they sway, stoop, and bend are sheer genius. Even when they don't utter a word, their messages are always understood.

Kinesics is the study and application of body movement. Your kinesic behavior can significantly reinforce your verbal message. Such movement adds variety to your overall delivery, as opposed to standing rigidly in one spot.

When speaking before a group, occasionally move back . . . then come forward. Move your upper body slightly to the left to address the left side of your audience, then slightly (you guessed it) to the right to give equal time to those on the right. Get really bold, take a full step or two to the right and then to the left of the lectern. I suppose we could call this speech or oral choreography. Want to get more personal with your listeners? Good. You can do that simply by moving closer to them, and if you wish to make emphatic points, take a step for each point, perhaps speaking in a lower voice for emphasis. Movement can also help you relax by releasing excess energy.

Move—but don't overdo it!

Remember, remaining motionless while you speak is like speaking in a monotone. It's not only boring, it will surely lose your audience's interest in your message.

Our Gestures

Gestures play a large role in our daily communication and are usually most effective when performed spontaneously. There's no question that effective gestures enhance and supplement verbal messages. A hitchhiker pointing his thumb, an umpire calling a player out at home plate, and an officer directing traffic at a busy intersection are examples of communicating explicitly without words, as is the sign language of the hearing-impaired.

However, if you constantly use the same hand or arm when making a point or if your gesturing becomes mechanical, then this activity can quickly become repetitious and boring. Strive for variety and spontaneity.

When giving directions, many people find it easier to accompany spoken words with hand movements—straight, to the right or left, up or down. We've probably all been shown, by the extension of the arms, the size of "the fish that got away." A scholar of nonverbal communication has aptly stated, "we respond to gestures with an extreme alertness and, one might also say, in accordance with an elaborate and secret code that is written nowhere, known by none, and understood by all."[8]

You must be especially wary when communicating with people from another culture. Don't be naive, like the Florida beauty queen who was "invited to participate in a parade in Port-au-Prince. She accepted graciously—but then spent the whole time atop her float, waving innocently to the crowd, unaware that in the language of Haitian gestures she was proclaiming 'Screw you! Screw you!' "[9]

As the world gets smaller and smaller, and the number of foreign students attending colleges and universities in the United States gets larger and larger, it's crucial to try to understand how nonverbal messages are perceived by students from other cultures. For example, according to Roger Axtell, author of *Gestures: The Dos and Taboos of Body Language around the World*,[10] the closed thumb and forefinger "OK" sign can represent an obscenity to a German, and to a Middle Easterner it could mean you're putting a curse on someone. Russians and Brazilians also take the OK sign as an insult. To the Japanese, it represents money and to the French, it means zero, zip.

In our culture the gesture of "thumbs up" means you did a ***top notch job,*** but to Nigerians and Australians, this gesture has vulgar connotations. To Germans it means the number one, and to the Japanese, the number five. Interestingly,

in other words:
top notch job— a performance of the highest quality

---

[8]Edward Sapir, *Human Message Systems* (New York: Harper & Row, 1976), 82.

[9]"The Language of Gestures Can Give You Away," *Elle,* May 1991, 198.

[10]Roger E. Axtell, *Gestures: Do's and Taboos of Body Language around the World* (New York: John Wiley & Sons, Inc., 1993), 43.

. . . in any language.

shaking our heads (no) and nodding our heads (yes) means just the opposite to Bulgarians.

In his book, Roger E. Axtell tells us that Queen Elizabeth II has developed certain body motions and gestures to transmit messages to her entourage. According to Raymond Fillager, a writer and lecturer about the royal family, Her Majesty uses her purse to convey some twenty different signals to her attending staff. For example, when she shifts her handbag from her right arm to her left, it's a signal to "Come and rescue me from this situation!"[11]

When students from other countries/cultures get up to speak, observe their nonverbal communication and don't hesitate to ask questions. You may be spared from embarrassing someone or being embarrassed.

Our Touch

Haptics is the study of communication through touch. Perhaps the most personal mode of communicating without words is **touch.** It can signal both positive (handshake) and negative (slap in the face) attitudes, depending on the individual being touched and his or her cultural patterns. For example, one study shows that students in the United States reported being touched twice as much as did students in Japan. It is unacceptable in Japan to be touched by

---

[11]Ibid., 12.

strangers, and, as a result, the Japanese make it a point to maintain their distance. In contrast, Middle Easterners, Latin Americans, and southern Europeans commonly engage in same-sex touching while speaking, whereas such actions are not common in Asia and northern Europe.[12]

Touching is a crucial aspect of most human relationships. It can communicate disapproval and punishment, tenderness and passion, approval and encouragement. Everybody—rich or poor, young or old, famous or unknown—is affected by touching. For instance, in his autobiography, former President Ronald Reagan recalls the moments right after he was shot in 1981 by a would-be assassin. "I was lying on the stretcher only half-conscious when I realized that someone was holding my hand. It was a soft, feminine hand. I felt it touch mine and then hold on tight to it. It gave me a wonderful feeling. Even now I find it difficult to explain how reassuring, how wonderful it felt."[13]

Here's another example of the power and, at times, therapeutic value of touching. In a *Newsweek* article about First Lady Laura Bush shortly after the 9-11 terrorist attack, it was reported how much of a calming and settling influence she has on the President's nerves in times of stress. The article went on to say that whenever President Bush "seems jittery, she'll brush his arm or touch the back of his neck, a simple act of reassurance that let's him know he's not alone."[14]

Touching starts at birth, when babies are introduced to the "outside world," and continues when parents take charge feeding, holding, cuddling, rocking, stroking, burping, bathing, and changing. Studies show the staggering importance of touch: orphaned babies placed in institutions have died because they were never cuddled or held.

Touching symbolizes different things to different people, depending on the specific situation, environment, time of day, and anticipated intent. Some individuals enjoy, and even crave, touching and being touched. Touching can be an expression of friendliness and affection and may signal sexual desires. Other people regard being touched as disrespectful and even offensive.

Our culture teaches us that it's improper for an individual of lower status to touch one of higher status unless encouraged to do so. For example, it may be acceptable for a professor to put an arm around a student, but not for a student to embrace a professor. A manager may touch someone from the mailroom but not vice versa.

Our culture frowns on a male hugging, embracing, or kissing another male. If you saw two women dancing or holding hands, you probably wouldn't think too much about it, but if you saw two men dancing or holding hands, you might interpret this as an act of femininity or homosexuality. However, in sports, a player who scores a winning touchdown, goal, or basket may be spontaneously hugged by his fellow players to show their joy.

---

[12]Joseph A. DeVito, *Human Communication* (New York: HarperCollins, 1991), 176.

[13]*An American Life, the Autobiography of Ronald Reagan* (New York: Simon & Schuster, 1990), 260.

[14]*Newsweek*, 3 December 2001, 36.

Although our culture has established certain taboos regarding male-to-male touching, there are times—for example, at a funeral—when no other action can equal a warm embrace to communicate affection, love, or sympathy.

How we touch, what part of the body we touch, and the duration of the touch are all important factors in interpreting a message. Notice people shaking hands, hugging, kissing, or pinching. Can you "read" them and their intentions? Touching, according to the messages communicated, can range from the very impersonal to the very personal.[15]

Our Vocalics

Vocalics is "how we say it," as opposed to what we say. Some elements of vocalics are voice quality, pitch, inflection, emphasis, rate of delivery, pauses, and tone of voice. For example, let's assume that your instructor had a female colleague from New England tape record the following message: "All of you are lucky to be in this speech course." After listening to this tape, the class would probably agree that the speaker had a message, it was conveyed in English, and everyone in the class understood it. Beyond this, the class would probably be able to say other things about the voice on the tape machine. They would be able to identify the voice as a white American female, probably from the Northeast because of her regional accent. They probably would agree that her voice sounded professional. Her diction was articulate and pleasant, she pronounced her words correctly, and she had no problem breathing. The class could probably tell if she were young, middle-aged, or older.

They might have received other messages as well, such as that her voice was soothing, she sounded alive and happy, and she would probably be fun to be with. Whatever it was that enabled the class to infer these messages—other than the actual spoken words—is paralanguage, or vocalics.

The quality of your voice—its pitch, rate of delivery, **inflection,** emphasis, and even pauses—plays an important role in helping you to deliver your message effectively. Take the simple question, "Where have you been?" Say it aloud four times, but put emphasis first on the word "Where," then on the word "have," then on the word "you," and finally on the word "been":

Where have you been?

Where have you been?

Where *have* you been?

Where have *you* been?

Where have you *been?*

You should have no difficulty interpreting the various messages received from the same sentence.

---

[15]R. Heslin, "Steps toward a Taxonomy of Touching." Paper presented to the Midwestern Psychological Association, Chicago, May 1974.

"<u>Where</u> have you been?" "Where <u>have</u> you been?"
"Where have <u>you</u> been?" "Where have you <u>been</u>?"

When preparing and practicing a speech, especially a talk designed to persuade, it is very important to go over your main points carefully to be sure that they're not only clearly identified, but also that the words are emphasized correctly. Emphasizing a wrong key word may significantly change the meaning of a sentence or even an idea, just as the tone of your voice can easily convey the direct opposite of what you intend to say.

Remember, *how* you say things can often be more important than *what* you say.

Other Codes

Other **codes** or elements, such as time, space, and artifacts (objects), are equally significant in nonverbal communication.

Time

Chronemics is the study of communication through the use of time. Most of us are very time-conscious, and time plays a vital role in the messages we convey. Many people consider time more valuable than money, and, indeed, most of our lives are influenced by a time schedule.

How important is time? To many people, time represents status and power. For example: A boss can keep a worker waiting, and can also be late for a meeting, without consequence. A doctor can keep a patient waiting. A college president can keep a dean waiting, who in turn can keep a division chairperson waiting, who can keep a department chairperson waiting, who can keep a professor waiting, who in turn can keep a student waiting. The more influential your position, the more command you have over your time and over other people's time.

Time should play an important role in the classroom. Be sure to be present on the assigned day of your talk and stay within the time limit of your talk. Always be on time for your class. Never enter the classroom while a classmate is delivering a speech, and always remain attentive to the speaker, even though class time may be running out. Don't start to collect your books or to reach for your jacket until your colleague is finished speaking. This is only common courtesy, which you should expect to receive under similar circumstances.

Being late or even last to arrive may be interpreted as a symbol of status, depending on a person's importance or popularity. I remember one time in college when my speech professor arrived late for class. As he approached the lectern, I foolishly told him he was late. Without hesitation, he slammed his books down on the lectern, glared at me, and bellowed, "As long as you're in my class, don't you ever forget this—instructors are *never* late. Only students can be late and that I will not tolerate. Do you understand?" Did I understand? *Did* I understand? Did *I* understand? Did I *understand?* You bet I did and I'll never forget it!

"I wonder if she forgot me?"

It's common knowledge that, on occasion, airline flights have been delayed for the arrival of a VIP. At a candidate's fundraiser, the candidate is usually the last to arrive. At a nightclub or concert, the star is usually the last to perform. At the theater, the leading performers are most likely to be the last to respond to curtain calls.

It's now time to turn our attention to how this element is perceived in other cultures. As in the United States, most Germans consider being "on time" important—it is a sign of respect. Punctuality is also an accepted way of life for Indians, Chinese, Japanese, and in most countries of Northern Europe. **On the other hand,** Indonesians, Saudi Arabians, and Nigerians enjoy the philosophy that what can't be done today can be done tomorrow. This ***laid-back*** philosophy regarding time is also enjoyed by people in southern Europe, Latin America, and the Middle East,[16] where ***closing up shop*** and taking an afternoon siesta is a daily way of life. (I'm all for that.)

What's interesting to note is that while the French are very time conscious, just across the channel, the Irish enjoy spending their time much more casually . . . which is clearly articulated in their famous quote, "When God made time, He made plenty of it."

Before we run out of time, you might find the following facts interesting and possibly useful for one of your talks. The average person squanders a total of thirteen years in meaningless activity. Five months of our lives are spent waiting for traffic lights to change, eight months opening junk mail, one year looking for things we've misplaced, two years trying to return phone calls, four years performing basic housework, and five years just waiting in lines.[17]

And far from being a meaningless activity, the average American spends six years eating. Speaking personally I must confess that I probably spend considerably more time than that on such a pleasurable activity.

Remember, you can "use time." You can "waste time." You can "kill time." You can "save time." You can "do time." You can "sell time." But you can't "buy time."

Space

How you use **space,** while speaking, can contribute to the overall effectiveness of your talk. Remaining behind the lectern while speaking can create a barrier between you and the audience. The lectern is a symbol of authority and is impersonal in nature. If you wish to become informal and more intimate during certain parts of your talk, then escape from the lectern and move closer to your audience. The usual nonverbal response of your classmates as you approach them should be more attentiveness.

Anthropologist Edward T. Hall coined the word **proxemics** to describe the study of space as a communicative mode. "Every living thing has a physical

in other words:

on the other hand—to mention the opposite

laid-back—very relaxed

close up shop—to temporarily close; to close for a few hours

---

[16]Donald W. Klopf, *International Encounters, The Fundamentals of Intercultural Communication* (Englewood, CO: Morton Publishing, 1991), 220.

[17]Letty Cottin Pogrebin, "It's about Time," *Family Circle,* 27 November 1990, 34.

"Excuse me, sir, can you tell us what time it is?"

boundary that separates it from its external environment."[18] He explains in his book, *The Silent Language,* that each of us has a personal area of space surrounding us, clearly established by an invisible boundary. This personal area, which he refers to as a "bubble," establishes distances at which we feel the most comfortable when interacting with people, and any attempt by another person to enter this area constitutes an intrusion. Notice how uneasy people become in crowded situations such as in an elevator, in a bus, or at the theater, when a stranger sits uncomfortably close. If you would like to experiment, the next time you're talking to a person, slowly inch a little closer, then a little closer—and observe that person's physical reaction.

And if you really want to have some fun, strike up a conversation with someone whose back is almost to the wall and start to advance slowly while you're talking. Then prepare to witness an interesting situation when he or she discovers that no further retreat is possible. The chances are that the individual will slowly depart. Hall's categories of interaction distance are listed in Table 3.1.

We take our space very seriously. We see signs declaring "No Trespassing," "Police Take Notice," "Keep Out," or "Private Property." These signs indicate private ownership, and intruders enter at their own risk. Throughout history, millions of people have been killed in wars over infringement on someone else's space. Territorial waters and air space are usually respected by all governments.

---

[18]Edward T. Hall, *The Silent Language* (New York: Anchor Books, 1973), 163.

TABLE 3.1

Space Distances Involved in Communication

	Intimate Distance (0–18 inches)
Close	(0–6 inches) Touching distance, whispering, confidential
Distant	(6–18 inches) Audible whisper, comfortable
	Personal Distance (18–48 inches)
Close	(18–30 inches) Within touching distance, friendly
Distant	(30–48 inches) Beyond touching range, courteous
	Social Distance (4–12 feet)
Close	(4–7 feet) Formal range, nonpersonal or occupational
Distant	(7–12 feet) More formal, barriers can appear
	Public Distance (12 feet and beyond)
Close	(12–20 feet) Across a room, strong voice required
Distant	(beyond 20 feet) Public speaking, shouting

Edward T. Hall, *Silent Language* (New York: Doubleday, 1981).

Territorial behavior is often evidenced in our daily lives. In a home, it's not unusual for each family member to sit in the same chair at every meal. When we walk down the street at night, it may bother us to sense a stranger approaching us from behind. While eating in a crowded cafeteria, some people resent a stranger asking permission to sit at the same table. How would you feel if you were waiting in line at a restaurant or theater and someone stepped in front of you?

Space may also indicate a person's status and authority. Many wealthy people live in very large homes and estates where the servants' quarters are removed from the rest of the house. At one time, a two-car garage symbolized status—now it's a three-car garage. Position and influence at work can usually be determined by the size of a person's office, its view, and the assignment of a private parking space.

And now, to take up a little more space, let's look at how some other cultures perceive space. We find that Latin Americans, Italians, and Puerto Ricans will stand noticeably closer to each other when communicating than Americans, Germans, Japanese, and Chinese. The latter prefer more distance between them when interacting. African Americans tend to stand closer to each other than do Caucasian Americans.[19]

---

[19]Klopf, *International Encounters*, 220.

"In case you haven't noticed—you're in my space!!"

And, according to author-researcher Mark L. Knapp in his book, *Essentials of Nonverbal Communication,* cultures in which people do interact more closely by touching each other more often, prolonging eye contact, and even speaking louder, include many Arab, Latin American, and southern European cultures. The opposite is true with most Asians, Indians, Pakistanis, northern Europeans, and North Americans.

A Colorful Section

Chromatics is the study and application of color as a mode of nonverbal communication. Color can and does play a significant role as a mode of nonverbal communication. If you're not familiar with the meanings of the red, yellow, and green colors on a traffic light, then I sincerely hope you are neither a driver nor a pedestrian, because in this case, ignorance could be fatal. Color is very much an intrinsic part of our daily vocabulary. How often do we use or hear such commonly used phrases/sentences as:

- "She was tickled *pink*."
- "Looking at life through *rose*-colored glasses."
- "Don't miss this *golden* opportunity."
- "The situation is not entirely *black* and *white*; you have to consider the *gray* area."
- "He was *green* with envy."

- "That only happens once in a *blue* moon."
- "I was so angry I saw *red.*"
- *Black* Magic
- "The coward showed his true color . . . *yellow.*"
- "Barbara has a *green* thumb; you should see her plants."

Color perhaps plays no greater a personal role than in the health field. Especially when it involves you. When you overhear a doctor or nurse say quietly, "She has good color," following your surgery, I'm sure those words are most comforting. Health care professionals are trained to detect, notice, and perceive a patient's "color"—whether facial, from hands, or even fingernails—at a glance, and then interpret and relate that color in assessing a person's health. No question—color can, at times, be a fairly good indicator of one's health.

When we buy clothes, color can not only enhance our appearance, but at the same time, can transmit powerful messages. Color experts tell us that different meanings may be conveyed from various colors. For example:

Red	Passion, excitement, warmth, aggression, love, danger
Yellow	Betrayal, cowardice, happiness, imagination, cheerfulness, optimism
Green	Jealousy, fertility, nature, good luck, health, relaxation, envy
Blue	Peaceful, stable, conservative, cold, trust, loyalty, calming
White	Sterile, purity, reverence, innocence, peace, humility
Black	Death, mysterious, fear, elegance, sexuality, wealth
Brown	Outdoors, earth, comfort, reliability, home, stability
Purple	Mystery, royalty, spirituality, arrogance, mourning, nobility

There's no question that color has an impact on our personality, emotions, moods, and behavior, and it's no wonder that color consultants have been retained by hospitals, penal institutions, schools, government offices, and factory managers to suggest color decor that would be most beneficial to the clientele or constituencies employed or being served.

Our Artifacts

The **artifacts,** or objects, in our possession transmit clear messages about us that can enhance or hinder a speaker's oral performance. When General Norman Schwarzkopf, the victorious commander in chief of Operation Desert Storm in the Persian Gulf, spoke to the Corps of Cadets at West Point in May 1991, he appeared before the student body dressed in his combat field outfit, rather than his full-dress uniform, for maximum effect. And he achieved it.

A firefighter or a police officer speaking before a group of local citizens will be more credible dressed in official uniform. But how persuasive would a public official be talking to a group of senior citizens about the government's plan to reduce the budget of low-cost housing units while wearing a $600 suit and a Rolex watch and sporting a 2-carat diamond ring after having arrived by chauffeured limousine?

Our clothes, furniture, paintings, cars, home, and jewelry are explicit indicators of our behavior and status. A wedding band says we're married. A ring on the right hand may say we're available. A police officer's badge shouts authority, and a uniform may announce a person's occupation.

Some people, on entering one room, feel comfortable and warm, whereas in another room they feel nervous. Is there any question that furnishings, including rugs, lamps, mirrors, and wall covering, contribute to the room's personality? People communicate more easily in comfortable surroundings than in uncomfortable ones.

A person driving a Mercedes 450 SL and one driving a dune buggy will communicate vastly different messages. And so will the individual who skippers a 45-foot yacht, as opposed to one who owns a 12-foot Boston Whaler.

Many people derive a sense of pride and self-worth from their collections. The wealthy may collect paintings, jewelry, diamonds, and gold worth a fortune. Other popular collector's items are cars, stamps, coins, dolls, trains, Waterford crystal, guns, butterflies, and fine wines. Many people enjoy their collections, but some also look on them as symbols of power, status, challenge, and accomplishment.

We Cannot Not Communicate

As we mentioned earlier, certain nonverbal cues can be faked and may contain different messages from what's actually being transmitted. It is easy to misinterpret parts of nonverbal language. Remember, nonverbal cues are not absolute. We must consider them in the total context of the situation in which they are produced.

Some revealing observations on nonverbal communication are contained in a published interview with a prominent Boston trial lawyer. He talks about the extreme importance of nonverbal communication in relation to selecting a jury. What does he look for and why? He prefers women jurors "because they're more attentive and sensitive" and jurors who smile because "[a] happy jury is a good jury."[20]

During jury selection, he observes how people walk to the jury box and how they are dressed. Is the walk positive and aggressive or slow and passive? Is the head held high or at half-mast? Are the shoulders slumped or is the posture erect? The attorney is looking for nonverbal clues to the potential juror's attitude and outlook on life. Knowing if a person is the nervous or calm type can be quite significant. From the individual's apparel and personal grooming, he may try to judge occupation, origin, living habits, and economic and social status.

---

[20]*The Patriot Ledger*, 31 May 1983, 1.

TABLE 3.2

Attitudes Communicated Nonverbally

Defensiveness
Arms crossed on chest
Legs crossed
Fistlike gestures
Pointed index finger

Evaluation
Hand-to-face gestures
Head tilted
Stroking chin
Peering over glasses
Pipe smoker gestures
Putting hand to bridge of nose

Suspicion
Arms crossed
Sideways glance
Touching, rubbing nose/eyes
Buttoning coat
Drawing away

Insecurity
Pinching flesh
Chewing pen, pencil
Rubbing thumb over fingers
Biting fingernails
Hands in pockets

Cooperation
Upper body in sprinter's position
Open hands
Sitting on edge of chair
Hand-to-face gestures
Tilted head
Unbuttoned coat

Openness
Open hands
Unbuttoned coat

Confidence
Hands in "steeple" position
Hands behind back
Back stiffened
Hands in coat pockets
Hands on coat lapels

Nervousness
Clearing throat
Whew sound
Whistling
Fidgeting in chair
Hand covering mouth while speaking
Not looking at other person
Jingling money in pockets
Tugging at ear
Perspiration
Wringing hands

Frustration
Short breaths
Tsk sound
Tightly clenched hands
Wringing hands
Fistlike gestures
Pointing index finger
Rubbing hand through hair
Rubbing back of neck

Gerard Nierenburg and Henry Calero, *How to Read a Person Like a Book* (New York: Pocket Books, 1973).

This trial lawyer knows more than just the law. He is keenly observant and proficient in understanding and interpreting people's nonverbal messages. They can be crucial not only in dictating how the lawyer will present his case to the jurors, but also in trying to anticipate how the jurors will react and make decisions.

Most of us tend to express certain behavioral attitudes with various nonverbal actions. Table 3.2 lists some common ways that we communicate such attitudes nonverbally.

Quick Clicks

Welcome to a "surprise search." To further enhance your research or simply to harvest more information about some of the things you studied in this
chapter, just drop in at any of the following addresses. What
you'll discover may be serious, educational, bibliographical, surprising, factual,
or even downright humorous. But it will definitely be informative.
  So, go ahead and give a "Quick Click."

www.presentersuniversity.com/courses/show_deskills.cfm? RecordID=29
www.members.aol.com/nonverbal2/diction1.htm
www.maria-brazil.org/gestures.htm
www.members.aol.com/katydidit/bodylang.htm
www.public-speaking.org

Things to Discuss in Class

1. Listen to a voice on the radio and jot down as much information as possible based on the speaker's vocalics. Discuss your findings in class.
2. While traveling to or from work or class, pay attention to the nonverbal messages around you. Then make a list of the messages you perceive. Discuss them in class.
3. The next time you're talking with a friend, slowly move closer and closer. Tell the class your friend's reaction.
4. Select someone in your neighborhood with whom you've never spoken. Tell the class as much as you can about that individual based on that person's nonverbal codes.
5. Explain to the class what nonverbal messages you think you transmit to others. The class may wish to respond with interpretations of your messages.
6. Discuss the verbal and nonverbal cues that your instructor employs in teaching this class.

7. If your class has access to a video camera and videocassette recorder (VCR), you may wish to record some of the following exercises as a learning experience in nonverbal communication. Play back the videotape to see how many members of the class received the nonverbal messages that you feel you actually transmitted. The exercises should not run more than a few minutes.
   a. Through facial expressions and with your eyes, try to convey different moods, for example, anger, fear, happiness, sadness, and surprise.
   b. Pretend that you're at a marketplace in a foreign country. The vendor, who doesn't understand English, shows you something. You admire it and try it on but feel it's too expensive. You want it. Nonverbally, communicate this to the vendor and bargain for a lower price.
   c. Again, you're in a foreign country where a language barrier exists. You're

at a restaurant, and, when the waiter arrives, you attempt to order a full-course breakfast nonverbally.

d. You're in a pet shop. Without words, convey to the class where you are and what you see. You look at various pets and then pick up the one you intend to purchase.

e. In silent language, demonstrate a line of work performed by a member of your family. First, you must identify the individual and then that person's occupation.

f. Using body language only, describe a vacation spot you would like to visit and the mode of transportation to get there.

g. Visually describe your favorite hobby.

h. If you have a full- or part-time job, describe it without saying a word.

i. Communicate, nonverbally, your major and your short- and long-term educational goals.

What Do You Remember from This Chapter?

1. Define nonverbal communication and give several examples.

2. Explain the statement. "We cannot *not* communicate."

3. What can posture tell us about a person?

4. List five gestures that convey explicit meanings.

5. Explain vocalics and give five examples.

6. Give an example of time being interpreted as a symbol of status.

7. What is proxemics?

8. List the four categories of interaction distance.

9. What is kinesics and its relevance to nonverbal communication?

10. List five phrases or sayings that demonstrate the importance of nonverbal communication.

11. Which nonverbal code can easily be misread? Explain.

12. List five types of messages that a person's eyes and facial expression can transmit.

13. List three synonyms for nonverbal communication.

14. Explain chronemics and haptics.

15. How is punctuality observed by the German and Japanese cultures as opposed to the Saudi Arabian and Irish cultures?

16. When the Irish proudly declare that, "When God made time, He made plenty of it," what does this convey?

Vitalize Your Vocabulary

A solid knowledge of synonyms (words that have the same basic meaning but may differ in tone and appropriateness) will impart vigor and variety to your speech. An excellent and proven source of synonyms and antonyms (words that mean the opposite) is *Roget's Thesaurus*. It does not, however, explain differences in meaning; for those shades of meaning you should consult a modern, authoritative dictionary.

Consider the basic meanings of the adjectives "slim" and "slender"; synonyms are "trim" and "svelte." These four adjectives are complimentary. On the other hand, synonyms such as "bony," "gaunt," and "skinny" are anything but complimentary and may even be insulting. The word "thin" falls somewhere between the first four adjectives and the last three. This example proves the vital importance of understanding different shades of meanings.

Each group of words in Table 3.3 is a set of synonyms; however, each group in column 2 represents antonyms for those in column 1.

TABLE 3.3

Synonyms and Antonyms

Column 1	Column 2
	Antonyms of Words in Column 1
big, huge, large, immense, vast, king-size, enormous, tremendous, colossal, mammoth, jumbo, gigantic, gargantuan, ample, abundant	small, little, tiny, petite, peewee, puny, miniature, diminutive, pocket-sized, minute, microscopic
brave, courageous, fearless, bold, valiant, heroic, game, valorous, gallant, lionhearted, spunky, plucky, dauntless, gutsy, audacious, adventurous, nervy, intrepid	afraid, cowardly, fearful, timid, yellow, fainthearted, lily-livered, weak-kneed, chicken-hearted, dastardly, pusillanimous
pleased, delighted, charmed, elated, intrigued, gratified, tickled pink, satisfied, sold on, carried away	complain, gripe, bitch, grouse, whine, beef, weep, bellyache, wail, crab, squawk, lament, mutter, fuss, moan and groan, grumble
genuine, authentic, valid, real, true, actual, bona fide, legitimate	fake, phony, artificial, counterfeit, mock, spurious, adulterated, make-believe, bogus, substitute, ersatz, pseudo-
pliable, flexible, tractable, yielding, bending, receptive, malleable, pliant, responsive, relenting	stubborn, obstinate, inflexible, rigid, immovable, bullheaded, adamant, unbending, unyielding, uncompromising, intransigent, resolute
slim, slender, lean, slight, frail, delicate, spare, underweight, gaunt, bony, skinny, scrawny	fat, stout, corpulent, obese, fleshy, beefy, plump, paunchy, full, rotund, tubby, roly-poly, pudgy, chubby, heavyset, portly, well-fed, thick-bodied, rich, swollen

Roget's International Thesaurus, 3rd ed. (Harper & Row, 1977).

You Can Overhear, but You Can't Overlisten

chapter 4

Nobody has ever listened himself out of a job.
—Calvin Coolidge, thirtieth President of the United States, 1923–1929

After reading and understanding this chapter, you should know:

- The difference between hearing and listening

- The importance of listening well

- Some major reasons why we listen

- Some ways to become a more efficient listener

- The different types of listening

- The vital correlation between vocabulary development and efficient listening

The act of listening comprises a significant portion of our daily activities. It is the other half of the communication process since, without listeners, we cannot communicate orally. Yet, few of us pay attention to improving our ability to listen.

Hearing is a passive biological function, whereas listening is, or should be, an active intellectual function that involves your mind, eyes, ears, and memory. As a listener, you influence speakers by your reactions. If you show interest through your facial expression or body language, you will see speakers perk up. If you show boredom or confusion through inattention or lack of eye contact, you will see that speakers tend to change their approach to avoid risking failure.

We listen for several reasons: to become informed, to understand, to evaluate, and to enjoy. Any intellectual activity that can affect your life to such an extent deserves to be done well. Suggestions for sharpening your listening skills are offered, but they will benefit you only if you make a commitment to improve yourself.

When you were a child, how often did your parents criticize you for not **listening**? As a parent, how frequently do you direct your children to listen? At one time or another all of us are guilty of not really listening to what's being said. Our inattention can lead to embarrassment, to argument, and, at times, to even more serious consequences.

All too often in interpersonal communication (between two or more people), we absorb only what we want to, at home, school, or play. Many times we choose not to pay attention to certain people because they are boring or **long-winded.** We have that arbitrary ability to *"tune out"* certain people, and let's face it, sometimes it can be beneficial. Nevertheless, it's safe to say that the rewards of effective listening are greater than those of "tuning out."

in other
words:

long-winded—
speaks too long

tune out—
ignore

Communication Activities

A study conducted by researchers at a leading university found that adults spend about 70 percent of their waking hours engaged in communication activities. It concluded that the average adult devotes 9 percent of this time to writing, 16 percent to reading, 30 percent to speaking, and 45 percent to listening.[1]

In the workplace, communication statistics are about the same. The average employee spends about 8 percent of the time writing, 13 percent reading, 23 percent speaking, and 55 percent listening.[2]

College students, however, spend almost 90 percent of their school time listening, which is not too surprising since, basically, that's what they're in school for. Yet studies show that the average college student listens at about 35 percent efficiency; certainly, nothing to write home about. And here's something else that's not too surprising: research indicates that students who listen effectively earn better grades and achieve beyond what their intelligence levels might have predicted.[3] From these figures we can say that we listen half again as much as we speak; we speak almost twice as much as we read; and we read almost twice as much as we write.

We can conclude, then, that of all the communication activities in which we participate daily, whether at home, at work, or at school, the predominant one is listening. It only makes sense, then, that we should strive to sharpen our listening skills to a higher level of proficiency.

Moreover, studies declare that after a ten-minute oral presentation, the average listener (and a large percentage of students rank below average!) hears, receives, comprehends, and retains only about 50 percent of the message. After

---

[1]James J. Floyd, *Listening: A Practical Approach* (Glenview, IL: Scott, Foresman, 1985), 2.

[2]J. Dan Rothwell, *In the Company of Others: An Introduction to Communication* (Mountain View, CA: Mayfield Publishing, 2000), 148.

[3]Walter Pauk, *How to Study in College* (Boston: Houghton Mifflin, 1989), 121–133.

That arbitrary ability to "tune out" certain people.

forty-eight hours most listeners remember only about 25 percent of what they heard.[4]

We wake up in the morning to the sounds of an alarm clock, a radio, or someone's voice. We may have conversation at breakfast, at work, at school, on public conveyances, or in a car pool. We might attend a business meeting, a lecture, or a luncheon. We might hear someone speak in person or on the radio, TV, or telephone. We might attend a concert, a movie, or a social or civic function. Think of all the times in one day, for example, that we listen. How much of that listening experience will we be able to recall? Are we actually *listening* and *understanding*, or are we just *hearing* things? There's a world of difference.

Despite these statistics, listening, the communication activity we engage in most of our waking hours (a third of our lives), is the one that our educational system ignores the most. In most colleges today, courses in basic writing are mandatory for all freshmen. Because of increasing alarm over our low national reading scores, reading courses are offered and, at some colleges, they're required. Courses in public speaking and oral communication are offered on most college campuses and, in some instances, taking at least one is a requirement for a degree. But how many institutions require a student to take a course in listening?

---

[4]Lyman K. Steil, Larry L. Barker, and Kittie W. Watson, *Effective Listening* (Reading, MA: Addison-Wesley, 1983), 88.

In your precollege education, your school's curricula probably emphasized writing skills over reading, reading over speaking, and speaking over listening. Perhaps because we spend so much time listening, we feel that we can do it efficiently. What a false conclusion this is!

The fact is that the business and educational communities complain that workers and students don't know how to listen. In the business world, where listening could mean making or losing money, employees spend about 60 percent of their workday listening, and executives spend approximately 57 percent of their business day listening.[5] One of the first companies to address this problem was a Fortune 500 international corporation, which took two steps.[6]

1. It set up special listening programs worldwide for all its employees who want to attend.
2. It invested hundreds of thousands of dollars in a two-page color advertising campaign in several national magazines, which ran for months. The theme was "We understand how important it is to listen."

The importance of this activity is effectively expressed in the following excerpt from their ad:

> The fact is, listening, like marriage, is a partnership, a shared responsibility between the person speaking and the person listening. And if the listener doesn't show genuine interest and sensitivity to what's being said, the speaker will stop talking. And the communication will fail.[7]

This program was a resounding success, as the company witnessed an increase in productivity and a decrease in employee accidents. Is it any wonder that many other corporations, both gargantuan and small, now offer similar "more effective listening" training programs for their employees?

I hope that more and more educational institutions "hear the call" and participate more actively in this very critical area of effective listening.

Listening as an Intellectual Activity

You can listen more effectively and improve your comprehension markedly if you work at it. Listening is just as important to interpersonal communication as is speaking; in fact, "listening is the other half of talking. If people stop listening, it is useless to talk—a point not always appreciated by talkers."[8]

---

[5]Andrew D. Wolvin and Carolyn Gwynn Coakley, "A Survey of the Status of Listening Training in Some Fortune 500 Corporations," *Communication Education* 40, April 1991, 153.

[6]Sperry Corporation, *Newsweek,* 20 October 1980, 89.

[7]Ibid.

[8]Stuart Chase, "Are You Listening?" *Reader's Digest,* December 1962, 48.

Listening is an intellectual activity.

While hearing is a biological activity, listening is an intellectual one because it requires more than just ears. In fact, it has been said that you hear with your ears, but you listen with your brain.

John H. Rhoades had some good advice when he said, "Do more than hear, listen. Do more than listen, understand." And Wilson Mizner makes a good point when he says, "A good listener is not only popular everywhere, but after a while he knows something."[9] Effective listening is a holistic activity that should include the following active efforts of your mind, eyes, ears, and memory:

- *Your mind.* You should summon your logical reasoning capacity to grasp the intended meaning of the speaker's message. Understand the differences between fact (something that is documented and known to be true), opinion (a personal view, not necessarily factual), and inference (drawing your own conclusions from or about something you have heard, read, or seen). We'll discuss logical reasoning in more detail in Chapter 11.
- *Your eyes.* You should observe the speaker's posture, facial expressions, mannerisms, and movements. All of these collectively communicate vital messages, including credibility. As we mentioned earlier, for a speaker to be totally effective, his or her nonverbal messages must coincide with the

[9]Lewis C. Henry, ed. *Best Quotes for All Occasions* (New York: Ballantine Books, 1995), 263.

verbal ones. So, be on the "lookout." Remember, also, that certain cultures, including many from Asia and the Middle East, generally refrain from direct eye contact, considering it inappropriate and rude. So, when listening to speakers from other cultures, be sure to take this into consideration.

- *Your ears.* Listen carefully to the speaker's voice. Is it pleasant, harsh, reassuring, authoritative, or weak? How about inflection, rate of speaking, pauses, loudness, and animation? Are they in "sync" with the message? In other words, is the speaker's nonverbal message enhanced or contradicted by the oral one?
- *Your memory.* Try to recall as much as you can about the topic at hand. Are you hearing new or contradictory information? Did the speaker omit anything? If so, what and why? By recalling as much as possible about the speaker's message, you should have a solid basis on which to compare or contrast the message with your own knowledge of the subject.

As a listener, you can help the speaker by communicating through your facial and body actions. When you're looking at the speaker, show interest: lean forward occasionally and appear to **catch every word;** even **jot down** a few notes or a question you may wish to bring up later. These positive responses tell the speaker that the message is **getting across** to you. If you slouch in your chair, whisper to your neighbor, read a book, or look just plain bored, the speaker will be well aware that he or she has problems.

Reasons for Listening

Following are some of the major reasons why we listen:

- To enjoy
- To become informed
- To understand
- To express sympathy
- To evaluate
- To understand and speak a new language better

To Enjoy

Listening for enjoyment is light listening—for example, engaging in a pleasant adult conversation with friends, family, neighbors, etc., listening to music, or watching a movie or TV show. Another example is listening to children introduce you to their imaginary friends or telling you what they want to be when they grow up. (This usually changes, daily.)

This type of listening should not involve any serious effort or strain, but should be casual and relaxed. This change of pace should be enjoyable and pleasant.

in other
words:

catch every word—to listen attentively and understand

jot down—write, make note of

getting across—being understood

To Become Informed

In the second type of listening, you seek new information. You listen to the radio for the weather report or school-closing announcement, you attend a class lecture or a business, social, or civic meeting. You establish in your mind the motive for listening, and then you direct complete interest in, attention to, and concentration on the speaker. If your instructor announces that there'll be a quiz following a short lecture, you're motivated to listen. "Know how to listen and you can learn even from those who speak badly," said Plutarch, Greek essayist and biographer, about 2,000 years ago.

To Understand

How often have you formed opinions of speakers and subjects before they have even begun or finished talking?

Many people find listening to understand most difficult because it requires restraint, fair-mindedness, and objective thinking. As a consequence, many of the world's problems have resulted from selfishness, disregard of other people's opinions, and failure to attempt honestly to understand another's viewpoint. Listening to understand doesn't mean that you must agree or disagree but that you must approach the subject with an unbiased, open mind. You must also listen totally to the message, striving to understand what is being expressed and why. Allow yourself to grasp the entire message before you react.

To Express Sympathy

in other words:

"sympathetic ear"—willing to listen to someone else's problems

"sound off"—to strongly express your views

breaking loose—express yourself strongly

attentive ear—someone who'll listen

If you're that rare person with a *"sympathetic ear,"* then probably every day you listen to someone *"sound off"*—a relative, friend, classmate, co-worker, stranger, or perhaps even your boss. To share or just listen to someone's pent-up feelings *breaking loose* can have a therapeutic effect on the talker and will distinguish you as a person who cares. This type of listening can be personally rewarding because practically everyone, sooner or later, needs an *attentive ear.* For example:

- Your good friend feels that his boss is exploiting his abilities while skimping on salary.
- A classmate is distraught because all sections of a course she wanted were closed.
- A family member didn't get the promotion he felt he deserved.
- On the way to work, someone slammed into your boss's brand new car and she wants to vent her emotions.
- Your neighbor just found out that his three children need dental braces.

To Evaluate

Of all of the types of listening, evaluative listening is the most difficult and the most important because it requires the most effort. There are a number of questions to bear in mind when listening to evaluate, whether in a speech or conversation:

- What is the main purpose of the talk?
- Is the talk informative, entertaining, persuasive, or inspirational? Is it meant to activate?
- Is the speaker making logical and valid points?
- Are the arguments convincing? Are they based on fact or on opinion?
- Is the speaker an authority on the subject or does he or she just *have an axe to grind?*
- To what needs of the audience is the speaker appealing?
- Can you clearly understand the speaker's message so that you can respond intelligently?
- Do the nonverbal elements of the talk coincide or conflict with the verbal message?

These are only some of the countless questions you should consider when listening to evaluate. You now have some idea of the complexity and depth of **evaluative listening.**

Do you usually take statements uttered by well-known people as the *last word,* or do you make an effort to seek out the other side before formulating an

in other
words:

have an axe to grind—have something to complain about

last word—absolute truth

Everyone needs a sympathetic ear.

opinion? If you're in a position to disagree with or question people, do you? Remember that you may disagree without being disagreeable. Whether the issues are international, national, local, business, educational, political, or social—evaluative listening is especially crucial.

A catastrophic breakdown in evaluative listening occurred not too long ago at the airport in the Canary Islands, near Spain. The pilot of a KLM jumbo jet either didn't hear or heard incorrectly the order to "stand by for takeoff." At the very same moment, the pilot of a Boeing 747 also didn't get the message. He taxied beyond the runway exit, placing his aircraft in the path of the KLM jet taking off without permission. Poor listening by both pilots caused the most tragic disaster in the history of aviation—581 people killed.

A similar catastrophe occurred in 1996 over Charkhi Dadri, India. New Delhi air controllers told a Kazakh cargo plane that it was flying straight at a Saudi Boeing 747 passenger jet. The pilot's acknowledgment was the last word the air controllers heard from either aircraft before they collided—death toll: 349 people. Transcripts indicated that the pilots were misled by their instruments or misunderstood the tower's directions.

Two other recent examples of extreme breakdown in communication (listening?) are drenched in controversy and bear tremendous political ramifications. They involve the infamous attacks on September 11, 2001.

One had to do with a memo, dated July 2001, that was e-mailed from a Phoenix FBI agent to FBI headquarters in Washington, D.C., urging the agent's superiors to investigate why so many Middle Eastern men were attending flight schools in Arizona to learn to fly large jets. The memo also suggested that these men could be followers of Osama bin Laden. FBI officials claimed the memo was never passed on to them, which evoked an outburst from a high-ranking member of the Senate Intelligence Committee, who declared, "They either went to sleep on it or they were inept in handling it."

The other incident concerned the August arrest of Zacarias Moussaoui, who became the object of suspicion at a flight school in Minneapolis. Notes from a Minneapolis FBI agent "speculating that Moussaoui might be planning to fly a plane into the World Trade Center were apparently ignored by higher-ups."[10]

Warning.   Poor communication or total lack of it could be injurious to your health. A leading health care agency strongly suggests that you be sure that your surgeon has a Magic Marker as well as a scalpel should you be contemplating surgery. Why? According to the president of the Joint Commission on Accreditation of Healthcare Organizations, during the past five years there have been over 150 instances of doctors operating on the wrong patient, wrong site, or performing the wrong procedure. Of the aforementioned cases, about three-quarters involved removing the wrong body part such as a kidney or the

---

[10]Kenneth T. Walsh and Kevin Whitelaw, "On the Spot," *U.S. News & World Report,* 27 May 2002, 20.

wrong leg, or operating on the wrong appendage. In one case a doctor operated on the wrong side of a patient's brain.[11] Not only is the yearly number of "wrong site" surgeries increasing, it is strongly recommended that patients refuse to go under anesthesia until surgeons properly mark the body part, with a Magic Marker—further confirming that physicians' notoriously bad hand-writing is "crystal clear." And, according to the report, the reasons given for the "sickening" errors: Poor communication and the pressure to do more work in less time.[12]

It pays to listen to someone who ***knows the score***—and then to evaluate correctly. As Oliver Wendell Holmes once proclaimed, "It is the province of knowledge to speak and it is the privilege of wisdom to listen."

To Understand and Speak a New Language Better

For students whose primary language is not English—and, for that matter, any student learning a foreign language—listening is an invaluable vehicle of learning. Listen carefully to how your instructor, as well as other speakers in class, pronounce words, syllables, vowels, and consonants to help your oral delivery. Watch their lips and mouth to observe how these sounds are formed. Listen to phrases, clichés, and idioms to become more familiar with the new language. (This book's feature, "In Other Words," explains common American idioms and phrases in the margin of the pages on which they appear.)

Don't be shy to question what you don't hear or understand. Just raise your hand. Instructors and student speakers are more than willing to repeat, use other words, slow down, or further explain something to assist your under-standability. (I also think it's an excellent idea to bring to class a small cassette tape recorder to record lectures and speeches for playback and study later. This handy little device is also useful for note taking, which will be discussed a little later.)

How to Be a Better Listener

Diogenes, a Greek philosopher who lived 2,300 years ago, demonstrated wis-dom when he said, "We have two ears and only one tongue in order that we may hear more and speak less."

To be a better listener you must first *want* to be one. You must realize the many benefits of improved listening, and you must be prepared to exert the re-quired effort. When you come to class, you know that you'll hear people talk,

in other words:

knows the score—knows what he or she is talking about

---

[11]Walter E. Williams, "Patients Advised: Mark Spot for Surgery," *Boston Herald,* 6 December 2001, 18.

[12]Katherine Hobson, "Medical Errors: The Right Cut," *U.S. News & World Report.* 17 December 2001, 49.

so prepare to listen. Develop a positive attitude toward the speakers. Tell your-self that you'll hear some exhilarating topics and that, in all probability, you'll learn something new. Motivation can spell the difference between just hearing something and listening and understanding it.

If you're planning to attend a lecture or to listen to a speech outside class, you can get ready for it by learning what you can about the speaker. Who is she? What's her background? Is she an authority on the subject? What's her mo-tive for speaking? What could you anticipate getting from the lecture? By in-creasing your interest in the speaker and her subject before the event, you can't help but listen more effectively. (This would be a good time to review some of the responsibilities of an ethical listener in Chapter 1.)

The following are some suggestions for honing your ability to listen:

- Develop your vocabulary.
- Concentrate on the message.
- Keep an open and objective mind.
- "Read" the speaker.
- Put yourself in the speaker's place.
- Take notes.
- Compensate for a speaker's flawed delivery.
- Get ready for the wrap-up.

Develop Your Vocabulary

Once you commit yourself to improving your listening efficiency, the best step you can take is to expand your vocabulary. Vocabulary development is so vital to effective listening that we have included a "Vitalize Your Vocabulary" sec-tion at the end of each chapter.

Fully understanding the meanings and inferences of words is crucial to your total comprehension of a speaker's intended message. Being able to put the speaker's language and message in proper perspective is a significant first step in developing your listening efficiency.

Concentrate on the Message

Interpersonal communication should be on a constant beam from the speaker to the listener and back to the speaker. Don't interrupt this beam by daydream-ing or succumbing to other kinds of distractions. Try not to think about last night, this morning, or tonight. If your thoughts begin to wander, take charge and direct them back to the speaker and his or her message. If the speaker is boring, challenge yourself to make the effort.

Another obstacle to total concentration is the fact that we think much faster than we speak. A comfortable speaking rate lies between 130 and 160 words per minute. The brain, however, can deal with approximately 500 words per minute. So you can see that, while we're listening, we have quite a bit of spare time. We must guard against becoming distracted during this spare time.

From the moment the speaker approaches the stand, rivet your eyes on him. Remember that eye contact is as important to the speaker as it is to the listener. Look interested and you will be interested. Watch his facial expressions and gestures while he's speaking. You can receive many clues to his meanings by observing his mannerisms. As discussed in Chapter 3, gestures can be eloquent.

Beware of distractions. Little things can ***throw you off:*** books dropping, people talking and coughing, fire sirens wailing. The speaker himself can be distracting. His outfit may be as loud as the fire siren, his gestures may be uncontrolled, or he may be constantly swaying. If these or any other distractions occur, then you must intensify your concentration on the message because nothing inspires a speaker more than an interested audience.

If the speaker is a student who's not completely at ease with the English language, you may want to double your concentration to ensure you understand the message—especially if the as-yet not-so-confident student chooses, for the most part, to read her or his speech verbatim.

Keep an Open and Objective Mind

Don't have the attitude, "I know what she's going to say and she's ***all wet.***" Preconceived opinions limit your ability to benefit from a true communicative experience. Be objective. ***Hear the speaker out.*** Then, if you disagree, ask her to clarify certain points. Give the speaker every courtesy that you would want if you were speaking.

Keeping an ***open mind*** is one of the more difficult techniques to master for effective listening because many people may be opinionated and make hasty judgments. They establish personal views even before the speaker opens her mouth. As mentioned in Chapter 3, a person's grooming, posture, walk, and eye contact, or lack of it, can nonverbally transmit positive or negative messages.

"Read" the Speaker

If the speaker gives his speech a title, grasp it. Closely follow the introduction and main points. In the introduction he should state what will be covered. Take note of the subject and anticipate the main points. How do they relate to the other points mentioned? Is he accomplishing what he set out to do? What about the soundness of his ideas? Are they valid? Are they logical? Does he have supporting material, and how does he use it? These are some thoughts to consider while you're listening.

Put Yourself in the Speaker's Place

You may be better able to understand and absorb a talk if you try to put yourself in the speaker's place (empathic listening). This means you must strive to feel, think, act, and react like the speaker. What motivated her to select this topic? What is her educational and professional background? What are her

in other words:

throw you off—distract you

all wet— mistaken

hear the speaker out— listen before forming an opinion

open mind— not prejudiced; giving it a fair chance

qualifications to speak on this subject? What action or reaction is she seeking from the audience and why?

If you can successfully *place yourself in the speaker's shoes,* not only will you understand her message better, but you will take a giant step toward becoming a more effective and responsive listener.

Take Notes

Taking notes can enhance your listening ability because it engages you in two activities—listening and writing. The secret to taking notes is to jot down only the main points. Whatever format of note taking works for you is the one you should use—complete sentences, phrases, or key words. Writing down key points as you hear them helps you grasp and remember them. As we mentioned in Chapter 1, taking notes is one way to provide the speaker with that all important feedback.

To enhance your note-taking proficiency, I recommend and encourage students to record the lecture on a small tape recorder. Then, at your first opportunity play the tape back and along with your written notes, you'll be able *to come up with* a more comprehensive documentation of the lecture for future review. How does that sound?

Compensate for a Speaker's Flawed Delivery

Not all speakers have read this book (what a shame!), thereby denying themselves some of our practical principles that might help alleviate bad delivery habits. Poor speech habits can detract from the message the speaker is trying to convey. He may talk in a monotone or pause often with *uh's, er's,* and *you know's.* Playing with notecards, eyeglasses, or a watch may discourage the audience from listening efficiently.

In this case, what you must do—and it isn't easy—is to separate the speaker from the speech. Just remember, many speakers have significant things to say but, unfortunately, erect obstacles that impede listeners. If you can discipline yourself to ignore the speaker's deficiencies, you may be rewarded with some valuable viewpoints and insights.

Get Ready for the *Wrap-Up*

Be ready for the conclusion of the talk. It will be the speaker's final chance to imprint her message in the minds of the listeners. At this time, she may repeat some important points that you may have missed during the talk. Listen for them and ask yourself the following crucial questions: Did I get the message? Do I agree, or do certain points need clarification? What were the strongest and weakest arguments?

Since some students—especially those whose first language is not English—may hesitate to ask questions, I would like to emphasize its importance for two

in other words:

place yourself in the speaker's shoes—put yourself in the speaker's situation; see it from his or her standpoint

to come up with—to produce

wrap up—the conclusion

reasons. First, asking questions will enable you to better understand the subject, and second, it will give you valuable experience in speaking. And if you're a beginner in our language, the more you speak it, the sooner you will master it. Remember, we are all friends and we all want each other to succeed in this course.

So, for all concerned, never be too embarrassed to ask questions. There is no more important process in education than asking questions.

Quick Clicks

Welcome to a "surprise search." To further enhance your research or simply to harvest more information about some of the things you studied in this chapter, just drop in at any of the following addresses. What you'll discover may be serious, educational, bibliographical, surprising, factual, or even downright humorous. But it will definitely be informative.

So, go ahead and give a "Quick Click."

www.listen.org
www.muskingum.edu/~cal/database/attention.html
www.cyberparent.com/talk/listen.htm
www.tufts.edu/as/stu_act/leadership/listening.html
www.historychannel.com/speeches/archive.html
www.va.gov/adr/listen.html
www.public-speaking.org

Things to Discuss in Class

1. Describe a job environment, school environment, or social environment that you consider ideal for listening.
2. Do you agree that attentive listeners help a speaker communicate better? Explain.
3. What distractions hamper your listening in this class? What can you do about them?
4. What have you observed to be the most common listening deficiencies? Prepare to discuss them.
5. Honestly evaluate your own listening habits. Can you improve them? How?
6. After another student has given a short talk, prepare a brief summary of the main ideas presented. You may do this on your own, or your instructor may call on members of the class at random for a response.
7. Find a very quiet spot at home and for several minutes relax, close your eyes, and try to listen to every sound. Attempt to identify the sounds, their sources, and the directions from which they come.

What Do You Remember from This Chapter?

1. Approximately what percentage of your waking hours is involved in listening?
2. How can a listener aid a speaker?

3. Name some types of listening.
4. List some hints for better listening.
5. What is the difference between hearing and listening?
6. How can vocabulary enhance your listening efficiency?
7. How can taking notes enhance your listening efficiency?
8. Give two reasons why it's beneficial to ask questions.
9. Name three speaker flaws that could detract from his or her message.
10. Explain "Getting ready for the wrap-up."
11. How can a tape recorder be useful in learning a new language?
12. How can we "listen with our eyes"?

Vitalize Your Vocabulary

Words from Japan

With the globalization of the world's economy and culture, many words from foreign countries have entered our language. In recent decades, as Japan has emerged as a world power and a leader in technological expertise and industrial productivity, many Japanese words have become part of American English.

Here is a sprinkling of Japanese words that you should know, together with their symbols.

banzai 万歳
Literally meaning a million, "banzai" is a carryover from the Chinese language, where it means something like "long live the king." Now, it means "three cheers" or "hip-hip hooray." It is said when celebrating something (usually three times in succession) and is accompanied by raising both arms.

bonsai 盆
A type of miniature tree.

futon 布団
A mattress placed on the floor.

geisha 芸者
A female entertainer who serves at a private party.

geta 下駄
Wooden sandals.

harakiri 腹切
Suicide by disembowelment.

hibachi 火鉢
A charcoal grill.

honcho 班長
Boss; literally, squad leader.

judo 柔道
Japanese art of self defense. The fundamental principle of judo is to utilize the opponent's strength to one's own advantage.

kamikaze 神風
A suicide pilot. A divine wind, specifically the typhoon that wrecked the Mongol invasion of Japan in the thirteenth century.

karate 唐手
The Loochoo (Ryukyu) art of self-defense, of hitting or jabbing opponents with one's fist or kicking them. It was introduced from China and gradually became a unique art of combat that uses no weapons.

kimono 着物
A traditional Japanese robe.

nisei 二世
Americans of Japanese descent.

rickshaw 力車
A man-pulled cart.

sake 酒
Wine made from rice.

sayonara さよなら
Good-bye.

sushi 寿司
Uncooked fish.

teriyaki 照り焼き
A type of marinade.

tsunami 津波
A tidal wave.

yen 円
Monetary currency.

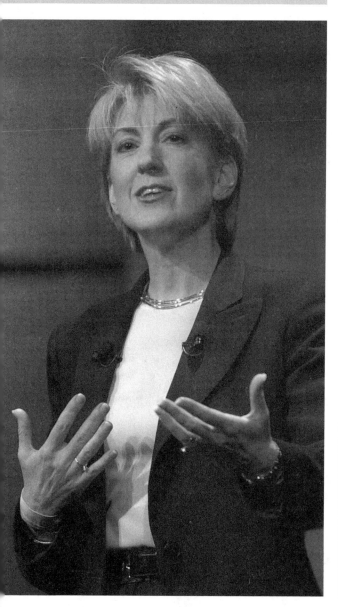

Make It Clear, Concise, Correct, . . . and Cohesive

First learn the meaning of what you say, and then speak.
—Epictetus, *Discourses* (2nd cent. A.D.), 3.23,
tr. Thomas W. Higgingson

chapter objectives

After reading and understanding this chapter, you should know:

- The skills that contribute greatly to effective delivery

- Ways to sharpen these skills

- The differences between articulation and pronunciation

- The importance of listening to yourself when you speak

- Ways to be more expressive in your speech

- The three major accents, or "dialects"

- The importance of pauses

- The importance of pacing

chapter preview

This chapter zeroes in on various aspects of delivering a talk: voice, pronunciation, articulation, rate of speaking pauses, and expression. Emphasis is placed on voice and pronunciation.

Your voice influences your speech and also your daily interpersonal communication. A pleasant, expressive voice is an asset in school, on the job, and in your social life. Such a voice is capable of inflection, the ability to go up and down comfortably in order to express different feelings, emotions, and ideas.

Almost all voices can be improved. Listening to your own voice on a tape recorder may spur you to act to improve it. Some practical suggestions on pitch, volume, and proper breathing are offered.

Your pronunciation and articulation immediately mark you as either an educated or an uneducated person. Sloppy speech and rigid lips result in omitted sounds, slurred syllables, and the addition of incorrect sounds. Ideas are presented to upgrade pronunciation and articulation to the standards recommended by authoritative dictionaries.

Other topics discussed in the chapter are the rate of speaking, the use of pauses, and the importance of expressing inner feelings and emotions.

Every spring, college campuses throughout the nation are visited by representatives from industry and government to recruit potential employees. Recruiters at several large state universities were asked to explain why they had rejected certain students. In almost 70 percent of the cases, the primary reason was that the rejected students did not "talk effectively during the interview."

My speech consulting practice affords me a rewarding opportunity to train men and women both in groups and individually, at all levels (from entry to top executive) in both the public and private sectors. Over the years, I have asked many executives, who have authority to approve an employee's promotion to a supervisory level, what qualities they considered paramount in making their final decision. The overwhelming response was the ability to communicate orally in clear and understandable language.

Clear and Understandable Language

How many times have you called a company, spoken to a salesperson, heard a lecture at school, or talked to someone on the telephone only to recoil in shock over gibberish which left you exclaiming, "I don't believe this!" You've found it almost impossible to understand the individual. Perhaps the person mumbled, ran words together, didn't articulate, talked in a monotone, took a breath midword or midphrase, or spoke too quickly or too slowly. It's amazing the number of people who communicate daily with the public and don't realize their speech shortcomings or who fail to improve their oral communication skills, especially many elected officials.

Through months and years of study, discipline, practice, trial and error, perseverance, and even failure, people can develop their speaking abilities. You should understand that Luciano Pavarotti was not *born* a great singer, Tiger Woods was not *born* a great golfer, Albert Einstein was not *born* a great physicist, and Michelle Kwan was not *born* a great skater.

The art of speaking to communicate knowledge, ideas, and feelings is no exception. All the theoretical knowledge of public speaking will not make you outstanding in the art, and it will not improve your ability, unless you're willing to commit yourself totally. It will take work, perhaps even a ***bit of needling*** from your family and friends, but if you have the will and motivation to sharpen your speaking effectiveness, nothing can deter you and it will be immensely worthwhile.

In my childhood, I wanted to become a radio announcer. I practiced reading, pronunciation, **enunciation,** interpretation, projection, and—the most difficult challenge of all—eliminating my Boston accent. I practiced in the bathroom, in the cellar, even in my brother's car. I took my share of ribbing, but even today I enjoy these reminiscences every time I appear before a microphone or TV camera. And you, too, can be successful . . . if you want to. It will, however, take determination and perseverance. As Ted Engstrom said, "The

in other
words:

**bit of
needling—**
small amount
of kidding

rewards for those who persevere far exceed the pain that must precede the victory." Rereading this quote several times will increase its meaning. If you want to do something, make up your mind to do it; then go at it **with gusto.**

Certain elements contribute to effective and lively delivery: your voice, breathing, pronunciation, articulation, rate of speaking, pauses, pacing, expression, and oral visualization.

Your Voice

There is no more versatile instrument in the world than your voice. Yet, as with any instrument, its effectiveness depends solely on the way you use it.

Listen to Yourself

The immediate reaction of most people when they hear their voices played back on a tape recorder is usually shocked disbelief. You may recall such statements as "That sounds horrible," "Good God, that's not *me*!" or "You mean I sound like *that*?" In almost all instances, the sad fact is that you *do* sound like that. If you're serious about speech development, you should use a good tape recorder to hear yourself as others hear you. It is an invaluable aid.

"I sound like that???"

Speech skill doesn't remain on a plateau; either it improves or it regresses. You must always work to improve it because that's the only way to banish poor speaking habits. Your tape recorder will "tell." The sound of your voice may play as great a role in getting your message across as do the words themselves.

There is no better way to eliminate bad speech habits than, first of all, actually to hear what you're doing wrong as you speak. You don't have to be a rocket scientist to realize that before you can correct a problem you must be aware of it and you must hear yourself saying it. This will not be easy. But, after much discipline and awareness, when you've reached the stage of not only recognizing your bad speech habit(s), but actually hearing them, then you'll be on the road to recovery. Listen very seriously whenever your speech professor offers suggestions, either orally or in writing, on how to improve your speech.

Some of the more common beginners' faults are: talking too fast; not opening your mouth enough to sound all the syllables in words; not pronouncing word endings; taking a breath mid-word, -phrase, or -sentence; and the repetitive meaningless utterances (vocalized pauses which we'll discuss later in the chapter) such as "OK," "like," "you know," and "I mean." (This might be a good time to review briefly the section on using correct English grammar in Chapter 2.)

Listening to yourself occasionally on a tape recorder is excellent—but you must discipline yourself to listen critically to every word and sound. Now let's briefly discuss some important characteristics of voice quality and delivery.

Here Comes the Pitch

Every voice has a **pitch.** Pitch refers to the highness or lowness of your tone, or sound. A person whose pitch is too high, too low, or monotonous (continuously on the same level) not only may transmit a negative impression but may risk losing listeners completely.

The Pitch Is Too High.   Your voice may sometimes be pitched too high because of nervousness (remember your first talk?), fright, or overanxiousness to respond. If you suffer no physical problems that affect your voice, the more often you speak, the more relaxed your throat muscles will become, resulting in more pleasant vocal sounds. A good exercise to lower a high pitch is to read aloud solemn passages very slowly.

The Pitch Is Too Low.   You may know some people who speak with a very low, bass sound. Usually they speak slowly. Reading aloud happy, lively material—children's stories, for example—at a fast pace is a good exercise that may help to raise a low pitch slightly.

The Voice Is Monotonous.   The person who speaks in a **monotone** is like *Johnny-one-note* on the piano. After a short while, the sound is boring, dull,

in other words:

Johnny-one-note—playing only one note

and lifeless. The voice lacks **inflection,** that is, the raising and lowering of pitch.

To avoid or eliminate a monotone, you must find your normal range. This is the vocal area that is most comfortable for you to carry on a normal conversation and from which you may easily raise or lower your pitch. One way to find your normal range is to match your vocal tones with the tones of a piano. Most women can usually start around middle C on the keyboard, and men an octave lower (if you're not familiar with the keyboard, ask someone who is). Your normal pitch range should be the notes in the scale that feel comfortable for you as you sound them, and from which you may comfortably go up and down. An acceptable range for a normal, healthy voice is about one octave, for example, C to C, or thirteen half-notes inclusive. (If you lack access to a piano, see your instructor about assisting you with this exercise, using a piano at your college.)

Once you establish your normal pitch range, use it. Listen to how it sounds and feels so that speaking in your full range becomes as natural as breathing. The up-and-down inflection of your pitch adds variety and vividness to your delivery. A good example of someone who speaks in a monotone is a hypnotist, someone who places a person under hypnosis (puts an individual into a deep sleep or a trance). If you have a monotonic delivery, you'll probably render the same effect on your listeners.

CAUTION *Your voice box is such a delicate, complex mechanism that abuse of it can lead to irreparable damage. Never force yourself to lower or raise your pitch drastically. Be sure to consult with your instructor before attempting to change your pitch.*

The Rate of Speech Is Monotonous.   A person who speaks each syllable, word, phrase, and sentence at the same rate of speed suffers from what speech authorities call **monorate.** The delivery, just like the monotonous voice, is boring, dull, and lifeless. It lacks variety and vividness. In other words, this type of delivery lacks pacing; this is discussed later in this chapter.

Volume

Some people have naturally loud or soft voices. If you speak too loudly or too softly, your audience will communicate this message to you nonverbally. For example, when you start to speak, do your listeners all move back in their chairs as if blown there by a gust of wind? Or do they move up to the edge of their seats, turning their ears in your direction?

The size of the room and the audience should determine your **vocal volume.** If you have a soft voice, start by asking the audience, "Can you hear me in back?" Speaking too loudly or too softly is not only annoying, it leads to a breakdown in speaker–listener communication.

Besides speaking too loudly or too softly, a speaker must be aware of a third aspect of volume—variety. When your loudness or softness does not vary, your voice becomes boring.

Breathing

Proper breathing is vital to speech communication because the outgoing breath provides the power for producing sound. Perhaps you know people who take several breaths in midphrase or midsentence. You feel that any minute they will require a tank of oxygen.

Learn to breathe deeply; practice filling your lungs with as much air as possible as quickly as possible. This healthful exercise will enable you to communicate a message-idea without interruption. Take a deep breath—mainly through your mouth—read something aloud, and stop when you have to breathe. Time yourself to see how long you can read.

Lung capacity varies widely among people. Some professional singers can hold a note comfortably from twenty to thirty seconds, and some seasoned speakers can complete a marathon sentence in one breath. The ability to speak from fifteen to twenty seconds on a single breath is attainable through deep breathing and should allow you to surmount any difficulty in finishing a sentence without gasping for air. As an added benefit, breathing deeply helps dispel nervousness by feeding your body with more oxygen.

Pronunciation

Nothing stands out more negatively in a speaker than mispronunciation. (If you have a question about the correct pronunciation of any word, consult a dictionary.) Pronunciation, **articulation,** rate of speaking, vocal volume, and proper breathing all contribute to the effectiveness of your communication. Defects in any of these areas can, unfortunately, impair your communication style.

Your environment—family, friends, city or section of the country where you live—has a tremendous influence on your pronunciation and speech habits. Regional accents, or "dialects," abound in our country. The three major accents are:

- General American—spoken by the largest segment of our population—includes the Midwest, the West, and parts of the Southwest. This dialect is most often heard on radio and TV and in movies.
- Northeast—includes the New England and Middle Atlantic states.
- Southern—includes the areas south of the Mason–Dixon line.

Each of these three major accents, or American dialects, has a beauty and style all its own, and none is superior to the others. They are all acceptable and

"You can pahk ova theya—just gimme the kah keez."

totally correct. Even within these geographic areas, local and regional dialects exist. Bostonians can easily be identified because they tend to overlook the letter *r* in the middle or at the end of words. For example, they say, "Pahk yah cah in the Hahvahd yahd." They also tend to sound an *r* when one doesn't appear, as in *Cuber* for *Cuba, Americer* for *America, delter* for *delta,* and *tuner* for *tuna.*

Here's an example of how a Boston accent caused not only bewilderment, but embarrassment as well. A very good friend of mine, a senior executive of a large global computer company, was addressing about six hundred employees at his plant in Germany. During his speech he observed that each time he mentioned the Saturn missile, a sea of blank looks stared at him from the audience. Himself puzzled from the strange feedback, he was greatly relieved when he finally concluded his presentation. His German host wasted no time bombarding him with many questions to learn more of the innovative and obviously revolutionary development of this "satin or cloth missile." It was only then that my American friend realized that by not pronouncing the *r* sound in the word *Saturn,* **it came out** satin.

An accepted standard dictionary can be a great aid in improving your pronunciation. Even though recognized dictionaries are accepted throughout the country, some of their recommended pronunciations are ignored in certain locales. Generally, it is wise to use the pronunciation typical of the region you're in, even though it may not be "correct," rather than to allow yourself to sound eccentric. Be flexible enough to bend a little to avoid embarrassment.

Another way to improve your pronunciation is to pay close attention to professional speakers and actors and then try to emulate them. A tape recorder

will verify your progress. Learning to sound words correctly and clearly will require time and effort, but once you achieve this goal it will pay you lifelong dividends at work and socially.

Articulation, or Diction

Articulation, **diction,** and enunciation have the same basic meaning. They refer to
clarity, intelligibility, and distinctness of your speech—in other words, the way
you produce **vowel** and **consonant** sounds: all the parts of words and nothing else.

Incorrect articulation usually results in leaving off parts of words, adding
parts to words, or slurring words together. It is possible, then, to articulate clearly
a mispronounced word. Misarticulation is quite different from mispronunciation.
Pronunciation pertains to standards of acceptability either of a particular region or
of a dictionary; articulation concerns only the distinctness or clarity of the words.

It's important to articulate sounds clearly. Voice each syllable carefully so
that the entire word sounds crisp and understandable. **Sloppy speech** results
from not taking the time to pronounce all the sounds in a word and from running words together. For example:

Whatimas zit?	for	What time is it?
What'sitdoin outside?	for	What's it doing outside?
How'ya doin?	for	How are you doing?
Ahdunno.	for	I don't know.
Whaja say ya name is?	for	What did you say your name is?
Howzitgowen?	for	How is it going?
Whatchadowen?	for	What are you doing?
Whujasay?	for	What did you say?
Whutsamatta?	for	What's the matter?

Here are some examples of slurred words:

kinda	for	kind of
becausa	for	because of
sorta	for	sort of
wanna	for	want to
needa	for	need to
hafta	for	have to
mindta	for	mind to
shoulda	for	should have
woulda	for	would have
coulda	for	could have
shouldna	for	should not have

"Jweetjet?" "No . . . Dijoo?"

Not opening the mouth enough is a major cause of poor diction, especially among neophyte speakers. Because the mouth is not opened sufficiently to allow all the sounds to evolve into clearly spoken words, the sounds seem to be struggling somewhere down in the throat. A beneficial exercise is to repeat vowel sounds aloud slowly, holding the sound of each vowel a full breath (AAAAAAAAAA—EEEEEEEEEE—IIIIIIIIII—and so on). Practice until you produce a full, forceful sound and can feel the muscles in your lips and mouth working. Don't hesitate to overexaggerate your lip and mouth movements. Do this every time you speak until the feeling becomes ***second nature.***

Nothing in our spoken language is more beautiful than fully stressed vowel sounds. When you sound them within a word, voice them a little longer. This is called an increase in **duration,** or length, of the sound. Notice the different durations of the *aw* sounds in the words "draw" "fog," and "sock." An increase in duration of vowel sounds adds color (variety and vividness) to your speech delivery.

Although we have five vowels in English, there are more than five vowel *sounds.* For example, note the different sounds produced by the letter *a* in the words aggravate, fat, hall, and bah; or the letter *e* in be, been, sex, feet, and term; or in the letter *i* in bin, high, kill, field, and evil; or the letter *o* in hot, go, out, order, and oil; or the letter *u* in cup, union, pure, fur, and guitar. **Prolongation** of these sounds adds interest and color to speech.

You can learn to produce more colorful vowel sounds, which can lead you to a more captivating delivery. However, it will take commitment, time, and effort. Practice the following vowel sounds aloud and listen to them carefully:

in other words:
second nature—
natural

A (ay)	betrayed	be-traayed
	delayed	de-laayed
	conveyed	convaayed
E (ee)	received	re-ceeved
	believe	be-leeve
	reprieve	re-preeve
I (eye)	divide	di-viide
	revise	re-viise
	coincide	coin-ciide
O (oh)	behold	be-hoold
	resold	re-soold
	foretold	fore-toold
U (you)	preview	pre-vyuu
	review	re-vyuu
	through	thruu

Another cogent reason to stress vowel sounds is that they impart carrying power to your voice. Relax your neck, throat, mouth, and lips; breathe deeply; open your mouth wide; and let these sounds roll out full and strong. As a result, your listeners will hear and understand you better, and appreciate you more.

The following are common pronunciation and articulation problems to be aware of:

Not Pronouncing All Vowels and Consonants

Bar*bra*	for	Bar<u>a</u>ra
bat*try*	for	bat<u>ter</u>y
boun*dry*	for	boun<u>d</u>ary
ca*ni*date	for	can<u>di</u>date
cho*clit*	for	cho<u>co</u>late
*di*mond	for	d<u>ia</u>mond
febu*ary*	for	Feb<u>ru</u>ary
go*va*ment	for	gov<u>ern</u>ment
gran*it*	for	gran<u>ted</u>
jew*lery*	for	jewe<u>lry</u>
li*bry,* Li*bary*	for	li<u>bra</u>ry
la*bra*tory	for	lab<u>o</u>ratory
p*leece*	for	<u>po</u>lice
r*a*member	for	<u>re</u>member

Running the Last Consonant of a Word into the First Vowel of the Next Word

your rown	for	your/own
her rauto	for	her/auto
your rinterview	for	your/interview
as zif	for	as/if
for rus	for	for/us
this sevening	for	this/evening
Near Reast	for	Near/East
the yumpire	for	the/umpire
her rage	for	her/age
his sage	for	his/age
her rapple	for	her/apple
his zonner	for	his/honor

Producing Incorrect Sounds of Letters

axe	for	a<u>sk</u>
dem	for	<u>th</u>em
dis	for	<u>th</u>is
exscape	for	<u>e</u>scape
git	for	g<u>e</u>t
jist or jest	for	j<u>u</u>st
nucular	for	nuc<u>lea</u>r
pitchah	for	pi<u>ct</u>ure
wid	for	wi<u>th</u>
winduh	for	wind<u>ow</u>
yestiday	for	yest<u>er</u>day
tuday	for	<u>to</u>day
tunight	for	<u>to</u>night
tumorrah	for	<u>to</u>morr<u>ow</u>

Eliminating Word Endings, Especially -ing in Verbs

walkin	for	walk<u>ing</u>
talkin	for	talk<u>ing</u>
coughin	for	cough<u>ing</u>
slep	for	sle<u>pt</u>
crep	for	cre<u>pt</u>

fine	for	fi<u>nd</u>
ben	for	be<u>nt</u>
sen	for	se<u>nd</u>
reveren	for	revere<u>nd</u>
fence	for	fenc<u>ed</u>

Adding or Reversing Vowels and Consonants

ath*a*letic	for	athl<u>e</u>tic
ath*a*lete	for	athl<u>e</u>te
alum*n*ium	for	alu<u>min</u>um
acro*st*	for	acr<u>oss</u>
*ca*lvery	for	<u>ca</u>valry
ev*u*ning	for	<u>eve</u>ning
in*ter*duction	for	int<u>ro</u>duction
laund*a*ry	for	laun<u>dry</u>
mischiev*i*ous	for	mischie<u>vous</u>
of*t*en	for	of<u>t</u>en (silent t)
p*er*duce	for	<u>pro</u>duce
p*er*vent	for	<u>pre</u>vent
wun*st*	for	on<u>ce</u>
skoo*w*ull	for	sch<u>oo</u>l
skejoo*w*ull	for	sche<u>dule</u>

It's important, however, not to go completely *overboard* and o-v-e-r-e-n-u-n-c-i-a-t-e, which will result in stilted and phony-sounding speech.

in other words:
overboard—to the extreme

Rate of Speaking

For most people, a comfortable **rate of speaking** lies between 130 and 160 words per minute. Speaking too fast can cause poor diction—running words together, slurring words, and dropping word endings—which could result in listeners' complaining, "What did he say?" A machine-gun delivery can easily lose your listeners.

On the other hand, talking too slowly may irritate your listeners even more than talking too fast. When speakers take what seems like five minutes to draaaaag out a phrase or sentence, they are setting up their listeners to yawn or lose interest. A sluggish speaker can easily convey an impression of shyness and lack of confidence or interest.

From this moment on, you should be conscious of your delivery rate. Listen to yourself on a tape recorder.

Pauses

Some reasons for pausing are to provide emphasis and variety in your delivery, ***pull your thoughts together,*** allow time for your audience to absorb an important point, and make transitions before stressing a major point or introducing new material.

Pausing is an art that every professional performer strives to master in order to achieve maximum effectiveness. Some of today's finest performers who have mastered the art of pausing include Denzel Washington, Meryl Streep, Barbra Streisand, and George Clooney. Certainly a master of this art is radio and television news commentator Paul Harvey.

Although pauses are the punctuation marks of speech, you must be careful not to pause excessively, which can lead to a staccato delivery. This can be abrasive to the ear and can ***short-circuit*** communication. With practice, determination, and the right number of pauses sprinkled at the right times, you can give your delivery more variety, excitement, and interest.

On the other hand, far too many speakers can't endure a moment of silence. Either from nervousness, habit, or both, they fill pauses with sounds or words such as *like, er, ah, um, OK, right, you know,* and *or something.* Very often they're not even aware that they're making these sounds called **vocalized pauses.**

Pausing is an art.

If you tend to sputter during pauses, don't despair. Become conscious of it, concentrate on conquering it, and try to keep your mouth closed during pauses. Here again, perseverance pays off.

Pacing

If you were on a long drive and kept your speed at exactly 55 miles per hour, chances are you would soon become bored and later, perhaps, drowsy. Wise drivers thus slow down, speed up for a while, then return to average speed. These drivers repeat this tactic until they reach their destinations.

World-class runners practice the same basic procedure. They may start out with a burst of speed, slow down a bit, pick up speed, continue at a *comfortable clip,* and then, when approaching the final stretch, exert a surge of energy and speed to propel them to victory.

Both drivers and runners perform a very important function of delivery—they pace themselves. It would be wrong to say that you should never talk quickly or slowly. It's only when you do either of these constantly that you sabotage communication.

To use **pacing** effectively means to speak at an interesting rate of delivery, with enough variety to hold your listeners' interest. To describe an exciting event, you would speed up your delivery. When quoting statistics or emphasizing several points, you would slow your pace. Speaking at a constant rate, either fast or slow, can only lead to monotony and the loss of your audience's attention.

Expression

When you speak, you communicate through facial expressions and body actions as well as by the words you choose and how you say them. Do your words convey exactly what you intend them to? Are you saying them with conviction and feeling, or are you just mouthing them? There is a difference between a person who bids you "good morning" with a warm smile and one who mutters it like a robot.

After you've prepared a speech, go over it carefully, noting the important points you wish to make. Review the title, opening remarks, main body, supporting statements, and transitional phrases. What points do you want to *drive home* in the conclusion? What is your appeal and to whom?

Understand what you want to say and practice saying it. Pause to attract attention, show your fingers to enumerate steps, raise an eyebrow to ask a question, frown to show disbelief, or lean toward the audience to make a personal point or to let it in on a secret. Don't hesitate to repeat a point several times if necessary.

What you are doing is making your talk come alive, and this effort will entice your audience to be more interested and motivated by your message. *Strive to convey emotions and feelings in your words and delivery.*

in other words:
comfortable clip—a comfortable pace

drive home—make clearly understood

Oral Visualization

A highly effective way to express yourself with animation is to recall first as many experiences as possible. Then select what you need for your talk and visualize it when you're communicating.

When was the last time you were frightened, lonely, depressed, or disappointed? Have you ever been hungry, cold, in pain, or grief-stricken? Can you remember experiencing moments of extreme joy, happiness, or pleasure? Do you remember any of your failures and successes? Hopefully, the latter outnumber the former.

Think about these and other experiences you may have had, if they relate to the topic about which you're planning to speak, until you're practically able to relive them.

If you're trying to convey some of these emotions and experiences, recall them again and again and try to visualize them as you communicate with your audience. Look at your listeners and, as you speak, feel, live/relive your words.

By mastering **oral visualization,** you'll not only communicate deeper meaning to your audience, but you'll also generate "electricity" from your message to your listeners, who will reflect it back to you through their expressions. You will have completed the full cycle of successful interpersonal communication. "Eloquence lies as much in the tone of voice, in the eyes, and in the speaker's manner, as in his choice of words."[1]

Quick Clicks

Welcome to a "surprise search." To further enhance your research or simply to harvest more information about some of the things you studied in this chapter, just drop in at any of the following addresses. What you'll discover may be serious, educational, bibliographical, surprising, factual, or even downright humorous. But they all will definitely be informative.

So, go ahead and give a "Quick Click."

www.pbs.org/greatspeeches/criticscorn/index.html
http://dir.yahoo.com/Education/Graduation/Speeches
www.iss.stthomas.edu/studyguides/orgstr3.htm
www.speech.cs.cmu.edu/cgi-bin/cmudict
http://oyez.nwu.edu
www.public-speaking.org

---

[1]La Rochefoucauld, *Maxims* (1665).

Things to Discuss in Class

As previously mentioned, no instrument is more useful in voice development than the tape recorder. Most speech classes have access to one—so use it, whenever possible, to record some of the following exercises. There's no better learning experience for personal and instructor evaluation than listening to your own voice.

1. Record about a minute of your voice on tape. The material may be preselected or impromptu. The purpose of this exercise is for you to hear your voice and delivery as others do. As you listen to the playback, be alert to your pitch, inflection, pronunciation, rate of speaking, breathing, and expression.

2. When you breathe, you should inhale as much air as possible to avoid taking a breath in the middle of a word, phrase, or sentence. Try reading each of the following sentences on a single breath:
   a. The future belongs to those who are willing to prepare for it.
   b. They say money isn't everything, but you must admit it sure beats poverty.
   c. Breathing is a basic biological process that continues as long as life is maintained.
   d. More people could enjoy much happier lives, if they could only learn to be more assertive.
   e. "Nature has herself appointed that nothing great is to be accomplished quickly and has ordained that difficulty should precede every work of excellence."—Quintilian

3. Here are some words that are often mispronounced and misarticulated; usually one sound is substituted for another. Use a dictionary, if necessary, to write the correct pronunciation beside each word before you record your voice.
   anesthetist _____
   chasm _____
   chiropodist _____
   diary _____
   et cetera _____

handkerchief _____
hearth _____
indict _____
jewelry _____
masochist _____
nuclear _____
picture _____
pronunciation _____
robot _____

4. Here are some words that are often mispronounced and misarticulated; usually one or more sounds/syllables(s) are omitted. Follow the same instructions as in exercise 3.
   accessory _____
   arctic _____
   asphyxiate _____
   casualty _____
   correct _____
   environment _____
   February _____
   figure _____
   length _____
   picture _____
   probably _____
   recognize _____
   regular _____
   twenty _____

5. Here are some words that are often mispronounced and misarticulated; usually one or more sounds are added to the word. Follow the same instructions as in exercise 3.
   accompanist _____
   across _____
   chimney _____
   disastrous _____
   escape _____
   film _____
   laundry _____
   athlete _____
   athletics _____
   monstrous _____
   often _____
   positively _____
   statistics _____

6. Here are some words that are often mispronounced and misarticulated; usually the

accent is placed on the wrong syllable. Follow the same instructions as in exercise 3.

admirable _____

amicable _____

autopsy _____

barbarous _____

comparable _____

guitar _____

impotence _____

incomparable _____

irreparable _____

magnanimous _____

mischievous _____

police _____

preferable _____

theater _____

7. Here are some words that are often mispronounced and misarticulated; usually two or more sounds are reversed. Follow the same instructions as in exercise 3.

asterisk _____

cavalry _____

hundred _____

introduction _____

irrelevant _____

perspiration _____

prescription _____

prevent _____

professor _____

solemnity _____

voluminous _____

For further practice in pronunciation, especially for students whose primary language is not English, see the list of some commonly mispronounced words in Appendix D.

8. As you read the following sentences aloud, prolong the vowel sounds to produce full, rich tones.

a. The most beautiful sounds in our language are produced when we open our mouths and prolong the vowel sounds within words.

b. Be nice to people on your way up the ladder, because you'll meet the same people on the way down.

c. The friendly, round-faced native traded corn and coffee for a large amount of cinnamon-flavored honey.

d. Noreene maintained that Gregory Wayne should not be blamed for the injury, which became inflamed.

e. Running into debt isn't so bad; it's running into your creditors that could produce problems.

f. Round and round went the wheel and when it came to a stop, it landed on my lucky number—13.

g. The orange was large, perfectly round, seedless, firm, deliciously juicy, and sweet.

9. Read the following sentences aloud with feeling and expression. Try to visualize the words and thought-ideas as you read.

a. The battalion of tall, determined waves slowly, but steadily, approached the unsuspecting, jagged shore like military columns. When they arrived, their fury was unleashed as they exploded against the rocks and ledges.

b. The raindrops happily tiptoed across the barn's metal roof almost in unison. Then, as if playing a game, they decided to slide off onto the soft, soggy ground.

c. "We shall fight on the beaches. We shall fight on the landing grounds. We shall fight in the fields and in the streets. We shall fight in the hills. We shall never surrender." —Winston Churchill

d. "If a free society cannot help the many who are poor, it cannot save the few who are rich." —John F. Kennedy

e. He rose, shivering, chilled, infected, bending beneath this dying man, whom he was dragging on, all dripping with slime. He walked with desperation, without raising his head, almost without breathing.

10. You may find the following two readings interesting because they contain all of the sounds of the English language.

It is usually rather easy to reach the Virginia Theatre. Board car number 56 somewhere along Churchill Street and ride to the highway. Transfer there to the Mississippi bus. When you arrive at Judge Avenue, begin walking toward the business zone. You will pass a gift shop displaying little children's playthings that often look so clever you will wish yourself young again: such things as books and toys and, behind the counter, a playroom with an elegant red rug and smooth, shining mirrors. Beyond this shop are the National Bank and the Globe Garage. Turn south at the next corner; the theater is to your left.

We have all heard the saying: "Laugh and the world laughs with you. Weep and you weep alone." Laughing is the sensation of feeling good all over, and showing it mostly in one spot. Nothing shows a man's character more than what he laughs at. To laugh means to love mischief, but with a good conscience. Man is the only animal who laughs and weeps, for he is the only animal who is struck with the difference between what things are and what they might have been. If animals suddenly got the gift of laughter, they would begin by laughing themselves sick about man, that most ridiculous, most absurd, most foolish of all animals. Life is not any use at all unless we find a laugh here and there.

What Do You Remember from This Chapter?

1. Name three elements that contribute to effective delivery.
2. How can you find your normal pitch range?
3. What is a good exercise that will help eliminate a monotonous delivery?
4. Why is proper breathing important to oral communication?
5. Explain the following terms: "oral visualization," "pacing," "duration," and "articulation."
6. Comment on the statement "She was a born singer."
7. Is it a good idea to listen to yourself when you speak? If so, why?
8. Name the three major accents found in the United States.
9. When speaking before an audience, how can you tell if you're speaking too loudly or too softly?

Vitalize Your Vocabulary

Words of Spanish Origin

Because of the continued growth of the Hispanic population and influence within our culture, many Spanish words or words of Spanish origin have been introduced to our vocabulary.

Here are some with which you may already be familiar:

adiós (interj.) Goodbye.

adobe (n.) Sun-dried bricks made of clay and straw and used to construct homes.

aficionado (n.) A great enthusiast or fan.

barrio (n.) A section of a city or town mainly inhabited by Spanish-speaking population.

bonanza (n.) Sudden prosperity.

canyon (n.) A deep valley with very high sides.

corral (n.) A fenced enclosure to restrict animals.

embargo (n.) A government order prohibiting certain ships from entering or departing certain ports.

desperado (n.) A notorious bandit.

fiesta (n.) A festival or celebration.

guerrilla (n.) A member of a small band of soldiers engaged in warfare.

hacienda (n.) A large estate.

junta (n.) A small group ruling a country or territory.

hoosegow (n.) A jail.

hurricane (n.) A violent storm with very high winds.

lasso or **lariat** (n.) A long rope with a noose at one end to capture a horse or other animal.

mantilla (n.) Lace or silk head covering.

mosquito (n.) Those nasty little insects.

patio (n.) A paved area beside a house used for outdoor entertaining.

piñata (n.) A papier-mâché figure filled with candy or toys that children break open on special occasions.

plaza (n.) A very large public place or open square.

ranch (n.) A large area maintained to raise livestock or a single crop.

renegade (n.) An outlaw or deserter.

rodeo (n.) A public display of cowboy skills.

siesta (n.) An afternoon nap (a favorite of your author).

sombrero (n.) A tall-crowned wide-brimmed hat made of either straw or felt.

vigilante (n.) A person who takes the law into his or her own hands.

Know Your Listeners and Speak Their Language

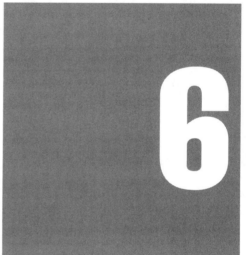

6

You will be successful only to the extent that you cast your thought in accordance with the make-up of your forum.
—Cicero, *Paradoxa Stoicorum* (46 B.C.)

After reading and understanding this chapter, you should know:

● The importance of audience analysis

● Some ways to research your audience

● The meaning and implications of ethnocentrism

● Some differences between oral and written communication

● The difference between concrete and abstract words

● Some examples of loaded words, clichés, slang, and vocalized pauses

● How to use words that motivate people

The words and sentences that flesh out your thoughts, feelings, and opinions critically influence your total impact on your audience. For that reason, audience analysis should rate top priority in preparing for any talk. Several ideas are given to help you with that analysis.

Your career can be helped or hindered by the way you use words in speech. Some examples of the power of words are sprinkled throughout the chapter. Many different kinds of words are discussed—specific and abstract words, short and pretentious words, loaded words, clichés, and slang.

Next, oral communication and written communication are compared. They share traits, such as clarity, accuracy, and appropriateness, but you should always be aware of differences between the two methods of communication.

As for sentences, some suggestions are advanced regarding their length, structure, and human warmth. Again, real-life examples spice up the text.

The chapter closes with several steps for developing your use of language to its full potential, including how to avoid sexist language.

Audience Analysis

Before you speak to any audience, you should learn as much about its members as possible. Only in that way can you best adapt the level of your language and the content of your talk to your listeners.

Where are you likely to speak? Certainly, in this class you'll give several talks, and since you know most, if not all, of the students, you should face no major problems in adapting your approach to them.

Another great advantage that you can enjoy in this scenario is topic selection. After initially coming up with several possible ideas for your classroom talk, you can converse with some of your classmates to ascertain their degree of interest, which, obviously, could help you make a final decision. Nothing like a "built-in" interesting topic.

Another speaking possibility exists in your workplace. For example, your department manager may ask you to explain and demonstrate a procedure to some fellow employees. Or you may be chosen to address your department on behalf of the local blood donor drive. In both speech situations—in class and on the job—you're familiar with your audience; you speak their language; you have things in common with them.

A third speaking possibility exists in any organization (social, cultural, athletic, and so on) that you belong to. You may be asked to speak at the next meeting or at the annual banquet. Here again, you know the people involved, their backgrounds, their education level, and their attitudes, and that's a tremendous advantage for you.

Since we're upbeat and positive in this course, we'll assume that you've given successful talks under all three circumstances, and with this course under your belt, you can do it again, only better. Since good speakers are hard to find and word about them travels fast, suppose that one day you get an invitation to speak to an organization in which you don't know a soul. What do you do now? If you feel able to ***handle the topic*** you're asked to speak on, accept this rare challenge. Here's where **audience analysis** *comes into play.* Be sure to ask the person who invited you for information about the members, information that encompasses a broad spectrum, such as in the following areas.

in other words:

handle the topic—know enough of

comes into play—becomes important

Age

Are the audience members recent college graduates, golden agers, or business executives in mid-career? Just remember, age exerts a powerful impact on people's attitudes, values, and motivations. Yes, they all speak English, but with differences based on occupation, education, and so on. Yes, they're Americans, but with different needs and interests. For example, back in the 1930s your grandparents, as young people, may have been ecstatic over President Franklin D. Roosevelt and his New Deal; as senior citizens in the 1990s, they may have switched to Republicanism. Back in the 1930s they probably romanced to music of the big bands, but chances are that you prefer another type of music. Age does make a difference.

A look around your classroom may instantly reveal classmates representing a wide range of ages—from high school graduates to golden age citizens (the new term for senior citizens). Studies show that the age of the average college student is rising. The average age of students in four-year colleges and universities is approximately twenty-four, and that of those enrolled at two-year colleges is around twenty-five. So when considering a topic and type of delivery, be sure that your speech is appropriate to listeners of all ages and not only your own age group.

Each member of your audience comes from an era or generation representing different cultures, values, and acceptable behavior, whether they're from Generation X, the twenty-somethings, baby boomers, post–baby boomers, echo boomers, or the golden agers. If your audience is comprised of mixed groups (different ages), then it's all the more essential to consider not only what you select to *talk* about but how you decide to *say* it.

Different ages can reflect attitudinal differences. Let's go back to mid-1998 and the biggest sex scandal in the history of the United States. The scandal took place within the White House and involved a sitting President, Bill Clinton; a young female intern, later an employee at the White House, Monica Lewinsky; and Federal Independent Prosecutor Kenneth Starr. Starr served the President a subpoena to give sworn testimony before a grand jury investigating

Know your audience and speak their language.

"I'll tell you my average age if you'll tell me yours."

whether he had had sex with Miss Lewinsky. Despite months of appearances before a Washington grand jury by White House aides, friends and associates, and others who might have had personal information concerning this scandal and the growing talk of possible impeachment, the President's popularity ratings remained surprisingly high. Why?

I think that you'll find the answers rather interesting. How about a little research project? (You may want to take a peek at the next chapter, dealing with research.) During your research, you may want to be on the lookout for such information as: What was the average age of the poll participants? How many national polls were taken? How did the men respond as opposed to the women? Were the respondents married or single? How many were disinterested in the scandal regardless of the President's innocence or guilt? How many felt he was guilty but should suffer no further punishment other than his public humiliation? Did the current state of the national economy play any role in the polls? How many thought the whole incident too embarrassing to the country or simply too trivial to warrant further attention? Your research should prove not only interesting but eye-opening. Look particularly carefully at how various age groups responded. Your effort could make for an interesting speech.

Sex

The sexual make-up of an audience is another important characteristic to consider. Are they all female or male, or are both genders represented? Quite often, audiences are mixed fairly evenly, although, at times, one sex may predominate. Let's say that you're going to speak to a group of women.

In today's world, as opposed to twenty or thirty years ago, women do just about everything that men do. They occupy high positions in business, government, education, and politics. They attend the same colleges, including the service academies, and they participate in just about all sports. Yet, there are differences between men and women that you, as speaker, should make allowances for in your preparation. You would not, for example, use the same anecdotes at a meeting of Women in Management as you would with a contingent of professional football players.

You also need to be careful about gender stereotyping. Be very sensitive about the exclusive use of "he," "him," or "his" when referring to political and business leaders, as well as to such occupations as pilot, doctor, car salesperson, engineer, and heavy-equipment operator. Be equally alert to the exclusive use of "her," and "she" when talking about elementary school teachers, nurses, secretaries, models, and librarians. (I'll have more to say on the subject of "nonsexist language" later in this chapter.) So, during your speech preparation, strive to communicate language that is not stereotypical and includes all members of your audience.

Interest in Topic

Are the members of the organization interested in the topic or are they required to attend, regardless of their interest? If the latter is true, what types of material will most likely pique their curiosity?

Attitude toward Topic

Do members of your audience have prejudices that will interfere with their listening or understanding? Are they sympathetic? If so, you should prepare material that will capitalize on that positive attitude.

Knowledge of Topic

The level of understanding possessed by the audience will largely determine the intellectual level of your talk. If the listeners know little, you should start with basics. If they know the basics, you should try to carry them at least a few steps beyond their current status. As mentioned earlier, take advantage of talking with classmates in speech class to acquire all sorts of pertinent information to help you in making decisions relative to topic selection and level of delivery.

Education

Having some idea of the audience's education level is crucial to any speaker. Your success as a speaker will depend, naturally, on your audience's ability to comprehend your message. The length of your sentences, your vocabulary, and the frequency with which you restate or repeat information during your talk will, obviously, have to be adjusted when addressing different groups such as high school or college graduates or a group of technical people, professional people, or laborers.

As you think about and prepare your talk, you may want to consider some of the interesting but depressing facts and statistics that were presented in a study, prepared for a 1998 education summit, by Dave DeSchryver, Mike Petrilli, and Sara Youssef:

- A 1992 survey estimated that about one-fifth of the adult population has only rudimentary reading and writing skills.
- The literacy level of young adults ages 15–21 dropped more than 11 points from 1984 to 1992.
- In 1994, 25 percent of twelfth-graders scored below "basic" in reading.
- In 1995, almost 30 percent of first-time college freshmen enrolled in at least one remedial course, and 80 percent of all public four-year universities offered remedial courses.
- According to U.S. manufacturers, 60 percent of all 17-year-olds lack the reading skills to hold down a production job at a manufacturing company.
- Seventy-six percent of professors and 63 percent of employers believe that "a high school diploma is no guarantee that the typical student has learned the basics."[1]

Would you like more alarming statistics? One-third of high school seniors couldn't identify Abraham Lincoln or the countries the United States fought during World War II. Only 6 percent could answer the following math question correctly: "Christine borrows $850.00 for one year and pays a simple interest rate of 12 percent. What will be the total amount of money she repays?" A major insurance company reports that 44 percent of its applicants couldn't read at the ninth-grade level. Some 80 percent of a major manufacturer's applicants flunked its fifth-grade math and seventh-grade English tests.[2]

Generally, a talk on tax shelter investments to assembly-line auto workers should be geared at a different level than the same talk given to computer analysts. Both groups probably know little about such investments, but the computer analysts are, on average, more educated and used to dealing with complex or technical information on a daily basis.

---

[1]The Center for Education Reform-Fifteen Years After "A Nation at Risk": Then and Now. Accessed from: http://www.edreform.com/pubs/then&now.

[2]Walter E. Williams, "Let's Fire Education Experts," *Boston Herald,* 12 May 1997, 19.

Cultural Interests

Do members of your prospective audience spend evenings watching TV movies and drinking beer at a local tavern, or do they read the Harvard Classics and attend concerts of Beethoven and Mozart? Do they play bingo and twenty-one, or do they pursue the intriguing intricacies of contract bridge and chess? Answers to questions such as these can help you choose the most appropriate material and language for your audience. Your choices can be crucial in determining the success or failure of your presentation.

Occupation

If, for instance, many members of your audience work in a particular field, say electronics, you'd be wise to include some references to that specialty. More often, however, audiences tend to represent a variety of occupations, and that fact ***rings a warning bell to you*** to make allowance for many differences among people. White-collar workers often differ in attitude and interests from blue-collar workers. Business employees and business owners have different values on many issues. Civil servants may well react differently from military personnel. A line of reasoning may succeed with one occupational group and fail with another. All these differences represent a challenge to you.

Economic Status

People's feelings and attitudes toward government policies, political parties, labor unions, and current happenings are deeply colored by their economic status. Individuals with high incomes are usually interested in stock market activities and tax legislation. People with low incomes, on the other hand, are more concerned about having enough to live on and a roof over their heads. You would approach people at these two economic levels in different ways.

Religious Affiliation

If you're not familiar with the religious beliefs held by members of the audience, you may say something that could offend some of them. Do most of them belong to the same religion? Don't forget that Protestants, Catholics, Jews, Mormons, and Muslims are likely to have different attitudes toward such issues as divorce, abortion, and the Middle East.

Race and Ethnicity

The United States is home to many racial and ethnic groups. For the first time in our history, Latinos (which include Cubans, Mexicans, and Puerto Ricans) have replaced African Americans as the largest minority group, followed by

Asian Americans and Native Americans.[3] Also, **_bear in mind_** that many ethnic groups define themselves through their common ancestry, for example, Italian Americans or Irish Americans.

in other
words:
bear in mind—
remember

If you're invited to speak to audience members from a particular ethnic group, you should try to get acquainted with its history, values, motivations, and achievements. You should also inquire about their command of English. If they've been in the United States only a few years, you should use simple English and avoid slang and idioms (regional expressions). Your audience will appreciate your efforts and you will be more understandable.

As we suggested at the outset of this discussion on audience analysis, you should be able to get most of the needed information from the person who invited you, from officers of the organization concerned, or from people who have spoken to the group in the past. What would really **_be "cool"_** is to get yourself invited to one of the group's meetings to observe **_firsthand_** your future audience.

be "cool"—be
good or be
great

firsthand—
personally,
or in person

In all probability, many excellent opportunities already exist at your college to learn more about various cultures, religions, and ethnic groups through the number of international clubs representing foreign cultures as well as diverse (traditional and nontraditional) social groups. Many of these student associations are open to anyone who is interested and not exclusively to members. Guests are usually welcome. So take advantage of these educational experiences. Also, throughout the academic year, many of these same clubs present cultural fairs or festivals displaying their unique customs, music, and ethnic cuisine. I'm sure that attending some of these events will prove to be interesting, exciting, and educational, especially the food-tasting adventures. Go forth to learn and enjoy.

Cultural Respect and Ethnocentrism

I would like to conclude this section with a note of caution. Be tolerant and open-minded of other cultures and customs. Don't feel that your culture is superior to others and that the way you do things is the only "right" way. Unfortunately, this obnoxious characteristic is frequently displayed by Americans traveling abroad. (While a tour director for groups visiting other countries, I found myself frequently reminding my group members, "Remember, when visiting other countries, _we_ are the foreigners.") There's a pretty big word to describe this negative attitude and it's (are you ready?) **ethnocentrism.** Now, aren't you glad that you came to class today? People who are ethnocentric consider other cultures and customs inferior to their own and will constantly express their views no matter to whom they're speaking. They feel quite comfortable displaying their attitude of superiority and righteousness. What you must never forget is that customs and habits of other cultures may be different

---

[3]U.S. Bureau of the Census.

from ours, but they're not either inferior or superior to ours. In many instances these "differences" go back thousands of years, and who are we to be critical or judgmental of them? That is why, as an educated person, you should do everything possible not only to learn about other cultures, but always to be fair and tolerant when exposed to them.

Language and Your Future

You can have a powerful delivery, an expressive voice, an attractive appearance, and thorough knowledge of your subject, but if your words are poorly chosen, your speech will fail to communicate.

With the right words, you can communicate your thoughts, your feelings, and your emotions. With the right words, you can teach people, give them understanding, entertain them, persuade them to change attitudes, and even persuade them to do your bidding. But before you can do any of that, you should learn as much as possible about words.

Words are double-edged tools of communication that can both help you and hurt you. They can make you happy or miserable; they can inspire you or depress you; they can propel you toward a full, useful life; or they can hinder your progress. Whoever said "Sticks and stones may break my bones, but words will never hurt me" lived in a world of fantasy, not in the real world of men and women, of love and hate, of success and failure, of hope and despair, of honesty and crookedness.

In the 1976 Democratic Presidential primaries, Georgia Governor Jimmy Carter said, "I see nothing wrong with ethnic purity being maintained" (in the suburbs). The expression "ethnic purity" outraged millions of black and liberal voters, and it shook up his smoothly functioning campaign. Carter later apologized for that blunder.

Eight years earlier, a similar incident occurred in the Republican Presidential primaries. This time, however, it ended in a shambles for George Romney, governor of Michigan and a powerful candidate. Powerful, that is, until he said that the White House had "brainwashed" him regarding the Vietnam War. That one word torpedoed Romney's campaign for the nomination, because anyone who could be brainwashed is not shrewd enough or strong enough to be President of the United States.

The way you use words will leave an indelible impression on people's minds. From your words, people will form opinions of your education, intelligence, credibility, and character, as well as your economic and social status. You may be highly intelligent, but if you trample on the English language, most bright, educated listeners will write you off as someone who's not going anywhere, someone who's a loser.

Mangling the language will place you in a predicament similar to that faced by Commodore Cornelius Vanderbilt, a nineteenth-century U.S. shipping and railroad tycoon. Because he had little formal education, he was embarrassed

"Sorry, we don't need no grammar books."

when he had to deal with "all them British lords. I know I am smarter than they are," he said, "but they sound smarter." Tape-record yourself sometime, and evaluate how your language sounds.

Before discussing words and their ways, let's first compare oral and written words, because some words are better suited to speaking and others are better suited for writing.

Comparison between Oral and Written Communication

There are many differences between communicating in written and spoken words—one to one or one to many. Because speaking is face to face and personal, it is much more direct than writing. Hand and body gestures, facial expressions, and vocal variety help greatly to support face-to-face communication. It is also reinforced by instant feedback from listeners in the form of smiles, frowns, applause, catcalls, clenched fists, and so on. An alert speaker who is sensitive to feedback can ***"shift gears"*** and adapt to changing circumstances.

Writing, however, depends solely on words and punctuation to deliver the message. Writing has no gestures and no voice, and if there is any feedback, it takes time to reach the writer.

in other words:
"shift gears"—be prepared to change to a different direction

Good talking is wordy, repetitive, and far less structured than efficient writing. (Perhaps that's why so many more people find talking well much easier than writing well.) A good speech, reproduced word for word on paper, usually does not read well because it rambles and repeats words and thoughts. It is not nearly as disciplined and organized as good writing.

Effective talking is aimed at people's minds and hearts through their ears, and ears prefer short, direct, conversational sentences. Long, involved sentences are acceptable in writing for two reasons: (1) The eye can absorb many more words in an instant than the ear can hear. (2) If readers stumble on a marathon sentence, they can read it again. Not so with spoken words—once uttered, they're gone, especially in a speech. If listeners miss a sentence, both they and the speaker have lost part of the message, there is no going back, except perhaps during the question-and-answer period. In a conversation, of course, a listener can ask the speaker to repeat. Table 6.1 summarizes and offers insight into the differences between speaking and writing.

Now let's focus on three standards that apply equally to talking and writing—*clarity, accuracy,* and *precise wording.*

Clarity

If the audience doesn't understand the message instantly, then the speaker has, to some extent, failed. Thus, every possible measure must be taken to ensure that all your words and thoughts are perfectly clear to the audience.

Throughout your talk, words are your prime means for helping your audience understand your message. And to harness the profound power of words, you should develop a lifelong habit of using a dictionary and a thesaurus. If you do not exploit these resources, you will fail to achieve your full potential as a listener, speaker, and conversationalist.

Another device that will help you achieve clarity in your talk is a summary. If your talk consists of three well-researched major points, list those points in your introduction so your audience will know at once what ground you will cover. Discuss them in depth in the body, then summarize them at the end of your talk, and emphasize any conclusions that they lead to; an example of such an ending is given in Chapter 8.

Another aid to clarity is the use of transitions—words that indicate the connections between ideas—which show whether you are continuing **in the same vein** or are about to shift to another topic. (Transitions are covered in more detail in Chapter 8, and many are tabulated there.)

A common speaking fault is failing to define technical terms, or *jargon.* For example, one student gave what could have been an interesting talk on his profitable hobby. He is a disc jockey and conducts dances for colleges and various organizations, and often performs at weddings. During his presentation, he frequently used esoteric terminology such as *pots, cans, fade, segue, equalizer, dBs, mixer,* and *control board.* As a result, very few students understood what he was talking about.

in other
words:
**in the same
vein**—on the
same topic

TABLE 6.1

Linguistic Differences between Speaking and Writing

Speaking	Writing
Wordy, repetitive	Concise, seldom repetitive
Tends to wander around topic	Better organized, sticks to topic, more relevant
Short sentences—roughly 5 to 20 words	Sentences usually longer
Simple sentence structure—usually S–V–O (subject–verb–object) sequence	More compound, complex, and compound, complex sentences
Informal style may be spiced with slang, contractions, sentence fragments	More formal style—very little slang, if any; few contractions and sentence fragments, if any
Depends heavily on personal pronouns—"we, us, you, they, them, I, me"	Depends less on personal pronouns
Is reinforced with facial and vocal expressions and hand, arm, body gestures	Depends on words and punctuation to get message across; format or layout may help
Feedback is usually instantaneous	Feedback may take days, weeks, or longer
Verbal transitions are same as in writing; pauses and change in body position can signify a new topic coming up	Verbal transitions are same as speaking
Can be marred with **vocalized pauses**—"er, ah, like, ya know"	No equivalent distractions
Planned strategic pauses can produce a powerful effect	No verbal equivalent
Uses more concrete words and shorter words	Tends to be more abstract and polysyllabic

Most hobbies, professions, trades, and sports have their own language, vernacular, shop talk, or jargon. Whether your subject is plumbing, carpentry, auto mechanics, sports, journalism, cooking, ceramics, or law, you must realize that the audience may not be familiar with your subject. You should, therefore, be prepared to explain uncommon terms and to ask if they understand your language. Confucius, the Chinese philosopher, said it all 2,400 years ago: "In language, clearness is everything."

Checking Accuracy of Research Material

As a conscientious speaker, you must see to it that your information is as current and as accurate as research can make it. The surest way for you to damage your credibility is to spew forth misinformation or outdated information.

How many times have you seen a story, a name, an important fact, or a charge against someone retracted in newspapers? Unfortunately, the damage was done when the misinformation first appeared in print. Such unwarranted embarrassment and mental anguish could have been avoided if someone had taken the time to recheck the information. If your talk is on a current or crucial topic, ***do your homework*** and ***arm yourself*** with quotations and sources to fortify your facts.

Here's a monumental example of consequences incurred when two respected media members failed to check and recheck their sources for accuracy. CNN (Cable News Network) and *Time* magazine reported an explosive story saying that the U.S. military had dropped lethal nerve gas in Laos in 1970 during the Vietnam War to kill U.S. defectors. A short time later CNN retracted the story when an independent investigator concluded that the story "could not be sustained." Result: two of the show's producers were fired, the senior executive producer resigned, and correspondent Peter Arnett was reprimanded. *Time* magazine retracted a print version of the same story, which it ran in conjunction with the news network.[4]

Remember, there is no substitute for accuracy . . . only damage to your credibility for the lack of it.

Precise Wording

Your language should be suitable to the subject, audience, and occasion. For example, a speaker who's addressing a Parent–Teacher Association should avoid the statistical and psychological jargon of advanced educational researchers. By the same token, he should not indulge in teenage slang. All good speakers analyze their audience first and adapt their language accordingly. (See Chapter 11 and the introduction to this chapter.)

Are you ready now for a historical anecdote relevant to the precise use of words? When Thomas Jefferson, author of the Declaration of Independence, presented his credentials, at age 36, as the U.S. minister (now called ambassador) to France, the French premier said, "I see that you have come to replace Benjamin Franklin."

"I have come to succeed him," corrected Jefferson. "No one can replace him."[5]

Later in his career, Jefferson was elected governor of Virginia and third President of the United States. However, even if you utilize words the way he

---

[4]*U.S. News & World Report*, 13 July 1998, 22.

[5]*Bits & Pieces*, March 1985, 2.

in other words:

do your homework—be well prepared

arm yourself—have at your disposal; gather together

did, I can't guarantee that you'll become governor of your state or President. But, then again, who knows?

Here's a more contemporary example in which a poor choice of wording led to the resignation of a high government official. While attending an academic conference, Assistant Secretary of the Army Sara Lister referred to the U.S. Marines as "extremists." "Whenever you have extremists," she said, "you've got some risks of total disconnections with society, and that's a bit dangerous." Several hours after reactions of indignation and outrage from the commandant of the Marine Corps and conservative leaders on Capitol Hill, she submitted her resignation.[6]

Command of the Language

We are concerned here with two goals—to capture and condense some insights and practices of the best oral communicators. From them we can learn a great deal about using words to get results. What follows is not the Ten Commandments on using language, but simply guidelines or suggestions on how to generate maximum power in your command of the language.

Concrete, Specific Words versus Abstract Words

For informative as well as persuasive speaking, there's no question that **concrete,** specific words carry a message most effectively. Concrete words pertain to tangible things—objects that we can perceive through our senses. The meanings of such words should be easily understood and leave little room for personal interpretation. Obviously, the more concrete words you use, the better your chances will be that the listener will comprehend your intended message exactly.

If **parallel construction** can be built into a sentence of such words, the emotional impact can be intensified. Here are two statements composed of concrete, specific, vivid words strengthened and immortalized with parallel construction. In 1933, President Franklin D. Roosevelt said to the Depression-battered American people:

> I see one-third of a nation ill-housed, ill-clad, ill-nourished.

Early in World War II, Prime Minister Winston Churchill declared to the English people, staggering under military setbacks and facing conquest by Hitler's Germany:

> . . . we shall fight on the beaches, we shall fight on the landing grounds, we shall fight in the fields and on the streets, we shall fight in the hills; we shall never surrender.

---

[6]Gregory L. Vistica and Evan Thomas, "At War in the Pentagon," *Newsweek*, 8 December 1997, 44.

Note the striking force of the parallel construction in that sentence. Note that the words are short and specific and that they permit instant understanding. Not even one abstract, nebulous word emasculates those sentences.

Here are some basic examples of concrete, specific words:

fruit	man	newspaper
taxes	college campus	hostage
suicide bomber	cyber security	sale
pedophile	syllabus	drugs
tuition	subpoena	restraining order
open-heart surgery	tidal wave	stocks and bonds
date rape	boat	court
woman	skyscraper	day-care center

You cannot, of course, avoid **abstract words** in public speaking. Sometimes they're necessary and serve a worthwhile purpose, but remember that they're subject to various interpretations and arguments depending on people's backgrounds, religion, education, nationality, and so on. When using abstract words, be sure to define and explain them to avoid any misunderstanding or misinterpretation of your message.

Abstract words pertain to intangible things, such as ideas, concepts, beliefs, attitudes, and values that cannot be seen. Here are some examples:

human rights	credibility	beautiful woman
handsome man	prejudice	tolerance
justice	punishment	democracy
morality	ethics	education
integrity	wealth	ideology
science	mercy	pain
generosity	devotion	fairness

As you speak, if there is any doubt whatsoever that some members of your audience may not fully understand a particular abstract word or phrase, be sure to repeat, define, redefine, or further explain the word or words in question. I'm sure that this consideration will be greatly appreciated by any students in your audience whose primary language is not English. It also shows interest and consideration to your audience if, on occasion, you ask them if they have questions and encourage them to raise their hand whenever they hear something they don't understand.

Short, Simple Words versus Long, Pretentious Words

For the purpose of informing or inspiring your listeners, simple, one- or two-syllable words are usually better suited. A classic example of using such words is Lincoln's Gettysburg Address. He delivered it not to inform people, but to inspire them. Of its 266 words, 195 consist of one syllable.

Here are two more examples, both from our good friend William Shakespeare. One of his more popular sonnets, which begins with "Shall I compare thee to a summer's day?," contains 114 words, and 92 of them contain one syllable. His classic Hamlet soliloquy, "To be or not to be . . . ," is comprised of 261 words, 205 of which have only one syllable. If Lincoln and Shakespeare can do it, so can you. (Do you appreciate the faith that I have in you?) These three masterpieces of literature appear later in this chapter. They are excellent exercises to be read aloud for practice in expression, diction, articulation, interpretation, pacing, and proper breathing.

Some audiences expect longer, more elegant words. The more you know about your audience, the better you can judge what kinds of words to use. Table 6.2 provides a sample listing of what some people refer to as pompous and pretentious words, together with their simple, direct equivalents.

TABLE 6.2

Comparison of Words with Similar Basic Meanings

Showy, Polysyllable Words	Short, Direct Equivalents
ablution	washing
ameliorate	improve
assimilate	absorb, digest
cognizant of	aware of
conflagration	fire
consolidate	unite, combine
contiguous with	touching
delineate	describe
designation	name
effectuate	carry out
enumerate	count, list
facilitate	make easy, simplify
expedite	speed up
incombustible	fireproof
initiate, institute	begin, start
innocuous	harmless
modification	change
optimum	best
progenitor	forerunner
subsequent to	later, next
termination	end

"Before we did anything, we had to extinguish the conflagration."

A glaring example of pompous, inappropriate language was given by the former U.S. ambassador to Great Britain, Walter H. Annenberg, when he was presented to Queen Elizabeth. She asked him a simple question about his housing arrangements and he replied: "We are in the ambassadorial residence subject, of course, to some of the discomfiture as a result of the need for elements of refurbishing and rehabilitation." He might have said, "We're redecorating now so the house is a bit messy."[7]

Equally verbose and pedantic is the following letter from a Houston, Texas, high school principal to a student's father:

> Our school's cross-graded, multi-ethnic, individualized learning program is designed to enhance the concept of an open-ended learning program with emphasis on a continuum of multi-ethnic, academically enriched learning using the identified intellectually gifted child as the agent or director of his own learning.
>
> Major emphasis is on cross-graded, multi-ethnic learning with the main objective being to learn respect for the uniqueness of a person.

---

[7]Barbara Walters, *How to Talk with Practically Anybody about Practically Anything* (Garden City, NY: Doubleday, 1970), 136.

The parent wrote the principal:

> I have a college degree, speak two foreign languages and four Indian dialects, have been to a number of county fairs and three goat ropings, but I haven't the faintest idea as to what the hell you are talking about. Do you?[8]

The kind of language the ambassador and the principal used has been called **gobbledygook.** It's been around a long time.

Another, more current, example of gobbledygook or *doubletalk,* and a real classic, is from a speech given by Federal Reserve Board Chairman Alan Greenspan at a black-tie dinner in Washington. Referring to the delicate condition of the stock market, Mr. Greenspan, in all seriousness, declared:

> But how do we know when irrational exuberance has unduly escalated asset values, which then become subject to unexpected and prolonged contractions, as they have in Japan, over the past decade?

In other words, "Stock prices are too high."[9]

This type of language—ostentatiously composed of pompous, superfluous, multisyllabic loquaciousness—abounds even more so today. Much of it is designed to confuse, confound, ***stretch the truth,*** alter the real meaning—and is really basically nonsense. Here are some words of wisdom by a top spokesman at the Justice Department referring to the explosive issue of forced busing. The Acting Civil Rights Chief wrote (and keep in mind we must assume that he was serious): "Forced busing is a misnomer. School districts do not force children to ride a bus, but only to arrive on time at their assigned school."[10] (Hell-O?) Other synonymous terms to denote convoluted speech include *political correctness* and *doublespeak.*

Here are a few more examples from a column written by John Leo:

- When requested for updated illegitimacy rates, a federal agency replied that it preferred

    . . . less judgmental terms such as nonmarital child-bearing or alternative mode of parenting.

- The athletic department of a major university expels players who steal, not for "theft" but for "violating team rules regarding personal property."
- Students no longer "flunk" tests in many schools, but have actually "achieved a deficiency."[11]
- And you "gotta love" this quote from an unidentified U.S. Army major explaining to a reporter the decision to bomb and shell a certain village in Vietnam:

    It became necessary to destroy the town to save it.[12]

in other words:
stretch the truth—to lie

---

[8]*Boston Sunday Herald American,* 6 February 1977, 23.
[9]*Newsweek,* 16 December 1996, 45.
[10]John Leo, "Language in the Dumps," *U.S. News & World Report,* 27 July 1998, 16.
[11]Ibid.
[12]Gorton Carruth and Eugene Ehrlich, *American Quotations* (Avenel, NJ: Wings Books, 1988), 569.

Being Politically Correct

Another area of communication similar to gobbledygook or doublespeak that has become increasingly acceptable to many people, but fortunately not all, is "politically correct" writing or speech—in other words, rephrasing things so as not to offend a certain class, segment, or specific populace of our society . . . no matter how ridiculous it may sound. Here are some examples from the publication, *The Official Politically Correct Dictionary and Handbook,* written by Henry Beard and Christopher Cerf:[13]

Incorrect	Correct
tax increase	revenue enhancement
old	chronologically gifted
prisoner	client of the correctional system
educational testing	needs assessment
lazy	motivationally deficient
bombing	armed reconnaissance
being fired	career change opportunity or outplacement
police brutality	inappropriate physical abuse
recession	meaningful down turn
slum	substandard housing unit

And from the *Quarterly Review of Doublespeak,* published by the National Council of Teachers of English, here are some entries to savor:

● U.S. soldiers should pay close attention to the Army's warning that exposure to nerve gas may cause "immediate permanent incapacitation"—that is, death.
● Colleges don't drop failing students, they "expedite their progress toward alternate life pursuits."
● Electric fans are now "high-velocity, multipurpose air circulators."
● A U.S. Department of Energy nuclear fuel dump is a "monitored retrievable storage site."
● The Environmental Protection Agency now refers to acid rain as "wet deposition."

And I can't tell you how greatly relieved I am to know that I'm no longer considered "elderly" or a "senior citizen" but, instead, I now am a "chronologically experienced citizen."[14]

I think you get the idea and can fully appreciate the statement that "simplicity is most conducive to understandability." Keep it simple.

---

[13]Henry Beard and Christopher Cerf, *The Official Politically Correct Dictionary and Handbook* (New York: Villard Books, 1995).

[14]National Council of Teachers of English, *Quarterly Review of Doublespeak,* Volume XXVI, Number 4, July 2000, 14.

"Homeless? No, just under-domiciled."

Although some of you may think the following bit of prose humorous, it's a pretty good example of what you can do with those wonderful things we call words.

> I used to think I was poor. Then they told me I wasn't poor, I was *needy*. Then they told me it was self-defeating to think of myself as needy, I was *deprived*. Then they told me deprived was a bad image. I was *underprivileged*. Then they told me underprivileged was overused. I was *disadvantaged*.
>
> I still don't have a dime. But I have a great vocabulary.[15]

Loaded Words

Some words that concern race, religion, and politics can provoke heated and sometimes overpowering reactions. **Loaded words** can either infuriate or humiliate people, and they can induce people to commit irrational acts. Loaded words are like a loaded gun; they can cause devastating damage. Here are examples of words that spell potential *danger* to you and to others:

Regarding race and religion: Whitey, Honky, Racist, Nigger, Wasp, Hebe, and Kike

Regarding nationality: Gringo, Spic, Harp, Wop, Dago, Polack, Chink, Jap, and Slant-eyes

Regarding political philosophy: Radical, Anarchist, Skin-head, Reactionary, Nazi, Communist, Right wing, and Left wing

---

[15]Jules Feiffer, *Jules Feiffer's America from Eisenhower to Reagan,* ed. Steven Heller. Copyright 1965 by Random House, Inc., and Alfred A. Knopf, Inc.

Terms such as "flag burner," "baby killer," and "do-gooder" could also prove to be incendiary.

Whereas loaded words are extreme in their potential for trouble, there are other words and their synonyms that can either be complimentary or belittling. Here are some examples:

Complimentary	Belittling or Disparaging
slender	skinny
inexpensive	cheap
imported	foreign
prudent	stingy
pre-owned	used
cocktail lounge	bar
discriminating	finicky
deliberate	indecisive
courageous	reckless
thrifty	tightwad

in other
words:
**make or break
you**—con-
tribute to
your success
or failure

In some situations your choice of words can either ***make or break you.*** Think before you speak.

We use approximately 2,000 words in our daily conversation. And of those 2,000 words, the 500 that we use most often have more than 14,000 different dictionary definitions.[16] How about that? Is it any wonder that we should be most vigilant when we search for the words we choose to use?

Clichés

Clichés are expressions that have been used so often that they have become meaningless. Since they reflect a sparse vocabulary and a pallid imagination, avoid them "at all costs." Below are a few examples:

clean as a whistle	easy come, easy go
good as gold	hard as a rock
light as a feather	ugly as sin
tough as nails	goes without saying
last but not least	in the final analysis
lean over backward	slept like a log

And, of course, the really stale and overused, "I wouldn't touch that with a ten-foot pole."

---

[16]Kathleen T. McWhorter, *Academic Reading*, 2nd ed. (New York: HarperCollins, 1994), 94.

Slang

The use of **slang** depends largely on the occasion of your talk and on the relationship between you and the audience. At a formal or even semiformal affair, slang would violate good taste even if you know most of the guests.

Slang terms can be generational, such as *hippie* from the 1960s or *yuppie* from the 1990s. (Can't wait to see what the new millennium will bring.) Other examples of slang include words like "neat," "cool," "awesome," and "wicked." And how about the use of the verbs "go" and "like" to mean "says," as in "He goes: 'Yeah, I was really lucky to get into Professor Vasile's speech class.' " or "She's like: 'Oh! That's cool, I had him last semester and he's really an awesome teacher.' " *In any case,* it's important to resist the temptation to overuse slang; too much of it can degrade any talk.

in other words:

In any case—no matter what happens

Use Nonsexist Language

Sexism refers to attitudes and behavior that are based on traditional stereotypes of sexual roles and usually result in the discrimination and degrading of one sex—most often, women. Sexist language is insulting and demeaning.

Nonsexist language is also called *gender-neutral* or *gender-free* language. An excellent set of guidelines to help you avoid sexist language, not only when speaking but when writing, as well, was published by the National Council of Teachers of English.[17] The following is based, in part, on that guide.

Whenever possible, use the word *man* exclusively to mean "male person," thereby avoiding the more inclusive meaning of "all of humanity." For example,

Instead of Using	Try Using
mankind	humanity, human beings, people
manmade	handmade, synthetic, manufactured
the best man for the job	the best person for the job
the common man	the average person

Try to use the same titles for both men and women when the jobs could be held by each of them. For example,

businessman/businesswoman	business executives or manager
chairman/chairwoman	chairperson, chair, moderator
policeman/policewoman	police officer

---

[17]*Guidelines for Nonsexist Use of Language*, published by the National Council of Teachers of English, 1111 Kenyon Road, Urbana, IL 61801.

Try to avoid sex-role stereotyping. That is, avoid words that conjure up a specific gender. For example,

Stereotyped Male Words	Stereotyped Female Words
doctor	nurse
professor	secretary
pilot	elementary school teacher
engineer	domestic help
mechanic	stitcher
barber	model
detective	librarian
heavy equipment operator	coed

Because of our environment, bad habit, prejudice, or just plain laziness, it's easy to communicate in language that is sexist. Some people are completely unaware of doing so. But, with effort and conscious awareness, you should have very little difficulty speaking in a manner that can earn you more respect and credibility.

(For an alphabetical partial listing of common sexist words and phrases and their suggested nonsexist alternatives, see Appendix C.)

Putting Words into Sentences

What else needs be said about spoken sentences? By all means, they should be of different lengths, mostly short, say from five to twenty words. These figures are merely estimates that stress the vital importance of short, conversational sentences.

Varied structure is another vital aspect. Try to avoid composing all your sentences in the same form. More than half of your sentences can follow the conventional *subject–verb–object* pattern, but if *all* of them are structured like that, you may lull your listeners to sleep.

In his immortal Gettysburg Address, Abraham Lincoln pointed up a third valuable lesson, that of the personal, human approach. Even though the occasion was most solemn, the dedication of a national cemetery, he touched his listeners with noble ideas clothed in personal pronouns and nouns in every sentence: ". . . our fathers . . . we . . . us . . . they . . . the brave men, living and dead, who struggled here . . . of the people, by the people, for the people. . . ." Such words breathe life and humanity into communication; use them. Here is the entire address. Read it from time to time to savor its beautiful thoughts expressed in majestic language.

Lincoln's "Gettysburg Address"

Fourscore and seven years ago our fathers brought forth on this continent a new nation, conceived in liberty and dedicated to the proposition that all men are created equal. Now we are engaged in a great civil war, testing whether that nation, or any nation so conceived and so dedicated, can long endure. We are met on a great battlefield of that war. We have come to dedicate a portion of that field as a final resting place for those who here gave their lives that that nation might live. It is altogether fitting and proper that we should do this. But, in a larger sense, we cannot dedicate—we cannot consecrate—we cannot hallow—this ground. The brave men, living and dead, who struggled here have consecrated it far above our poor power to add or to detract. The world will little note nor long remember what we say here, but it can never forget what they did here. It is for us, the living, rather to be dedicated here to the unfinished work which they who fought here have thus far so nobly advanced. It is rather for us to be here dedicated to the great task remaining before us—that from these honored dead we take increased devotion to that cause for which they gave the last full measure of devotion; that we here highly resolve that these dead shall not have died in vain; that this nation, under God, shall have a new birth of freedom; and that government of the people, by the people, for the people, shall not perish from the earth.

William Shakespeare's Eighteenth Sonnet

 1 Shall I compare thee to a summer's day?
 2 Thou art more lovely and more temperate.
 3 Rough winds do shake the darling buds of May,
 4 And summer's lease hath all too short a date.
 5 Sometime too hot the eye of heaven shines,
 6 And often is his gold complexion dimmed,
 7 And every fair from fair sometime declines,
 8 By chance or nature's changing course, untrimmed;
 9 But thy eternal summer shall not fade,
10 Nor lose possession of that fair thou ow'st,
11 Nor shall Death brag thou wand'rest in his shade,
12 When in eternal lines to time thou grow'st.
13   So long as men can breathe or eyes can see,
14   So long lives this, and this gives life to thee.

Hamlet's Soliloquy "To Be or Not to Be"

To be, or not to be: that is the question:
Whether 'tis nobler in the mind to suffer
The slings and arrows of outrageous fortune,
Or to take up arms against a sea of troubles,
And by opposing end them? To die: to sleep;
No more; And by a sleep to say we end
The heartache and the thousand natural shocks
That flesh is heir to, 'tis a consummation
Devoutly to be wished. To die, to sleep,
To sleep: perchance to dream: Ay, there's the rub;
For in that sleep of death what dreams may come
When we have shuffled off this mortal coil,
Must give us pause: there's the respect
That makes calamity of so long life;
For who would bear the whips and scorns of time,
The oppressors wrong, the proud man's contumely,
The pangs of despised love, the law's delay,
The insolence of office, and the spurns
That patient merit of the unworthy takes,
When he himself might his quietus make
With a bare bodkin? who would fardels bear,
To grunt and sweat under a weary life,
But that the dread of something after death,
The undiscovered country from whose bourn
No traveller returns, puzzles the will
And makes rather us bear those ills we have

Than fly to others that we know not of?
Thus conscience doth make cowards of us all;
And thus the native hue of resolution
Is sicklied o'er with the pale cast of thought,
And enterprises of great pith and moment
With this regard their currents turn awry,
And lose the name of action.

Your thoughts and the way you phrase them are often influenced by context—by surrounding circumstances—and by events preceding your talk. A relevant example is the attention-getting introduction often used by Jimmy Carter in the 1976 Democratic Presidential primary campaign. In 1976, Watergate, one of the worst political scandals in U.S. history, dominated American newscasts and newspapers, and the principal perpetrators of that shame were mainly lawyers based in Washington, D.C. Here are the opening remarks of many of Carter's campaign speeches:

> Hi, I'm Jimmy Carter and I'm running for president. I am not a lawyer. And I am not from Washington, D.C.

Also, in his vote-winning speeches Carter said something that struck a responsive chord among Americans wearied and angered by deceit in high office:

> I will not lie to you.

He communicated—and the voters sent him to the White House. Short, personal sentences can be very convincing.

One more outstanding introduction comes to mind: the one used occasionally by President Harry S Truman in the nip-and-tuck Presidential campaign of 1948. The pollsters tabbed him as a loser to Republican nominee Thomas E. Dewey, governor of New York. Here is Truman's no-nonsense, no-doubletalk introduction:

> My name is Truman, I'm president of the United States, and I'm trying to keep my job.

He communicated—and the voters sent him back to the White House.

Another example of a blockbusting statement was President Ronald Reagan's answer regarding the very sensitive issue of age. During the second TV debate with his opponent Walter Mondale, in response to a question referring to his ability to keep up with the demanding schedule of his office (an obvious attempt to introduce the age question), President Reagan confidently declared:

> And I want you to know that I will not make age an issue of this campaign. I am not going to exploit for political purposes my opponent's youth and inexperience.[18]

---

[18]*Newsweek*, November/December 1984, special issue, 109.

What a **comeback.** He communicated—and the voters sent him back to White House.

Straight talk is something to which we should always aspire. Again, if I may quote the newly sworn-in President Harry S Truman on how he felt the morning after President Roosevelt died, he confided to the press:

> When they told me yesterday what had happened, I felt like the moon, the stars and all the planets had fallen on me.

Could the average American relate to that quote? You can bet your life on it. While we're on a roll, here, would you like some more examples of "straight talk"? When John F. Kennedy was asked how he became a hero in the South Pacific during World War II, without hesitation, he replied:

> It was involuntary; they sank my boat.

More recently, following the 9-11 terrorist attacks, President George W. Bush, at Ground Zero, his arm around a New York firefighter, and holding a bullhorn, confidently declared:

> The people who knocked these buildings down will hear from all of us soon.

As *U.S. News & World Report* columnist Gloria Borger wrote, "Americans wanted to believe him, and they did." Another example of telling-it-like-it-is, comes from Secretary of Defense Donald Rumsfeld. He was asked, at a press conference, why cluster bombs were being used in Afghanistan. His simple reply:

> Because we're trying to kill Al Qaeda and Taliban troops, to be perfectly blunt.

To further illustrate the power of using carefully chosen short, simple words, here's a handful of famous quotes that enjoy a comfortable niche on the bookshelf of U.S. history. They were uttered by some of our country's "word masters." Although the quotes are identified, you might enjoy, as a learning experience, doing some research to discover *when* these words were articulated and under what circumstances. Who knows, perhaps you may find one that could be developed into an informative, interesting speech.

1. "The eagle has landed."—Neil Armstrong
2. "My fellow Americans: ask not what your country can do for you—ask what you can do for your country."—John F. Kennedy
3. " . . . of the people, by the people, and for the People."—Abraham Lincoln
4. "Nuts!"—General Anthony McAuliffe
5. "I know not what course others may take; but as for me, give me liberty or give me death."—Patrick Henry
6. Here are two big ones from Harry: "The Buck Stops Here." and, "If you can't stand the heat, get out of the kitchen."—Harry S Truman
7. "The only thing we have to fear is fear itself."—Franklin D. Roosevelt
8. "I shall return."—General Douglas McArthur
9. "I have a dream."—Martin Luther King, Jr.

10. "I feel your pain."—Bill Clinton

11. "Read my lips."—George Bush

Notice the number of words with only one syllable.

Speaking of words, let me leave you with something I read a while ago.

God wove a web of loveliness, of clouds and stars and birds,
but made not anything at all so beautiful as words.

Quick Clicks

Welcome to a "surprise search." To further enhance your research or simply to harvest more information about some of the things you studied in this chapter, just drop in at any of the following addresses. What you'll discover may be serious, educational, bibliographical, surprising, factual, or even downright humorous. But it will definitely be informative.

So, go ahead and give a "Quick Click."

www.pbs.org/greatspeeches/wordchallenge/index.html
www.speechtips.com
http://presentersuniversity.com/courses/show_codefining.cfm? RecordID=85
www.racerelations.about.com/library/weekly/aa052499.htm?terms
=Art+Of+Conversation
www.public-speaking.org

in other words:

over the heads of—hard to understand

talked down to—overly simplified, to the point of being insulting

Things to Discuss in Class

1. Tell the class about a recent experience in which you felt that the speaker either talked **over the heads of** or **talked down to** the audience.

2. Give an example of the power of words and how it affected people's lives.

3. Relate to the class an experience in which a speaker received negative treatment from the audience because of insufficient audience analysis prior to the presentation.

4. Identify a speaker (a professional on TV or radio, a professor, and so on) whose ability to communicate successfully with an audience you greatly admire and explain how that person communicates effectively.

5. Try to think of someone in public life who is an excellent communicator. Prepare to discuss that person in class.

6. Try to think of a speaker who is successful as a communicator who uses a large number of concrete words. Prepare to discuss that person in class and list several examples of concrete language.

What Do You Remember from This Chapter?

1. Explain the importance of researching and analyzing an audience.
2. Explain two differences between oral and written communication.
3. What types of words carry the message most effectively in informative speaking?
4. What is a danger in using abstract words in communication?
5. Explain two ways to research an audience effectively.
6. List two ingredients critical to achieving clarity in your talk.
7. Give two examples each of abstract and concrete words.
8. What historic speech contains 266 words, 195 of which consist of one syllable?
9. Explain the term "gobbledygook."
10. What is sexist language. Give five examples.
11. List five stereotypical male words and five stereotypical female words.
12. Explain the meaning of ethnocentrism and give five examples.

Vitalize Your Vocabulary

Words of Native American Origin

Many words have entered the English language from dozens of Native American dialects. Here are some of the more common ones:

barbecue	papoose	squaw
canoe	pecan	tepee
cougar	potato	tobacco
hickory	pow-wow	toboggan
hominy	raccoon	tomahawk
moccasin	skunk	wampum
moose	squash	wigwam

Some less well-known Native American words are

calumet (n.) A pipe smoked as a token of peace.

caribou (n.) Deer found in the arctic regions of North America.

caucus (n.) A closed meeting of members of a political party to decide on policy and to select candidates for office.

chautauqua (n.) An annual summer recreational and educational program.

mackinaw (n.) A short double-breasted coat of heavy woolen material, often plaid.

maize (n.) Corn.

peyote (n.) A drug derived from cactus.

sachem (n.) The chief of a tribe or the head of an organization.

sequoia (n.) Giant redwood trees of California.

There are hundreds, possibly thousands of Native American names of places in the United States—for example:

Allegheny	Manhattan	Potomac
Appomattox	Mashpee	Saratoga
Biloxi	Miami	Scituate
Buffalo	Milwaukee	Seattle
Catskill	Mobile	Seneca
Cayuga	Mohegan	Spokane
Chesapeake	Mohave	Susquehanna
Cheyenne	Muskogee	Tallahasee
Chicago	Nantucket	Texarkana
Conestoga	Narragansett	Tuskegee
Cucamonga	Nauset	Waco
Dakota	Niagara	Walla Walla
Erie	Oneida	Wichita
Kalamazoo	Penobscot	Winnebago
Kennebec	Pensacola	Yakima
Malibu	Peoria	Yuma

To show that the United States had been "the land of the Indians,"[19] the early settlers recorded the names of 27 of the 50 states that are derived from Native American words. Here they are with their general meaning:

Alabama "clearers of the thicket"

Alaska "great land"

---

[19]"Naming the Hunting Grounds." *U.S. News & World Report*, 8 July 1991.

Communicate with confidence.

Arizona "place of little springs"

Arkansas "the people who live downstream"

Colorado "red river"

Connecticut "at the long tidal river"

Idaho "the sun is coming up"

Illinois "superior men"

Iowa "sleepy ones"

Kansas "people of the south wind"

Kentucky "meadowland"

Massachusetts "people near the great hill"

Michigan "big lake"

Minnesota "sky-tinted water"

Mississippi "big river"

Missouri "people with the dugout canoes"

Nebraska "flat water"

New Mexico from the Aztec "Mexica," followers of the war god Mexitli

North Dakota "friends"

South Dakota "friends"

Ohio "beautiful river"

Oklahoma "red people"

Tennessee "area of traveling waters"

Texas "ally"

Utah "land of the sun"

Wisconsin "gathering of the waters"

Wyoming "upon the great plain"

Finally, consider the name of the largest recreational lake in Massachusetts:

Chargoggagoggmanchauggauggagoggchaubuna-gungamaugg

The Nipmuck Indians gave this lake the longest name of any waterway in the world.[20] The name means: "You fish on your side of the lake and I'll fish on my side, and nobody fishes in the middle."

---

[20]*The Boston Herald,* 19 January 1988, 7.

Selecting a Speech Topic and Doing Research

Nature has herself appointed that nothing great is to be accomplished quickly, and has ordained that difficulty should precede every work of excellence.

—Quintilian, eminent Roman teacher of speech (A.D. 30?–96?)

After reading and understanding this chapter, you should know:

- How to go about selecting a topic

- Several ways to conduct research

- How to use library tools and resources

- How to use online subscription and World Wide Web (WWW) resources

- How to summarize, paraphrase, and select apt quotations

- How to take research notes and compile a bibliography

chapter
p r e v i e w

If you're asked to select your own speech topic, choose one that interests you, one that you can handle, and one that suits your audience. Your next step usually involves paring down the topic to a manageable size that you can cover in a short talk. When the topic is focused clearly in your mind, its time to seek solid information—very often the only basis of effective interpersonal communication in business and professional careers.

There are several ways to find information, and you should feel free to use the ways that will suit your needs best: dredge up your own experiences, opinions, and observations; contact various organizations and agencies, both public and private; consult nonprint media (television, radio, documentary films, and recordings); interview specialists from all walks of life; utilize libraries and on-line electronic information resources.

You'll find the bulk of your information in print and online—newspapers, websites, journals, magazines, and books. It is vital that you read and take notes with a critical eye. Question constantly. The fact that a statement is published does not guarantee its accuracy. Your evaluation and critical thinking skills are especially challenged when using World Wide Web resources, where direct author publishing without review is possible and postings can change overnight.

Criteria for Selecting a Topic

Before you can give a brief, stimulating talk, you need a topic and information on it. Your instructor may assign a topic and ask you to research it. At other times the assignment may specify a general area—for example, taxes, welfare, spouse abuse, or illegal aliens—and call on you to select a particular facet of it. Some students prefer to have a specific topic selected for them because it's easier than having to choose one themselves.

If the instructor tells you to choose your own topic, your first reaction will probably be, "What will I talk about?" Without question this is the most common response by students. With a little thought and with the suggestions in this chapter, you may find that selecting a topic is not as difficult as you first imagined. In any event, you should weigh the following guidelines in searching for a topic:

- Your interest in it
- Your ability to handle it
- Its appropriateness to the audience

The Topic Should Be Interesting to You

If you're not interested in the topic, chances are that nobody else will be, and your talk will probably fizzle. Interest, enthusiasm, or zeal—call it what you will—is reflected in your voice and by your nonverbal communication. Audiences sense enthusiasm, or the lack of it, in a speaker, and they respond accordingly. Remember Ralph Waldo Emerson's statement, "Nothing great was ever achieved without enthusiasm!"

If you're deeply interested in a particular topic, chances are your audience will be, too. Your enthusiasm can't help but be transmitted to your listeners because it's contagious. If you can get totally ***wrapped up*** in your subject, the end result could be electrifying.

in other
words:
wrapped up—
become totally
involved

Audiences sense enthusiasm, or the lack of it.

John Wesley, founder of the Methodist church in the eighteenth century, was once asked how he attracted such large audiences and held them spellbound. "I set myself on fire," he replied, "and they come to watch me burn."

The Topic Should Be within Your Capability

In other words, can you ***handle the topic*** on the basis of your personal experiences, book learning, firsthand knowledge, family background, personal convictions, and acquaintances in specific fields? If some or all of these factors are in your favor, then the odds are that you'll be able to prepare for and speak intelligently on your selected subject.

For example, let's assume that you're planning a talk on the operation and safety of a nuclear power plant. Nuclear safety has been a vital concern since the Three Mile Island accident in Pennsylvania in 1979; our concern has been further intensified by the Chernobyl disaster in the Ukraine in the former Soviet Union in 1986. To handle this kind of topic, you need a strong technical background, several visits to a nuclear plant, and interviews with engineers and administrators. Then, you face the challenge of compiling all this scientific information and translating it into a level of English that your audience can understand.

in other words:

handle (the topic)—to know enough about (the topic)

The Topic Should Be Suitable to the Audience

Knowing the make-up of your listeners will help you shape a more effective person-to-person communication. To know your listeners, you should try to answer several questions about them: what are their average ages, ethnic background, occupation, financial status, sex, and educational level; and what other elements may affect your performance?

Consider a speaker at a meeting of the National Organization for Women. If he or she explains innovative tactics that would help qualified women break into public school administration, higher echelons of civil service, or corporate executive suites—the three areas in which women have traditionally been shut out—the audience may respond with a standing ovation.

In other words, try to assess the problem from the standpoint of the audience. Put yourself in the role of an active listener and ask yourself these questions: What do I expect from this speaker? Will the message be interesting, informative, and understandable? Will I want to hear more? (Audience analysis is discussed in depth in Chapters 6 and 11.)

Selecting Material and Narrowing the Topic

A common tendency among beginning speakers is to select a subject that is so general it cannot be covered thoroughly in a short presentation. Suppose you find a subject that arouses your curiosity, for example, how to cope with violence in a permissive society. Should you use this subject for a talk? Definitely not, because it's so vast and complex that you couldn't even dent it in a half-hour. You must restrict the subject so that you can discuss it in the allotted time, usually four to six minutes.

What you need now is a statement that focuses your talk into one clear, concise sentence (a **thesis statement**)—for instance:

> To reduce the amount of violence in U.S. society, our judicial system must begin to impose much stiffer prison sentences.

in other words:
sink your teeth into—develop

Now you have a vital, current statement that you can ***sink your teeth into*** in a short speech. In addition, this statement will save you much library time because it will help restrict your research to relevant information. From a speaker's viewpoint, a talk without solid, current information isn't worth giving, and from an audience's viewpoint, it isn't worth listening to. Your next step is a quest for knowledge, in other words, research.

Doing Research

The difference between a speech stocked with the latest accurate information and a speech lacking it can be the difference between acceptance and rejection

"I'd like to talk a minute about intergalactic exploration. . . ."

by the audience. We say "acceptance" because most audiences listen to and respect a knowledgeable speaker. This hard-won knowledge will give you an injection of self-confidence, and, together with your listeners' respect, ***you're off and running.*** The following ideas will help you ferret out information on any topic.

Probe Your Own Knowledge, Experience, and Observations

If you stop to think, you'll probably discover opinions, ideas, and knowledge that you didn't know you had. ***Jot them down***—they may form the basis of your research. And don't forget to question friends and acquaintances, because some of them may know a good deal about your topic.

Try to recall as many experiences as possible—lectures that you've heard, both in and out of school, as well as impressions and comments about those lectures. What do you remember about their question-and-answer sessions? Jot them down. How about your workplace? Are any of your associates from another country or culture? Have they ever expressed opinions? Jot them down. Have you ever been in the military service—perhaps stationed overseas? What do you remember about your assignment, the people, and their culture? Jot these memories down. Probing your own mind, you'll be amazed at what you'll be able to ***come up with.***

in other words:

you're off and running—
you're prepared to proceed

jot them down—write them down

come up with—discover

Contact Government Agencies and Private Organizations

Some federal agencies, such as the Departments of Health and Human Services, Housing and Urban Development, Transportation, and Labor Statistics, publish many reports on special topics. Surf the Web to see what is posted for federal and state department and agency information. Often, you will find the facts and statistics just right for supporting your topic. Consider content links on the site, including the FAQ (Frequently Asked Questions) sections. Using the e-mail links posted to the site can help you get the specific details you need quickly. However, remember to watch your deadlines. Sometimes, because of the volume of information requests or other behind-the-scenes complications, a website may be no faster than a telephone call or using traditional postal routes. If you do decide to call (ask for the public information office), or write, be very specific in your request. The only ***drawback*** is that you may have to wait a long time for an answer. Some state agencies will also provide you with information.

Research the Visual Media

Check out TV and radio documentaries and talk shows, audio- and videotapes, films, film clips, and cassettes. These nonprint media have been assuming more and more importance as carriers and recorders of vital information.

Audio and video files are also available on the World Wide Web and can be heard and viewed using free applications such as Real Audio and Real Video. Here are a few basic programs that can easily be downloaded to most computers connected to the WWW to make multimedia web files easy to use:

www.sdc.shockwave.com/shockwave/download/frameset.fhtml? (Shockwave®)

www.adobe.com/products/acrobat/readstep.html (Acrobat Adobe Reader®)

www.real.com (RealPlayer®)

Your library probably has a collection of audio and video tapes on all kinds of subjects. Check with a librarian to see if any tapes deal with the topic of your talk. If you're lucky, a television channel (especially cable) may show a documentary on your topic. If you can watch it or even tape it with a **video-cassette recorder (VCR),** you're that much ahead in your quest for knowledge and understanding.

Speaking of cable TV, it offers a multitude of excellent educational research resources. For example, when you get a chance, tune into The History Channel, The Animal Channel, The Discovery Channel, C-Span, and, of course, the award-winning series *Biography* on the A&E Channel, to mention a few. Do some research to locate others.

Talk to People

Authorities on various subjects are everywhere, and many of them are willing to share their expertise. Be sure to have a list of questions ready, so that you won't waste experts' time. After they have answered your questions, thank them and leave immediately.

A tape recorder can be used in a face-to-face information quest because it is a time saver, but first request permission from the interviewee to use the recorder. Some people are "allergic" to being taped and tend to ***clam up.***

Don't feel that you must always seek out authorities sitting on top of the organizational pyramid. Some of them tend to be "long" on administrative plans, policies, and procedures but "short" on ***street smarts.*** On the other hand, many people in everyday positions essential to the functioning of society can brief you on problems in specialized areas, and they may do so if you ask. You'll be astonished at what you can get simply by asking.

Remember, you've added the Internet to your communication tools. Chat rooms are often anonymous. Even if you have a screen name, you probably won't be able to verify the identity of the person behind it simply by sending

Talk to the "woman in the street."

chat mail messages, so be careful not to depend too much on a source that can't be confirmed. Listservs tend to be more dependable in that users need to register and usually belong to the online community in a more stable and committed way.

Read

The most dependable and extensive of all information sources, reading opens endless horizons to you. Just about "everything you ever wanted to know about anything but were afraid to ask" can be found in books, magazines, journals, newspapers, government reports, almanacs, encyclopedias, dictionaries, diaries, and so on.

Reading is like having a passport to anywhere in the world and an invitation to conversations by the finest men and women of past centuries.

How much information should you garner? Far more than you need. Learn from the best filmmakers. They normally shoot at least five times more film than they'll use; then they select the best footage and splice it into a unified package. By the same token, the best speakers usually gather and master two or three times more material than they'll use. This extra knowledge *pays dividends* in the confidence and fluency with which they deliver their talks and answer audience questions.

Learn to Use the Library and the Virtual Library

To extract the maximum benefit from the printed word, you must know how to use the library. With the growth of the Internet and the World Wide Web, the library isn't limited to its physical space anymore. Most libraries offer a rich bank of information in paper, microfilm and microfiche, audio and video cassettes, CD-ROMs, as well as links to electronic information by linking users to subscription and other online resources. Traditional sources of information (shelves of books and racks of magazines) are supplemented, not replaced, by a wide range of electronic information resources referred to as the *virtual library*. So, let's touch on the highlights of exploiting your library's resources.

Card catalogs have been replaced by online book catalogs called OPACS (see the vocabulary at the end of the chapter), which greatly enhance the searcher's ability to identify and put to use keywords and subject headings to increase the efficiency of even novice researchers.

One of the strongest advantages to having a book catalog online is that people can search library holdings from any computer connected to the Internet. Most libraries belong to consortiums, which means that through lending and borrowing agreements, a member of one library can tap into the resources of many libraries using a service called "interlibrary loan."

A database of books is only the beginning of what schools, colleges, and public libraries have to offer information seekers. Many libraries subscribe to dozens of databases that provide information on countless numbers of specific areas and subjects. This information is accessible to you not only through computers in your college library, but also from off campus. You can usually get instructions on how to access and use the various databases by participating in library instruction opportunities or using the online tutorials and context-relevant search tips offered as part of the databases themselves.

Databases can save you hours of arduous manual research because they'll search through thousands of information resources in seconds. The computer will display on screen the titles of all articles and books related to your search and will provide you with all the reference information needed to locate the source material. Computer reference retrievals can usually be printed using a nearby printer or downloaded (transferred) onto a computer floppy disk (a small flexible disk for storing data) or sent via e-mail to your personal account.

Database searches can scan for titles, authors, subjects, and keywords or phrases. When you initiate a database search using keywords, you must use very precise keywords (descriptors) relevant to your topic to narrow the number of retrieved references. If you run into a roadblock—and most students do at times—don't hesitate to ask the librarian for guidance. Some typical database titles are *Lexis Nexis, Proquest, InfoTrac,* and *Dialog.* Also available are programs on **CD-ROM** (Compact Disc—Read Only Memory). The list of available programs in the CD-ROM Directory continues to grow, but Web-based online services are leading the group of electronic information resources.

Entire volumes of multimedia encyclopedias and programs are now available on CD-ROM for research at home or in your dorm room, and most have an equally comprehensive version online. Recognizable names include *Britannica, Encarta,* and *World Book.* In addition to quality content and references, most offer photos and multimedia files, taking advantage of the possibilities of the still-evolving formats and technologies.

To connect to online Web resources from off campus, you'll need an **ISP** (Internet Service Provider) such as America Online, Juno, Earthlink, or MSN. Internet access can bring more information than you need to your desktop in seconds, and since no one controls what moves from one computer to another across the Internet, the challenges to the information seeker are greater than ever. The Internet is an incredible communication tool that brings to the world of information things like **e-mail** and the **World Wide Web.** These have a profound effect on the way data is stored, organized, and retrieved. Quite frankly, **between you and me,** the multimedia accessories available on many computers make research a fun and entertaining activity while improving the quality of what can be accomplished. But more about that later.

Let's get back to the basics of finding a book in the library using the online catalog. Begin by looking at how books in libraries are located using an **online** library catalog. Remember, periodicals are also routinely accessed using electronic means. Learning how to use the book database will help you when you expand your library search to locate magazines, journals, and newspapers.

Library holdings information is held in computerized **databases** (large collections of data organized in a computer so that the data can be expanded,

in other
words:
between only
us

**how sharp you
are**—how

Megahours of spellbinding sight and sound entertainment.

updated, or retrieved in seconds). The three major ways to find materials in a library are by title, author, and subject. The electronic databases, however, make it possible to search by keywords (descriptors) as well. Keyword searches require precision, but with a little practice you will discover how to retrieve efficiently an increased number of references per search.

Figure 7.1 shows a typical library holding record from an online public access library catalog. Each record contains a call number that indicates the book's location in the library. The note **field** of a record will usually provide some details about the physical description of the book and the subject field will provide alternate headings under which you might find books on the same or closely related subjects. Don't miss the subject heading links usually found at the bottom of the record on the screen. This is one of the reasons why the catalog actually serves information seekers better by being offered via the WWW. The use of **hypertext** links means that you can easily move from one subject heading to another, taking advantage of a range of different organizational approaches to ideas related to your subject.

Once you find the book on the library shelf, you can save time by skimming the table of contents and the index for the particular phrases of a topic that you plan to discuss. Take the time to browse the shelves while you are there, since you are likely to discover related materials stored in the same location.

Indicates if the book is currently available for use

Location and call numbers lead you straight t the book

Subject fields offer alternative terms for further searching

Details about the book

FIGURE 7.1

Record from an Online Library Book Catalog

North of Boston Library Exchange (NOBLE)

Check out Periodicals (Magazines, Journals, and Newspapers). In the periodical section you'll find the latest authoritative information on countless specialized fields. Timeliness is the tremendous advantage that periodicals offer—information that may be only weeks or days old, in contrast to books that require several months to a year to publish.

To find articles in periodicals relevant to your topic, turn to the indexes, especially *Readers' Guide to Periodical Literature*. This guide lists, by subject, the contents of more than two hundred popular U.S. publications. Without question, it is the best source of general information on current topics and is an excellent aid in getting your research off the ground. The *Guide* is published bimonthly in green paperback and annually in green hard cover. Here's a sample listing of magazines indexed in the *Guide: Atlantic, Business Week, Down Beat, Ebony, Esquire, Forbes, Glamour, Harper's, Ladies' Home Journal, Money, Nation's Business, Popular Science, Reader's Digest, Sports Illustrated, Time, U.S. News & World Report, Vital Speeches of the Day,* and *Writer.* An electronic version of the traditional paper index can be found online if the library subscribes. It is usually offered through an online service called *FirstSearch* through a company called OCLC. Check with the librarian to discover your options.

Check out Indexes. Remember, there are both paper and electronic versions of these and other indexes, so don't be afraid to explore. Some are subscription databases that require you to be in the library or to have an ID and password combination for access. Others are offered free from wherever you can connect to the Internet, so take the time to find out. If you're searching for material on business, industry, education, or public affairs, consult some of the following indexes:

Bibliography Index

Business Periodicals Index

Christian Science Monitor Index

Dun & Bradstreet

Education Index

Humanities Index

New York Times Index

Psychological Abstracts

Public Affairs Information Service

Social Services Index

Ulrich's Periodical Directory

United Nations Documents Index

Wall Street Journal Index

For science and technology, use the following:

Applied Science & Technology Index

Aviation and Space Technology

For statistical data, you might dig into various government publications as well as the following:

Information Please Almanac

United Nations Statistical Yearbook

U.S. Statistical Abstracts

World Almanac

To learn about people, consult the following:

Current Biography

Dictionary of American Biography

International Who's Who

Leaders in Education

Who's Who in America

Who's Who in Finance and Industry

Who's Who in Law

Use Quotations from Authorities and Use Anecdotes.   In the following list, some of the sources are available free online and others are available only in paper format; still others are subscription services available online, but only with a user ID and password combination. For example, *Bartlett's Familiar Quotations* can be found on the library reference shelf or on the Web at www.bartleby.com/100, but the *Oxford English Dictionary* (online at www. dictionary.oed.com) requires a paid subscription for access. So, if you're searching for appropriate quotations and anecdotes relevant to your talk, consult the following excellent sources wherever they can be found:

Bartlett's' Familiar Quotations

Little, Brown Book of Anecdotes

Oxford Dictionary of Quotations

Stevenson's Home Book of Quotations

The International Thesaurus of Quotations

Treasury of Women's Quotations

Look at Encyclopedias.   For general information and for an overall view of thousands of subjects, check out what is available via www.libraryspot.com/ encyclopedias.htm, and look in the reference section of your library for the same titles and other online subscription offerings. Remember, you can't beat the following standard encyclopedias on- or offline:

Collier's Encyclopedia

Encyclopedia Americana

Encyclopedia Britannica

Use a Dictionary and Thesaurus.   To attain a versatile and descriptive vocabulary—a deeply envied asset—you should use various types of word-books throughout your life. An entire range of resources is available in the library and online via the Bartleby site at www.bartleby.com. Watch on- and offline for these titles:

Funk & Wagnall's New Standard Dictionary

Random House Dictionary of the English Language

Roget's International Thesaurus

Webster's Dictionary of Synonyms

Webster's Third New International Dictionary

Read Newspapers and Magazines.   Daily and weekly newspapers are the most common sources of supporting material. Many papers have earned national and international reputations as authoritative sources of information on current and past topics and issues. You'll strengthen your talk considerably if you can quote from such highly respected newspapers as the *New York Times, Washington Post, St. Louis Post-Dispatch, Atlanta Constitution,* and *Wall Street Journal.* They give superb coverage of political, social, and business topics in the United States and around the world. The *New York Times* even has an index that dates back to 1913.

If your talk concerns local or state issues, you should examine local, daily, and weekly papers. Some of these papers publish columns on various issues by nationally prominent journalists.

Other excellent sources for supporting information are weekly national news magazines such as *U.S. News & World Report, Newsweek,* and *Time.* Many other magazines and publications (some general and others specialized) are also available at your college or local library and offer endless possibilities for conducting research.

More about the Virtual Library— Your Best Bet May Be the Internet

The **Internet** links one network of computers to another to another, bringing together information sources from around the globe. The World Wide Web is a hypertext information system that organizes information in a format that's easy to deliver and access. Integration of text with graphics, audio, and video, which the average layperson is able to navigate using inexpensive or free browsers, is revolutionizing the world of facts and information. It is also making the job of the information user more challenging in that it is more important than ever for each individual to know how to critically assess and evaluate information in efficient and effective ways.

Take the time to learn about the tools available to researchers. Whether you're looking for information to bring credibility and dimension to your talk or you're looking for examples of how great orators deliver their material, the World Wide Web is a good place to go for information. You can listen to Martin Luther King's "I Have a Dream" speech online, or tap into U.S. government statistics from the most recent Census.

Becoming computer literate is intertwined with being information literate. This will not happen during one or two trips to the library or the computer lab. If you intend to use the Internet for research, save yourself some time and aggravation by learning the basics. Before you begin using online resources, it helps to know and gain experience with:

● Using a personal computer
● Using a keyboard and a mouse
● Using a graphical **browser** such as Explorer or Netscape to navigate the WWW
● Using Web-based e-mail to store and sort information
● Using **search engines** such as Google

- Using an online index such as the Digital Librarian
- Printing and **downloading** files to a disk
- **Citing** information from an electronic source so it can be found again

A lot of the information found on the Web is the same information found in books on the library shelves. So why use the Internet? First, there is already more information on the World Wide Web than what could be stored in the largest of libraries, and it's increasing every day. Second, an electronic medium has the ability to sort and search far beyond human limits.

With that having been said, it's important to realize that the search for information is not a choice between paper and electronic resources. The Internet hasn't made hardbound books and paper versions of magazines extinct. The Internet brings us more information, faster, in a format that makes the information more manageable than ever before; but by itself it can't do it all, at least not yet. Looking for information is as much an art as a skill. Using only one tool to access and sort information seriously limits the scope and quality of your research. The Internet and the World Wide Web outperform other tools for speed and quantity, but quality research is more about range, depth, and scope—not just volume. Don't limit yourself by relying on one tool, any more than you would rely on one set of encyclopedias or one person for information.

Here's one final hint for exploiting your library and the virtual library. Get acquainted with reference librarians. No matter *how sharp you are,* research is a time-consuming process that librarians can speed up by guiding you to the right reference aids. However, don't expect them to do your research; that's your task.

Making a Bibliography

At this point you're primed to dip into reference works in order to locate sources of information. Magazines, journals, newspapers, books, and Internet sources are all fair game in the hunt. Whether you plan to refer to a few sources or to a dozen, you should number and list them on notepaper or 5-by-7-inch **note cards.** This list (Figure 7.2) is your preliminary **bibliography**—the list of sources that you actually use in your talk is your final bibliography.

If you decide to use the Internet for research, it is particularly important to keep an accurate record of what you find, including when and where you found it. Unlike a paper source, electronic sources may change overnight, making it difficult, sometimes impossible, to retrieve the information again. To avoid wasting time and relying on sources that cannot be verified later, you should use the most current guidelines published by the American Language Association for creating a bibliography, so that your list of sources is a useful and valid one.

AFFIRMATIVE ACTION IN EDUCATION
  Back to square one: [minority admissions at the University of Texas and University of California, Berkeley]. A. Cohen. il *Time* v151 no15 p30–1 Ap 20 '98
  Don't get hysterical [minority education at University of California after end of affirmative action] J. Leo. il *U.S. News & World Report* v124 no16 p12 Ap 27 '98
  Exam question [affirmative action via government test prep aid to minority students] C. Lane *The New Republic* v215 no15 p6 Ap 13 '98
  How to even the score: test prep [minority access to LSAT tutors] R. Ratnesar. il *Time* v151 no15 p31 Ap 20 '98
  In defense of preference [cover story] N. Glazer. il *The New Republic* v218 no14 p18–21+ Ap 6 '98
  Lies, damn lies and racial statistics [University of California overplays drop in minority admissions] C. Krauthammer. il *Time* v151 no15 p32 Ap 20 '98
  Testing Texas [impact of Hopwood v. University of Texas Law School decision] J. Traub. *The New Republic* v218 no14 p20–1 Ap 6 '98

FIGURE 7.2

Preliminary Bibliography

Evaluating Your Sources

Try using the four basic evaluation guideline categories that Web experts consult.

- Accuracy?
  1. Does the content contain numerous spelling errors and/or typos?
  2. Is the Web page's creation date present?
  3. Is the information current or outdated?
  4. Is the content detailed or too general?
  5. Are arguments well supported?

- Credibility?
  1. Does the page contain the author's name, position, or occupation?
  2. Is the author affiliated with a well-known organization?
  3. Is there a means of contacting the creator (e.g., e-mail or phone)?
  4. Are the writer's credentials on the page?
  5. Are the credentials relevant to the topic?
  6. Is the page peer-reviewed?

- Documented?
  1. Is the original source of the content material apparent?
  2. Is there a bibliography?
  3. Are statistics' sources identified?

● Appropriate?

1. What is the scope of the page in terms of its topic's coverage?
2. Is only one view presented, or are others noted and/or represented?
3. Does the author's writing style seem more emotional than objective?

For example, an article dealing with international news in the *New York Times* or *Los Angeles Times* carries far more **clout** than a similar article in a small-town newspaper. Admittedly, one or both of the last two yardsticks may be difficult to apply, but they do help in comparing one work against another and in deciding which would make a better source.

Evaluating what you find using the Internet is not as easy as it seems since, as we considered earlier, no one is **in control** of the Internet. E-mail headings aren't always accurate representations of where the information originated, since aliases can be used and points of origin distorted electronically. Graphics are easily tampered with using image-editing software, and text is easily manipulated using word-processing programs and text editors. (Talk about ethics!)

Although there are no foolproof methods for considering the credibility of a website, there are some elements common to most reliable sites. Figure 7.3 shows a typical World Wide Web page. As with paper sources, you are considering the origin of the page. For example, if the American Psychological Association

FIGURE 7.3

A World Wide Web Page

provides material on mental health, your source is much more credible than an e-mail message from a listserv on which a group is discussing various forms of neurotic eating disorders.

Taking Notes

The purpose of taking notes is to record accurately information and ideas that you believe will be useful in developing your speech. Since using someone else's words without giving proper credit, known as **plagiarism** (see Chapter 1), is considered a major form of cheating/stealing, you need to be careful to record information, not words, whenever possible. There are times, of course, when a writer's words are so striking that you will want to use them. Quoting occasionally from your sources is permissible, provided that you indicate that you are quoting. In writing, quotation marks serve this purpose. In speech we usually say "quote" and "unquote" to signal the beginning and end of a quotation: "The professor described the student's paper as quote, dramatic but unconvincing, unquote."

Whenever you write down the exact terminology of a writer, be sure that you place the borrowed words in quotation marks in your notes. If you fail to do so, you can find yourself plagiarizing without knowing that you are doing it.

Take a few notes.

Well-publicized cases of plagiarism by politicians and professional writers have focused attention on plagiarism in recent years. Two columnists of the *Boston Globe,* among others, have recently lost their jobs because of accusations of plagiarism. In the classroom, the consequences of plagiarism can be a failing grade or even suspension.

Figure 7.4 presents an original passage and Figure 7.5 shows notes taken from that passage.

Here's a time-tested tip on using research note cards. Indicate the following on each card: a brief heading, information from one source and on one topic, and the source (for example, magazine name, author, title of article, volume number, date, and page number).

As a modern researcher, you enjoy a tremendous advantage over historical information seekers such as Thomas Jefferson, Charles Darwin, and Winston Churchill. Say, for example, that you run across a few pages full of meaty, relevant information in a book, magazine, or encyclopedia that can't be borrowed. You could easily waste an hour or so copying the pages in longhand.

[Source: Charles N. Barnard, "Blimps: Big, Beautiful, & Everywhere You Look." *Smithsonian,* June 1998, pp. 32–33.]

Visionaries have always seen a future for airships that goes far beyond advertising, however. In South Africa, the Hamilton Airship Company has formulated plans for a luxury dirigible of near-*Hindenburg* proportions. It would carry 30 passengers across the Atlantic from Johannesburg to New York in 10 days at speeds of up to 100 miles per hour. In New York City, Donald Trump recently conceived a plan to ferry 160 high rollers a day to his casino in Atlantic City aboard a luxury airship. The exorbitant cost, not any lack of engineering feasibility, caused him to shelve the idea.

A company called Airship Management Services (AMS) is working with a company in Saudi Arabia to provide a blimp for surveillance during the hajj, the annual gathering of millions of Muslims in Mecca and Medina. AMS blimps have already helped with crowd management at the Los Angeles, Seoul and Atlanta Olympics—examples of what many believe will be a growing airship market: police work and border patrols.

A German company, CargoLiftr AG, is planning to build a gigantic cargo-carrying airship capable of flying 80 mph. When fully inflated, it will be longer than the Washington Monument is tall. It's aimed at the $9-billion-a-year market for transporting freight to places where planes can't land and for carrying cargo—turbines and power-generating equipment, for example—that is too bulky and heavy (up to 150 tons) for airplanes.

FIGURE 7.4

Original Passage from *Blimps: Big, Beautiful, & Everywhere You Look*

Several ideas have been advanced for the use of blimps:

1. Transatlantic passenger flights from Johannesburg to New York. Speeds up to 100 mph.

2. "Ferry 160 high rollers" from New York to Atlantic City. Plan by Donald Trump abandoned because of cost.

3. Surveillance during the hajj, the annual gathering of millions of Muslims in Mecca and Medina.

4. Crowd control at the Olympics—already done at Los Angeles, Seoul, and Atlanta.

5. "Growing airship market: police work and border patrols."

6. Transporting cargo to places where planes can't be used.

FIGURE 7.5

Notes on Original Passage in Figure 7.4

Since almost all libraries have photocopy equipment, use it to save time. Reading important information into a cassette tape recorder can also save time. (Be sure to document the source.) And, of course, the biggest time saver at the library is the computer, where you come, you search, you find, and with a press of a key or mouse—***voilà***—you have a printout. Isn't modern technology marvelous?

in other words:
voilà—(French) there it is, to express success or satisfaction

CAUTION *When you quote, summarize, or paraphrase an individual or published source without giving due credit, you are guilty of* plagiarism, *a very serious offense, especially since passage of the copyright law of 1978. An update to the U.S. Code enacted in 1997 provides greater protection in the area of intellectual property by addressing criminal infringement of copyright.*

A major concern for everyone is the idea of intellectual property rights. Using other peoples' ideas or taking words written or spoken by someone else and calling them your own are serious considerations. If people couldn't access and use other people's inventions and discoveries, performances, and writing, then much of what is accomplished in the scholarly, scientific, and artistic arenas would never happen. But to use or build on the accomplishments and productions of others without acknowledgment or credit is a serious form of thievery: it's plagiarism.

Acknowledging source material is an important skill for people who make presentations in front of audiences. A good place to get started is to make sure that you understand the rules of citing information and that you concern yourself with the details of following formats published by one of several authoritative bodies that concern themselves with the rules of publication. Two of the most prominent guidelines are published by the Modern Language Association, "How do I document sources from the World Wide Web in my works-cited list?" www.mla.org (MLA), and the American Psychological Association, www.apastyle.org/elecref.html (APA). Consult the website of either organization or get some practice by using an online tool called Noodlebib at www.noodletools.com/noodlebib/index.php. Noodlebib is a Web application that allows you to create and edit an MLA bibliography online. The site includes examples of the guidelines for using online materials.

If you want to try writing citations on your own before checking out the formal guidelines, get a magazine article in front of you and ask yourself a few questions.

- Who wrote the article?
- What is the title of the article?
- What is the name of the magazine the article was in?
- What is the publication date on the magazine?
- What page(s) was the article on?

Keep your answers in order because, along with punctuation, the order is what provides the format.

The citation format is the formal organization of the details that describe the article and its source. A typical magazine citation begins with the author's name, which is followed by the title of the article, the name of the magazine it was published in comes next, followed by the date the magazine was published, and the page(s) it was on. And punctuation matters, so move slowly at first and notice the specifics of how citations come together. Periods and quotation marks make a difference later on when citations get more complicated, so don't lose track of what goes where.

Let's now cite an article from *National Fisherman Online*, edited by Jerry Fraser. Here's the basic format for citing a magazine article:

Author. "Title of Article." Title of Periodical Date: First page–last page.

The informal citation is then

Fraser, Jerry. "The Highliners." National Fisherman Online: December 2001 pg. 1.

The trick to writing good citations is in following the guidelines. The above example is an informal approach that gets the job done but, as in most things worth doing, there's more to it than that. The correct citation if following MLA guidelines is

"The Highliner." National Fisherman Online Dec. 2001: 1. 21 Jan. 2002 <www.nationalfisherman.com/mag/pastissues.htm>.

The difference is in the details. Jerry Fraser is the editor of the magazine, and no author was given a byline on the article. The publication the magazine

article came from was an electronic version accessed online and not a traditional paper copy. The rule is to include the access date as well as the publication date and the URL (the Web address) used to retrieve the article. And don't
miss that five-space indent that precedes the second line! It's a rule of MLA
citation format, so it has to be there.

Learning how to acknowledge when you are using someone's words and/or
ideas isn't particularly difficult, but it does require a sincere effort to pay attention to detail. A formal citation is created by your commitment to follow an
agreed-upon guideline designed to ensure that words or ideas that belong to
someone else can easily be traced back to the source from which they were taken.

In other words, if you take a sentence or paragraph from a book or magazine
article and include them in an essay, a presentation, or a website, you have to let
your audience know where the material came from and provide the information
in a way that is easy to follow so they can locate the original work for themselves.

Don't forget to consult the formal guides as needed. Citation formats are not
the sort of thing people need to memorize, but if you make presentations regularly, you'll find that people are often interested in where your material came
from and are looking for sources to do additional reading on the subject on
their own. A list of source material, a bibliography, is a routine tool for people
who work in the world of words and ideas.

No question about it, conducting research can be a prolonged, difficult, and
sometimes discouraging activity, but the overall results will be most rewarding.

Quick Clicks

Welcome to a "surprise search." To further enhance your research or simply to harvest more information about some of the things you studied in this
chapter, just drop in at any of the following addresses. What
you'll discover may be serious, educational, bibliographical, surprising, factual,
or even downright humorous. But it will definitely be informative.

So, go ahead and give a "Quick Click."

MLA website: www.mla.org/www_mla_org/style/style_index.asp?
   mode=section
Federal gov site (Thomas): www.thomas.loc.gov
University at Albany Library Internet Tutorials: www.library.albany.edu/internet
California Library Instruction: www.lib.calpoly.edu/infocomp/modules/index.html
ListServ website: www.western.tec.wi.us/voice/discuss/lists.htm
Evaluation website: http://milton.mse.jhu.edu:8001/research/education/
   net.html
Search Engine Watch: www.searchenginewatch.com/resources/reviews.html

Things to Discuss in Class

1. List two subjects that interest you but that, because of your lack of knowledge, would require research if you were planning to talk about them.
2. Would you prefer to select your own topics or to have them selected for you? Why?
3. List a speech topic that would apply only to one specific audience. Explain your reasons for choosing it.
4. Select a topic that would interest the class and list some possible sources of information on it.
5. Research one significant event that took place on the day you were born.
6. List two topics that you think would make interesting talks. Make sure that you narrow each topic so that it can easily be covered in a four- to six-minute speech.
7. Discuss the types of information you can find in the *Readers' Guide to Periodical Literature.*
8. Select what you feel is an interesting topic, then go to the library and prepare a bibliography on it.

What Do You Remember from This Chapter?

1. After you've decided on a topic for your talk, what should your next step be?'
2. List several ways to find information.
3. Name two sources that provide statistical data.
4. Explain the difference between a summary and a paraphrase.
5. When using the Internet for research, why is it so important to keep an accurate record of what you find, including when and where you found it?
6. Name the two most prominent formal guideline sources for correctly citing information during your research.
7. What are the four basic evaluation guideline categories that Web experts consult?
8. What's the difference between a dictionary and a thesaurus?
9. What information can you expect to find from online book catalogs?
10. Explain how the Internet has revolutionized the activity of researching information.

Vitalize Your Vocabulary

Basic Computer and Internet Terms

back up (v.) To make a copy of important data to be used if your current file is destroyed.

boot (v.) To start the computer.

browser or Web browser (n.) A client application that allows a user to view HTML documents as well as graphics on the World Wide Web.

byte (n.) The amount of computer memory needed to store one character of a specified size, usually 8 for a microcomputer and 16 for a larger one.

CD-ROM (Compact Disk—Read Only Memory) (n.) Term applied to a variety of storage formats by which audio, text, and graphics are retrieved from the disk by laser beam.

chat room (n.) Communication service used on the Internet in "real time." Participants can enter text by typing on the keyboard; the message appears on the other user's monitor.

cursor (n.) The movable symbol on the computer monitor (screen) that indicates the place where the operator is working.

cyberspace (n.) The universe of environments, such as the Internet, where people interact via connected computers.

database (n.) A large collection of information stored in a well-organized format that can be retrieved by specific software.

debug (v.) To eliminate a mistake within a computer program or its electrical system.

download (v.) To transmit data from a central to a remote computer, from a file server to a workstation, or from a computer to a floppy disk.

e-mail (n.) Electronic mail. Tool for sending messages over the Internet.

FAQ (n.) Acronym for Frequently Asked Questions, a website section that contains basic information of general interest to visitors of the site.

field (n.) One of many sections that come together to constitute an electronic record.

file (n.) A collection of data considered a single unit.

floppy disk (n.) A small, inexpensive removable disk used to record and store information.

font (n.) A set of type characters used for printing information.

format (n.) The arrangement by which data are stored or displayed.

hard copy (n.) Printed computer output.

hard disk (n.) A metal disk covered with a magnetic recording surface usually installed inside PCs for added storage capacity.

hardware (n.) Equipment that makes up a computer, such as chips, boards, wires, and transformers. Term also applies to other computer-related pieces of equipment, such as printers, modems, keyboards, and monitors.

HTML Abbreviation for HyperText Markup Language.

http Abbreviation for HyperText Transfer Protocol, used to access information on the Web.

hypertext (n.) A section of web-page text that responds to a user command by establishing a connection to a file of information.

interface (n.) Interaction between hardware, software, and operator.

Internet (n.) An electronic network linking computers together, originally called ARPANET, the Advanced Research Projects Agency of the U.S. Department of Defense.

ISP (n.) Internet Service Provider. Establishes connections between computers and the Internet.

keyboard (n.) A set of keys (like a typewriter) used to type data into a computer.

links (n.) A hypertext screen section, usually underlined words or a framed graphic, that responds to a user's command to move from one file of information to another on a web page or to another website.

Listserv (n.) An automatic mailing list server. Messages are automatically broadcast to everyone who subscribes to the list.

load (v.) To put information or data into the computer.

megabyte (n.) A unit of measure for the information stored in either the computer's hard drive or floppy disk; 1 megabyte equals 1 million characters (bytes) of data.

memory (n.) The computer's storage capacity.

menu (n.) Programs, functions, etc., displayed on the monitor for user selection.

modem (n.) A device used to transfer computer information over phone lines.

mouse (n.) A palm-sized device with one or more buttons that when rolled across a flat surface points at and selects items on a computer screen for input.

netiquette (n.) (Are you ready for this?) Short for network etiquette.

network (n.) Terminals and computers linked together for the purpose of interacting with each other.

online (adj.) Connected to the Internet.

OPAC (n.) Online Public Access Catalog. Often a Web-based system allowing for the use of hypertext links among subject headings.

operating system (n.) The main control program that runs the computer, such as Macintosh, OS-X, Windows XP, or Linux.

PC (n.) Personal computer.

power surger (n.) An electrical device into which the computer is plugged to prevent loss of data or information due to a sudden jolt or loss of electric power; a surge protector.

printer (n.) A device that prints data and graphics from the computer.

RAM (n.) Random Access Memory.

ROM (n.) Read-Only Memory.

screen (CRT, monitor) (n.) A screen for viewing what's being displayed by computer.

search engine (n.) A World Wide Web tool designed to look for and display information in response to a user's query.

software (n.) Programs for directing the operation of a computer.

terminal (n.) A keyboard or video display unit used for entering information into or receiving information from a computer.

URL (n.) Uniform Resource Locator, another name for a website address.

user friendly (adj.) Not intimidating; easy to use.

Username (n.) The name you use to log onto a computer system or network. Many people use it as their e-mail name as well.

virus (bug) (n.) A destructive program that is secretly attached to an existing program that can alter or delete data and can cause other computer malfunctions.

website (n.) A collection of "pages" on the World Wide Web providing detailed (graphic) information about an organization, company, or individual that/who owns and maintains the site. The first visual that is shown on the screen, when entering a site, is called a home page.

window (n.) A separate viewing area on a display screen.

word processor (n.) A program to allow an operator to write, edit, and correct text or documents on the computer.

workstation (terminal) (n.) A PC that serves a single user.

WWW (n.) World Wide Web. An international collection of information searchable using text or graphic browsers.

chapter

8

Putting It All Together

Order and simplification are the first steps toward mastery of a subject.
—Thomas Mann, *The Magic Mountain* (1924)

After reading and understanding this chapter, you should know:

- The two principal types of outlines

- The six parts of an outline

- How to prepare an outline

- The four parts of a talk and how to bond them together

- How to come up with a title for your talk

- How to prepare an introduction to your talk

- How to prepare a conclusion to your talk

- What transitions are and how to use them

chapter
preview

At this stage you've done your research and you know your subject. Now you must plan, or outline, your talk. In the long run, a good outline will save you far more time than you will devote to preparing it. The two most common types of outlines, the topic outline and the sentence outline, are explained and illustrated.

When you construct your talk, you may work on the body first and then the introduction or conclusion. A well-thought-out introduction will usually win audience goodwill and interest. Numerous suggestions for effective introductions are given, and all of them appear in introductions quoted from actual speeches. In addition, some ideas for forming conclusions are listed, and excellent examples are included.

Since every talk should have a title, actual titles of many speeches are listed, along with pointers on their distinguishing characteristics.

In every talk you give, the introduction, body, and conclusion should be linked smoothly to each other by means of transitions. Examples of transitions, together with the conditions that call for their use, appear in a table at the end of the chapter.

NOTE *The way you organize your talk can make or break your overall perfor-mance. For that reason, this chapter deserves a great deal of your time and effort.*

Preparing an Outline

in other words:

turned over in your mind—thoroughly reviewed

inside out—thoroughly, completely

You've done your research, you've uncovered more than enough material (al-ways a wise policy), you've **turned the material over in your mind,** and you understand it **inside out.** Where do you go from here?

What you need now is a plan to organize all the information you've gathered. In a sense, you're in the same position as an architect about to design a building, an airline pilot about to fly the Atlantic, or a motorist about to drive from New York to San Francisco. To accomplish these objectives, the architect needs blue-prints, the pilot needs a flight plan, and the motorist needs road maps.

By the same token, you need a plan, or **outline,** of your talk. Before grimacing at the thought of preparing an outline, weigh the advantages of doing so:

● It helps you decide what information to use, how to sequence it, and what information to omit.
● It helps you classify information and separate main ideas from subordinate ones.
● It helps you see the relationships between main ideas and their supporting materials and helps you determine whether those relationships are logical.
● It saves you time by revealing possible gaps or redundancies in your body of information.
● It helps you organize your talk and therefore makes your message more easily understood. And, after all, isn't that the point? Of course it is.

An outline, whether it's for a five- to seven-minute talk (quite likely in this course) or a twenty-minute talk, should consist of six parts: a **title;** a **purpose** (what you want your audience to get from your speech); a **thesis statement** (the main idea of your talk); an **introduction** designed to win the attention of your audience; a **body,** or discussion; and a **conclusion,** which is comparable to the punch line of a joke. You'll recall that there are only four parts of a talk as op-posed to six parts of an outline. The purpose and thesis, by themselves, are not part of the talk but should be woven into the introduction. They are included in the outline to help you keep in focus the response you seek from your audi-ence and the message that you wish to communicate.

The body of your outline should encompass three to five main points, each supported by data. Strive to use various types of data, such as statistics, quota-tions, definitions, anecdotes, contrasts, comparisons, and examples. Keep in mind, however, that everything you include must be relevant to the **topic at hand.**

topic at hand—the topic being discussed

dip our toes—to begin

Before we **dip our toes** into the sea of outlining, let's spend a little time on the important aspects of the purpose and thesis statement.

"This is just the outline—wait 'til you hear the speech!"

Purpose and Thesis Statement

The purpose of a talk is the speaker's objective, that is, what the speaker hopes to achieve by giving the talk. The purpose may be informative, persuasive, or entertaining. The statement of purpose should be developed around a strong verb and should be stated as an infinitive: to convince, to demonstrate, to urge, to defend, to clarify. You should never attempt to give a talk without a clear understanding of what your purpose is. The purpose is the glue that holds the various parts of a talk together. If any element does not contribute to achieving the purpose, it doesn't belong in the talk. If you're trying to convince your audience that your team is going to win the championship this year, you shouldn't get involved in describing the stadium. If you're explaining the nutritional value of vegetables, don't waste time talking about the cholesterol content of eggs.

The thesis statement is a sentence that summarizes the content of the speech. It must agree with the purpose. If the two do not match, they should be revised; chances are that you haven't thought enough about what you're going to say. If you forget the thesis statement and try to jump from your topic to your introduction, you're heading for trouble.

The importance of the purpose and thesis statement, as well as the difference between them, can be observed in the following examples. Let's assume that you've decided to give a talk on the subject of going to college. That's a good first step. What you need next is a purpose and a thesis statement. Here are some possibilities:

Purpose: To encourage the listener to attend college.

Thesis statement: There are many reasons why you should seek a college education.

Purpose: To explain the benefits of a college education.

Thesis statement: A college education provides a number of important benefits to the student.

Purpose: To weigh the pros and cons of going to college.

Thesis statement: There are both advantages and disadvantages involved in going to college.

Purpose: To show that not everyone should go to college.

Thesis statement: It is a myth that everyone should go to college; there are a number of reasons why any given individual should not go.

Purpose: To outline the costs of going to college.

Thesis statement: Going to college requires a substantial financial investment.

Purpose: To suggest ways to reduce the costs of going to college.

Thesis statement: There are many sources of financial support available to help the college student reduce costs.

Each of the above examples, and many others that you might come up with, represents a very different speech. As you can see, it isn't enough simply to know that you're going to give a talk about going to college.

Once you have settled on your purpose and thesis statement, you're ready to develop an appropriate outline. At this point, you may find it helpful to expand the thesis statement to include your major points: There are many sources of financial support available to help the college student reduce costs—scholarships, loans, part-time jobs, attending a publicly supported college, commuting. OK, let's now wade into the very exciting and stimulating topic of outlining.

Principles of Outlining

Applying the following principles of outlining will help you achieve the benefits discussed above.

- Use a standard numbering system for main points and supporting points. A popular system uses Roman numerals (I, II, III, etc.) for main points, capital letters (A, B, C, etc.) for first-level supporting points, and Arabic numerals (1, 2, 3, etc.) for second-level supporting points.
- Use one symbol for each point.
- Be sure that topics numbered at the same level are equal in importance.

● Keep your outline fairly simple. If it becomes complicated, you know that your speech will be too involved.

The outline below illustrates these principles.

    I. Main point or idea
       A. First-level supporting point or idea or Major supporting detail
          1. Second-level supporting point or Minor supporting detail
          2. Second-level supporting point or Minor supporting detail
       B. First-level supporting point or idea or Major supporting detail
    II. Main point or idea

This numbering system and its indentions clearly highlight relationships among items in an outline. For example, main points I and II above are equal (sometimes called *coordinate*) in importance or value. Likewise, first-level supporting points I.A. and I.B. are also equal to each other but are subordinate to main point I. In turn, second-level supporting points I.A.1. and I.A.2. are equal to each other but are subordinate to first-level supporting point I.A.

If your outline sticks to the principles of equality and subordination explained here, you're on your way to a logically organized outline.

It's absolutely vital that topics numbered at the same level be equal in importance. The following example, inserted here as a caution to you, violates this cardinal rule:

    I. Use of telephones is increasing worldwide (the world).
       A. It is increasing in South America (a continent).
       B. It is increasing in North America (a continent).
       C. It is increasing in the United States (a country).
       D. It is increasing in Asia (a continent).

Just as first-level supporting point I.A. (South America) is subordinate to main point I. (the world), so first-level supporting point I.C. (a country) is subordinate to a continent (North America). Therefore, I.C. doesn't belong here; it belongs at the next lower level—I.B.1.—and should be indented further. The outline should look like this:

    I. Use of telephones is increasing worldwide (the world).
       A. It is increasing in South America (a continent).
       B. It is increasing in North America (a continent).
          1. It is increasing in the United States (a country).
       C. It is increasing in Asia (a continent).

Your English professor may have told you that in a formal outline you should not have a single subpoint because subpoints represent divisions of the points they are supporting and you can't divide something into one part. An outline for a short talk, however, can be a bit more informal.

Let's assume you've decided to give a talk encouraging your listeners to consider a career in real estate. As you brainstorm the topic, you jot down the following outline:

in other
            words:
tied to—
confined to

You should consider real estate as a career for the following reasons:

I. It can be very rewarding financially.
II. You're not ***tied to*** a desk all day.
III. You have to have a car.
IV. There will always be a demand for your services.
V. It's a great job.
VI. You have to pass a state examination to get a license.
VII. You meet a lot of interesting people.
VIII. The commissions are substantial.
IX. You have the chance to help people.

As you go back over the outline, you see that you've developed a list of points related to a real estate career, but not all of them are advantages. First of all, you realize that point III, although true, isn't an advantage of a real estate career. (Being able to deduct car expenses on your tax return may be an advantage, but not the need to have a car.) You strike that line from the outline.

Continuing down your list, you see that point V isn't a supporting point for your argument either. Rather, it is a restatement of your main point. So you remove it from the outline.

Next you realize that having to pass an exam is not an advantage but rather a requirement. You drop that from your outline too. You're left with the following:

I. It can be very rewarding financially.
II. You're not tied to a desk all day.
III. There will always be a demand for your services.
IV. You meet a lot of interesting people.
V. The commissions are substantial.
VI. You have the chance to help people.

On closer scrutiny you see a lot of overlapping among your points. Lines III and V support point I. Lines IV and VI both relate to working with people and should be combined under an appropriate heading. You think of additional supporting points and hopefully end up with this:

I. It can be very rewarding financially.
  A. There will always be a demand for your services.
  B. The commissions are substantial.
    1. Though salesmen share commissions with brokers, they do quite well.
II. You're not tied to a desk all day.
  A. You spend a lot of time in your car.
  B. You can do much of your phone work at home.
III. You have the chance to work with people.
  A. You get to meet a lot of interesting people.
  B. You have the chance to help them.

Types of Outlines and Sample Outlines

Speakers most commonly use sentence and topic outlines. You will want to use both. You should use the sentence outline in planning your talk because it will force you to think through the point you want to make about each of the topics you plan to discuss. But when you present your talk, you will be much better off with a topic outline. Having a sentence outline in front of you while you're speaking will tempt you to read it. And you don't want to do that if you want to give an effective speech. Listeners want to be spoken to, not read to. Moreover, a paper on which you have written a sentence outline will be too cluttered to permit you to find your place readily.

Coming up now is a subject for a sentence outline. Let's say that a year ago you went on a health kick that has drastically changed your lifestyle, especially concerning diet. You've read up on these topics because you want to be healthy, and now you're eager to tell the class about a diet that pays off in better health and appearance. The following outline is suitable for a five- to seven-minute talk, and its title is even spiced with a touch of slang:

Title

If You Want to Be Healthy, You Gotta Eat Smart

Purpose

To explain why a sound diet is important to one's health and what makes up a healthful diet

Thesis Statement

To get the nutrients you need for good health, you should eat daily, in varying amounts, from the four basic food groups.

Introduction

   I. Sensible nutrition, based on eating from the four food groups, is vital to achieving good health and keeping it.
   II. An essential nutrient is any food in the diet necessary to maintain life, to carry on normal functions, and to promote growth and repair of the body.
   III. The Japanese diet is the exact opposite of ours. The Japanese people live longer than we do and have fewer cases of cancer and heart disease than we do.

Body

   I. According to the U.S. Department of Agriculture,[1] you should base your daily diet on the following food groups:
     A. Pastas, rice, cereals, whole-grain bread—6 to 11 servings
     B. Vegetables—3 to 5 servings; fruits—2 to 4 servings

---

[1]*Newsweek*, 27 May 1991, 48.

C. Milk, yogurt, cheese—2 to 3 servings; meat, poultry, fish, dry beans, eggs, nuts—2 to 3 servings

D. Sweets, oils, fats—use sparingly

Conclusion

Because of this diet, I feel much better and look much better. It can do the same for you. Start today.

The following partial sentence outline carries the numbering system one step further and, at the same time, illustrates another pitfall for you to beware of. Assume that a speaker is to argue that Los Angeles—or any large metropolitan area, for that matter—is facing a crisis in traffic congestion and desperately needs more public transportation. Let's say that the outline looks like this:

I. Traffic congestion is on the brink of strangling the entire city.

A. Every 24 hours more than 1.3 million autos enter, leave, or pass through Los Angeles.

1. Most autos carry only one person; the average is 1.3 persons.

2. Most rush-hour traffic is inbound between 7 and 9 A.M. and outbound between 4 and 6 P.M.

3. Autos cause air pollution.

B. Public and private parking facilities are inadequate.

in other
words:
tossed out—
omitted

Notice that item I.A.3., air pollution, has nothing at all to do with traffic congestion and should be ***tossed out.***

Earlier we mentioned two types of outlines: sentence and topic. The topic outline, except for the thesis statement (main idea), consists only of key words or phrases. As an example of a topic outline, let's convert the above sentence outline on big-city traffic to a topic outline:

I. Los Angeles on verge of collapse from traffic

A. 1.3 million autos in and out daily

1. One person in most autos; average 1.3

2. Rush hour traffic: 7–9 A.M., 4–6 P.M.

B. Parking areas inadequate

Observe above how each indention represents a narrowing down of information. All outlines should adhere to this principle; that is, they should move from general information to more and more specific information.

So far we've emphasized the benefits of sentence outlines because, by their very nature, they contain more detailed information than topic outlines. However, to show you ***the other side of the coin,*** here's a complete topic outline that could serve as the basis of a four- to six-minute talk.

**the other side
of the coin—**
another way of
doing the same
thing

Title

The Many Costs of Buying a Car

Purpose

To explain the many expenses involved in buying a car

Thesis Statement

If you are thinking about buying a new car, be sure to consider all of the many expenses involved.

Introduction

    I. Alternatives to consider before buying a new car.
       A. Public transportation
       B. Borrowing or leasing a car when you need it
       C. Taking cabs
       D. Sharing a car
       E. Buying a used car

Body

    II. Don't overlook any of the following expenses:
       A. Initial costs
          1. Down payment
          2. Sales taxes
          3. First-year insurance premium
          4. Registration
       B. Ongoing expenses
          1. Monthly payments
             a. Principal
             b. Interest
          2. Upkeep
             a. Gas and oil
             b. Periodic routine maintenance
             c. Unexpected major repairs
          3. Insurance beyond the first year
          4. Annual taxes and fees
       C. Hidden expenses
          1. Depreciation
          2. Denial of other things the money could buy
          3. Loss of opportunity to invest

Conclusion

If you decide that you can afford all the expenses I have outlined, shop wisely—and happy driving!

Because of the great importance of having the knowledge of and being able to prepare an effective outline, here's another topic outline. This one covers the topics of this chapter and you can use it to study.

Putting It All Together

    I. Prepare an Outline
       A. Types of Outlines and Sample Outlines
    II. The Body of Your Talk
       A. From Simple to Complex

Topic outlines are also well suited to help you deliver your talks. Simply convert your sentence outline into a topic outline, type it double-spaced onto one or two 5-by-7-inch cards, and lay them on the lectern. Glancing occasionally at the card for a second or two should ***trigger*** your knowledge and memory of the subject so that you can keep on talking and still maintain eye contact with your audience.

in other words:

trigger—
stimulate

The Body of Your Talk

Since every talk should have four parts—a title, an introduction, a body, and a conclusion—your outline must reflect that arrangement of elements. In preparing your talk, however, outline the body first and then the introduction or conclusion. The reason for this sequence is that you need to know your message before you can introduce it.

As mentioned before, the main points and subpoints (major and minor supporting details) that support your thesis statement comprise the body, or main discussion, of your presentation. For short talks, such as you'll probably give in this basic course, three or four main points should be enough.

Clearly, it's impossible to know in advance how many points and subpoints you'll end up with or, for that matter, how many paragraphs each point will require for adequate coverage. You'll find the answers when you translate all the bits and pieces that form your outline into sentences and paragraphs. You can arrange your main points in any one of the following sequences:

● From simple to complex—a much-used strategy in teaching
● From cause to effect
● From effect to cause
● From problem to solution
● According to space or location
● According to time

From Simple to Complex

If, for example, you're explaining and demonstrating various tennis strokes to your class, you'd logically start with the basic forehand and backhand. You'd then cover more advanced strokes such as the serve, smash, and volley. If you were to begin with the smash and the volley, you would confuse and discourage most novice players; they'd lose interest. In other words, when discussing

Be sure to start with elementary concepts.

something technical or new to an audience, be sure to start with elementary concepts and then move to the more difficult.

From Cause to Effect

Reasoning from cause to effect involves a situation, event, or condition (an effect) that will happen in the future. For example, in a speech on energy conservation, you might reason that if you insulate your house or apartment (install storm windows and doors, caulk them, lower the thermostat, use an economical shower head, and so on), your heating bill will decrease substantially. All these causes, but especially insulation, will result in an effect—a lowered heating bill.

Here a caution is in order. An effect is usually produced by more than one cause. For example, to win most of its games, a football team needs a sharp, hard-driving coach, talented players who are willing **to go all the way,** some "cooperative" opponents, and a smidgen of luck.

in other words:
to go all the way—to exert maximum effort

From Effect to Cause

"Effect to cause" reasoning involves finding a cause for an event that has happened. Suppose you witness an auto accident and notice that one of the two drivers moves unsteadily, slurs his or her words, and has slightly glazed eyes. You might conclude that the accident was caused by a driver under the influence of alcohol.

For another example, suppose that the number of burglaries in your city has doubled in the past two years, and in the same period your police force was cut 40 percent. In a speech, you might assert that the increase in crime (effect) was caused, at least partially, by the cutback in police protection.

These simple cases illustrate the kinds of thinking that we do throughout life. Some cases, however, are not so clear-cut; because they combine many causes and effects, they will require hard, straight thinking.

From Problem to Solution

Pollution of air and water is a critical problem in today's industrialized societies. Some of the steps being taken to solve the problem are: improving the internal combustion engine, controlling the exhaust of industrial smokestacks, and restricting the dumping of waste into bodies of water. In your speech, first state a problem, then suggest possible solutions.

According to Space or Location

Let's say that you want to discuss the mountain ranges in the United States. A logical approach would be to start with the White Mountains in New Hampshire and move westward to the Sierra Nevada in California. Or you could go the other way around. But you would surely not go from New Hampshire to California and then back to the Rockies in Colorado.

According to Time

Suppose you decide to give a talk on how our economy has evolved historically. You would go back to the eighteenth century to discuss our trailways and waterways; next you would move to the nineteenth century with the advent and proliferation of our railroads; you would then ***point out*** how the twentieth century gave us not only superhighways but larger, faster, and more efficient aircraft; and finally, you would prophesy (with considerable confidence) that our new millennium (the twenty-first century) will see an explosion of electronic and other technological innovations to develop informational and communication services further.

in other words:

point out—
mention

The Introduction to Your Talk

Now that you know what the substance of your talk will be, you're in a much better position to forge a strong introduction. Such an introduction is vital to the success of your talk because it can win over your audience immediately. Since the first few sentences are crucial, you should consider memorizing them. Rehearse them until you can speak smoothly and confidently.

Your introduction should serve three major functions:

● To divulge the purpose of your talk
● To gain audience goodwill
● To arouse audience interest

To achieve those aims, your introduction may include any one or a combination of the following:

● A startling statement
● Reference to the occasion and sponsor
● Reference to the audience
● Reference to the speaker
● Reference to literature
● Questions to the audience
● An anecdote
● Quotation from an authority
● Statistics
● A look to the future

All these suggestions are illustrated in the following examples from actual speeches.

A Startling Statement

Suppose you're to speak about a few very wealthy and generous people who believe in helping poor youngsters get an education, and you begin like this:

> In the largest gift of its kind in Massachusetts, a Connecticut couple has pledged $2.5 million to put 67 East Cambridge second graders through college.
>
> The gift to the entire second-grade class of the Harrington School will provide motivational counseling, tutoring, mentoring and a summer school program through the next 10 years as well as free tuition for four years of college or vocational school.[2]

This introduction should grab your audience's interest immediately.

Reference to the Occasion and Sponsor

> Good afternoon. It's a pleasure to be here today. And it's especially appropriate that the YWCA should be sponsoring this seminar on civic responsibility and the corporate woman. Few organizations have put themselves on the line quite the way the "Y" has in its concern to provide equal opportunities for growth and development to everyone.
>
> Looking back through history, whenever there's been an important women's issue, or relevant needs to be addressed, the "Y" has been there. This includes being in the forefront in initiating programs for women returning to the labor market after absences of many years; offering career-oriented workshops for teenagers; and using "Y" buildings, which were formerly dormitories, as shelters for battered women or as senior citizen centers.[3]

Reference to the Audience

> Madam Chairman, Distinguished Guests, Ladies and Gentlemen.
>
> Thank you for that kind introduction. It is indeed an honor for me to have been invited to address the Empire Club of Canada. Before I begin my prepared text, I'd like to ask all war veterans in the audience to please stand up at their places, and remain standing.
>
> Now, would everyone who has ever taken a Red Cross First Aid or Water Safety course please stand.
>
> Would those who have ever volunteered for the Red Cross, are Red Cross employees or have ever made a donation to a Red Cross international appeal, a local Red Cross or United Way campaign please join those already standing.
>
> And finally, of those still seated, if you have ever donated blood or received a blood transfusion, would you also please stand?
>
> Ladies and Gentlemen, it gives me great pleasure as Secretary General to dedicate my presentation to the constituents of the Red Cross. Please be seated.[4]

---

[2]*The Boston Globe*, 15 June 1991, 1, 20.

[3]Mary M. Gates, "The Changing Role of Women in Voluntarism: Individual Growth and Worth." Speech delivered to the YWCA, Seattle, Washington, 27 February 1981.

[4]George B. Webber, "The Red Cross—Our Path into the 21st Century." Speech delivered to the Empire Club of Canada, Toronto, Ontario, Canada, 19 February 1987.

"I rise so you can see me—speak so you can hear me—
and sit down so you can like me."

Reference to the Speaker

I did not want to come to Los Angeles to give this lecture for many reasons. I am neither a philosopher nor a political activist. However, because of the heated debate between biomedical scientists and antivivisectionists, I felt an obligation to speak on behalf of the right of the incurably ill to hope for cures or relief from suffering through research using animals. I am crippled—by paraplegia—which today is incurable. Those of us who have an incurable disease or have permanently crippling injuries can only hope for a cure through research. Much of this experimental work will require the use of animals, and accordingly, we must find some compromise that defends both human rights and animal welfare. In the determination of a compromise between the reduction of human suffering and the violation of animals' welfare, which at times includes causing pain or discomfort; I unequivocally choose to reduce human suffering.[5]

Reference to Literature

Thank you for this chance to keynote Kent State's honors week events. We gather this week to recognize academic achievement. Oddly, the theme of these proceedings

---

[5]Dennis M. Feeney, "Human Rights and Animal Welfare," *American Psychologist*, June 1987, 593–594.

is the approach of 1984, the year George Orwell made a metaphor for totalitarianism. I say "oddly" because the central feature of Orwell's *1984* was the mass mind—whole populations thinking in state-imposed uniformity. Such uniformity strikes me as the antithesis of the individual intellectual excellence that we gather to honor this week, the excellence that René Descartes celebrated in saying, "I think, therefore I am."[6]

Questions to the Audience

Many of you—maybe most—have seen poverty at close range, have had contact with people who are homeless, hungry, ill, who subsist on low wages or insufficient welfare grants, who live in miserable surroundings that are shocking and repulsive. . . .

You have asked yourself: what is wrong, why isn't something done about it? Are those appalling conditions to be blamed on an evil economic system, on a heartless society, on an unconcerned government, on powerful, malevolent forces? If our social-economic system is so bad, how did it make the great majority of our people better off than most of the rest of mankind? Evidently, it does produce the greatest good for the greatest number. Why do millions of people, especially the needy from all over the world, envy us Americans and would like to come here if they could? Why, as we found out in the past few months, do so many people in overseas countries view the United States with admiration, why do they try to find a way to adopt or copy our political-economic system, so they might be able to live as well as most of us do? Our living standards are drastically higher than those in most of Africa, Asia, South America and even ahead of much or most of Europe.

Should we then conclude that we Americans, smug in our comfort, neglect the less fortunate in our midst—that we just do not care about people who income-wise are the lowest 10 percent or 20 percent of our population?[7]

An Anecdote

They've asked me to give you some advice this morning on *service*. I am always a little reluctant to give this speech because I remember the grade school student who wrote,

"Socrates was a Greek philosopher who went around giving people good advice. They poisoned him."

Last week I heard of a discussion that actually occurred between a banker and his customer in Texas. The farmer came in and told the banker he had some good news and some bad news. The banker said, "Well, let's hear the bad news first." The farmer said, "You know the crop loan I've taken out from you every year the last ten years?" The banker said, "Yes." "Well, this year I can't pay it back. And

---

[6]Alton W. Whitehouse, Jr., "The Misinformation Society: Renewing Our Commitment to the Power of Education." Speech delivered at Kent State University Honors Week, Kent, Ohio, 20 April 1981.

[7]Roger A. Freeman, "Does America Neglect Its Poor." Speech delivered to the Stanford Alumni Association, San Francisco, California, 14 March 1990.

you know the mortgage I have on my land?" "Yes." "I can't pay it back either. And the couple of hundred thousand I still have outstanding on my tractor and the other equipment?" "Yes." "They're all yours." There was a moment of silence. And then the banker said, "Well, what's the good news?" The farmer smiled: "I want you to know that I'M GOING TO KEEP ON BANKING WITH YOU!"

Well, the good news from here is that I'm going to keep talking![8]

Quotation from an Authority

With the publication of his book, *The Making of the President—1960*, the late Theodore White achieved instant recognition as one of America's foremost political writers. The success of his book was so great that it insured the favorable reception of his subsequent books that followed each presidential election through 1980.

One of the things that Teddy White did so well was to paint a verbal picture of the United States, a picture based on his personal observations along the campaign trail combined with the then available statistical data.

His last book was written after the 1980 election and contained a dramatic sentence that I have never forgotten. This is what White wrote:

"At the end, with all the attention and programs, big cities were on their way to tragedy: they had become warehouses for the very poor or enclaves of the very rich, while common civility had become a memory."

The significance of White's description of the big city is that it is painted in terms of rich and poor with no reference to the middle class which has historically been the foundation of the city.[9]

Statistics

Mr. President, Mr. Speaker, fellow delegates, colleagues and friends: I stand before you today not only as your president-elect, but also as a dean and as a professor. As a professor, I am programmed, once started, to speak for fifty-five minutes. However, I have been reminded that the story of the creation of the world is told in Genesis in 400 words, that the world's greatest moral code, the Ten Commandments, contains only 297 words, that Lincoln's immortal Gettysburg Address is but 266 words in length and that the Declaration of Independence required but 1,321 words to set up for the world a new concept of freedom. I think I get the point."[10]

A Look to the Future

Today the Soviet Union is disaggregating and the U.S.A. has shed her imperial role, abandoned her economic dominance and is turning inwards. At one and

---

[8]Robert Williams, "The Do's and Don'ts of Service." Speech delivered to the American Banker Conferences, New York, New York, 19 June 1990, and Los Angeles, California, 28 June 1990.

[9]James C. Gardner, "The Changing American City." Speech delivered to Premier Mortgage "Breakfast Brigade," Shreveport, Louisiana, 16 October 1990.

[10]C. John Tupper, "A New American Revolution: Do Your Own Thing vs. Guaranteeism." Speech delivered to the California Medical Association, 12 March 1979.

the same time, we are losing both our great enemy and our great friend. Locked in struggle, they have remained locked in decline.

What is more, America has chosen a different path. As *Time*, that very American magazine, recently wrote, and I quote,

> by 2020, a date no further into the future than John F. Kennedy's election is in the past, the number of U.S. residents who are Hispanic or non-white will have more than doubled to nearly 115 million.

Only a short time later, the population of European descent will be a minority. To quote *Time* again, "the 'average' U.S. resident, as defined by Census statistics, will trace his or her descent to Africa, Asia, the Hispanic world, the Pacific islands, Arabia—almost anywhere but white Europe. . . ."[11]

The Conclusion to Your Talk

With your main discussion and introduction ready to go, you should be all set to work out a conclusion. Two cautions are in order: (1) a conclusion should not drag on and on; and (2) it should not contain any new material.

Here are some ideas to incorporate in your conclusion:

- A summary of key ideas
- A prediction
- A quotation, either emotional or factual
- A quotation from an authority
- An anecdote or question, or both
- A challenge to the audience
- A call to action
- A historical reference

All these suggestions are illustrated in the following conclusions from actual speeches.

A Summary of Key Ideas

> In conclusion, I feel sure that these programs of communication are proving of great benefit to both managers and employees. Even if they were expensive, *which they are not*, it would still be worth it. *The cost of economic ignorance would be much, much greater.* After all, better communication reaps the following benefits for a corporation:
>
> - Employees know decisions and the reasons for them.
> - Less misunderstandings occur.
> - The possibility of cooperation with change is greatly increased.

---

[11]James Goldsmith, "Europe—Why and How." Speech delivered at the Institute of Directors Annual Lecture, London, England, 12 June 1990.

- The damaging effects of rumor are lessened.
- The role of management is reinforced.

Managers, union leaders and rank-and-file employees readily understand the need for these improvements in their relationships. And, as the Japanese have proved, whether working with their own nationals, or American or Australian workers, employee understanding and involvement works for everybody's benefit. Certainly we are experiencing these benefits in some corporations in Australia.

> Enterprise Australia is proud to have contributed toward these advancements in employee communication.[12]

A Prediction

In reality, I believe, we will evolve along a more conventional and prosaic trajectory. Barring some cataclysmic developments on the energy front, the automobile is likely to remain the preferred means of transportation of most Americans well into the next century—although, as we have noted, it will be a vehicle vastly different in design and performance. At the same time, public transportation—or, I should say, collective transportation—will assume a much more significant role in our daily lives. Transit of tomorrow will have more varied forms and utilize a wider range of vehicles, service modes, and operating arrangements, as it tries to serve a broader, more differentiated market.

While public transportation will tend to become more flexible and personalized, the automobile will. . . .

Rail transit of the surface variety may. . . .

Finally, pedestrians will have regained some of the territory they lost to the automobile during the last fifty years, as cities and suburbs impose more stringent requirements on the use of cars in congested centers and residential neighborhoods.

And—oh yes—we will still have rush-hour traffic and potholes. They will be there to remind us of the good old days back in the late 1980s, when gasoline was still only one dollar a gallon, when parking in government buildings was still free, and when one could still afford the luxury of driving to work in one's own automobile.[13]

A Quotation, Either Emotional or Factual

In conclusion, we need to be reminded of the famous words of the Protestant minister who recounted the prevailing attitude during the Holocaust:

> . . . They came first for the Communists, and I didn't speak up because I wasn't a Communist.

---

[12]J. T. Keavney, "Australia: Turning away from Socialism." Speech delivered to the Board of Trustees of the American Economic Foundation, New York, New York, 19 January 1981.

[13]C. Kenneth Ovski, "Urban Transportation: A Profile of the Future." Speech delivered at the NASA Colloquium on Profiles of the Future, Washington, DC, 11 September 1979.

You might conclude with a prediction for the future.

Then they came for the Jews, and I didn't speak up because I wasn't a Jew.

Then they came for the trade unionists, and I didn't speak up because I wasn't a trade unionist.

Then they came for the Catholics, and I didn't speak up because I was a Protestant.

Then they came for me, and by that time no one was left to speak.

Thank you.[14]

A Quotation from an Authority

I want to conclude my talk by quoting in its entirety a brief but, I think, superb exposition of what I've been trying to say. The author is Leo Rosten, and, believe it or not, I once worked with him too. He called his little essay *The Power of Words,* and it goes like this:

---

[14]R. Y. Woodhouse, "Equality Faces a Dangerous Decade: Defend Our Beliefs and Speak Out." Speech delivered at the Naval Supply Systems Command Human Resource Management Conference, Seattle, Washington, 18 November 1980.

They sing. They hurt. They teach. They sanctify. They were man's first immeasurable feat of magic. They liberated us from ignorance and our barbarous past. For without these marvelous scribbles which build letters into words, words into sentences, sentences into systems and sciences and creeds, man would be forever confined to the self-isolated prison of the scuttlefish or the chimpanzee. 'A picture is worth 10,000 words,' goes the timeworn Chinese maxim. 'But,' one writer tartly said, 'it takes words to say that.' We live by words: Love, Truth, God. We fight for words: Freedom, Country, Fame. We die for words: Liberty, Glory, Honor. They bestow the priceless gift of articulateness on our minds and hearts—from 'Mama' to 'infinity.' And the men who truly shape our destiny, the giants who teach us, inspire us, lead us to deeds of immortality, are those who use words with clarity, grandeur and passion. Socrates, Jesus, Luther, Lincoln, Churchill.

The power of words. . . .[15]

An Anecdote or Question, or Both

And I'll close with a true story to illustrate how we *are* set apart and what our values really are. During the days of the Soviet triumph with their first Sputnik, a grade school class in Russia was discussing that remarkable feat—eclipsing the whole world in scientific genius. The teacher asked the class if they were thrilled with the prospect of a Russian satellite probing space and perhaps some day landing a Russian on the moon.

The class smiled with pride and agreed it would be a great achievement to go to the moon. But one thoughtful student broke the silence and spoke a different kind of response.

"Yes, it would be wonderful to go to the moon," he said. "But I would like to know—when may we go to Vienna?"[16]

A Challenge to the Audience

So, one of the challenges in the 1990s is to structure ourselves to deal with this "interdependent independence" that will be necessary for twenty-first century existence.

The technologies of communications and third-generation computers provide us the opportunity to pursue individuality to a degree not possible before. At the same time, they allow us to share and access the experience and knowledge of others. Most important, they provide the only analytical resource capable of dealing with the incredible environmental, economic and other structural interdependencies of the world.

Again, the transition to a fully integrated third generation has more profound implications than all computer history to date. It will be a challenging, exciting, potentially rewarding new era.

---

[15]Melvin J. Grayson, "The Last Best Hope: Words." Speech delivered to the Society of Consumer Affairs Professionals in Business, New York, New York, 3 April 1981.

[16]Harvey C. Jacobs, "Finding Your Way through the Woods: It's a Lifelong Challenge." Speech delivered at the Defense Information School, Fort Benjamin Harrison, Indianapolis, Indiana, 24 January 1981.

Henry Ford said, and I quote: "A generation ago there were a thousand men to every opportunity, while today there are a thousand opportunities to every man." Ford made that statement in 1927. I don't really know about then. But I do know about now. The Third Computer Generation will open up more opportunities than ever before. Not to every man and woman, perhaps, but without question, to those who are prepared. Whether you are or not is up to you.[17]

A Call to Action Now

It's time for action for *all of us*.

Here's what *you* can do.

First, we can all follow Lyn Banke's admonition and take this opportunity to raise the level of concern among our legislators.

Write to them. Let them *know* what the need is. Let them *know* how child care will benefit our society and our economy.

And second, start an active effort in your own organization or company to identify and address child care needs.

And while we're at it, we need to focus on what we can do, *not* just complain about what we *can't*.

It's clear to me, and I hope to you that the child care that's provided in this decade—and into the next century will be no better than we make it.

Thank you.[18]

A Historical Reference

Mr. Lincoln would not offer government as the *first* alternative for dealing with problems. He would focus government action where it could be used best: to break down barriers to freedom and opportunity: to enable every man and woman to fulfill their potential, develop their God-given talent, and pursue their inalienable right to human happiness.

After all, isn't that what the terrible battle fought here was really about—the noblest effort any people ever made to dismantle the cruelest barrier to human freedom?

One hundred and twenty-seven years after Gettysburg, Lincoln's belief that all human beings are created equal and endowed with inalienable rights—the faith upon which liberal democracy is based—is beginning to prevail around the world.

Because of democracy's long march from Independence Hall through Gettysburg to the very streets of Moscow, the *world* knows the simple yet profound truth: the yearning for freedom cannot be extinguished, the struggle for inalienable rights will never end short of victory; nothing can deny the transcendence of democracy.

---

[17]Robert M. Price, "Computers in the '90s." Speech delivered at the Minnesota Executive Speaker Series, University of Minnesota, Minneapolis, Minnesota, 13 February 1990.

[18]Stephen E. Ewing, "Nourish Thy Children." Speech delivered to the Child Care Coordinating Council, Livonia, Michigan, 30 March 1990.

As Americans, we cannot rest until the blessings we enjoy are shared by all. Let us fulfill our Nation's destiny by making Mr. Lincoln's great proposition of democracy—set forth on this battlefield—into a self-evident truth for every man, woman, and child on this earth.[19]

The Title of Your Talk

Just as every book has a title and every newspaper story a headline, so every talk should have a title. Your title is an ad, a billboard for your speech. And audiences generally appreciate knowing immediately what they are about to hear rather than waiting to find out your message. They usually learn the title of your talk either from a printed program, the chairperson, or the **MC** (master of ceremonies). In class, your instructor may have you write your title on the chalkboard. If you try to imagine a movie without a title, you can appreciate the importance of a title for your talk.

Usually, the most propitious time to consider a title is after you've developed the main ideas of your speech. It's possible, however, that during the process of building the introduction, body, and conclusion of your talk, a striking title may suddenly appear, seemingly out of nowhere. If it does, you're lucky. If it doesn't, try to create one that meets these criteria:

1. It should be provocative enough to pique your listeners' interest.
2. It should be short and simple; say, from three to ten words.
3. It should indicate the purpose and content of your talk.

Table 8.1 (p. 192) lists some titles taken from speeches published in the journal *Vital Speeches of the Day*, along with their outstanding traits.

Transitions, or Connecting Links

Just as a brick wall needs cement to keep it intact, a speech needs something to hold it together. That "something" is **transitions**—statements, questions, or phrases that allow you to smoothly connect one idea to the next—moving from the introduction to the body, from the various major points within the body to their supporting details right into the conclusion. Transitions also show the relationships between ideas.

You see transitions in daily communication, but when you speak to a group, you may forget them. Don't. They help your listeners follow your train of thought and, thus, make your communication task easier.

---

[19]Jack Kemp, "Lincoln's Vision of Democracy." Speech delivered to the Lincoln Fellowship of Pennsylvania, Gettysburg, Pennsylvania, 19 November 1990.

TABLE 8.1

Types of Speech Titles

Traits	Titles
Questions	"How Can We Control Teen-Age Crime?" "Where Is This Black Progress?"
Alliteration	"Inventors, Invention, and Innovation" "Private Property and Perestroika"
A complete sentence	"Nothing Much Happens without a Dream"
A famous title	"The Ten Commandments of a Quality Community"
Similar last syllables	"Foundations, Traditions, and Directions in U.S. Health Care"
Imagination	"I Touch the Future—I Teach"
Fairy tale opener	"Once upon a Time"
Startling statement	"Raising Corn and Beans and Hell"
Brevity	"Welcome Home"
Words that rhyme	"Town and Gown" "TV's Jiggle and Wiggle"
A play on words	"Today's Dollar Doesn't Make Much Sense" "If You Don't Think Dieting Is Serious Business What Do Its First Three Letters Spell?"

Table 8.2 lists some simple transitional words and phrases that can be used to connect sentences and the conditions that call for their use.

The most important type of transition in an effective speech is the smooth movement from one section of the speech to the next. Since inevitably the attention of listeners will wander, if you want to be understood easily, you will need to provide reminders of where they've been and where they're going as your speech unfolds.

To help your listeners follow you, you should adopt the habit of the country preacher who was asked how he managed to come up with a first-rate sermon every Sunday. He said, "It's really quite simple. You have to do just three things for the congregation: first, tell them what you're going to tell them; then tell them; then tell them what you told them." Adhering to the preacher's formula will supply much of the help your listeners will need to follow you. Reinforcing the structure with phrases and sentences that guide your audience from one of your points to the next will provide the rest. The following excerpts from a speech demonstrate how the preacher might have handled a recommendation of his favorite restaurant:

1. *Tell them what you're going to tell them:* At the end of your introduction preview your main points.

TABLE 8.2

Transitional Words and Their Uses

To indicate	Use these transitions
Place	adjacent to, on the opposite side, diagonally across, diametrically opposite
Time	after a few hours, meanwhile, in the meantime, afterward, immediately, earlier, later, then
Purpose	for this reason, to this end, with this goal
Concession	of course, to be sure, naturally
Comparison and contrast	on the other hand, nevertheless, on the contrary, in contrast, in the same way, conversely, however, in like manner, similarly, whereas
Summary or repetition	in other words, to review briefly, in short, on the whole, to sum up, as previously noted, here again, in summary, in brief, if I may repeat
Explanation	for example, in particular, more specifically
Addition	furthermore, in the second place, besides, moreover, again, in addition, equally important, finally, also
Cause or result	on that account, therefore, as a result, thereupon, for this reason, consequently, accordingly, under these condition, hence
Conditions	although, because, even though, since, if, unless, under these circumstances, nevertheless, otherwise, this being so

I recommend Nana Vasile's because [main point #1] the food is outstanding, [main point #2] the atmosphere is charming, and [main point #3] the prices are right.

2. *Tell them:*

[transition] First, [main point #1] let me tell you about the Nana Vasile's awesome food. [Descriptions of the speaker's favorite dishes follow.]

[transition] But you expect more than good food from a first-class restaurant. You also want to enjoy it in [main point #2] a quiet, home-like atmosphere. [Details about the atmosphere follow.]

[transition] So far I've talked about the good food and the pleasant atmosphere. For the college student on a restricted budget, however, the greatest attraction of Nana Vasile's may well be [main point #3] its reasonable prices. [Examples of reasonable prices follow.]

3. *Tell them what you told them (conclusion):* After the discussion of prices, recapitulate your main points.

[transition] In summary, the next time you are looking for a restaurant where [main point #1] you will find delicious food [main point #2] served in a cozy atmosphere [main point #3] at prices that won't even make you use your credit card, pay a visit to Nana Vasile's. You'll be glad you did!

After you've selected and narrowed your topic, performed your research and apply what you've learned from this chapter, you should feel quite confident about putting together an interesting and effective talk. Good luck.

Quick Clicks

Welcome to a "surprise search." To further enhance your research or simply to harvest more information about some of the things you studied in this chapter, just drop in at any of the following addresses. What you'll discover may be serious, educational, bibliographical, surprising, factual, or even downright humorous. But it will definitely be informative.

So, go ahead and give a "Quick Click."

www.startingpage.com/html/quotations.html
www.westegg.com/cliche
http://curry.edschool.virginia.edu/go/multicultural/lanugage/quotes.html
http://curry.edschool.virginia.edu/go/multicultural/sites/hisspeeches.html
www.bartleby.com/100
www.public-speaking.org/public-speaking-articles.htm

Things to Discuss in Class

1. Give the class an example of a sentence outline and a topic outline. Explain why you prefer one over the other.
2. Find two speech titles you consider outstanding. Explain why you think so.
3. Write an outline for a short talk on any subject you could give in class. Don't forget the title.
4. Consult the journal *Vital Speeches of the Day* for an outstanding introduction and/or conclusion. Bring either one to class for discussion.
5. In your library, investigate several sources, such as *Vital Speeches of the Day*, and bring

to class a few examples of the various ways that speakers arranged their main points during their talks.
6. Bring to class a short speech and point out its transitions.
7. Select two general topics that you feel would make an interesting talk, and suggest two titles for each topic.

What Do You Remember from This Chapter?

1. Why should you outline your talk?
2. Describe the two principal types of outlines.
3. List a few characteristics of a good title.

4. What are the chief purposes of an introduction?
5. Explain the main parts of a speech.
6. Mention a few ways to prove your main points.
7. What elements should be present in a conclusion?
8. What are transitions and why should you use them?
9. What two cautions should you keep in mind regarding the conclusion of your talk?
10. Explain the difference between a main point and a subpoint.

Vitalize Your Vocabulary

Because thousands of English words are derived from Latin words, there's no question that the study of Latin would strengthen your English vocabulary. But you don't have to study that ancient language in order to benefit from it. To increase your word power, we suggest that you learn the meanings of some Latin prefixes and roots. By doing this, you'll improve your command of the English language in speaking, writing, reading, and listening.

To get you moving, below are a few Latin prefixes and roots, along with their meanings, and some sample English words that use them:

Prefixes	Meanings	Sample Words
ambi	both	ambidextrous, ambiguous
anti	against, opposite	antifreeze, antibiotic
circum	around, on all sides	circumference, circumlocution
equi	equal	equidistant, equilibrium
intra, intro	within	intramural, intrastate, introvert
sub	under, beneath	subcontract, subhuman, submarine
super, supra	above, over	superhighway, supersonic, supernatural

Now let's do the same with some Latin roots:

Roots	Meanings	Sample Words
aqu	water	aquarium, aquatic, aqueduct
aud, audit	hear	audio, audience, auditorium
ben, bene	good, well	benefactor, benefit
cid, cis	cut, kill	homicide, incision, suicide
cred	belief, trust	credible, credit, creed
flu, fluct	flow	fluctuate, influence
leg	law	legal, legislate, legitimate
medi	middle	medieval, mediocre, medium
nov	new	innovate, novelty, renovate
tors, tort	twist	contortion, distort, torque
viv	life, lively	vivacious, vivid

If some of these sample words are not clear to you, poke your nose into that dust-covered dictionary.

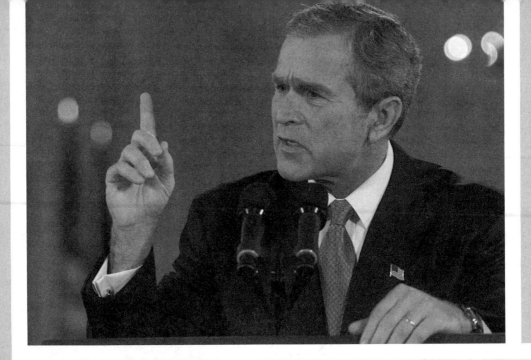

9

Delivering Your Speech

All the great speakers were bad speakers at first.
—Ralph Waldo Emerson, "Power," *The Conduct of Life* (1860)

*After reading and understanding
this chapter, you should know:*

● The various methods of
delivering a talk

● The advantages and
disadvantages of each method

● The difference between an
extemporaneous and an
impromptu talk

● How to deliver a talk that you
have prepared

● The importance of speaking
with enthusiasm

● The importance of practicing
your talk

● How to cope with nerves
before you speak and while
you're speaking

● How to develop your style and
confidence as a speaker

chapter
preview

There are four methods of delivering a speech: speaking extemporaneously, reading from a manuscript, speaking from memory, and speaking impromptu. For most people, an extemporaneous talk is the most effective. It requires you to know your subject in depth and allows you to use note cards. You can also look at your listeners and speak in the language most appropriate to them and to you.

Those who have significant statements to make to the public or to a special audience often read from a manuscript. Beginning speakers who need 110 percent security also tend to read. The disadvantages of reading are that usually, the talk sounds "read," eye contact is lost, and the speaker may become addicted to reading all the time. If, however, you must read your talk, try to follow the suggestions given in this chapter.

Speaking from memory invites trouble. What do you do if you forget a word? In addition, this method of delivery can sound cold and mechanical. Memorizing, however, can help you in your introduction and conclusion. Memorizing is also recommended for very short talks, such as introducing a speaker or presenting or accepting an award. (See Chapter 13.)

However, there is another way of speaking. If you are called on to say a few words—without prior notice—you are speaking impromptu. The best advice on speaking impromptu is to have some remarks prepared if there is any likelihood you might be called on without warning.

Other topics discussed in this chapter are the importance of practicing your talk, ways to relieve tension before and while speaking, and developing style and confidence as a speaker.

Speaking Extemporaneously

The most successful speakers in business, politics, religion, and education speak extemporaneously. After analyzing the audience in advance, they perform the following regimen:

- Select a topic and limit it to the time available.
- State the purpose of the talk.
- Decide on three or four main points and a few subpoints under each.
- Research the topic and prepare a bibliography.
- Gather supporting material.
- Prepare an outline.
- Put it all together.
- Prepare an introduction and conclusion, sometimes memorizing them.
- Prepare note cards.
- Practice the speech aloud two or three times, with or without note cards, and, preferably, to a few critical listeners.

By doing these tasks, successful speakers smooth their **delivery** and bolster their self-confidence. If you follow this method of preparing your talk, you should be so immersed in your topic that you need refer only occasionally to your note cards or outline.

An **extemporaneous** talk enables you to speak in your own style, even to the extent of choosing some words on the *spur of the moment.* Thus, your presentation will not sound memorized, or "canned." Since note cards reinforce your memory and give you confidence, you'll be able to maintain that all-important eye contact and, at the same time, convey sincerity and spontaneity. You can even move away from the lectern because you're not chained to a written manuscript. With these advantages, you can talk in your own conversational style and, thus, establish a rapport with most audiences.

As you can see, extemporaneous delivery offers you a great deal of latitude. If you wish to quote someone, you can read the quotation verbatim or recite it from memory. Be sure to cite the source. If you give the talk more than once, chances are that you will not use the same wording each time. The talk will be conversational and spontaneous—the reward for advance preparation.

On the other hand, there are pitfalls to be aware of: looking at note cards too often or playing with them can distract an audience; and a weak, limited vocabulary will not result in a spontaneous, vivid, and attention-getting speech.

All things considered, extemporaneous speaking is the most effective method of delivery and the one that you should try to master.

Using Note Cards in Extemporaneous Speaking

After you've studied your topic and know it well, it's time to prepare note cards if you need them. Suitable notes consist of key words and phrases that will

in other
words:
**spur of the
moment—**
immediately,
without
preparation

The talk will be conversational and spontaneous.

remind you of your main points and subpoints. Keep your notes as concise as possible and print them, on one side only, in large capitals, so you can skim them in a flash and resume eye contact with your listeners.

Utilizing 3-by-5-inch note cards is recommended because if you don't have a lectern or speaker's stand on which to lay them, they will conveniently fit in the palm of your hand, hidden from the audience. If you know there'll be a lectern present, then you may consider using 4-by-6-inch note cards. You want to keep your notes hidden from your audience so as not to create any distraction. Another thing, number your cards in the event that you either drop or misplace them. (We discussed using notes at the end of Chapter 2.)

Speaking with Enthusiasm

One of the most significant elements of oral delivery is speaker **enthusiasm.** If you're genuinely excited and stimulated by your topic, then the chances are excellent that you can conduct this "electricity" to your audience.

Having enthusiasm for your topic means speaking with sincerity about your topic and speaking with **empathy** for your listeners. It means talking with excitement—elevating your voice here, then lowering it a bit there. (Remember our discussion on inflection in Chapter 3?) It means talking quickly on occasion, and slowly at other times. (Pacing is covered in Chapter 5.) It means emphasizing action and descriptive words and phrases. (Oral visualization is covered in Chapter 5.) It means pausing just before making an important point or two, or after making important points, to allow the audience time to let the message *sink in.* (You will find more on pausing also in Chapter 5.) And it certainly means looking directly at members of your audience to make your listeners active participants in the speaking event.

Enthusiasm comes from believing in yourself and what you have to say. Enthusiasm means being excited about being able to share your message with your audience. Your enthusiasm should be clearly revealed through your eyes, your facial expression, your movement, your body gestures, your voice and, yes, your carefully chosen words. You should be able to almost feel this remarkable sensation tingling from your fingertips. Enthusiasm is contagious.

Other Methods of Delivery

The other three methods of delivering a speech—reading from a manuscript, speaking from memory, and speaking impromptu—do not approach the extemporaneous method in overall effectiveness; however, they are useful in certain speaking situations. We now turn to a discussion of these three methods.

You can conduct "electricity" to your audience.

Reading from a Manuscript

We strongly urge beginning speakers to refrain from reading their entire talks. There are, however, circumstances in which very limited reading may be helpful, such as when you're presenting statistics or a quotation.

When accuracy is extremely important, speakers will often read from a **manuscript.** For example, officials who must make policy statements don't want to risk omitting points or being misunderstood or misquoted. Reading from a manuscript also allows them to use precise, polished language and helps them comply with time limits. For example:

- The President of the United States addressing the Congress and the nation on budget cuts or the need to increase taxes
- A judge announcing a very important, perhaps a landmark, decision
- A corporate spokesperson explaining to stockholders why he or she recommends a merger
- A school committee spokesperson announcing the reason for the massive layoffs of teachers and administrative personnel

These speakers are fully justified in reading their statements; they can't afford a wrong word. For you, as a nonprofessional, however, reading your entire speech word for word could create one or more of the following problems:

- Your speech may sound read and, therefore, lack spontaneity and enthusiasm. It could sound dull.
- Your delivery could become staccato (choppy) instead of flowing smoothly.
- You may, occasionally, hesitate, creating annoying and meaningless pauses. (This definitely will diminish your credibility.)
- You may make mistakes, such as mispronouncing, skipping, or repeating words.
- You may read too fast, making it difficult for your audience to understand you.
- You may become so engrossed in your manuscript that you forfeit rapport with your audience by not looking at them.
- You may be so "glued" to the manuscript that you can't move about and gesture.
- You may communicate only isolated words instead of whole ideas.
- You may become so dependent on reading your talks that you will not develop skill in other methods of delivery.

If, however, you feel compelled to read your speech verbatim, then consider the following tips.

1. Don't use words you don't normally use, because you'll ***run the risk*** of mispronouncing them or hesitating when you approach them.
2. Be sure that your sentences are short and understandable. A listener has only one chance to hear what you're saying (unless, of course, you repeat very important points). Keep this in mind when you write your speech.

in other words:
run the risk—
take the chance

Remember that you're writing for the ear—which likes short, conversational sentences—and not for the eye, which can go over material several times.

3. Type your speech in all caps, either double-spaced or triple-spaced. Number each page and type only on one side of the paper. For ease of reading and quickly finding your place again after looking at the audience, use large print. When you finish a page, turn it or slide it aside quietly.

4. Practice reading your speech aloud over and over until you know it so well that you can look at your audience more than at your manuscript and so that your speech will sound conversational. This will take a great deal of practice, but it'll be worth the effort.

Rehearsing is imperative. Once I listened to a speaker who read his entire speech and had not practiced sufficiently. The last line at the bottom of one page was repeated as the first line of the next, and he read both! It hardly sounded as though the speaker was in command.

Speaking from Memory

The riskiest method of delivering a talk is to memorize it and to speak completely from memory. This method often lacks warmth, feeling, and enthusiasm because the memorized words usually pour forth very mechanically. The chilling risk is that forgetting a word or key phrase could throw you into a state of panic.

Very few people can deliver memorized speeches effectively. Those who can are very likely professionals who have been speaking this way for years because they have trained and developed their memory.

Many years ago, as a college student in a speech class, I was assigned a short memorized talk. I chose to speak on memory development, since I was interested in improving this ability. I started by explaining how important memory can be in everyday living, how it is a God-given talent to some but one that can be developed with perseverance and application by others. I stated, "Basically there are three important factors involved in the development of memory. One is association." On the blackboard I wrote the words "One—Association." "Two," I continued, "is repetition." Again, approaching the blackboard, I wrote "Two—Repetition." Then, facing the class, I announced, "And three!" . . . dead air, silence. I drew a blank. The silent seconds seemed like horrendous hours and, for the life of me, I couldn't remember the third point.

The class thought my performance was humorous, as I stood motionless with a look of desperation. After ***getting myself together,*** I embarked on an impromptu talk on the fallacy of attempting memorized speeches.

Memorizing can help you with introductions and conclusions, the two most crucial parts of a talk. Memorizing your opening and concluding remarks allows you to begin and end confidently and enables you to look at your audience directly instead of glancing at notes. By the same token, it may be wise to

in other
words:
**getting (one-
self) together**—
regaining
composure

Suppose you forget a word.

memorize a short talk (a minute or so), for example, introducing a speaker or presenting or accepting an award (discussed in Chapter 13).

If you happen to be gifted with a highly retentive memory, speaking entirely from memory does offer a few other advantages: you're free to move around the platform and use gestures; you can more accurately meet time limits; and you can phrase your opinions, ideas, and facts in precise, polished language. We must add, however, that very few people can deliver a memorized talk spontaneously and enthusiastically.

It's interesting to note that in some countries/cultures, such as China, Japan, Korea, and some Middle Eastern countries (where eye contact is usually avoided), an integral mode of educational delivery and acquisition is by memorization. It is therefore not only natural, but understandable, that students from these countries/culture prefer and find it quite comfortable to memorize their speeches.

Speaking Impromptu

An **impromptu talk** is one for which you've had no previous notice, so you're denied the advantage of preparation. Yet, if you analyze your daily conversation, you'll find that most of it, by far, is impromptu: in class, over coffee, at home, on the phone, with a date (or somebody else's date), on the job, and during interviews. In all these cases, except interviews, you may be conversing with one or a half-dozen people. You talk, they listen; they talk, you listen. Interaction is taking place.

Because of your experience or degree of involvement in a group or organization, you should have a pretty good idea whether you may be called on "to say a few words" at a formal meeting. Before going to a meeting, banquet, or any other gathering, ask yourself, "If I were called on to speak, what would I say?"

An impromptu situation doesn't require a fifteen-minute talk. Driving home one sharp point in a few minutes of a carefully prepared *"off-the-cuff"* talk can make you look like a pro. If there's any possibility, no matter how remote, that you may be asked to say a few words, prepare some comments. It's better to be prepared and not be called on than to be called on and not be prepared.

Although you may be ready to say a few words, you must focus your thoughts on a specific topic. Here are some ideas that may help.

- Refer to what previous speakers have said and add your own opinion.
- Comment on some of the topical views expressed by people at your table. They could be a fertile source of ideas.
- Compare the past and present, with possibly a word on the future.
- Compare certain advantages and disadvantages.
- State the problem and a possible solution. (Perhaps you may wish to recommend that a special committee be named to investigate the matter further and then file a report at the next meeting.)
- State the importance of the problem and its effect on your daily lives.
- Consider the topic from the viewpoints of childhood, adulthood, and old age.
- Consider the topic from political, economic, or social aspects.
- Consider the topic geographically—by city, state, country, or the world.

One or more of these approaches should work for you, because your obligation is to speak only two or three minutes. But you have to think fast; make no mistake about that. And under no circumstances should you start by apologizing for your lack of preparation.

If you're completely unprepared to speak about a particular topic and don't wish to address the group, bow out as gracefully as possible (again, prepare a short statement ahead of time). Something like the following will do: "Thank you very much for asking me to speak, but quite frankly, I'm not prepared at this time and will have to pass. However, I'll be prepared at the next meeting and, if you so desire, will be more than happy to speak then."

We have discussed four methods of delivery—speaking extemporaneously, reading from a manuscript, speaking from memory, and speaking impromptu. Since the most effective speech delivery may contain a combination of all of these, experiment with them to establish the style most comfortable for you.

in other words:

"off the cuff"—impromptu, without preparation

An "off-the-cuff" talk can make you look like a pro.

"Practice Is Nine-Tenths"

You've just studied the major methods of delivering a talk, but one crucial step still remains before you face your audience—rehearsal.

Facing an audience is not theory. It's your *moment of truth,* and there's no better way to prepare for that moment than to practice aloud beforehand. Many beginning speakers skip this exercise and then regret it. Ralph Waldo Emerson, the "Sage of Concord," *struck the bull's-eye* when he said, "Practice is nine-tenths."[1] He knew the truth of that aphorism because he made outstanding speeches in public for fifty years.

Unique proof of Emerson's words was the acceptance speech delivered by President Gerald Ford at the Republican National Convention in August 1976. It was "the best speech of my life," he said later. It electrified the delegates and gave them hope of victory. It changed Ford's life-long image as a bumbling, stolid, lackluster speaker to a powerful, dynamic, fighting-mad speaker who could inspire an audience.

---

[1]Ralph Waldo Emerson, "Power," *The Conduct of Life* (1860).

in other words:

moment of truth—that time when you must accept reality of the situation; when one's courage and skill is about to be tested

struck the bull's-eye—made an excellent point

How did he do it?

First of all, the speech was planned for many weeks. President Ford spent more time rewording and polishing it than any other speech he had given in his thirty-seven-year political career. For two weeks, with the aid of a speech coach, he practiced delivering it. In addition, he went through two complete videotaped rehearsals, always concentrating on delivery. As a result of all this work, he was able to maintain almost constant eye contact with his audience and to use powerful, spontaneous gestures at the right moments. The main ingredients that made the speech a smashing success were Ford's efforts—the importance he placed on it and his emotions of the moment. No wonder he was interrupted with cheers more than sixty-five times.

Great speakers are made, not born. If Gerald Ford could do it at age 62 you can do it at 22, 32, or whatever.

Preparation and practice are the keys to successful speaking. The purpose of practice is to ensure, as much as possible, that your talk in front of the audience will flow smoothly. Try to practice your talk before at least one person who will offer a suggestion or two. If you can't find a volunteer, use a tape recorder (a videotape recorder is even better, because you see and hear yourself as an audience does), and then listen to the playback. It's a sobering and educational experience. Another idea is to speak before a mirror; you'll benefit from this once you get over feeling self-conscious about doing it.

If you can't find a volunteer. . . .

You have three choices for practice: a live audience, a tape recorder (audio or video), or a mirror. In fact, why not use all three? Whichever method you choose, *practice* before you face your audience.

And don't forget to devote attention to seemingly minor details. In 1962 President John F. Kennedy made a historic speech in Berlin (see Appendix A). The following four words in that address helped win over the Germans: *"Ich bin ein Berliner"* ("I am a Berliner"). JFK practiced at least ten minutes to master the German accent in its two-second delivery. And a half-million Berliners exploded with tumultuous approval during the speech.

Regarding your delivery, remember, if there are students in the class who are still learning English, be sure to speak slowly and try to maximize your eye contact. In an attempt to better understand you they may be closely watching the movements of your lips as you form your speech sounds and, at the same time, studying your facial expressions while you speak.

Coping with Nerves

Whichever method of speaking you select, one condition is predictable—you'll suffer the jitters: butterflies in the stomach, trembling knees, parched mouth, sweaty palms, and thumping heartbeat. But don't be alarmed, because these are normal reactions that grip most speakers, even seasoned ones. (Review this topic in Chapter 2.)

If the jitters torture you, then shake hands with Michael Douglas, superstar actor-producer. When he was a college student, like you, and studying acting, he suffered such intense nervousness that he kept a wastebasket offstage; he used to vomit in it and then continue acting. "I've worked hard," he said, "both as a person and as an actor, to fight my way through stage fright."[2]

It might be helpful for you to know that other famous people who have been struck by nervousness, stage fright, speaker apprehension, or whatever you want to call it, include Franklin Roosevelt, Ronald Reagan, Lily Tomlin, and Sir Laurence Olivier. There! Don't you feel better already?

Many students have confided to me that while they were speaking they were so nervous at times that they didn't think they could finish their talks. But in most cases they never looked one-quarter as nervous as they felt. Many speech instructors from all over the country have conveyed similar experiences, and fellow students generally agree that their classmates don't look even half as nervous as they claim to be.

Many communication scholars believe that stage fright, or speech tension, is the result of anxiety rather than fear.[3] Fear is a spontaneous reaction to a

---

[2]*Parade* Magazine, 14 February 1988, 5.

[3]J. A. Daly and J. C. McCrosky, *Avoiding Communication: Shyness, Reticence, and Communication Apprehension* (Beverly Hills, CA: Sage, 1984), 188.

present negative event, whereas anxiety involves the anticipation of a future event. How many times can you recall being upset over something you had to do or that you expected to take place, only to find the actual situation was nowhere near as negative as you had anticipated? For example:

- Perhaps when you were in junior high school, one Friday afternoon your teacher told you that the principal wanted to see you first thing on Monday morning. Can you recall that ruined weekend, during which you conjured up all of the worst scenarios possible, only to find out that the principal wanted to ask you if one of your parents could accompany the class on a field trip?
- Just before going to lunch you receive a telephone message from your boss's secretary stating that your boss would like to see you at 2:30 P.M. to discuss an important matter. Instead of enjoying lunch (if you even have one), you spend the time upsetting yourself to the point of indigestion, only to discover that your boss merely wants to discuss the vacation schedule.
- You're one of three finalists for a job you want very much. The salary is generous, the hours are compatible with your school schedule, and the location is close to home. You have been told that a final decision will be made in a few days and you will be notified by phone. Will you experience any anxious moments waiting for the call?

Being anxious is a common and normal reaction to certain situations. By now you have probably found that the degree of anxiety you experienced while waiting to give your first talk was far worse than actually giving it.

Some Suggestions for Relieving Your Tension before Speaking

1. Be sure that you're deeply interested in your topic.
2. Prepare thoroughly so that you know your topic very well. Most professional speakers master much more information than they need.
3. Think positively. As you prepare and practice your talk, keep telling yourself that you will do a good job and that the audience will be deeply interested in what you have to say.
4. As soon as your name is called, take a few very deep breaths while you're still sitting and a few more while walking to the front of the class. It helps to get a healthy supply of oxygen into your system.
5. Just remember, your audience wants you to succeed.

Some Physical Exercises to Help Alleviate Tension before Speaking

1. Sit straight in your chair and relax your head, letting it droop forward until your chin is touching your chest (or is as close to it as possible). Then

s l o w l y move your head to the left and upward as you continue moving it to the right in a circular motion; then lower it to its original position with your chin resting on your chest. Pause about five seconds, then repeat the exercise two or three times. After the third time, pause for about five seconds and then repeat the exercise three more times but in the opposite direction. Take long deep breaths during this exercise.

2. Sitting upright and relaxed, lower your head so your chin is resting on your chest. Then, as you slowly inhale, slowly raise your head to an upright position. Then, as you slowly lower your head, slowly exhale until your head is resting in its original position. Repeat this exercise several times, making sure that you are taking deep breaths as you slowly raise your head and slowly exhaling while lowering your head.

3. Sitting straight up, let your shoulders slump forward and let your arms hang loosely at your side. While taking slow deep breaths, shake the fingers on your hands as though you're trying to free them from something sticky.

To obtain the maximum benefit from your deep breathing, you want to be sure that you're breathing from your diaphragm, which is the muscle that separates your chest cavity from your abdominal cavity. By placing both hands flatly and firmly on your abdomen, you should be able to feel your abdomen expand when you inhale and contract as you exhale. If you have any questions regarding diaphragmatic breathing, don't hesitate to ask your professor.

The following exercises can be conducted while breathing normally.

4. While sitting relaxed in your chair, clench your fists and hold them tightly for about three or four seconds, then relax. (If you have long fingernails, WHOA!!) Repeat this exercise several times.

5. Repeat the above exercise using one fist at a time.

6. While sitting relaxed, firmly push down on the seat of your chair with both hands for several seconds and then relax. Repeat this exercise several times.

Exerting physical pressure and expending your energy should result in eventual and dramatic reduction of your body tension. I think that you'll find these exercises to be quite helpful.

Some Suggestions for Relieving Your Tension while Speaking

1. Just before you begin to talk, place your notes on the speaker's stand; look around at the entire class, take another deep breath, and, with a smile, greet your audience.

2. Use vigorous, but not constant, gestures with your hands, arms, shoulders, head, and body. Such physical actions will channel your nervous energy constructively, attract attention, and fortify your oral message.

3. As you look around the class, don't just scan the audience with your eyes. Move your entire head to the left, then to the right, and back to center. Fully moving your head in this manner should considerably ease neck tension.

4. Don't rivet yourself behind the lectern. Take a few steps to the left and remain there for ten or fifteen seconds before returning to the center position. Then, after a while, repeat this movement in the opposite direction. Deliberate movement is an excellent aid in lessening tension.

5. Focus on your message and audience. Try to become message-conscious, not self-conscious, and your nervousness should diminish, allowing you to communicate more effectively.

6. If you suddenly feel tension building or muscles tightening while you're at the lectern, try gripping the sides of the lectern and squeezing, then slowly releasing the grip and squeezing again. Repeating this exercise several times can be quite effective and hardly noticeable to the audience.

7. Act confident and you'll begin to *feel* confident.

8. Many students find it helpful to admit their nervousness at the beginning of their talk. There's nothing wrong with doing so. Such an admission to your classmates can gain you sympathy and understanding because soon it will be their turn to speak.

Developing Style and Confidence as a Speaker

The way you deliver a speech is critical to its total effectiveness. Poor delivery can largely negate the many long hours that you've invested in researching, planning, organizing, and outlining your talk. Someone once said: "Speeches are like babies—easier to conceive than to deliver."

You can begin immediately to develop your speaking style and confidence. You don't have to wait until you've finished this exciting course. Putting into practice the following suggestions can help you to *get off to a flying start.*

in other words:

get off to a flying start— begin in a positive way

- Speak at every opportunity.
- Observe capable speakers and learn from them.
- Read good literature.
- Use a dictionary and thesaurus to strengthen your vocabulary.
- Practice writing, including your talks.
- Know your subject and feel deeply about it so that you can speak with enthusiasm.

Speak at Every Opportunity

Each day and evening of your life present countless opportunities for you to converse. Talk to members of your family about the kind of day they had at work or at school. Discuss their successes, failures, and accomplishments. Share yours with them as well. On the way to and from school or work and while you're there, strike up conversations with your instructor, classmates, supervisor, colleagues, friends, and acquaintances. *This is particularly important if you're a foreign student trying to improve your American grammar and pronunciation.* (You may find Chapter 15 on conversation especially helpful.)

If you belong to a club, organization, or community group (if you don't, join one), speak whenever you can. Whether in your community or on campus, volunteer to become a member of a committee, or campaign for a friend who's running for office. Better yet, run for an office yourself. Within a short time, you'll realize that speaking often can not only be fun but a learning experience as well. And really, isn't that what a fruitful life should be all about?

Aristotle put it wisely back in 4 B.C. when he said, "To learn is a natural pleasure, not confined to philosophers, but common to all men." You only need the will and the motivation.

Observe Capable Speakers and Learn from Them

Another superb learning exercise is to observe and listen to outstanding speakers. Speeches given by many great orators that were originally recorded on film have been transferred to videotape. Such invaluable collections are available at many libraries, perhaps even on your campus. Here you can witness some excellent examples of orators such as Winston Churchill, Franklin Delano Roosevelt, and Adolph Hitler (although he spoke German, watch his fiery delivery and dramatic gestures). Other great speakers of the past include Everett Dirksen, John F. Kennedy, Martin Luther King, Jr., Adlai Stevenson, and Harry S Truman. Some contemporaries include Rudolph Guiliani, Congresswoman Nancy Pelosi, Mitt Romney, Condoleezza Rice, Elizabeth Dole, Ted Kennedy, and Hillary Rodham Clinton.

Your librarian or instructor will be able to recommend other well-known communicators, past and present, who may be found on videotape. Look around your local video store and watch the TV listings, including PBS and cable. Take the initiative to *look, listen, and learn.*

Read Good Literature

in other words:
dish up—make available

Again, your school or local library can ***dish up*** an excellent menu of literature from which you may select, savor, and digest. Taking certain "lit" courses can quickly dispel the idea that literature is dull and boring.

With a little inquiry and some independent research, you can experience the fulfillment of enjoying some of the greatest works of the literary masters, both prose and poetry. Avail yourself of some of the writings of such masters as Aristotle, Cicero, Confucius, and Shakespeare. Turn the pages of some of the masterpieces by authors such as Jane Austen, Rudyard Kipling, Robert Louis Stevenson, and John Keats. Why not sneak a peek at some of the works of Louisa May Alcott, Henry Thoreau, Walt Whitman, Emily Dickinson, Herman Melville, and Edgar Allan Poe? And don't forget titans of the twentieth century—William Faulkner, Ernest Hemingway, F. Scott Fitzgerald—and those still living—John Updike, Joyce Carol Oates, Ann Beattie, and Saul Bellow.

Referring to the reading of fine writings, someone said, "that man is known by the company his mind keeps." Particularly poignant is the quotation from the philosopher Francis Bacon, who said, "Some books are to be tasted, others to be swallowed, and some few to be chewed and digested." Please, help yourself, and **bon appétit.**

Use a Dictionary and Thesaurus

We cannot overemphasize the importance of expanding your vocabulary. We feel so strongly about this that we have incorporated vocabulary development as an integral part of this book (in the "Vitalize Your Vocabulary" sections in all chapters of the text). A strong, descriptive vocabulary indicates an educated (formally or not) person who usually draws praise and admiration. One of the surest ways to expand your present knowledge of words is to use an authoritative dictionary and **thesaurus** frequently.

You're bound to hear unfamiliar words every day. Start carrying a small notebook, one that can easily fit into your pocket or pocketbook. Whenever you hear a new word, write it down. You may hear such words in conversation, listening to a lecture, watching TV, listening to the radio, or you may see them in print. Jot them down, look them up in a dictionary, record their meanings, and most important, use your new words whenever you can. You'll be amazed how quickly your vocabulary will flourish. There are also a number of helpful paperback vocabulary development books available.

While a dictionary basically contains an alphabetized list of words with definitions, etymologies (if you don't know the meaning of this word, here's a good place to start—look it up and write down its definition), and pronunciations, a thesaurus is a book containing synonyms, antonyms, and, in some instances, slang, idioms, and colloquialisms (aha, another new one). A thesaurus can help you find the exact word to express your exact meaning. For example, in one such publication, the word "student" has over one hundred different classifications.

Words can announce life. Words can execute death. Words can bring happiness. Words can instill misery. Words can declare war. Words can welcome peace. Words can announce success. Words can proclaim defeat. Be sure of not only what you want to say but the words you choose to say it. And you gotta love this quote from Adlai Stevenson in a 1952 campaign speech: "Man does not live by words alone, despite the fact that sometimes he has to eat them."

Practice Writing, Including Your Talks

Another excellent exercise for developing your style and confidence as a speaker is to practice writing, including your talks. By writing your talks you'll be able to revise, change, or make any necessary improvements in language and content before making out your note cards. But remember, you don't want to read your talks verbatim.

Effective writing requires a great deal of effort and discipline, as many of you already know from having taken some writing courses. Writing requires you to think and evaluate and may also involve research, note taking, summarizing, paraphrasing, quoting, outlining, drafting, editing, and rewriting.

Writing can also help further develop your grammar and syntax skills as you sharpen your ability to communicate orally more accurately, clearly, coherently, understandably, informatively, and persuasively. From experience and research, we believe that a good writer has a better chance of becoming a good speaker, rather than vice versa.

Know Your Subject and Feel Deeply about It So That You Can Speak with Enthusiasm

Giving a talk is much easier when you have something worthwhile to say. If you have strong opinions based on personal experience that are contrary to the speaker's or if someone belittles or insults you or a member of your family, the chances are ***pretty solid*** that you would have little difficulty in counterattacking swiftly and with a vengeance.

This is how you should approach and prepare for every speaking assignment. Consider it a crusade and believe that what you will say to your listeners will be the most important or most inspirational message they will ever hear.

Knowing your topic inside out, researching and preparing more than you think you'll need, and being firmly convinced that your message will be entertaining,

in other
words:
pretty solid—
very good,
excellent

in other words:

sell yourself short—underestimate your abilities

informative, or persuasive should enable you to deliver your talk with a degree of enthusiasm that may even surprise you. Don't *sell yourself short.*

If you have believed, as many people do, that great speakers are born and not made, we hope that reading this chapter has changed your mind. For one final example of a speaker being made through years of effort, let's flash back to Boston in 1947. Sometime in that year, I was in a small audience of World War II veterans listening to a speech on foreign policy by freshman Congressman John F. Kennedy. He was witty and knowledgeable, but his voice lacked depth and variety, his language contained *er's* and *ah's,* his Boston accent was strong, and his hands were stuck in his pockets much of the time.

JFK was aware of his limitations. He knew that great speakers are made, not born. He knew that President Franklin D. Roosevelt and Prime Minister Winston Churchill struggled for years before they reached their full potential as speakers. He knew what he had to do and he did it.

Kennedy gave speeches often, read good literature to strengthen his vocabulary, and received coaching from a Boston University speech professor. In addition, he rehearsed his speeches, used a tape recorder to improve his voice and diminish his Boston accent, observed competent speakers, and wrote newspaper articles on social and political problems. He spoke before live audiences, on radio, and on television. As a result of his strenuous efforts, by 1960 he was ready for the crucial television debates with Vice President Richard Nixon. Many historians agree that Kennedy's performance won the Presidential election for him.

Granted, JFK had many things going for him—wealth, education, family contacts, a brilliant mind, a sense of humor, good looks, personal drive—but if you do half of what he did, you will greatly improve as a communicator.

Quick Clicks

Welcome to a "surprise search." To further enhance your research or simply to harvest more information about some of the things you studied in this chapter, just drop in at any of the following addresses. What you'll discover may be serious, educational, bibliographical, surprising, factual, or even downright humorous. But it will definitely be informative.

So, go ahead and give a "Quick Click."

www.speech.cs.cmu.edu/cgi-bin/cmudict
www.historychannel.com
http://dir.yahoo.com/Education/Graduation/Speeches
www.bartleby.com/100
www.pbs.org/greatspeeches

Things to Discuss in Class

1. Which methods of delivery do you think are used by political campaigners? Discuss this.
2. As a listener, which method of delivery do you prefer? Why?
3. Cite two speakers you've recently heard, and discuss their methods of delivery. In your opinion, which delivery was the most effective? Why?
4. Select a short passage and read it aloud in your normal delivery. Then, try reading the same passage aloud with enthusiasm, using inflection, feeling, and excitement in your delivery. Notice the vast improvement. Use of a tape recorder would be invaluable.
5. Recall for the class several instances in your life in which anticipating an event was far worse than the actual event.
6. If you've ever seen a speaker deliver a presentation without benefit of a lectern, tell the class how the speaker used his or her hands and notes.
7. To develop your ability to speak with enthusiasm and to improve your interpretation of the spoken word, read poetry and children's stories aloud and record them.

What Do You Remember from This Chapter?

1. List four methods of delivering a talk.
2. Explain the advantages and disadvantages of each method of delivery.
3. Is it permissible to use more than one method of delivery in the same talk?
4. Explain two differences between extemporaneous and impromptu talks.
5. Is it possible to prepare for an impromptu talk? Explain.
6. Why is practicing a talk important?
7. Is it a good idea to memorize the introduction and conclusion of a talk? Explain.
8. What role, if any, does enthusiasm play in speech delivery?
9. List three suggestions for relieving tension prior to speaking.
10. List three ways to help develop your speaking style.

Vitalize Your Vocabulary

Government and Politics

bipartisan (adj.) Representing members of two parties.

bureaucracy (n.) The whole body of nonelected government officials, often accused of red tape and insensitivity to human needs.

caucus (n.) A closed meeting of a political party to decide policies.

conservative (adj.) Tending to oppose change and to favor traditional ideas and values; (n.) a person who holds such views.

constituent (n.) A voter in a politician's district.

electorate (n.) The people qualified to vote in an election.

grass roots (n.) The local level, as opposed to the centers of political power.

gubernatorial (adj.) Pertaining to the governor.

impeach (v.) To legally charge a public official with misconduct in office.

incumbent (n.) The current holder of an office.

independent (n.) A voter who does not belong to a political party.

left wing (adj. and n.) See "liberal."

legislate (v.) To enact laws.

liberal (adj.) Favoring civil liberties and the use of government power to promote social reforms; (n.) a person who holds such views.

lobby (n.) Usually a group of people trying to influence lawmakers in favor of the group's special interest.

plank (n.) An article or principle in the platform of a political party.

platform (n.) A formal statement of a political party's goals and principles.

primary (n.) When voters select candidates from a field of candidates to run in the final election.

radical (adj.) Extreme, as in an approach to social, economic, and political problems; can be either left wing or right wing; (n.) one who holds such views.

referendum (n.) The practice of submitting a measure to the voters rather than to the legislature.

registration (n.) The official enrollment of citizens eligible to vote; if not registered, they cannot vote.

right wing (adj. and n.) See "conservative."

Let's Be Informative

10

To live effectively is to live with adequate information.
        —Norbert Wiener, *The Human Use of Human Beings* (1954), 1

After reading and understanding this chapter, you should know:

- The purposes and types of informative talks

- Four principles that help people learn better

- How to use statistics effectively

- How to prepare the introduction, body, and conclusion of an informative talk

chapter
preview

In this age of widespread college education, of national computer networks, and of endless research into the unknown, information has evolved into a national resource. By the same token, information has become an invaluable asset to individuals who can absorb it and share it through talking with their peers. In other words, speaking to convey knowledge and understanding can help you advance your career.

Adapting the knowledge level of your talk to the knowledge level of your audience is of supreme importance. Three kinds of audiences are described from this viewpoint, and, in order to help you meet their needs, various types of informative talks are explained.

Certain principles of learning that help you are discussed briefly. If you apply them, your informative talks will get better results, but applying these principles is not enough. First you need to acquire knowledge, information, and understanding in order to flesh out your talk. And that means doing your homework.

Many down-to-earth suggestions are given for preparing the introduction, body, and conclusion of your informative talk. After you finish your presentation, a question-and-answer period is an excellent way to tie up loose ends.

The chapter ends with a speech by Nelson Mandela.

Knowledge Is Power

Because the words *information* and *knowledge* appear throughout this chapter, let's define our terms:

> **information** (n.) Facts, data, news; knowledge communicated by others or obtained from study, instruction, or investigation.

> **knowledge** (n.) Comprehension, learning, information, an organized body of facts, or ideas inferred from those facts.

Americans have always set a high value on knowledge. We believe that democracy functions best when its citizens are armed with sound knowledge on which to base intelligent decisions. Because of this belief, the United States has developed the most extensive system of public education that the world has ever known. Because of this belief, the United States has more colleges and universities than do England, France, Germany, and the Commonwealth of Independent States combined. Because of this belief, the United States has more newspapers, magazines, book publishers, radio stations, television channels, computer networks, and public libraries than those same countries put together.

Such media, both here and abroad, have created a revolution in the handling of information and an explosion of knowledge in countless specialized areas. As a result, information is now regarded as "a new basic resource that supplements the familiar natural resources of matter and energy."[1] Matter and energy change with use, while knowledge does not. On the contrary, the more that knowledge is used and shared among people, the more valuable it becomes; for example, the knowledge needed to produce and use antibiotics and other "miracle" drugs has probably saved millions of lives.

Information is more accessible today than at any other time in our history, and our quest for it is insatiable. We have desktop, laptop, and notebook computers; the Internet; World Wide Web sites; e-mail; cell phones (both analog and digital, yet); pagers; faxes; and even hand-held organizers.

In a *Newsweek* article by Jennifer Tanaka, she writes that a single daily edition of the *New York Times* newspaper contains more information than the average person living in the seventeenth century would have been exposed to in a lifetime.[2]

Another article informs us that the "average American office worker sends or receives 201 messages a day,"[3] whether e-mail, voice mail, cellular phone, pager, hand-held computer (electronic notebook), Post-it®, or fax. I bet that you just can't wait to enter the corporate workforce (if you're not already employed in that environment).

---

[1]*Encyclopedia Britannica*, 15th ed., s.v. "information processing."
[2]Jennifer Tanaka, "Drowning in Data," *Newsweek*, 28 April 1997, 95.
[3]"Does America have ADD?" *U.S. News & World Report*, 26 March 2001, 14.

Unfortunately, this information mania is not confined strictly to the workplace. We appear to have an obsession with cell phones; they're everywhere—people walking down the street, on public conveyances, in cars, in restaurants, restrooms, and classrooms; at sporting events, in stores, athletic clubs and non-athletic clubs; at the beach, pool, or golf course. Even elevators and escalators are not immune to their presence. The constant display and use of cell phones without consideration for others can certainly create or perpetuate an "annoyance factor." Talk about information overload?

The continued commitment of the United States to this philosophy is clearly visible by our global dominance in such high-tech informational industries as computers, software, fiber optics, HDTV (high-definition television), and telecommunications. The world sees the United States ignoring all speed limits on the Information Superhighway. As one economist noted, "We're in the midst of the third industrial revolution."

Some Purposes of Informative Talks

Despite the multiplying numbers of computers (personal, business, and scientific) and databases, we still exchange astounding quantities of information orally. Much of our talking—on the job, in politics, at home, or in social contacts—is focused on one major objective: to present information so that it will be understood, remembered, and possibly utilized.

**in other
words:**

**open new
horizons**—
present
new areas
of interest

talk down—
speak in a
degrading
manner

**cover too
much
ground**—over-
whelm, present
too much
material

(an) "out"—
way of escaping
from a difficult
situation

**"showing (you)
up"**—trying to
embarrass you

Briefly, you want to ***open new horizons*** for your listeners, to give them new perspectives and understanding. In light of this goal, most audiences fall into three categories that may overlap: not informed, generally informed, and well informed.

With listeners who are not informed, you should deal in elementary matters and explain any jargon or specialized concepts. Here's where relevant comparisons and statistics (discussed later in this chapter) can help your audience understand your presentation. Just be careful not to ***talk down*** to them and not to ***cover too much ground*** at one time.

With a generally informed audience, you should use fundamental knowledge sprinkled with advanced material. The perplexing question is this: How much of each is appropriate? (For ideas on researching your audience, see Chapter 6.) Since some of your listeners may resent basic information as an onslaught against their egos, you may explain that you're simply laying a foundation on which to build deeper understanding. Another diplomatic ***"out"*** for you is that you're reviewing fundamentals for a few people whose memories may need refreshing.

With well-informed listeners, you're free to skip fundamentals and plunge into advanced information in depth. Listeners armed with knowledge are usually easy to handle, but a warning belongs here—know your subject, or a few sadistic members of the audience may revel in ***"showing you up."***

Be careful not to talk down to your audience.

Some common types of audiences you are likely to address include:

- Classes in school
- Decision-making individuals or groups on the job
- Voters assessing candidates at an open forum
- Consumers listening to purchasing experts for tips on stretching the dollar or conserving energy
- People listening to radio and television newscasts, documentaries, and so on

Someday, at school, on the job, in your community, you may find yourself giving an informative talk to one of these audiences and attempting to describe a person or place; to report an event, a problem, or a situation; or to explain a concept, device, process, theory; or giving directions.

An evaluation guide for **informative talks** appears near the end of this chapter. Since the guide reminds you to include important items in your informative talk, you should consult the guide before you speak.

Some Major Types of Informative Talks

Among the major categories of speeches—those to entertain, to inspire, to persuade, to actuate, and to inform—by far the most often presented is the speech to inform. What does this mean to you? Simply that the way you handle your storehouse of information and share it with others can have a significant impact on the direction of your career.

Let's clarify the use of speech categories. Because a speech is labeled "informative" doesn't mean that it's boxed in a neat compartment called "information." An informative speech may contain elements of persuasion, entertainment, or both, and those extras will, very likely, make it a more effective speech. The point is that, although speeches belong primarily to one category, they often include elements of other categories.

There is no better example of overlapping categories than the speech delivered by President George W. Bush to a joint session of Congress, the American people, and the world, on September 20, 2001, regarding the 9-11 terrorist attacks. Basically an informative speech, it contains elements of persuasion, inspiration, and a call to action. So emotional, dynamic, and moving was this speech that it is included in Appendix A of this text for you to study and to read aloud for practice in delivery, emphasis, and understandability.

The general objective of the informative speech is to convey understanding and knowledge, because humans have an instinctive need to understand themselves and their surroundings. And remember, to be successful this must be done in clear, understandable language. From that general objective, let's now focus on some of the more common types of speeches to inform: reports, instructions, demonstrations, and lectures.

Reports

A chief function of committees in business, education, politics, the armed forces—you name it—is to give reports on projects and problems. A neighborhood committee, for example, may investigate the need for traffic lights at a dangerous intersection, report its findings, and make a recommendation for or against traffic lights. At the other end of the spectrum, the President of the United States reports, once a year, on the State of the Union. Oral reporting goes on in all walks of life. How many oral reports have you given or heard in and out of school?

Instructions

Today you may tell an out-of-state tourist how to find the new shopping mall at the other end of town. Tomorrow your instructor may explain how to do a research paper. Handouts with specific steps to follow may supplement the oral instructions. Very often, written instructions help clarify the oral how-to-do-it phase. If you're a parent or grandparent—need I say more about the frequency of giving instructions?

Demonstrations

When you show someone how to use a camera, how to perform a card trick, or how to operate a computer terminal, you are demonstrating. This kind of informative speaking is so important that it rates a chapter of its own—Chapter 12.

Lectures

In addition to class lectures, this type of informative speaking includes talks at professional seminars, radio and television talks on travel and politics, and book reviews at club meetings. These talks are often given after luncheon or dinner; their prime purpose is to enhance the listeners' knowledge and appreciation of a particular subject.

Four Principles of Learning

Before you embark on your first informative talk, let's review some key findings on how people learn. Teachers in the past few thousand years and psychologists in the past hundred or so years have discovered that the following principles, when applied, speed the learning process.

1. *People learn better when you, as a speaker, involve as many of their senses as possible.* For example, suppose that you're demonstrating how to make a new kind of spaghetti sauce. You cut and mix the ingredients (seeing), fry them (smelling), explain the procedure (hearing), and then hand out samples to your listeners

Involve as many of their senses as possible.

(tasting). With four of their senses involved in this learning experience, your listeners will remember far more than if you used only words to convey the message.

Of course, this example is an extreme case because you won't always be able to involve four senses in the same talk. Often, however, you'll be able to involve the sense of seeing (with videotapes, photographs, maps, and models) and the sense of hearing (through the spoken word), and the sense of feel as you pass out objects.

2. *People learn better when salient points of information are repeated a few times or are restated in different words.* Here is an example of this principle.

> Doctors and dieticians tell us that breakfast is the *most important meal* of the day. Yet, millions of Americans skip this *crucial meal* daily, to save time, to pare off pounds, or both. After seven to nine hours in bed, these people may be rested sufficiently, but physically and mentally they need the *energy*—"fuel," if you don't mind—that a *well-balanced breakfast* can provide. Without that *energy*, their bodies and minds cannot operate at top efficiency through the morning. That is why, for most people, a *good breakfast* is a *key element* in nutrition that can lead to a healthy and more productive life.

Notice that the significant idea (italicized) in the preceding paragraph is mentioned seven times.

3. *People learn better when they're motivated to do so.* Your listeners pay close attention to you when you answer the often unspoken question that most people ask: "What's in it for me?" Tell them how to get a better job, reduce their income taxes, be healthier, live longer, or be more attractive to the opposite sex, and you can be sure that they will ***hang on*** every word you utter.

4. *People learn better when new, relevant information is presented in small, well-organized amounts.* If you're explaining the basic causes of World War II to an audience that knows little about the subject, you might organize your material according to political, economic, and military causes. You could discuss each category separately but not deeply, and in your conclusion, you could point out how all three types of causes combined to trigger the most devastating war in history.

How to Select a Topic

Although this subject is pretty well covered in Chapter 7, a couple of ideas bear repeating. Choosing a topic that interests you will enable you to better communicate your message with enthusiasm, credibility, and confidence. And, if you're excited about your topic, the chances are your audience will be, too.

From the moment you start considering potential topics you should start flashing positive messages across your mind such as, "My audience will find my topic interesting" and "My audience will benefit from what I plan to say." Positive messages can greatly enhance your confidence in the topic selection–research–planning–delivery process.

in other
words:

hang on—
listen very
closely to

Obviously, the best place to start your search is with yourself. Conduct an inventory of your experiences. Your work. Your travels. Your hobbies or your goals may make for interesting listening. You might have read a best-selling book, seen a memorable movie, attended a cacophonous (head for the dictionary) concert, or heard a lofty lecture. Perhaps, you met a celebrity or someone with an unusual occupation . . . all good topic possibilities.

A fruitful source that many students overlook—and that could provide very helpful information—is the number of student-related activities, programs, and services that your college offers. These include: student athletic activities and various clubs, advising and counseling, career services and, perhaps, internships and cooperative education, the Learning Center and External Studies. What about the Financial Aid office? (Yes, what about it?)

And don't forget the source of sources . . . the library with its multitude of books, magazines, newspapers, and electronic reference material. This might be a good time to quickly review the sections "What's This about Ethics" in Chapter 1 and "Doing Research" in Chapter 7.

No matter what topic you finally choose, be sure that:

- It's not too broad (limit your main points to four or five).
- You've established the specific purpose and thesis statement. (See Chapter 8.)
- You're able to present your message in the allotted time.

Getting into Your Informative Talk

The talk to inform, by its very nature, dictates that you do your research and that you know your subject. After all, your primary purpose is to convey information and understanding that your listeners didn't have before.

Because a strong introduction is crucial to any talk, before you plan your opening remarks you should review the ideas listed in Chapter 8. Most of those ideas apply to introductions to all kinds of talks. At the very least, in the introduction to your informative talk, you should:

- State the purpose of your talk.
- List the three or four main points orally and, if possible, write them on a chalkboard. However, if writing takes unduly long, your listeners' attention may wander. You may consider highlighting the main points on a poster, which is excellent visual reinforcement for your oral listing.
- Stress the subject's importance to your listeners; if it will save them time or money, make their lives easier, or help them get better grades, say so immediately.

Because first impressions are powerful and lasting, you should practice your introduction aloud many times so that you can deliver it fluently and still maintain eye contact. A well-spoken introduction can perform miracles for you in one or two minutes.

Moving into the Main Discussion

You're now ready to launch into a discussion of the main points mentioned in your introduction. As you know from Chapter 8 (organizing your information), each main point requires subpoints for support: facts, examples, quotations from authorities, incidents, anecdotes, comparisons, statistics, and so on. Ample research should provide you with many of these supports (which, except comparisons, are illustrated in Chapter 8). Now let's look at comparisons, statistics, audiovisual aids, and questions as supporting elements for your informative talk.

Comparisons

If you're explaining concepts that are new to an audience, try to compare them with something familiar to the audience. A few apt comparisons can bring your explanation to life. For example, let's assume that you plan to give a talk about the importance of saving for the future. (Something that should be of interest to everyone.) Your ***chances of connecting*** with your audience would be greatly enhanced if you included some of the following observations:

- If you went out for dinner and a movie twice a month at a cost of $75 each time, that would total $1,800 a year. If, instead, you invested that money over 30 years and received 10 percent interest per year, you would have $339,073.[4] If you splurged only half as much, you would have $169,536.
- By spending just $1 a day (whether on a soft drink, gum, or a candy bar) for 40 years, by the time you're ready to retire you'll be short about $190,000.[5]
- Smoking a pack of cigarettes a day could burn a hole in your retirement account to the tune of $330,000.[6]

Here's another example of how money can quickly multiply (although not too many of us could completely participate): if you took 1 penny and doubled it each day of the month for 30 days you would have $5,368,709.12—that's 5 million, 368 thousand, seven hundred nine dollars and 12 cents. What would you have if there were 31 days in the month?

The following are two concise comparisons, one dealing with specific amounts of money and the other with imagery and science; both can be grasped easily:

1. In 1984 the federal government spent $2.6 billion daily. "Piled flat, one atop the other, 2.6 billion $1 bills would stack 176 miles high—745 times as tall as New York's Empire State Building."[7]

---

[4]Ric Edelman, *The Truth about Money* (Washington, DC: Georgetown University Press, 1996), 299.

[5]Ric Edelman, "The No-Spending Plan," *U.S. New & World Report*, 20 October 1997, 82.

[6]Ibid., note 5.

[7]*U.S. News & World Report*, 24 December 1984, 25.

2. Sun flares sprayed streams of particles into space, sweeping the solar system *like streams of water from a revolving lawn sprinkler.*

Statistics

The use of statistics supplies concrete information that may perk up your audience's interest and, at the same time, may help establish you as a credible speaker. Try to observe the following cautions in using statistics:

● Don't throw reams of figures at your audience; they're too difficult to remember.
● In addition to giving statistics orally, present the key figures with a visual aid—a chalkboard, flip chart, poster, or slide.
● Repeat the most important figures at least once.
● Round off long figures. Instead of saying "$1,000,359," say "a little over a million dollars." Your audience will appreciate it. (The exception, of course, is if you intend to be very specific in order to make a dramatic point, as illustrated in the previous section when I discussed saving money.)
● Use only the most accurate and most recent statistics.

Notice how the following example dramatizes and clarifies the distance of the moon from the earth, about 239,000 miles:

If you could drive your car nonstop to the moon at 55 mph, you'd get there in 182 days.

Here's a comparison among one million, one billion, and one trillion:

One million seconds is about 12 days.

One billion seconds is about 31 years.

One trillion seconds is about 31 thousand years.

Notice how effective the following comparisons are regarding waste product statistics:

Recycling is gaining popularity, but currently only 11 percent of U.S. solid waste lives again as something else. And still the volume of garbage keeps growing—up by 80 percent since 1960, expected to mount an additional 20 percent by 2000. Not including sludge and construction wastes, Americans collectively toss out 160 million tons each year—enough to spread 30 stories high over 1,000 football fields, enough to fill a bumper-to-bumper convoy of garbage trucks halfway to the moon.[8]

Another effective method of ***getting your message across*** is to use short, factual statements, such as:

1. The amount of energy that escapes through our doors and windows each winter is equal to all the oil that flows through the Alaska pipeline each year.

---

[8]"Buried Alive," *Newsweek,* 27 November 1989, 67.

in other
words:
**getting your
message
across**—com-
municating so
people will
understand
you

2. The average American uses the equivalent of seven trees in packaging and paper products each year.[9]

Let's say that you plan to give a talk on our currency. Notice the interest factor and impact that the following short factual statements could have on your audience.

1. There are 490 bills in a pound.
2. It costs 4.2 cents to make a bill.
3. The average life of a $1 bill is 18 months.
4. The average life of a $50 or $100 bill is 9 years.[10] (But not in the Vasile household.)

Many people are interested in the subject of probability and statistics. If you plan to give a speech on job opportunities for the next decade, for example, it might be not only interesting, but shocking, if you included short factual statistics regarding the odds of dying at work while in a particular line of employment. (It may even cause some students to consider a change in their majors.) Here's a short list of jobs and the odds of dying while employed in that particular occupation.

School teachers	1 in 200,000	Electricians	1 in 9,700
Accountants	1 in 145,000	Police	1 in 8,200
Registered Nurses	1 in 125,000	Firefighter	1 in 6,500
College teachers	1 in 96,000	Pilots	1 in 1,000
Social worker	1 in 52,000	Fishermen	1 in 925
Construction	1 in 10,000	Sailors	1 in 825[11]

What do you say we conclude this section on statistics with one that you may have helped to make possible? That is, if you wear Levi's. According to Levi Strauss, the largest manufacturer of jeans in the world, the company uses about 1.25 million miles of thread each year, or enough to wrap around the world more than fifty times.

Audiovisual Aids

Be sure to "spice up" your informative talk with audiovisual aids, such as recordings, CDs, videos, multimedia graphics, photographs, and maps (see Chapter 12). Say, for example, you are discussing the various types of automobile antitheft devices. Photographs and, perhaps, even a video would certainly be interesting and effective, but the most compelling visual aids would be to display the actual pieces of equipment. Reality "grabs" people.

---

[9]*Masspirg Report,* September 1991.
[10]*The Patriot Ledger,* 14 May 2001, 7.
[11]*The Boston Sunday Globe,* 11 November 2001, E8.

Questions

A foresighted tactic to use while researching and preparing for your speech is to anticipate relevant questions that your listeners may want to ask at various stages of your talk. Asking such questions and answering them during your talk often stimulates your audience to think along with you and to bring up new ideas. If your talk is a lecture, you may wish to allow questions during your presentation. Then again, you may decide only to accept them after your talk, during the question-and-answer session. Be sure to clearly state the **_ground rules_** in your introduction.

Remember, understandability is synonymous with communication. If members of your audience are having difficulty understanding your message, then you're failing as an effective communicator. Although the topics of clarity and understandability are covered in Chapters 5 and 6, they warrant another brief mention. Since 9-11, more and more government agencies, and their abbreviations, are mentioned daily in the print and nonprint media. But, remember, not all of your classmates partake in the daily menu of reading or listening to the news media. So, if your talk is about current events (health/welfare, economy,

in other words:
ground rules—
format of the presentation

"To clarify . . . the IRS, OSHA, SSA, EEOC, and USHSA have us up a tree."

environment, the Middle East, or whatever), the chances are excellent that it would include references to such federal agencies as the

| FBI | BATF | FAA | EPA | SSA |
| CIA | IRS | SEC | FEMA | INS |

Some government agencies are not as well known as others, and many are unfamiliar to students new to our country/culture, Consequently, when referring to such an agency for the first time in your speech, be sure to follow the agency's initials by its name. For example, if you're talking about the BATF say, "The BATF, that's the Bureau of Alcohol, Tobacco, and Firearms," or, "The FBI, that's the Federal Bureau of Investigation," or, "The INS, that's the Immigration and Naturalization Service." (For a list of some government agencies that frequently appear in the media, see the Vitalize Your Vocabulary feature at the end of this chapter.)

Remember the Vasile axiom: if you have any doubt whatsoever that any member of your audience may not understand what you're saying, then take the time to clarify it.

And, again, for students whose primary language may not be English, if you hear something that you don't understand, raise your hand and ask the speaker to explain it further.

Winding Up Your Informative Talk

At the end of your main discussion, you might pause a few seconds and move a step or so to either side. The pause and movement signal that your talk is about to end. Then you may say something like:

- In conclusion (or before concluding), I would like to emphasize the following points.
- If you leave with only one thought, I hope that it will be. . . .
- And now I would like to close with a quotation from . . . (an anecdote about . . . , a comparison between . . . , a poem about . . .).
- Let me briefly summarize. . . .

Again, you may stress the importance of the subject and the benefits that the listeners may derive from the knowledge you've shared with them. Remember that a conclusion should be brief and to the point. Don't drag it out or trail off by muttering, "Well, I guess that's about it."

Another idea for your conclusion is to encourage listeners who want to learn more about the subject. You can list, on the chalkboard, relevant titles of magazine articles or books. Better still, prepare this information as a one-page **handout** that you can distribute on the spot. Most people like handouts because they're free and can be useful as lasting reminders of your key points.

Whereas other categories of talks seldom require a question-and-answer period, the informative talk does for these practical reasons: (1) if your treatment of a particular topic was foggy or incomplete, you have a second chance to clarify it; and (2) if you omitted a facet of the subject that concerns some of the listeners, you can supply the missing information.

Former President Harry S Truman summed up the value of the question-and-answer session in these words: "I know of no way of communicating more information in shorter time than the question-and-answer method."

Sometimes question-and-answer periods begin with a resounding silence that embarrasses both speaker and listeners. Almost everyone **shies away** from being the first to ask questions, for fear of sounding stupid. Planning can avert this silence. Ask a few questions—thought out beforehand—and answer them yourself if nobody in the audience cares to try.

Or you can do what many professional speakers do—"plant" a question or two with a friend in the audience; it's perfectly legitimate. If nobody speaks up, your friend can "break the ice." Then other listeners will very likely pop questions at you.

If you've done enough research, you'll be able to answer almost all queries, which should give you a feeling of accomplishment for a job well done. If a question stumps you, don't try to bluff around it. Admit that you don't know the answer but that you will try to find it. Most of your listeners will appreciate that you're an honest and ethical human being who doesn't pretend to be a know-it-all.

in other words:

shies away—to hesitate or to withdraw

"Of course, (gulp) I know the answer to your question . . . but first let's hear what you think."

A Sample Informative Speech with Outlines

As mentioned earlier, it is common that the various types of speeches do intertwine. An informative talk could contain elements of persuasion, and motivation, as well as inspiration. And such a speech took place on May 10, 1994, when Nelson Mandela, newly elected president of South Africa, delivered his inaugural address to the people of South Africa and the world at Pretoria. This historic event, for the first time, proclaimed the end of Apartheid (racial segregation in the Republic of South Africa).

After you read Mandela's stirring speech, review the two outlines—sentence and topic—to see how it might have been constructed.

▪ Glory and Hope[12]

Let There Be Work, Bread, Water, and Salt For All

Mandela gets to the point immediately, with no long-winded introduction.

He provides a stirring use of parallelism: "reinforce humanity's belief . . . , strengthen its confidence . . . , sustain all our hopes. . . ."

He links the reactions of South Africans to those of the rest of the world, establishing a common response from all listeners.

1   Your majesties, your royal highnesses, distinguished guests, comrades and friends: Today, all of us do, by our presence here, and by our celebrations in other parts of our country and the world, confer glory and hope to newborn liberty.

2   Out of the experience of an extraordinary human disaster that lasted too long must be born a society of which all humanity will be proud.

3   Our daily deeds as ordinary South Africans must produce an actual South African reality that will reinforce humanity's belief in justice, strengthen its confidence in the nobility of the human soul, and sustain all our hopes for a glorious life for all.

4   All this we owe both to ourselves and to the peoples of the world who are so well represented here today.

5   To my compatriots, I have no hesitation in saying that each one of us is as intimately attached to the soil of this beautiful country as are the famous jacaranda trees of Pretoria and the mimosa trees of the bushveld.

6   Each time one of us touches the soil of this land, we feel a sense of personal renewal. The national mood changes as the seasons change.

7   We are moved by a sense of joy and exhilaration when the grass turns green and the flowers bloom.

8   That spiritual and physical oneness we all share with this common homeland explains the depth of the pain we all carried in our hearts as we saw our country tear itself apart in terrible conflict, and as we saw it spurned, outlawed and isolated by the peoples of the world, precisely because it has become the universal base of the pernicious ideology and practice of racism and racial oppression.

---

[12]President Nelson Mandela, "Glory and Hope." Speech delivered to the People of South Africa, Pretoria, South Africa, 10 May 1994.

9   We, the people of South Africa, feel fulfilled that humanity has taken us back into its bosom, that we, who were outlaws not so long ago, have today been given the rare privilege to be host to the nations of the world on our own soil.

10   We thank all our distinguished international guests for having come to take possession with the people of our country of what is, after all, a common victory for justice, for peace, for human dignity.

11   We trust that you will continue to stand by us as we tackle the challenges of building peace, prosperity, nonsexism, nonracialism and democracy.

12   We deeply appreciate the role that the masses of our people and their democratic, religious, women, youth, business, traditional and other leaders have played to bring about this conclusion. Not least among them is my Second Deputy President, the Honorable F. W. de Klerk.

13   We would also like to pay tribute to our security forces, in all their ranks, for the distinguished role they have played in securing our first democratic elections and the transition to democracy, from bloodthirsty forces which still refuse to see the light.

14   The time for the healing of the wounds has come.

15   The moment to bridge the chasms that divide us has come.

16   The time to build is upon us.

17   We have, at last, achieved our political emancipation. We pledge ourselves to liberate all our people from the continuing bondage of poverty, deprivation, suffering, gender and other discrimination.

18   We succeeded to take our last steps to freedom in conditions of relative peace. We commit ourselves to the construction of a complete, just and lasting peace.

19   We have triumphed in the effort to implant hope in the breasts of the millions of our people. We enter into a covenant that we shall build the society in which all South Africans, both black and white, will be able to walk tall, without any fear in their hearts, assured of their inalienable right to human dignity—a rainbow nation at peace with itself and the world.

20   As a token of its commitment to the renewal of our country, the new Interim Government of National Unity will, as a matter of urgency, address the issue of amnesty for various categories of our people who are currently serving terms of imprisonment.

21   We dedicate this day to all the heroes and heroines in this country and the rest of the world who sacrificed in many ways and surrendered their lives so that we could be free.

22   Their dreams have become reality. Freedom is their reward.

23   We are both humbled and elevated by the honor and privilege that you, the people of South Africa, have bestowed on us, as the first President of a united, democratic, nonracial and nonsexist South Africa, to lead our country out of the valley of darkness.

24   We understand it still that there is no easy road to freedom.

25   We know it well that none of us acting alone can achieve success.

He paraphrases the U.S. Declaration of Independence by using the phrase. "We, the people of South Africa. . . ."

Having linked South Africa with the other nations of the world, he invites the latter to share in his country's destiny.

He wins support by acknowledging the efforts of those who brought about the achievement being celebrated.

The appeal to healing wounds and the promise to consider amnesty help to overcome the resistance of those who in the past have been adversaries and thereby enlist their participation in the new government.

The evocation of the Declaration of Independence is reinforced with the use of the term "inalienable rights."

Mandela demonstrates humility, portraying himself as servant of the people whose action placed him in his present position.

He uses slightly unnatural expressions to elevate his statements to a loftier rhetorical level: "We understand it still . . . ," "We know it well that. . . ."

He again uses rep-
etition and paral-
lelism: *"for* national
reconciliation, *for*
nation building,
for the birth of a
new world."

The repetition and
parallelism con-
tinue in a stirring
litany: four succes-
sive sentences
begin with "Let,"
following the
model of King's
speech. Three of
these "Let . . ."
sentences end with
"for all." (Is this
suggestive of "with
liberty and justice
for all"?) He also
repeats the words
"again" and
"never."

He offers a juxta-
position of oppo-
sites: the high-level
abstractions of "jus-
tice," "peace," and
"work" against the
basic physical ele-
ments of "bread,"
"water," and "salt."

The parallel to
King's speech is
carried out at the
end, where Man-
dela refers to a
well-known patri-
otic American
song, as King ends
with the words of a
famous spiritual.

26   We must therefore act together as a united people, for national reconciliation, for nation building, for the birth of a new world.

27   Let there be justice for all.

28   Let there be peace for all.

29   Let there be work, bread, water and salt for all.

30   Let each know that for each the body, the mind and the soul have been
freed to fulfill themselves.

31   Never, never and never again shall it be that this beautiful land will again
experience the oppression of one by another and suffer the indignity of being
the skunk of the world.

32   The sun shall never set on so glorious a human achievement!

33   Let freedom reign. God bless Africa!

Analysis

To an American ear, this speech is suggestive of such prominent U.S. documents as the Declaration of Independence, Lincoln's "Gettysburg Address," and
the speeches of Franklin D. Roosevelt and John F. Kennedy—and especially
Martin Luther King, Jr.'s, "I Have a Dream" speech, which is presented in Appendix A and which you will want to compare to Mandela's address to discover the striking similarities of both content and style.

Throughout the speech, Mandela uses simple but eloquent language; short,
cadenced, epigrammatic sentences that have the ring of slogans—saved from
monotony by interspersed longer sentences of more fluid rhythm. Forceful one-
syllable words predominate.

He makes frequent use of the "We" structure to establish a oneness between
himself and the rest of the South African people. Like Lincoln, he knows that
repetition can be highly effective rather than boring, especially when wrapped
in parallel structure.

The style will also suggest a Biblical tone to many listeners.

You can no doubt identify other ways in which this speech achieves its
special effect.

Now, here's a sentence outline of the speech:

Title

Glory and Hope: Let There Be Work, Bread, Water, and Salt for All

Purpose

To celebrate the birth of a new South Africa and to inspire confidence in its
future

Thesis Statement

Through the efforts of many, a new order for South Africa has arisen out of
the pain of the past; though the future will not be easy, it holds the promise
of fulfillment, dignity, and freedom for all

Introduction

I. Welcome guests
II. Acknowledge significance of the occasion and issue challenge to South Africans

Body

I. Establish inclusiveness of the new order
II. Describe pain of the past
III. Acknowledge South Africa's return to the community of nations, welcome participation of other countries in sharing this historic event, and invite their support in South Africa's struggle to meet the challenges of the future
IV. Give credit and express gratitude to the masses of South Africans, to F. W. de Klerk, and to our security forces
V. Call for national healing
VI. Pledge ourselves to liberation of our people, to peace, to a secure society for both black and white
VII. Promise to address the issue of amnesty
VIII. Dedicate the day to those who made freedom possible
IX. Express awareness of the difficulties awaiting us

Conclusion

I. Call for justice; peace; work, bread, water, salt; self-fulfillment; and freedom from oppression
II. God bless Africa!

Here is a topic outline of President Mandela's talk.

Title, Purpose, Thesis Statement

Same as in sentence outline

Introduction

I. Welcome
II. Significance of occasion and challenge

Body

I. Inclusiveness
II. Pain of the past
III. Role of other nations
IV. Credit and gratitude
   A. To masses of South Africans
   B. To F. W. de Klerk
   C. To security forces
V. National healing
VI. Pledges

A. To liberation
B. To peace
C. To security for all
VII. Amnesty
VIII. Dedication
IX. Difficulties of the future

Conclusion

I. Goals for the future
II. Benediction

Some Suggested Topics for Informative Talks

1. Racial and ethnic profiling
2. Terrorism—who, what, and where?
3. Child sexual abuse by the clergy
4. Soccer mania in the United States
5. Soft money in politics
6. Business and corporate ethics
7. The difference between plagiarism and paraphrasing
8. What's wrong with plagiarism and cheating?
9. Vouching for school vouchers
10. Big business misconduct
11. Porn in the library
12. Generic vs. name-brand drugs
13. What is a liberal/conservative court?
14. Insider trading
15. CEOs' golden pocketbook
16. Newly acquired women's rights in Pakistan
17. What's all this cloning business talk
18. Corporate welfare
19. Al Qaeda—what it represents
20. A day in the life of a Washington lobbyist
21. Managing your money
22. DNA and the death penalty
23. Gas-electric vehicles
24. A national ID card
25. Identity theft
26. A cashless society
27. Cell phone etiquette
28. Remember the first three letters of the word diet
29. Political pork, or bringing home the bacon
30. The right to bear arms

For more suggested topics, see Appendix B.

Quick Clicks

Welcome to a "surprise search." To further enhance your research or simply to harvest more information about some of the things you studied in this chapter, just drop in at any of the following addresses. What you'll discover may be serious, educational, bibliographical, surprising, factual, or even downright humorous. But it will definitely be informative.

So, go ahead and give a "Quick Click."

http://gwis2.circ.gwu.edu/~gprice/speech.htm
www.pbs.org/greatspeeches/timeline/index.html
http://gos.sbc.edu
http://seaborg.nmu.edu/clouds
www.tamu.edu/scom/pres/archive.html
www.onlinenewspapers.com
http://newslink.org

Things to Discuss in Class

1. Prepare a short informative talk on one of the following:
   a. A concept or device
   b. A process or theory
   c. An event
   d. A problem
   e. A situation
2. Be prepared to discuss some principles that speed the learning process.
3. Prepare a short talk (a minute or two) giving specific directions on how to get somewhere. Be as concise and explicit as possible.
4. Prepare a five- to ten-minute talk on one of the following topics:
   a. The organizational structure of a business
   b. The organizational structure of an educational facility
   c. The organizational structure of a political campaign

What Do You Remember from This Chapter?

1. What are the prime purposes of informative talking?
2. List several categories of speeches. Which one is presented most often?
3. List some principles which, when applied, speed the learning process. Give examples of these principles.
4. What are some elements that should be included in the introduction of your informative talk?
5. What cautions should you observe when you use statistics?
6. Is it a good idea to follow an informative talk with a question-and-answer period? Explain.
7. Can an informative speech contain elements of persuasion or entertainment? Explain.
8. When explaining concepts that are new to an audience, what type of comparisons should you make?

Vitalize Your Vocabulary

Appearing more and more in the print and non-print news media are stories referring to various government agencies. To help you become acquainted with the more frequently mentioned agencies, here is a listing of some of the more common ones, preceded by their abbreviations.

BATF Bureau of Alcohol, Tobacco, and Firearms

CCR Commission on Civil Rights

CIA Central Intelligence Agency

DHHS Department of Health and Human Services

EEOC Equal Employment Opportunity Commission

EPA Environmental Protection Agency

FAA Federal Aviation Administration

FBI Federal Bureau of Investigation

FCC Federal Communications Commission

FDA Food and Drug Administration

FDIC Federal Deposit Insurance Corporation

FEC Federal Election Commission

FEMA Federal Emergency Management Agency

FRS Federal Reserve System

FTC Federal Trade Commission

GAO General Accounting Office

INS Immigration and Naturalization Service

IRS Internal Revenue Service

NASA National Aeronautics and Space Administration

NLRB National Labor Relations Board

NRC Nuclear Regulatory Commission

NTSB National Transportation Safety Board

OSHA Occupational Safety and Health Administration

SBA Small Business Adminstration

SEC Securities and Exchange Commission

SSA Social Security Adminstration

USITC United States International Trade Commission

USPS United States Postal Service

Let's Be Persuasive

11

Speech is power: Speech is to persuade, to convert, to compel.
—Ralph Waldo Emerson

After reading and understanding this chapter, you should:

● Appreciate the importance of speaking to persuade

● Know the purposes of speaking to persuade

● Be familiar with methods of analyzing an audience

● Know how to use statistics effectively

● Understand the meaning of facts, opinions, "expert" opinion and inferences

● Understand the various strategies and principal methods to help you persuade an audience to accept your views

● Understand the Motivated Sequence of persuasion

chapter
preview

A form of communication crucial to the achievement of your career goals is persuasive speaking. Several examples of persuasive speaking are given, to show how practical and how valuable it can be to you.

Persuasive speaking has three purposes: to convince people to take action that you want them to take, to change their attitudes or beliefs, and to strengthen or weaken their current attitudes or beliefs.

Before you can persuade your listeners to change their stance and do what you want them to do, you must analyze your audience. Several relevant questions are asked; if you can find answers, you'll stand a good change of winning the audience to your side.

Armed with some understanding of your audience, you're now in a position to plan strategy. Two types of audiences are considered: (1) friendly and (2) neutral or passive.

Authorities on persuasion, starting with Aristotle 2,200 years ago, agree on three ways to persuade:

1. Through logical argument by using evidence and reasoning
2. Through speaker credibility
3. Through appealing to basic social, biological, and psychological needs and desires

Another method of persuasion—the Motivated Sequence—is also discussed. Each of the four methods is highlighted, and specific examples are given.

The chapter ends with an electrifying speech by Elizabeth Dole at the 1996 GOP National Convention in San Diego on behalf of her husband, Senator Bob Dole, who was chosen to be the Republican Party Presidential nominee.

The Importance of Persuasive Speaking

Is the ability to persuade important to you, your family, your career? Instead of simply answering "yes," we'll list some examples of **persuasive speaking** that occur all around you. Maybe you've already been involved in one or more of the following situations:

● Representing yourself in Small Claims Court
● Persuading a professor to admit you into her already overenrolled course
● Convincing your manager that you should be chosen for a promotion to a position that has ***just opened up***
● Presenting your case to borrow the family car
● Presenting your case for denying the request for use of the family car
● Selling yourself during a job interview
● Listening to political candidates ask for your vote
● Strongly presenting your views, as a parent, on the subjects of sex education and condom distribution in the public schools
● Trying to convince a person to go on a date
● Trying to persuade a politician why you need a new sidewalk
● Insisting that your child attend the local neighborhood school instead of being bused across town
● Asking the court for more liberal visitation rights for your child
● Settling a claim with your insurance company
● Trying to convince your professor that your final grade should have been an A instead of B+

We're sure that you get the point that persuasive speaking is a valuable skill to develop. Although there are no magic formulas or ***rules of thumb*** to transform you overnight into an accomplished persuader, there are several suggestions in this chapter to help you sharpen your ability. Of course, before you can convince anybody of anything, your body, your voice, your facial expressions, and your gestures should reflect the fact that you yourself are convinced. Audiences sense whether speakers are convinced of the truth of their arguments or are faking it.

Don't forget the extremely crucial point made back in Chapter 3, that when a person's actions and words appear contradictory, the actions often communicate the true feelings. That's why you must always be conscious not only of what you say, but also of your nonverbal messages transmitted from your facial expressions, gestures, body movements, and eye contact. These messages need to coincide with your verbal ones.

The Stanford University Graduate School of Business, one of the foremost school of its kind in the world, conducted research on successful managers and found that they have five major characteristics in common. "Oral persuasiveness" leads the list because "the successful manager is primarily an effective speaker . . . he is interested in persuading others to his point of view."[1]

---

[1]*Nation's Business*, June 1976, 6.

in other words:

just opened up—just became available

rules of thumb—certain rules based on experience or common sense

Before we begin, remember these powerful words from Lord Chesterfield, written in 1739 but still true today: "To please people is a great step towards persuading."

The Purposes of Persuasive Speaking

All the examples of persuasive speaking listed in the previous section have one common aim: to convince people to take a form of action. Therefore, they're called speeches to **actuate,** and the best way to accomplish that is through motivation (discussed later in the chapter).

Another purpose of talks to persuade is to reinforce or strengthen, listeners' existing attitudes, beliefs, behavior, opinions, or values. Let's say, for example, that you strongly oppose the distribution of condoms (birth control devices) in the public schools and you're to speak to a group whose views coincide with yours. You would simply reiterate a few powerful arguments to reassure your listeners and fortify their position.

A third purpose of persuasive speaking is to convince people to *change* their attitude toward a particular subject. Suppose you're speaking to a group that is neutral on the subject of condom distribution in the public schools and open to discussion. In your introduction, try to capture their goodwill immediately (see the section on introductions in Chapter 8). You would now follow

The importance of persuasive speaking.

with some strong arguments for your position and elaborate on them. Then you might introduce statistics and other evidence accompanied by visual aids as you discuss ethics, morality, parental responsibility, health issues, etc.

Analyzing Your Audience

In order to persuade your listeners, it is crucial that you learn as much as possible about your audience's beliefs and attitudes toward your topic and your position. If your listeners' beliefs and attitudes are fixed, perhaps you should settle for a chance to speak your piece and hope that they'll give you a fair hearing. Realistically, you cannot expect to change their minds with just one speech, no matter how convincing you are. If, however, your listeners are open minded, you may be able to swing some moderates among them to your banner.

It might even be presumptuous, on your part, to feel that if your speech didn't totally persuade or convince your audience, your efforts were a failure. As I mentioned in the preceding paragraph, this is just not true. If you got only some members of your audience to "give some serious thought," or "think twice" about what you had to say, then you should feel positive and successful. Persuasion, occasionally, can occur over a period of time, as opposed to being instantaneous.

Figure 11.1 shows the range (from strongly opposed to strongly favorable) of audience feelings, attitudes, and beliefs toward any speaker and subject. Sometimes an audience is polarized at one inflexible position, especially on emotional issues that cut deeply into their lives, such as unemployment, busing, gun control, abortion, and the high cost of energy. At other times an audience may be so fragmented that its members span the entire spectrum from strongly opposed to highly favorable.

No question about it—it's important to study your audience beforehand. (Refer to Chapter 6.)

Strongly opposed	Opposed	Neutral, uninterested, no opinion	Favorable	Highly favorable

FIGURE 11.1

The Range of Beliefs and Attitudes of Listeners

in other
words:
turning an
audience
around—get-
ting the audi-
ence to agree
with your
position

Turning an audience around is a devilishly difficult task, much tougher than selling an automobile or a house. Convincing an audience to make even a slight change in direction requires a carefully planned approach, anchored in a shrewd assessment of the audience's position. Think of lawyers who practice criminal law and who attempt to do this on a daily basis. Many citizens/jurors enter a courtroom thinking the defendant is probably guilty. Often, confronting deep-rooted prejudices, the criminal attorney must try to convince jurors that there is a particular way to see the facts, evidence, testimony, and circumstances that leads to no other conclusion but that the government has not proven the lawyer's client guilty.

The planning and attention to detail are crucial. It is paramount that each juror is persuaded. The defense lawyer must assess what facts will convince some jurors (audience analysis); what government errors or omissions will influence some jurors (audience analysis); what is the most effective way to present all of the facts, but especially those that may be unpleasant to hear and to deal with; how best to characterize and simplify the information the jurors will be discussing together so as to focus their understanding and clarify their responsibility; how best to convince the jurors that they cannot be convinced beyond a reasonable doubt by the evidence presented by the government that the defendant is guilty of the crime charged, no matter how powerful or distasteful some of the evidence might be. Because a life may be at stake in a criminal trial, and imprisonment (rather than a bad grade) may be the result of poor planning, the attorney's attempt to convince a jury is probably the ultimate attempt to persuade.

Thinking of the jurors as your audience and the attorney as you, the speaker, should give you a better understanding of the seriousness and the challenge with which you're confronted when attempting to convince or persuade.

While you're not carrying the same responsibility that a defendant's attorney carries when she gets up to address the jury, it would be wise to aim for the degree of care in your persuasive speeches that the attorney employs when she is preparing the closing argument. Always aim for precise attention to detail; always aim for clear understanding of your facts and a clear and logical presentation of them; always aim to reach and develop a rapport with each member of your audience (eye contact) so that each sees your point of view, even if he or she was convinced otherwise before you began your speech.

Let's wrap this up by saying that, in the same way the attorney assesses his or her audience—the jury—you must assess yours.

Before you can make that assessment, however, you should try to answer the following questions and any others that pertain to your particular situation.

1. What are you trying to accomplish? In other words, what is your specific purpose in speaking?
2. How does your audience feel toward your purpose and position?
3. What emotional or psychological appeals will move these people? (This is discussed later in this chapter.)

Turning an audience around can be a difficult task.

4. What logical reasoning will "reach" them?
5. Are they willing to accept new ideas?
6. Why should this audience listen to you?
7. Do you know anyone who has had previous experience with this audience? Can that person help you answer these questions?

While these questions may seem simple or obvious, they are the same questions that the defense attorney must consider. She shapes these questions to her circumstances. You should do the same thing at the outset of your planning.

After you've analyzed your audience in terms of these questions, you will better understand their attitudes, feelings, and motives. Only then will you be prepared to plan your overall strategy.

Speech Strategy

Because this is a basic speech guide, we will delve into strategy just deeply enough to help you cope with some typical situations. For example:

● If the audience agrees with your position, discuss a few major issues so that you will reinforce your audience's position and erase any doubts that may plague them.

in other
words:

nudge it over
the line—move
it in your favor

"sitting on
the fence"—
undecided

● If the audience is interested but undecided, use a few of your strongest arguments, both logical and emotional, to **nudge it over the line** into your territory. If an audience is **"sitting on the fence,"** sometimes a gentle prod is all that is needed to spur them to make a decision favorable to your point of view.

● If your audience is not interested in your subject, try to appeal to some aspects of their self-interest (discussed later in this chapter).

● If your audience disagrees with you, don't be aggressive in the introduction. Instead of using a strong, positive statement, phrasing your proposition or solution in the form of a question or two may be a more tactful approach. Let's say that you're to speak to hard-pressed taxpayers (is there any other kind of taxpayer?) in your town about raising taxes to finance a cleanup of the town's polluted lake. You might start by asking, "Do you want your children to have a safe, healthful place to swim, fish, and sail? Or do you want them to hang around street corners, pizza parlors, pool halls, or video game arcades?"

● Under the same circumstances, another approach to discuss areas of agreement first—if there are any—and then move to areas of disagreement. You might start like this: "We taxpayers all agree on the need for a family recreation area in town. Fortunately, we have a lake and we should use it for family fun. After we clean up the lake, our taxes will return to normal. In other words, this proposed tax increase will last only as long as the cleanup project lasts."

● If your audience understands the problem, spend less time on it and more time on your solution. Let's continue with the lake situation. Since your lis-

Try to anticipate objections.

teners, the taxpayers, understand the problem, you should devote most of your efforts to describing the benefits that they will enjoy from the restored lake. Be sure to stress that the tax increase is temporary and will stop after the lake is cleaned up.

● Spot your most convincing arguments at the beginning and end of your speech. Arguments in the middle tend to be forgotten. Playwrights know this, which is why the best plays usually open with a bang and close with a crash.

● Try to anticipate questions and objections. Plan your answers beforehand. This tactic applies to all speech situations, not just to persuasive speaking, and it can spare you many a headache.

● The opportunity to participate in a question-and-answer session may win over some hostile listeners. If you've studied your audience, you know who its influential members are. While you're speaking, focus special attention on them, because the other members tend to follow their lead.

How to Select a Topic

Although selecting a topic is pretty well covered in Chapters 7 and 10, several ideas bear highlighting. Obviously, selecting a subject about which you feel very strongly will enable you to better communicate your position with confidence and credibility.

Remember, that in a speech to persuade, nothing is more essential than transmitting credibility; because you're not only offering your audience *accurate* information but you're trying to:

● Convince them to take a form of action
● Reinforce or strengthen their existing attitudes, beliefs, behavior, opinions, or values
● Change their attitudes or opinions to agree with your position

Let's start by looking at some of the resources available to you.

Personal

As I mentioned in Chapter 10, an excellent starting point in selecting a topic is with yourself by reviewing your own experiences.

● Perhaps you applied for a job and were turned down because of Affirmative Action policies in place at the company or public institution.
● Maybe you were told that the neighborhood school within walking distance from your home is full and your children must be bused across the city to another school.
● Maybe you have a ***real beef*** about the registration process at your college or the college's policy of canceling classes due to low enrollment even though that particular class may be required in order for you to graduate.

in other
words:
real beef—
gripe

● If you're from another country, perhaps you have a problem with our immigration laws or our foreign policy in general.

Print Media

Another rich source of acquiring ideas is from the print media.

● All major newspapers offer editorials as well as a section on Letters to the Editors, where anyone can express his or her opinion simply by writing to the newspaper.

Here are some addresses you may want to visit for some ideas:

The New York Times	www.nyt.com
The Chicago Tribune	www.Chicago Tribune.com
The San Francisco Chronicle	www.sfgate.com
The Wall Street Journal	www.wsj.com
The Washington Post	www.washingtonpost.com
USA Today	www.usatoday.com

● Equally as prolific as a source for topic selection are the weekly news magazines such as *Newsweek, U.S. News & World Report,* and *Time,* as well as various liberal and conservative publications. Check them out on the Internet.
● And, of course, the omnipresence of national and local radio and television talk shows.

Electronic Media and Library

● Don't forget the inexhaustible resources available on the Internet.
● And the good old reliable (always-there-when-you-need-them) source . . . your college or public library staff.
● Try the *Guinness World Records, The World Almanac, The Time Almanac.*

in other words:

coming up with—deciding on

By now, you should at least have a pretty good idea on how to get started on ***coming up with*** a topic to persuade.

No matter what topic you select, remember the previously mentioned triad for an effective persuasive performance:

● Narrow the topic and present four or five main points.
● Clearly establish your specific purpose and thesis statement.
● Be sure you're able to present your message in the allotted time.

Methods of Persuasion

Speech authorities, psychologists, politicians, trial lawyers, and master salespeople know that there are four principal methods of changing people's attitudes or actuating people to do what you want:

1. Persuading through evidence and **reasoning.** (The formal term for this action is **argument.**)
2. Persuading through speaker credibility or **ethos.**
3. Persuading through appeals to basic social, biological, and psychological needs, wants, and desires.
4. Persuading by using the Motivated Sequence (MS, explained on pages 263–264.).

In most cases of successful persuasion, all four methods are mixed in varying degrees, depending on the speaker's analysis of the audience and on the speaker's character and style.

How to Persuade through Evidence and Reasoning

Let's consider these methods, starting with argument and its components, evidence and reasoning. **Evidence,** as you know, consists of facts and expert opinions.

A fact is information that can be proved, is documented, and can be verified. Here are some examples.

Fact:	More women than men are getting A's in this class.
Opinion:	Women are smarter than men.
Fact:	There has been an increase in the number of motor vehicle fatalities caused by drunk drivers.
Opinion:	The sale of alcohol beverages should be illegal.
Fact:	Professor Vasile's textbook, *Speak with Confidence,* is used on college and university campuses in almost every state in this nation.
Opinion:	Professor Vasile's textbook *Speak with Confidence,* is a great speech book.
Fact:	Among the highest paid people in the country are professional athletes.
Opinion:	Professional athletes are overpaid.
Fact:	The *New York Times* has one of the largest circulation figures of any newspaper in the United States.
Opinion:	No question, the *New York Times* is a great newspaper.
Fact:	The cost of going to college is astronomical.
Opinion:	College tuitions should be tax deductible.

Using Opinions Wisely.   **Opinions** may be either your own or those of other people. As with facts, some opinions are convincing and others are not, depending on their sources. Your opinion of the causes and probable cure of inflation will carry weight only if you're an expert economist who has a reputation for sound thinking. Therefore, if you're using opinions in your speech to persuade, identify the sources and their qualifications.

The most valid type of opinion is the **"expert opinion."** This is expressed by a recognized authority in a particular field. Expert "testimony" may differ but, nonetheless, is admissible in a court of law. (And you can't get much more valid than that.)

On the other hand, using "nonexpert" opinion can jeopardize your talk. In a Presidential TV debate, watched by 90 million people in October 1980, President Jimmy Carter committed a gaffe that cost him dearly. During an exchange with California's Governor Ronald Reagan, the Republican nominee, on whether or not to increase our stock of nuclear arms, he mentioned his daughter Amy's fear of nuclear proliferation. That statement not only ***turned people off,*** it made President Carter the butt of countless cutting comments. The voters couldn't have cared less about 11-year-old Amy's opinion on nuclear weapons. The President should have quoted a world-famous nuclear physicist; that opinion would have been credible and persuasive.

At the close of that same debate, Governor Reagan showed how to use people's own opinions to win votes by asking questions that hit Americans where it hurt most—in their pocketbooks: "Is it easier for you to go and buy things in the stores than it was four years ago? Are you better off now than you were four years ago?" That masterful use of questions to persuade an audience helped catapult Reagan into the White House.

Such a key question helped another Presidential candidate capture the White House. In 1960 Senator John F. Kennedy faced a formidable obstacle—prejudice against Catholics. Never in 180 years had the United States elected a Catholic President, and JFK was determined to alter the course of history. In a landmark speech to a prejudiced audience—the Ministers' Association in Houston, Texas—he made this persuasive point:

> Today I visited the Alamo where, side by side with Davy Crockett and Sam Bowie, died Bailey and Carey and McCarthy. . . . But no one knows whether they were Catholic or not, because there were no religious tests at the Alamo.

"Why, then," JFK asked, "should there be a religious test for the White House?"[2]

Inferences mean drawing a conclusion or generalization based on observation, experience, and/or logic. ***In other words,*** when you infer something, you come to a conclusion or generalization based on what you see, hear, or read, but which may not be specifically evident or stated. For example, let's say you're driving home late one night after studying at the library. As you approach your house, you observe a police car in your driveway. Whoa! You may conclude one or several theses (inferences). A member of your family is ill and they're waiting for the ambulance. Perhaps there was a burglary. Maybe your kid sister got into ***a little jam*** and the police took her home. It isn't until you enter the house that you learn (with great relief) that the police officer is a friend of your dad's and he stopped in to say hello.

---

[2]*Boston Globe,* 20 November 1983, A37.

in other words:
turned people off—made people angry or disinterested

in other words—say in another, more understandable way

a little jam—a little trouble

As you can see, when you make an inference it isn't necessarily a valid one. Inferences may prove to be correct, false, or elsewhere in between.

To sum up, remember that **facts** are statements that are documented and can be verified. Everyone is entitled to his or her opinion, but the only authoritative ones are offered by experts or authorities in their specific fields. And inferences are conclusions or generalizations based on your experience, observation, and/or logic which may be true or, best, an educated guess.

Types of Reasoning.   If you have facts and authoritative opinions, you're in a position to carry out some reasoning. So now let's discuss some common types of reasoning: inductive, deductive, causal, and analogic.

Inductive reasoning, the reverse of deductive reasoning, starts with specific *examples* or *cases* and ends with a general *conclusion* based on the examples or cases. For instance, much U.S. food lacks taste and food value; canned produce and packaged bread are notorious in this respect. Compared to European breads, most U.S. bread is flat, tasteless, spongy mush. In addition, most of our canned fruits and vegetables are "embalmed" with chemical preservatives and additives that may cause serious health problems. Most of these foods are produced, processed, and packaged by giant farm corporations. From these examples, we may draw the general conclusion that these farm corporations are impairing the health of the American people.

This discussion of U.S. food can be condensed into the following syllogism:

Much American food (bread, canned fruits and vegetables) lacks taste and nutritional value. (specific example)

Most of these foods are produced by giant farm corporations.

These corporations are harming our health. (general conclusion)

Here's another example of inductive reasoning:

Some federal laws and regulations promote clean air and water. (specific example)

Clean air and water are essential to good health.

Therefore, we should support these laws and regulations. (general conclusion)

A common weakness in inductive reasoning is illustrated in the following generalization.

The Professional Air Traffic Controllers Organization and another union went on strike in violation of their contracts.

Therefore all unions are bad and should be outlawed.

That generalization is weak and invalid because it is based on a very limited number of examples. There is no rule about how many examples you need, but the more you can cite, the stronger your case will be.

Sometimes you can observe all of the cases in a particular situation. For example, you can poll your speech class and determine how many students have small children; you could go even further and poll the students in all of your classes. As a result of the information you receive, you can form a reasonable conclusion: of the 115 students in my classes, 73 have children under five years of age. If your poll was more focused, you could also determine how many of the students with children under five are concerned with child care. Do problems with child care affect their ability to select classes and/or concentrate on their classes? Would a day care center on campus be advantageous for those students?

You might want to draw a conclusion from your little poll. If you have enough specific examples to support your conclusion, and if the examples are typical or representative of all working students in your college, and if your information is current or recent, you may be able to draw a sound generalization:

> A substantial number of students at College X are distracted from their studies by concerns about day care for their small children.
>
> If day care concerns were removed, these students would experience a boost in their efforts to achieve academic success.
>
> College X should provide an on-site day care facility for students.

Most often, however, we're not able to make definitive observations about things. Even when we have evidence that we or other reliable witnesses have collected, there may be unexplained situations that will negatively affect our conclusions. Therefore, our conclusions can only be probable, not definite or certain.

Deductive reasoning is the type of reasoning that moves from a general premise, or principle, to a specific conclusion. If the premise is true, then the conclusion is most likely true. As we mature over the years, we learn lessons of life from which we make deductions. For example, we may deduce, from experience, that people who smoke in elevators and other closed-in places are more concerned with their own immediate satisfaction than with the comfort of others.

Unlike inductive reasoning, which attempts to arrive at the truth (probable conclusions), deductive reasoning guarantees that your conclusion must be true.

In formal terms, deductive reasoning is structured as a *syllogism* that consists of a major premise, a minor premise, and a conclusion. The classical syllogism is this:

Major premise:	All men are mortal.
Minor premise:	Socrates is a man.
Conclusion:	Socrates is mortal.

Here's another example of deductive reasoning:

Major premise:	People who eat fatty, cholesterol-laden junk food are asking for health problems.

"Relax, son—I'm just delivering tickets to the Police Benefit Show."

Minor premise: The Smith family lives on that kind of diet.

Conclusion: The Smith family will face health problems.

Sometimes, in conversation or in a talk, one of the parts of a syllogism may be omitted. Consider these statements, for instance: "Whenever tuition and fees at colleges are raised, many students drop out. Next year the tuition and fees at this college will go up 25 percent." The conclusion implied, but not stated, is that a lot of students will be forced to leave college.

Beware of one potential pitfall in using deductive reasoning: you must be certain that both premises are true. If they're not, the conclusion will be unreliable, as in this syllogism:

Having a college degree is the surest way to get a well-paying job.

Charles Ross will soon have a college degree.

Charles Ross will get a well-paying job.

As we all know, having a college degree is only one factor in achieving a well-paying job and, therefore, the conclusion is invalid.

Careful attention to detail and precise wording will lessen your chances of making inaccurate statements. Your major premise should have been stated: Having a college degree is an important factor in getting a well-paying job. Then, your conclusion might have been more effective if it stated: Charlie Ross has taken a major step toward getting a well-paying job.

Keep in mind that the major premise in a syllogism may be the result of induction or observation of particular instances or cicumstances. The notion that all men are mortal comes from our astute observation that people die (women as well as men). Although we know that there are people alive who are over 100 years old, I think that you'll agree that there are none over 150. Based on what we and our scientists and observers of people have noticed throughout time, no people are around from the Stone Age or the Enlightenment: they have died. So, based on this observation of particular incidents of the deaths of human beings, we come to the conclusion that all men are mortal. (Bear with me, now.) We now take that conclusion and make it a major premise. We can then reason about a particular individual or member of the class described in the major premise, Socrates, and make a statement, a minor premise, that Socrates is a man. The conclusion links the two statements together: all men are mortal; thus, because Socrates is a man, Socrates is mortal.

The problem lies in the formulation of the premises. In order for your argument to be sound, your premises must be sound. Make sense? "Having a college degree is the surest way to get a well-paying job" is not sound. It's just not true. There are other ways to get jobs that pay well. Alternatively, in this technological world, you might have a degree in general studies and have a hard time getting a well-paying job. Thus, my friend, if the major premise is false, the conclusion is also false.

Causal reasoning, also discussed in Chapter 8, moves from cause to effect (result). For instance, doctors and scientist have proved, through thousands of experiments, that smoking heavily (cause) shortens your life by a certain numbers of years (effect).

Here's another common-sense example of causal reasoning:

When mortgage rates decline, people are more willing to buy homes. (cause)

Mortgage rates are now declining.

Sales of homes will soon increase. (effect)

The danger in causal reasoning is to oversimplify, to rely too heavily on one cause; in the real world, most effects are brought about by several causes. In the smoking example, it is important to consider that other factors—heredity, environment, and lifestyle—influence longevity.

To avoid oversimplification in causal reasoning, keep the following two questions in mind:

1. Did the alleged cause, in fact, result in or contribute to the effect?
2. Is the alleged cause the only cause of the effect?

In **analogic reasoning** (reasoning based on analogy), you predict that, because two things or situations are similar in several important respects, they will be similar in other respects and will therefore produce similar results. For example, suppose you argue that a one-way traffic system in your city would relieve congestion and reduce the number of injuries and fender-benders because that system achieved these results in another city. To make a convincing case, you must prove that the two cities are alike in most vital aspects: number of vehicles and traffic officers, weather, population, condition of streets, traffic lights, and so on.

Experts who try to predict the behavior of the stock market will sometimes warn that stocks can be expected to decline because the prevailing economic conditions are comparable to those that existed just prior to some past major decline. The success rate of such predictions is not very good, usually because even though there may be many similarities between economic conditions of two different periods, there are always other conditions that are not the same.

We can see that analogic reasoning is often subject to error because the things compared may be too different. We must remember that no two things are identical. The persuasiveness of any argument based on comparison depends on very close similarity between the things compared. In other words, the points of similarity must far outweigh the points of dissimilarity.

If analogic reasoning is of limited value as a form of proof, it can be useful as description or explanation. A good way to describe something your audience is not familiar with is to compare it to something that they know well. You could, for example, prepare someone who is going to a hockey game for the first time by explaining that hockey is a lot like basketball. Similarly, you could describe the British system of government by pointing out the many ways in which it is similar to our own.

Neither of our descriptions would be complete, however, unless we pointed out the differences between hockey and basketball and between the British and U.S. systems of government. This realization suggests a very useful variation of analogic reasoning. The *comparison and contrast* form of reasoning combines similarities and differences and is a more accurate way to describe most things.

Whichever type of reasoning you choose to use—deductive, inductive, causal, or analogic—you should be able to handle your evidence (facts and authoritative opinions) effectively.

How to Persuade through Statistical Credibility

If you think that statistics (see statistics in Chapter 10) play an important role in the informative talk (and you do think that, don't you?), then ***firing off*** statistics in a persuasive speech can be crucial. Although Disraeli is credited for espousing, "There are three kinds of lies—lies, damn lies, and statistics,"[3] they are only as effective as they are accurate.

When searching for statistics, keep the following three points in mind:

1. *Sources.* Does the information come from the original source such as a governmental or private agency/study, or is it secondhand, such as from a newspaper

in other words:

firing off— stating or saying many

---

[3]Benjamin Disraeli, "The Dictionary of Human Quotation," edited by Evan Esar, (New York: Dorser Press, 1989), 66.

**in other
        words:**
secondhand—
not from the
original source

pay off—bring
results

or a news magazine quoting from the original source? If it's **secondhand,**
be sure it's complete and accurate.

2. *Reputation of the source.* Is the source a recognized authority in the field,
reflecting credibility? In other words, are you quoting from the U.S. Bureau
of the Census, the *Wall Street Journal,* or the *National Enquirer*?

3. *Recency of data.* Be sure to document the latest statistics. And you do this
by researching several sources. This extra effort will **pay off.**

Statistics alone can be boring and dry. Inject life into them. Paint them in
language that is understandable. For example, if you're talking about the gigantic $6 trillion national debt (that's with 12 zeros—want to see what it looks
like?—$6,000,000,000,000),[4] you could spark your listeners by declaring that
the debt for each man, woman, and child in the United States is almost $21,000
and it would take the U.S. Bureau of Engraving and Printing roughly 170 years
just to print the total amount.

Another approach to grab an audience's attention is to "telegraph" a litany
of short, pungent statistics.

In a nationwide survey of almost 4,500 high school students:

- 90 percent who had plagiarized from the Internet admitted that this was
  not the first time
- 74 percent had cheated on a test at least once
- 72 percent had cheated on written work
- 52 percent had taken some material from a web site without submitting
  any citation
- 30 percent cheated on a regular basis
- 15 percent had turned in papers mostly acquired from the Internet[5]

The final example of statistics below would forge an extremely persuasive
argument on the dire need to find a solution to the prodigious alcohol problem
facing the United States.

- 14 million people in the United States are problem drinkers
- $185 billion are expended yearly for treatment
- 100,000 deaths per year are attributed to alcohol
- 53 percent of adult Americans (or 93 million people 18 or older) have a
  family history of a drinking problem[6]

As we conclude this section on statistics, remember—their efficacy is only
proportional to their accuracy.

How to Persuade through Speaker Credibility

During the Watergate crisis in the 1970s, the credibility of the White House
plummeted to its lowest ebb in U.S. history. The word "credibility" was bandied

---

[4]Executive Office of the President and Office of Management and Budget, 2002, 1.
[5]*The Patriot Ledger,* 19 February 2002, 1.
[6]National Institute on Alcohol Abuse and Alcoholism of National Institutes of
Health, 2002.

"Statistically speaking, 50% of all married people are women."

about daily—in newspapers, in magazines, on television, on radio, and in conversations everywhere. The scandal had reached such alarming proportions that people no longer believed any statements issued from the White House. Its credibility, an intangible but vital resource, was utterly destroyed.

When an audience believes a speaker and has faith in him or her, the speaker enjoys **credibility.** Credibility doesn't just happen; it has to be earned through such personal characteristics as

- Sincerity and concern for listeners
- Tact and friendliness
- Reputation and character
- Self-confidence and poise
- Experience and special knowledge of the subject

A crisis reminiscent of Watergate was the 1987 Iran-Contra scandal, in which it was revealed that members of the Reagan administration had made arms deals with Iran and had used the proceeds to finance the Contra rebels in Nicaragua. At congressional hearings, the key figure was Marine Lt. Col. Oliver North, who admitted carrying out the highly questionable deals. It appeared that North was slated to be the scapegoat for his superiors, the hapless victim of his congressional inquisitors.

What actually happened? After four days of testimony, North emerged a folk hero. He became as famous as Lee Iacocca, who, as president of Chrylser Corporation, saved the company from bankruptcy and possible extinction, and better known than Secretary of State George Schultz. He drummed up more

He really enjoys credibility.

support for the Contras in four days than President Reagan had done in six years. For a short time, at least, "Olliemania" gripped the nation; T-shirts, bumper stickers, and even pop music sang his praises.

How can we account for this sudden reversal, in which the expected victim became the victor? It was, in fact, a triumph of overwhelming credibility. We Americans admire and respect a man of courage. Colonel North appeared in uniform, wearing a chestful of combat medals and decorations. We also admire and respect a man who is dedicated to his wife and family. Colonel North insisted that not only had he been a faithful husband, he had accepted the gift of a home security system only in order to protect his loved ones. We admire and respect a man who shows loyalty to his superiors, especially if one of those superiors is the President. Colonel North made it clear that his loyalty was absolute. And finally, abandoning both military and bureaucratic jargon, Colonel North spoke in simple, folksy English that proclaimed him to be "one of us."

In short, Colonel North fully understood the elements that impart credibility to a speaker and exploited them to his advantage.

And why do you suppose that when John Walker Lindh, the "American Taliban,"[7] was returned to the United States from Afghanistan to face prosecution, he requested that his hair and beard be cut?

---

[7]*Newsweek*, 17 December 2001, cover.

We're certainly not recommending that you use a manipulative approach when you speak in private or in public—but you would be foolish not to consider the impression you're making.

Speaking of "appearance," let's consider the impression that former President Bill Clinton made throughout the Monica Lewinsky scandal. President Clinton is a very effective public speaker, some even say charismatic, and in an effort to win the American public to his side, he made every effort to appear sincere and truthful. His manner is engaging and warm; his style simple, direct, and as folksy as that of Colonel North. However, he was shown to have lied when he denied his liaison with Ms. Lewinsky. He deceived his closest aides, the Congress, the public, and his family. Thereafter, as much as he may be respected for any accomplishments associated with his Presidency, his image as a liar colors everything he did or will ever do. Even when a liar tells the truth, the nagging doubt exists. His gifts for persuasion are tainted; he is hard to believe.

To enjoy credibility, you cannot take any shortcuts or bypass any rules. If you do, and you are discovered, there is no recovery. Once you establish credibility, your reputation accompanies you whenever you enter a room, begin a conversation, or attempt to persuade someone.

A reputation as a liar drags you down, whereas a reputation for honesty and good character helps you to develop your full potential.

You'll recall that in Chapter 1 we discussed ethics. I suggest that you carefully review the subject when you are preparing your persuasive speech.

How to Persuade through Appeals to Basic Human Needs, Wants, and Desires

We all have a certain amount and degree of basic needs, wants, and desires. And these important ingredients of life have no age barrier. Many older people wish to be younger, and many younger people wish to be older. People seek a higher standard of living, ways to live longer, ways to enjoy greater health, ways to make more money, ways to be more socially acceptable and respected, and ways to be more appealing to the opposite sex.

Audience members are more easily persuaded when you can suggest ways to fulfill their basic needs, wants, and desires, such as those that follow.

Self-Preservation.   We all need food, clothing, and shelter. We want to escape accidents, fires, violence, and other risks to our well-being and our family's well-being. These needs are reflected in the escalating sales of fire and smoke detectors as well as hurricane and flood insurance. In the same vein, the demand for burglar alarms and other security systems in motor vehicles, as well as in homes and industry, has prompted some manufacturers to include them as standard equipment.

In a persuasive appeal to this need, you can assert that your position fulfills your listeners' need for self-preservation. For example, you might try to persuade the audience to buy smoke detectors by pointing out their life-saving feature.

Sexual Attraction.   Most of us want to be admired and fulfilled by the opposite sex. It's a normal desire that lasts a lifetime. This sexual need is responsible for the multibillion-dollar-a-year cosmetic and apparel industry supported by both sexes. These industries are able to persuade potential customers (audience members) that their cosmetics and apparel satisfy customers' desire to be attractive. How else can you explain the popularity of such services as mate-matching, computer dating, singles clubs and trips, and male and female escort services?

Feeling Good and Looking Good.   Again, this is a universal want, and if you can unlock the secrets of good health and grooming, you will always have an audience. Today more and more men go to hair stylists, enjoy facials, and seek the services of plastic surgeons, once patronized mainly by women. According to *Fortune* magazine, each year men spend $9.5 billion on face-lifts, eyelid lifts, hair pieces, make-up, and (are you ready for this?) even girdles.[8]

Male and female America has never been more weight-conscious. Books and articles on controlling or losing weight are everywhere—in public and private waiting rooms, in libraries, trains, planes, and buses, in our homes, and regularly (it seems) on bookseller lists. It's estimated that approximately 40 percent of all women and 25 percent of men in the United States are on a diet at any given moment, and we spend over $33 billion (that's with a "B") a year on goods and services to look more svelte.[9]

You may also be aware of the dynamic growth in the number of health clubs and weight salons that welcome both sexes and the rising consumption of fresh and natural foods, herbs, and vitamins to improve health and looks. Interest in nutrition has never been higher. At the same time, people are drinking fewer alcoholic beverages and smoking less than they used to.

in other
words:
**don't "make
it"**—don't
succeed

Social Acceptance.   Most people crave acceptance by their peers at school, at work, and in social activities. Some people continually strive for acceptance and **don't "make it"**; other people bask in acceptance without appearing to exert much effort. Some individuals would go to any length to become members of exclusive clubs, societies, or organizations or to have their children attend "very" private schools. This strong desire for social acceptance is probably the reason that so many people are taking self-help courses and purchasing record numbers of self-development books. Such resources offer ways to become socially acceptable; you can use the same technique in your persuasive speech.

Acquisition of Wealth.   Just about everyone wants wealth in some form— jewels, stocks, land, real estate, art objects, or just plain old cash. Tell your

---

[8]Margery Eagan, "Quest for Body Beautiful Crosses the Gender Line," *Boston Sunday Herald,* 15 September 1996, 6.

[9]John Langan, *Ten Steps to Building College Reading Skills,* 3rd ed. (Marlton, NJ: Townsend Press, 1998), 151.

listeners how to acquire wealth, or how to save on income taxes, and you'll have them ***eating out of your hand.***

Curiosity.   People need knowledge about many topics—science, business, sports, government, entertainment, other people, and especially themselves. If you can answer their questions, audiences will be mesmerized by your every word. This curiosity accounts for the popularity of biorhythms, psychics, numerologists, tea leaf and palm readers, and astrology. Radio and TV talk shows, as well as newspaper and magazine columns featuring these topics, enjoy large participatory audiences.

Altruism.   Altruism is the generous urge to help others without any motive of self-gain. It is on this basic urge that the United Fund, Heart Fund, Salvation Army, and various cancer research funds base their appeals for financial aid and the Red Cross bases its appeal for blood donations. The desire to be altruistic also explains why such programs as the Peace Corps and VISTA have been so successful. Fortunately, many people feel a compulsion to help others—to do something for humanity. Many of them remain anonymous, like the countless firefighters, police officers, emergency medical personnel, and other volunteers from New York and around the country who were part of the prodigious rescue operation at the World Trade Center on 9-11.

Patriotism.   Many people who don't respond to other appeals may react generously when asked to help their country. This is especially true in times of war or other national disasters. Although our sense of patriotism dipped to a low ebb during and after the Vietnam War, that antipatriotic mood reversed itself sharply during the Persian Gulf War. A tremendous surge of men and women volunteered to serve in Operation Desert Storm. This patriotism is further documented by the increasing number of public and private colleges offering ROTC military training programs and some high schools offering Jr. ROTC programs.

Identification of Speaker with the Audience.   Let's say you're going to speak to a gathering of farm workers about joining a union. If you once spent a summer picking lettuce or grapes, you should mention that experience in your introduction. Then you can relate to the farmworkers, and they will more likely feel that you understand their day-to-day problems and that you're concerned about their welfare. They will be far more inclined to accept your ideas than if you had never experienced their long hours, meager pay, and spartan housing.

Belonging.   We all belong to a family and feel loyal to it as well as to friends, schools, social clubs, political parties, and neighborhood organizations. Most of us feel a very strong loyalty to our profession and place of employment. These networks of loyalties and interrelationships strongly influence our actions and attitudes. Most people want to belong.

in other
words:
**eating out of
your hand**—
completely
captivated

So compelling is this burning need to belong that many people escape society's mainstream to join communes and cults. And some have even voluntarily participated in group suicide rituals.

Adventure.   Traveling to faraway, exotic places or experimenting with a new sport (bungee jumping, sky diving, or hang gliding) are examples of fulfilling the desire for adventure. Some people feel a compulsion for adventure laced with clear-cut danger—for example, climbing a challenging mountain or exploring a fearsome glacier, big game hunting in Africa, diving perilously deep for ship wreckage or treasure, or sailing across the Atlantic singlehandedly. To exploit this urge for adventure, travel agencies publish vivid advertisements that show people climbing mountains or hiking across glaciers. Our history is distinguished by families and individuals with a penchant for adventure—from our early pioneer settlers to our pioneers in space travel.

Since all these motives (needs, wants, desires) affect people in different ways, when you speak to persuade, you should try to appeal to your listeners through as many motives as possible.

This very basic discussion of human needs, wants, and desires merely ***touches the surface*** of the vast, tremendously complex subject of human **motivation** and persuasion. It is a fascinating area with endless frontiers.

Remember this: to convince people, you should appeal to their minds and emotions; one reinforces the other.

in other words:
touches the surface—only approaches the subject; lacking in depth

How to Persuade by Using the Motivated Sequence

The Motivated Sequence (MS) of persuasion was created by Alan Monroe, late professor of communication at Purdue University. He distilled this method of persuasion from many years of conducting sales training programs in the business world. Basically, the MS method consists of five steps:

1. *Arouse attention to the need or problem.* State how this problem affects your listeners—their health, happiness, security, financial savings, etc.
2. *Describe the need or problem in its various facets.* Explain to your listeners the reasons why they should be concerned about the problem and the urgent need for its resolution.
3. *Satisfy the need.* Present a plan of action that will meet the needs or solve the problems of your audience. Provide evidence that the plan of action has helped others.
4. *Visualize the results.* Show listeners how adopting your plan of action will change their lives for the better. On the other hand, if they reject the plan, show how their lives will get worse.
5. *Call for action.* Challenge your listeners to take action, if possible, right then and there, to start changing things. Since getting started is usually hard, try to get them to take one specific step—such as signing a protest statement or making a pledge not to smoke anymore—and the next step will be easier.

CAUTION *You must know where your listeners stand on the problem or issue. They may need reinforcement or encouragement on just one or two of the five steps. If that's the case, concentrate your efforts there.*

Let's see how the Motivated Sequence can be applied to a speech. You will remember that in Chapter 8, we presented the skeleton of a talk attempting to persuade the audience to visit Nana Vasile's restaurant. Here is another perspective on that same talk, showing how it can be adapted to follow the steps of the Motivated Sequence:

Introduction

You've just come home from an exceptionally difficult day. You're exhausted, your blood sugar is low, and you're starved. But the last thing you want to do is go out to the kitchen and slave over a hot stove to prepare dinner.

[Arouse attention to the need or problem.]

You need to be pampered. Your jaded appetite requires a special treat and your jangled nerves need to be soothed—but an inspection of your wallet reveals that you don't have very much money to last you until payday.

[Describe the need or problem in its various facets.]

Body

I know just the solution: go out for dinner at Nana Vasile's. I recommend Nana Vasile's because the food is outstanding, the atmosphere is charming, and the prices are right. [Describe the food, the atmosphere, and the prices.]

[Satisfy the need.]

Conclusion

[Visualize the
results.]

Picture yourself relaxing while you and the special someone in your life feast on your favorite meal in the tastefully decorated, romantically lit dining room to the accompaniment of soft background music—without having to be nervous about the inevitable arrival of your check.

[Call for action.]

　　If the picture I've just painted appeals to you, pay a visit to Nana Vasile's. You'll be glad you did!

A Sample Persuasive/Nominating Speech with Outlines

Just because we categorize a speech as entertaining, informative, persuasive, nominating, actuating, or inspiring doesn't necessarily mean that it is boxed in a neat compartment and features only elements of that particular category. Categories can and do overlap.

　　For example, a major nominating speech will include some elements to persuade as well as to inform because, obviously, you're trying to convince your audience not only to look favorably on your nominee, but actually to vote for him or her. The speech may also include elements to entertain as well as to inspire.

　　I am not saying that all these elements should be included in one speech, but, when you think about it, you can see how such overlapping can and does occur.

　　Can you imagine the reception of a speech that effectively includes most or all of the above categories and is brilliantly delivered? That's exactly what happened on August 14, 1996, at the National Republican Convention, when Elizabeth Dole nominated her husband, Senator Robert Dole, as the Republican candidate for President of the United States.

　　To personalize her speech and maximize its emotional content, she delivered it from the convention floor, among the delegates, rather than from behind a lectern on stage. To say that her speech literally held the audience spellbound would be an understatement.

　　Before I present Elizabeth Dole's speech, "This Is a Defining Moment in Our Nation's History," here's a brief analysis of it for you to study and use as a guide as you read over her speech.

　　In nominating her husband, Bob Dole, to be the Republican candidate for the Presidency, Elizabeth Dole chose not to give a traditional speech stressing his qualifications for the office. Instead, she opted to humanize a man who had been widely perceived as austere and unemotional. Through a series of human-interest anecdotes, she portrayed Bob Dole as compassionate and deeply concerned for the less privileged members of society.

　　In addition, she focused on the "character issue" by presenting an extensive series of testimonials to her husband's integrity. Throughout the speech she also invoked themes that appeal to large segments of the Republican party. Her extended reference to Bob Dole's serious war-inflicted injuries maintained a tone of patriotism, while references to his humble origins and the final mention of his relationship with her own mother played up the "family values" theme so popular with many Republicans.

Here, now, is Elizabeth Dole's speech, followed by a sentence and topic outline.

▨ This Is a Defining Moment in Our Nation's History

1 Tradition is that speakers at National Republic Conventions remain at this imposing podium. I'd like to break with tradition for two reasons. I'm going to be speaking to friends and secondly I am going to be speaking about the man I love. Just a lot more comfortable for me to do that down here with you.

2 Now for the last several days a number of men and women have been painting a remarkable portrait of a remarkable man. A man who is the strongest, the most compassionate and tender person, I've ever known. A man who is quite simply my own personal rock of Gibraltar. Tonight I want to put the finishing brush strokes on that portrait, if you will.

3 Bob Dole, if you're watching, let me warn you that I may be saying some things that you in your modesty would never be willing to talk about. I think the people you've been serving all these years in America deserve to know, they have the right to know.

4 This is not a time to be silent. This is a defining moment in our nation's history. This election is about the vision and values that will shape America as we move into the next Century; about the character of the man who will lead us there.

5 Now Bob Dole, as you know, was born in a small Kansas town. His parents were poor, in fact at one point, when Bob was a boy, they had to move their family, parents and four children, to the basement and rent out the small home upstairs, just to make ends meet.

6 But while they were poor, perhaps, in material things, they were rich in values—values like honesty, decency, respect; values like personal responsibility, hard work, love of God, love of family, and patriotism. These are the values that led Bob on the battlefields of Italy. These are the values that helped sustain him in over three years in the hospital.

7 Now I didn't know Bob back then, but Pat Lynch did. Pat stand a moment if you will. Pat Lynch is from Boone, Iowa. Pat was one of Bob's nurses in Percy Jones Hospital, Battle Creek, Michigan. Pat has told me about Bob's good humor and how they would wheel him from ward to ward to cheer up other soldiers. She also told me that Bob was very patient, and that he tapped his inner resources so that he could endure not just day after day but month after month.

8 Also, Pat told me that when Bob was totally paralyzed and people thought he would never walk again, he willed himself to walk. He was a person of great

perseverance and determination and drive. He recovered fully except for the use of his right arm, in his three years in the hospital.

9   During that period of time I think Bob's sensitivity to problems of others was certainly deepened as well, because he's been there, he's been through adversity, he's known pain and suffering.

10   It was at this time in his life that he got to know Dr. Kelikian. Dr. Kelikian was a great surgeon of Chicago, Illinois. Dr. Kelikian had fled war-torn Armenia as a young man. Three of his sisters were not so fortunate. But he came to the United States with only $2.00 and a rug from his home land under his arm. Dr. K, at that time a young boy, worked on a farm. The owner of that farm was so impressed that he paid his way through college. He went to medical school and became a great surgeon, a master of bone and joint surgery.

11   Bob Dole went to Dr. Kelikian looking for a miracle because he wanted to be the person he was before the war, a great athlete, a person that was on his way to study medicine. Dr. Kelikian performed a number of operations and then administered tough love. He had to say to Bob, "you are not going to find a miracle. Now the choice is up to you, Bob, you can continue to feel sorry for yourself or you can get on with your life and work to make the most of what you do have.

12   Dr. Kelikian would not take a penny for any of the operations and did the same for many young veterans coming back from the war who couldn't afford the medical care they needed. So you can imagine how we cherish the friendship of Dr. Kelikian's widow Alice Kelikian and her daughter Alice.

13   Certainly Bob has known the struggle of making ends meet and he couldn't have had a college education if it were not for the GI bill. So he is going to protect and preserve and strengthen that safety net for those who need it. Also he has dedicated his life to make a difference, a positive difference for others, because of his own experience. Whether it's on the battlefield, on the Senate floor, or whether it's in his personal life. He is going to make that difference for others.

14   You know it was only about 12 years ago that I recall so well Bob coming home from a trip to Kansas. We were sitting in the bedroom talking and he said, "Elizabeth my plane was late and they were trying to rush me into a meeting out there and there were these two young people who were waiting outside the door to talk to me. They were severely disabled and they were there with their parents, Tim and Carla were their names. Tim said to me "Senator Dole, we found a source of help for people that have a disability such as ours in another state, can you help us get there?"

15   As Bob was telling me about it, I can't stop thinking about Tim and Carla. "Elizabeth, I have been meaning to start a foundation for people with disabilities for years and I haven't done it yet." Well, very soon thereafter the Dole Foundation was up and running and Bob has raised millions of dollars to help people with disabilities. Tim, thank you for inspiring Bob Dole to start the Dole Foundation for people with disabilities. Tim, I want to thank you for your courage and your spirit. Thank you, and we love you.

16   I remember about 10 years ago Bob and I were about to celebrate our birthdays, which are 7 days apart in late July. Bob suggested a reverse birthday party. He said, "Let's go to Sara Circle," which is a very special place in inner-city Washington that houses and administers to elderly poor. He said, "Let's find out what the 30–40 residents most need and want and give them the gifts, and give them the party.

17   So that is what we did, and we have had many wonderful visits there with cherished friends, the most recent about three weeks ago. And I remember a Thanksgiving about three or four years ago. Bob called up and he said, "You know, Elizabeth, I would like to do something different this Thanksgiving," and he sounded kind of sheepish, because he had already put the plan in motion. I said "Bob, what would you like to do?" He said, "I have invited 25 young people and their church sponsors to have Thanksgiving dinner with us." He had already reserved places for us and he had TVs put in so the kids could watch the Redskins game.

18   But I think what touched us so deeply was after they had finished their Thanksgiving meal and they had finished watching the game, they began to talk about their life stories. The common thread that ran through so many of their stories was that these kids had until recently never heard someone say, "I care about you. I care about you."

19   Ladies and Gentleman you never read about that Thanksgiving dinner in the paper or heard about it in the media, because Bob Dole never told anyone about it. He did it from his heart. He wants to make a difference, a positive difference for others because he cares. Because that is who he is.

20   I will certainly not forget his last day as majority leader of the United States Senate. I was seated up in the balcony, you know, and I was watching as Senator after Senator, Democrat and Republican, stood and paid tribute to my husband on the Senate floor.

21   They talked about his countless legislative achievements. How he had led the United States Senate to successfully pass the largest tax cut in the history of the United States of America. They talked about how he saved Social Security. I want to quote from a letter.

22   This is Claude Pepper, as you know he was champion of seniors. He wrote to Bob on May 11, 1983, and thanked Bob for his extraordinary contributions, saying, and I quote, "You never lost hope and faith in our accomplishing the immeasurable task in saving Social Security. We could never have produced these results without your skill and sincerest desire to make a meaningful contribution.

23   That's leadership ladies and gentleman.

24   They also talked about how Bob had led the Senate just last year to save Medicare, to increasing spending 62%, only to have the White House veto the legislation, providing no other alternative for saving the system, except a multi-million dollar ad campaign to scare our senior citizens.

25   They talked about Bob's incredible ability to bring people together and his sense of humor. That reminds me of the time I was up for confirmation hearings before one of the committees of the Senate for Secretary of Transportation and my husband introduced me.

26   You know what he did to me? He sort of did a take-off on Nathan Hale, 'And I regret that I have but one wife to give for my country's infrastructure!' That's Bob Dole. But above all these, Senators, Democrats and Republicans talked about Bob's character, his honesty, his integrity.

27   I remember Senator Pete Domenici, the beautiful speech that you gave and when you concluded your speech you said, "The next majority leader of the United States Senate had better know that he had better be honest, he had better tell the Senate the truth because Bob Dole knew no other way." Remember that Pete?

28   Diane Feinstein, Democrat of California said that "Bob Dole's word," listen to this now, "Bob Dole's word is his commitment and his commitment is a matter of honor and we often disagree on issues," she said, "but even when we disagree I know where I stand with Bob Dole and I know I can trust his word."

29   And that is why ladies and gentlemen, why Bob Dole's fellow Senators elected him 6 times to be their leader. Because they know he is honest and trustworthy, a man of his word, and his word is his bond, and they know he has exceptional leadership skills.

30   Isn't that exactly what we want in the President of the United States? You see these are the people, just think about this, these are the people who know him so well that they have worked with him day after day, year after year. They know what his judgment is like under pressure, that is why they continued to put their faith and trust in him, making him the longest serving Republican leader in Senate history, 11 years.

31   I am also very proud of the fact that the employees of the United States Senate, the waiters and waitresses, and others who work there, voted Bob twice—4 years apart—two surveys—as the nicest, friendliest Senator of all 100 Senators.

32   These are employees like Trudy Parker, who is a member of the United States Capital police. Trudy, bless your heart, Trudy was the first person that Bob saw on his way to work every morning while he was in the Senate.

33   On that final day, I can still see you and I will always remember it forever. You threw your arms around my husband with tears streaming down your face and you said, "Elizabeth, everywhere you go people tell you that they love Bob Dole because he always had a kind word for everyone," bless you Trudy, thanks.

34   Now let me just say I could go one and on sharing stories about this loving husband and father, this caring friend, please indulge a very proud wife this one final story that neither I nor a 95-year-old mother will ever forget.

35   When Bob was dating me, he used to go to North Carolina a lot and visit my parents. One morning unbeknownst to me he left his bedroom and went down to where my mother was fixing breakfast in the kitchen. He had a towel over his arm and shoulder that had been disabled in the war. He said, "I think, Mrs. Hanford, you ought to see my problem." Mother said, "Bob, that is not a problem, it is a Badge of Honor."

36   My fellow Americans I believe that in the years to come future generations will look back to this November, and say, "Here is where America earned a Badge of Honor.

37   Here is where we elected a President who gave us more opportunity, a smaller and more efficient government, and stronger and safer families.

38   Here is where we elected a better man who led us to a better America, because here is where we elected Bob Dole.

39   God Bless You All.

Her speech was a great success, prompting many columnists to proclaim that it was one of the greatest speeches ever delivered at any national political convention.

Here is a sentence outline of that speech:

Title

This Is a Defining Moment in Our Nation's History

Purposes

I. To support the nomination of Bob Dole as the Republican candidate for the Presidency

II. To humanize a man frequently perceived as severe

III. To emphasize the "character issue" in the 1996 presidential campaign

Thesis Statement

As we move into the next century, America needs a president who has vision and character; a president rich in in values like honesty, decency, respect, and patriotism; a president who accepts personal responsibility and has an enviable record of extraordinary leadership.

Introduction

I. Because the content of my remarks is intimate, I am going to speak down here with you, away from the podium.

II. I am going to fill in the details of a remarkable portrait of a remarkable man.

III. This is a defining moment in our nation's history.

Body

I. Bob Dole comes from humble origins: poor in material things but rich in values.

II. Bob spent three years in the hospital recuperating from war injuries.

   A. Through that ordeal, he demonstrated his good humor, strength, determination, and sensitivity to others.

   B. He was fortunate enough to come under the care of Dr. Kelikian.

     1. Dr. Kelikian had transformed himself from a penniless immigrant into a great surgeon.

     2. After his surgery on Bob, Dr. Kelikian challenged him: "Get on with your life and work to make the most of what you . . . have."

III. Since Bob took advantage of the GI Bill to pursue his education, his gratitude ensures that he will protect and preserve and strengthen the safety net for those who need it.

IV. Bob's compassion can be seen in several typical acts:
   A. His encounter with two disabled young people led Bob to establish the Dole Foundation to help people with disabilities.
   B. He once held a "reverse birthday party" at Sara Circle.
   C. Another time, he invited twenty-five young people and their church sponsors to join us for Thanksgiving dinner.

V. Bob's integrity and determination to make a difference are revealed by numerous testimonials:
   A. His Senate colleagues credited him with passing the largest tax cut in history and enacting legislation to save Medicare.
   B. Claude Pepper thanked Bob for saving Social Security.
   C. Diane Feinstein cited his honesty and trustworthiness.
   D. The U.S. Senate elected him six times to be its leader.
   E. Employees of the Senate twice voted Bob the nicest, friendliest of all 100 Senators.

VI. One final story: Bob once showed my mother his badly injured arm and shoulder, telling her "you ought to see my problem."

Conclusion

Future generations will look back on this election and say, "Here is where America earned a Badge of Honor."

Here is a topic outline of the same speech:

Title, Purpose, and Thesis Statement

(Same as in the sentence outline)

Introduction

  I. Speak away from podium to be intimate
 II. Portrait of a remarkable man
III. Defining moment

Body

  I. Humble origins but rich in values
 II. Hospitalized for war injuries
    A. Courage through his ordeal
    B. Under the care of Dr. Kelikian
      1. Doctor's background
      2. Doctor's advice to Bob
III. Bob's education and caring philosophy

IV. Examples of compassion
    A. Establishment of Dole Foundation
    B. Birthday party anecdote
    C. Thanksgiving dinner anecdote
V. Integrity and determination shown by testimonials
    A. Largest tax cut in history and Medicare legislation
    B. Claude Pepper tribute
    C. Accolade from Diane Feinstein
    D. Six times was elected leader
    E. Tribute from Senate employees
    F. Final story of Bob and my mother

Conclusion

VI. Future generations and "Badge of Honor"

Some Suggested Topics for Persuasive Talks

1. What's all the fuss about stem cell research and cloning?
2. Military tribunals should (not) be allowed during times of national crisis.
3. Colleges that receive federal funds should (not) be required to offer ROTC programs on campus to students.
4. The federal government should (not) insure employee pension funds from companies that go bankrupt.
5. The United States and energy independence
6. Whoever believes the "customer is always right" also probably believes in the tooth fairy.
7. Internet addiction—good or bad?
8. The efficacy of "home schooling."
9. Cell phones should (not) be banned from restaurants and other public places.
10. You can (cannot) be a career woman and an effective mother.
11. Olympic judges should be paid professionals rather than volunteers, in an attempt to eliminate all possibility of improprieties.
12. Libraries should (not) be responsibile for protecting children from Internet pornography.
13. Convicted rapists should (not) be castrated.
14. We should replace the income tax with a flat tax or a national sales tax.
15. We should do away with plea bargaining.

For more suggested topics, see Appendix B.

Quick Clicks

Welcome to a "surprise search." To further enhance your research or simply to harvest more information about some of the things you studied in this
chapter, just drop in at any of the following addresses. What
you'll discover may be serious, educational, bibliographical, surprising, factual,
or even downright humorous. But it will definitely be informative.
    So, go ahead and give a "Quick Click."

www.historychannel.com/speeches
www.mbcnet.org/debateweb/html/index.htm
http://douglassarchives.org/directory/General_Collections_of_Speeches_
    and_Historical_Docs
www.historyplace.com/speeches/previous.htm
www.startingpage.com/html/quotations.html
www.onlinenewspapers.com
http://oyez.nwu.edu/
www.intrepidsoftware.com/fallacy/toc.htm

Things to Discuss in Class

1. List two topics for a persuasive speech that would affect members of your class. Explain what methods you would use to win their sympathy and motivate them to react the way you want them to.
2. Excluding the topics previously listed, give two topics for speeches to persuade.
3. Evaluate two TV commercials as to their intended audience and the persuasive appeal(s) used. Did the commercials accomplish their purpose?
4. Prepare a five-minute gripe talk about something at your school or place of employment. Present a solution to the situation and conclude by suggesting a form of action for your audience to take.
5. Give an example of how you would persuade an audience using appeals to self-preservation and sexual attraction.
6. Give an example of how you would persuade an audience using appeals to feeling and looking good and social acceptance.
7. Give an example of how you would persuade an audience using appeals to acquisition of wealth and curiosity.
8. Give an example of how you would persuade an audience using appeals to altruism and patriotism.
9. Bring to class two newspaper or magazine advertisements and discuss the appeal(s) used to influence the intended audience.

What Do You Remember from This Chapter?

1. List three purposes of talks to persuade.
2. What is the benefit of anticipating questions and objections?
3. Name three ways to persuade people.

4. List three elements that contribute to a speaker's credibility.
5. Is credibility the sole requirement for persuading people? Explain.
6. Name three basic needs of individuals to which speakers might appeal.
7. List three questions that you should ask yourself concerning an audience for whom you are planning a persuasive talk.
8. List two speakers you consider to have credibility and defend your choices.
9. Give an example of inductive reasoning.
10. Give an example of deductive reasoning.
11. Give an example of causal reasoning.
12. Give an example of analogic reasoning.
13. Explain the Motivated Sequence.
14. Explain fact, opinion, and inference.
15. List two things to keep in mind when researching statistics.

Vitalize Your Vocabulary

When you communicate, you often use number words or number ideas, but did you ever wonder where the numbers come from? Most English number words derive from either Latin or Greek (L or G). For example:

Source Words	Meanings	Number Words
semi (L)	half	semicircle, semicolon
hemi (G)	half	hemisphere
uni, from unus (L)	one	unit, union, unison, unilateral
primus (L)	first	primary, primate
monos (G)	single, solitary	monarch, monocle, monogamy, monolog
sesqui (L)	one and a half	sesquicentennial
bi, bin (L)	two	bigamy, binary, binocular
tri (G)	three	tripod, triad, trilogy
quadr, quadri (L)	four	quadrangle, quadrant, quadrille
penta (G)	five	pentathlon, Pentagon, pentateuch
quin, quint (L)	five	quintet, quintuplets
decem (L)	ten	decade, decathlon, December
deca, deka (G)	ten	decalogue
decimus (L)	tenth	decibel, decimal
centum (L)	100	centennial (see "Bi"), centipede
mille (L)	1,000	millennium
kilo (G)	1,000	kilometer, kiloton
mega (G)	1,000,000, extremely large	megaton, megabuck
myriad (G)	a large, indefinite number	myriad is used as an English word
micro (G)	1/1,000,000, extremely small	microscope, microeconomics

Roman Numerals

Roman numerals, although centuries old, are still used today. They may indicate the order of rulers, political or religious, such as King Louis XIV or Pope John XXIII. They can be seen on some ships as the Queen Elizabeth II and might also be used by some publishing houses. (Look at the page numbers at the beginning of this book from the Table of Contents through the Preface.) Roman numerals can often be seen during the credits of some motion pictures, and displayed on gravestones and buildings. They're even used in the Superbowl and the Olympics. Now let's review how to read them.

I = 1	C = 100
V = 5	D = 500
X = 10	M = 1,000
L = 50	

1	I	12	XII	23	XXIII	60	LX
2	II	13	XIII	24	XXIV	70	LXX
3	III	14	XIV	25	XXV	80	LXXX
4	IV	15	XV	26	XXVI	90	XC
5	V	16	VXI	27	XXVII	100	C
6	VI	17	XVII	28	XXVIII	200	CC
7	VII	18	XVIII	29	XXIX	250	CCL
8	VIII	19	XIX	30	XXX	500	D
9	IX	20	XX	33	XXXIII	700	DCC
10	X	21	XXI	40	XL	900	CM
11	XI	22	XXII	50	L	1,000	M

You'll notice that when a smaller number is placed before a larger number you subtract, e.g., IX = 9 and XIX = 19; and when a smaller number is placed after a larger number you add, e.g., XXXI = 31 and LX = 60. When you put a horizontal line over a number you multiply that number by 1,000, so $\overline{X}$ = 10,000 and $\overline{M}$ = 1,000,000.

Show and Tell . . . Adding Sight to Sound

In one of the most famous and fateful incidents in the Bible, the Lord summoned Moses to the top of Mount Sinai. There He appeared to Moses in the form of a fiery cloud, and there—to the appropriate accompaniment of thunder and lightning—He presented Moses with the Ten Commandments. That, so far as I know, is the earliest recorded use of audiovisual techniques for mass education.

— Harold Howe II, former U.S. Commissioner of Education, addressing the National Audiovisual Association

After reading and understanding this chapter, you should:

- Understand the power of audiovisual aids to persuade an audience

- Understand the value of using audiovisual aids to enhance and complement your talk

- Become familiar with the various types of audiovisual equipment and basic computer technology and know what to be aware of when using them

- Be able to select a topic and present a demonstration talk on it

chapter
preview

Specialists in modern educational psychology agree on at least one principle: the more senses are involved in learning, the greater the learning. That is a convincing reason to use audiovisual aids whenever you think they will enhance your presentation.

This chapter reviews historic events that graphically display the power and impact of audiovisual media.

Audiovisual aids described in this chapter include charts and graphs, flip charts, photographs, chalkboards, slides, overhead transparencies, audiotapes and videotapes, document cameras, records, models, and maps. Several points on how to use and operate projectors and similar equipment are presented. Among the most significant are computers. Advances in technology make it practical and convenient to integrate live online materials as well as prepackaged segments to many types of presentations, including multimedia.

Also discussed is the demonstration talk: what it is, how to prepare for it, and how to present it.

How Visuals Can Aid You

You may recall that in Chapter 10, the first principle of learning we discussed was that people learn better and retain information longer when you, the speaker, involve as many of their senses as possible. This chapter is devoted entirely to adding visuals to your speech, to help make your presentation more interesting, educational, memorable, and even, perhaps, more entertaining. Using visual aids effectively can help capture and hold your audience's attention, create a pictorial image in their minds, and greatly enhance their ability to retain what they're viewing.

If your primary language is not English, visual aids can provide additional meaning and value as you speak. If you are concerned that you may not be completely understood, you can fortify your message and your confidence by displaying key or troublesome words along with your visuals to enable your audience not only to *hear* what you have to say but also to *see* what you're saying. In other words, allow the visuals to share the spotlight, so that all the attention won't be exclusively on you.

Consider the Impact of Audiovisual Aids

The power of pictures (moving or still) to persuade can be overwhelming. Permanently branded in the memories of countless millions of people throughout the United States and the world are vivid photographs, films, or videos of such tragedies and historical events as:

- The sickening spectacle of the Space Shuttle *Columbia* breaking apart on reentry February 1, 2003, somewhere over Texas and killing all seven astronauts. (Do you remember the *Challenger,* January 28, 1986?)
- The diabolical countenance of John Walker Lindh looking at us from the cover of *Newsweek* magazine (Dec. 12, 2001). The 20-year-old American went to Afghanistan and fought for the Taliban and was later discovered and captured in an Afghanistan prison with a group of Al Qaeda and Taliban fighters.
- The revealing and repulsive videotape of Osama bin Laden and a sheik (released in Dec. 2001) proudly making a number of gleeful references to the infamous 9-11 attacks.
- The gaping hole in the side of the U.S. destroyer, the *U.S.S. Cole,* as a result of a terrorist bomb (Oct. 2000) as the ship refueled in the port of Aden in Yemen. The attack killed seventeen sailors and wounded forty-two.
- The countless death scenes of innocent women, children, and men caused by terrorist activities in Israel, Palestine, and Northern Ireland.
- The incredible conflagration in a Lima, Peru, shopping area in which over 265 people perished (Dec. 2001).

"Let's talk about the great floods of 1993."

- The explosion, fire, and crash of France's *Concorde* flight #4590 just after take-off in Paris (July 25, 2001), which killed all 109 aboard and five on the ground.
- The death camps and crematoria of Nazi Germany, in which millions of Jews and others were murdered during World War II.
- The shoot-out and total destruction by fire of the Branch Davidian cult compound in Waco, Texas, where at least seventy-two men, women, and children were consumed by the inferno in 1993.
- The nuclear power plant "meltdown" at Chernobyl in the Ukraine in 1986.
- The massacre of Chinese students who raised the Statue of Liberty during a pro-democracy demonstration in Tiananmen Square in Beijing, China, in 1989.
- The assassination of President John F. Kennedy in Dallas in 1963.
- D-Day, June 6, 1944.
- The car crash in Paris, France, in August 1997, which took the life of England's Princess Diana, and the billions who mourned at her globally televised funeral.

You may have viewed on TV or have seen in various publications some of these horrific events. If not, grab this opportunity to do a little research to expand your knowledge of history. Any one of these events could be "developed and pictured" into an interesting and dynamic speech.

Finally, who can or will ever forget the U.S.'s Second Day of Infamy (do you know the first?), September 11, 2001, when an enemy launched an attack on the United States. Two hijacked passenger jets crashed into the World Trade Center (WTC) in New York, collapsing the twin towers and a third building in the WTC. A third hijacked passenger jet crashed into the Pentagon in Washington, D.C., and a fourth, which some government officials believe was headed for the White House, crashed instead (thanks to some passenger and staff heroics), into a field in Somerset County, Pennsylvania.

Live television and radio (sight and sound) transmitted these incredibly devastating and heart-shattering scenes into our homes and cars. Actually to see the two planes crash and explode into the towers; to view some desperate people in the buildings, some as high as ninety stories up, jumping to escape the charging flames; to witness the horrified and panicked expressions frozen onto countless terrified faces as people covered with ashes and soot fled from the collapsing towers; to watch the unimaginable heroics of the New York firefighters, police officers, emergency personnel, and many volunteers as they searched for survivors; all this almost defies description.

By evening on September 11, 2001, approximately:

- 3,000 people had died in and around the World Trade Center
- 260 people had died in the four hijacked planes
- 120 people had died at the Pentagon

Live television from the scene followed by the graphic and mind-numbing photographs in newspapers and magazines only magnified the awesome power and "jolting" impact these events had on us. (For a moving and hard-hitting "War on Terrorism" speech to a joint session of Congress, to the American people, and to our enemies, see President George W. Bush's speech in Appendix A.)

Now, let's explore how to use this incredible power in your presentations.

Igniting Your Presentations

After speaking with numerous business executives and managers, I learned how amazed they are at the huge number of sales presentations that fizzle. Yet, with a little more effort and imagination in the use of **audiovisual aids,** such presentations can convince associates at a business conference, win over potential clients to the speaker's viewpoint, or close a crucial sale. Remember, hearing and seeing fortify believing. (That rhymes.)

Fortunately, more and more companies are realizing the importance of making presentations with audiovisual aids and have established in-house media departments. Some of the larger insurance, utility, and industrial companies have media production studios that rival commercial radio and TV stations.

Familiarize yourself with the resources available to you. Photos taken with a simple camera, for example, can be scanned and saved to a floppy disk or e-mailed without a lot of extra expense. A basic Internet connection and a standard Web browser simplifies access to all sorts of audio and video files that can be easily integrated into a presentation. Although you may not have access to a first-class team of media production professionals, with some preparation, imagination, knowledge of visual aids, and computer graphics you can offer a successful audiovisual presentation or demonstration talk.

Because of the increase in TV viewing, acquiring information visually is, to a disturbing extent, replacing reading. This fact is substantiated by the dismally low reading scores in the public schools. Another depressing fact is that many adults rely so much on their TV sets for news and informational programs that the degree of illiteracy in this country is growing at an alarming rate.

How alarming? This should ***ring some bells.*** In a survey involving 180 million adults, most of whom attended twelve years of public school, over 95 percent (or 174 million) couldn't read, write, and figure well enough to go to college; two-thirds (or 120 million) didn't have the "literacy proficiency" to go to high school; and nearly 25 percent (one-quarter, or between 40 and 44 million) just couldn't read.[1] Another survey, entitled *Adult Literacy in America*, reports (and I'm glad that you're sitting down) that approximately 90 million Americans over the age of 16 are, according to most workplaces, basically unfit for employment.[2]

Just so you'll know ***what's going on*** in some other countries, consider these further facts. In Japan, there is virtually no illiteracy. In Germany, the school year is two months longer than ours. And in South Korea, students go to school on Saturdays.

Most U.S. high school graduates have seen 15,000 hours of TV and, as a result, expect speakers to use visual aids.

The addition of a few graphs (see Figure 12.1), charts, pictures, models, slides, movies, videotapes, audiocassettes, or records, together with a dash of creativity, can transform an average presentation, whether in the classroom or at a sales meeting or business conference, into an exciting and highly motivating event.

The use of audiovisual aids is supported by an established principle of psychology: people learn far more through two senses—hearing and seeing, for example—than through one (hearing or seeing) alone. A study by psychologists shows that 85 percent of what we learn comes through our eyes and only 11 percent through our ears.[3] If some of your aids—for example, models or small objects—can be handled by your audience, then the sense of touch reinforces hearing and seeing.

---

[1]Regina Lee Wood, "Our Golden Road to Illiteracy," *National Review*, 18 October 1993, 54.

[2]*Time*, 20 September 1993, 75.

[3]Robert L. Montgomery, *A Master Guide to Public Speaking* (New York: Harper & Row, 1979), 36.

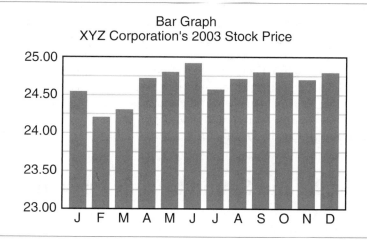

Bar Graph
XYZ Corporation's 2003 Stock Price

Line Graph

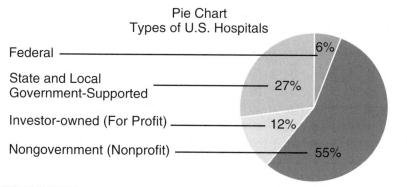

Pie Chart
Types of U.S. Hospitals

Federal ——————————————————— 6%

State and Local
Government-Supported ————————— 27%

Investor-owned (For Profit) ———————— 12%

Nongovernment (Nonprofit) ————————— 55%

FIGURE 12.1

Graphs Like These Make Very Effective Visual Aids

The American Management Association, which conducts management training sessions worldwide, tells us that from an average lecture we retain about 10 percent of the information. Using visual aids, the retention jumps to 50 percent. And, when we combine visual aids with audience participation, our retention capability soars to 70 percent. Remember, the more senses are involved, the greater the learning. (This principle is also discussed in Chapter 10.)

Another powerful reason for using visual aids is that they arouse and maintain audience interest and reinforce the message. There's no question that the effort you put into preparing visual aids pays off handsomely.

Adding Sight and Sound to Your Presentations

If you're required to give a presentation that involves using audiovisual aids, you'll probably find it challenging and rewarding, because it is informative and, in some cases, entertaining. Using audiovisual aids requires planning and practice and can result in a performance that will be a credit to you. It will afford you a rich opportunity to further develop your self-confidence, for it will place you in the role of expert lecturer.

Computers are among the easiest tools to use for delivering effective audiovisual aid. Although we'll explore the use of slides, transparencies, and audio and video materials individually, you may decide to use several of these at once. If you do, then a computer—laptop or PC—and specially designed software programs can save you a lot of time and work and, at the same time, inject more life and excitement into your presentation.

Among the options available for presentation software, Microsoft's Power-Point® is the most common. For those of you not already familiar with Power-Point, this excellent program can serve as a simple graphics display tool or a memorable multimedia presentation vehicle. Novice users can attractively present the outline of a speech by displaying one slide after the next while the verbal presentation is delivered. More experienced users can fully exploit the features of PowerPoint software to animate slide content, or integrate audio sound bites and video clips that enhance the content and delivery of speech. (Who knows, you may become another Walt Disney.) We'll look more closely at the uses of presentation software later in this chapter.

Here's something to keep in mind. Regardless of how sophisticated presentation software and hardware can be, the basics for what goes into preparing to deliver a quality presentation remain rooted in common sense.

Be sure that the physical surroundings are adequate for your audiovisual aids. If a table is needed to hold your models, be sure one is there. Check that an electrical outlet (with sufficient power) for your projector is within reach, or that you have an extension cord. Computers don't require any special electrical connectors, but, a power strip with a built-in surge protector is a good idea. If the room is wired with a jack to connect to a telephone line, or better yet a digital line (***you're golden***), then you might consider including an online portion to your presentation. You can be sure that your class will be very impressed.

in other words:

you're golden—you're making the most of a situation

Try to avoid displaying visual aids before you refer to them in your presentation. If you're going to use charts, graphs, photos, and so on, set them up beforehand but keep them covered or out of view so that your listeners will not get a sneak preview and be distracted.

Always rehearse your presentation a few times, using the same equipment you plan to use in your talk. The key to a flawless performance is practice, practice, practice. It's the only way to counter "Murphy's law": if anything can go wrong, it will. Nothing is more embarrassing in the middle of a presentation than fumbling with a piece of equipment because you haven't practiced using it.

Of course, no one is immune to the plague of Murphy's law—not even the "high and mighty" of government. Early in his administration, President Bill Clinton was scheduled to deliver one of the most important speeches of his young Presidency to a joint session of Congress. Because of last-minute editing changes, a top aide rushed the final version of the speech to the operator of the TelePrompTer just moments before speech time. In his haste, he inadvertently hit the wrong button on the computer and combined the new speech with an old one already in the system.

No one realized the blunder until President Clinton himself reached the podium, looked at the TelePrompTer, saw the old speech, and with stricken terror turned to Vice President Al Gore and declared, "We have to get this fixed."

It took almost seven minutes (which I'm sure seemed like hours) to correct the problem. Meanwhile, the eloquent and confident (and, we might add, well-prepared) Chief Executive started his critical speech on national health care to Congress and the nation using only his rough notes until the TelePrompTer caught up with him.[4] A looming disaster was averted by a calm, ***"cool,"*** and confident President.

"cool"—in complete control

Would you like another classic example of Murphy's law at work? Bill Gates, the founder and chairman of the giant computer software company Microsoft, was planning to unveil his new Windows 98 software to a large and major computer show audience in Chicago. After a brief introduction extolling the virtues of his new product, and right on cue, one of his assistants went to plug in a scanner when, you guessed it, the system crashed. Zero, nada, blank, poof! A very confident Mr. Gates quipped without missing a beat, "I guess we still have some bugs to work out. That must be why we're not shipping Windows 98, yet."[5] He, then, proceeded to another computer to complete his demonstration.

Now, allow me to present "Vasile's law." Vasile's law states that to break Murphy's law, you should perform a full-dress rehearsal of your presentation.

---

[4]*Newsweek,* 4 October 1993, 4.

[5]Cliff Edwards, AP, "Windows 98 Crashes during Gates's Show," *Boston Globe,* 21 April 1998, C7.

in other
            words:
on hand—
nearby and
available for
use

In other words, plan, prepare, and practice—several times, if necessary—to avert delay and embarrassment. Bill Gates's being prepared by having standby equipment **on hand** and displaying a quick sense of humor averted what could have been a humiliating experience, which can work for you, too.

Consider Using an Easel

Easels are useful for displaying a variety of visual aids, including large cards or poster boards bearing charts, graphs, or other information; flip charts; and photographs.

To Display Large Cards.   Charts, graphs, simple statistical tables, and the like may be prepared in advance using pieces of poster board about 3 feet by 4 feet. Place all of your cards on the easel, and as you finish with each card, remove it and place it on the floor. When preparing these cards or boards, use stiff paper that won't curl down and fall off the easel. If the cards are thin, glue or tape two of them together. Number them in case they get out of sequence, and use two or more colors for a more eye-catching presentation. You can also use different colors for headings, subheadings, and overall emphasis.

Since the audience will tend to direct its attention to portions of the visual aid that you're not discussing, prepare the material in a way that allows you to cover what is not being currently discussed. Each unit can be covered with a strip of paper or a piece of cloth that can be removed when you're ready to discuss that point.

To avoid blocking people's view, use a 3-foot pointer or a telescoping one. This will enable you to remain at arm's length from the cards and still reach the material comfortably with the pointer. Remember to hold the pointer with the hand closest to the easel and never turn your back on the audience.

Now, here are some pointers for using your pointer. As tempting as it may be, don't play with the instrument. In other words, don't tap or slap the pointer against your leg, don't rub or stroke it, don't swing it between your legs and don't continually drop it on your foot or on the floor. Remember, the purpose of the pointer is to point *at* and not play *with*. I hope you **get the point.**

get the point—
understand

To Use a Flip Chart.   A flip chart is a pad of paper approximately 27 inches by 33 inches, normally containing about fifty sheets. This form of visual aid allows you to flip each page up and over the easel when you're finished with it. You may prepare it in advance of your presentation or write on it during your talk. In either case, be sure to use a marker that won't bleed through to the pages underneath. Large blotches on pages are distracting and look amateurish.

Don't talk to the pad of paper while writing on it. Keep your attention focused on the audience. Again, the information you're putting on the pages can be made more interesting and emphatic by using more than one color.

To Display Photographs.   Photographs are an excellent medium for conveying information, especially to a small group. Size is a critical element; make sure

If there's a "bleed-through" problem, use two sheets at a time.

that the photographs are large enough to be seen by everyone. For a larger group, you may need to have enlargements made (this can be quite expensive).

A famous example of the persuasive power of photographs took place during the Cuban missile crisis in October 1962, before the United Nations Security Council. The U.S. ambassador, Adlai Stevenson, confronted the Soviet ambassador, showing him and the world enlargements of aerial photographs which proved that the Soviet Union was building offensive missile bases in Cuba. In light of this overwhelming evidence, world opinion forced the Soviet Union to dismantle the missiles and bases, thus averting a possible nuclear war.

Consider Using a Chalkboard

A chalkboard is a simple visual aid that is readily available in most classrooms. Before you write on it, be sure that it's completely erased. If possible, write before you give your presentation and cover your material with a large piece of paper or cloth so that the audience is not distracted by it. For added effectiveness and interest, use a second color of chalk along with the traditional white. Headings and major points, for example, may be written in yellow, pink, orange, blue, or purple. You can purchase a box of chalk in mixed colors. Again, a little imagination can produce a more interesting and memorable presentation. I suggest, however, not using more than two colors.

If your presentation requires writing on the chalkboard, try to minimize the amount of writing so that you can devote maximum attention to your audience. Don't speak while writing on the board. Speak either before or after, and when you do, use a pointer and stand sideways so that you can look at your listeners.

Speaking of pointers, if you really want to be *"classy,"* instead of using a wooden or metal retractable one, use a **laser pointer.** This state-of-the-art piece of equipment emits a beam that produces a red dot on surfaces up to a couple of hundred feet away. Although I doubt you'll ever be that far from your visual, you can appreciate the advantage of mobility between you and your audience.

CAUTION *When using a laser pointer, never point it at the audience and, above all, avoid direct eye exposure, because laser radiation can be dangerous.*

Although we've advised you not to speak while writing on the chalkboard, also try to avoid long periods of silence, because silence causes interest to lag. Remember to write clearly and large enough for all to see—and try to write on a straight line. Be sure to hold the chalk at a sharp angle (30 to 40 degrees) to the board; otherwise, the moving chalk will cause nerve-wracking squeals and make your audience want to run for cover.

Converging Technologies

Pretty fancy heading, but what **converging technologies** means is simply taking all the technological components that you plan to include in your presentation—the audio as well as the visual and the various equipment—and putting it all together.

Most colleges and universities have audiovisual departments and technology centers that are well stocked with various types of projection equipment that can be used with PCs, laptops, PDAs (Personal Digital Assistants), document cameras, overhead projectors, and VCRs. Usually staffed by professionals, these resource centers make it possible for you to put the finishing touches on a presentation while allowing you to retain your individual style. Maintaining your own individuality is not only important to you, but critical to your credibility.

Media resource center staff members can help you learn to use what is at your disposal in ways that really benefit your presentation. There's nothing worse than adding pictures, sound, and the bells and whistles of presentation software without applying a clear sense of how the features enhance your content. Things that flash and go pop without reason soon distract and annoy the audience instead of assisting them in their job of listening and understanding the content of your presentation.

Another way media center staff can help is by *clueing you in* to the rules. Taking the time to understand what you need to know about a certain piece of equipment or the details of how a software program works saves time, frustration, and what can sometimes become costly fumbles.

Consider Using Projectors

One of the main uses of projectors when speaking in front of an audience is for the projection of transparencies. A lot is said about the creation of **transparencies** in this chapter, since presentation software packages are making it so much easier to design effective and attractive transparencies even if layout and other graphic skills are not your strong point. Images projected via transparencies or otherwise are invaluable as a means of getting ideas across to an audience, so you'll want to find out all you can about using projectors.

A projector can take an image from any number of different sources and, by using light and lenses, enlarge and relocate the image so your entire audience can view it at the same time. You get quite a different result from passing a photograph around the room while you talk about its content than you do by projecting that same picture up on a wall or a screen so that you and the entire audience can view it together.

The type of *format* your image is in—for example, an image on disk, a paper photograph, a film clip or slide, a video, or an oil painting on canvas—usually determines your options on how you can project that image. In the recent past, pictures targeted for use in making presentations were often converted into slides in the processing lab. The projected image was clear and slide projectors helped the presenter to organize and deliver the images without a lot of fuss. Slides and carousel slide projectors are still a viable option, but the process of **digitization** has moved them to the back shelves of audiovisual departments. You may still see filmstrip projectors designed to guide strips of 35-millimeter (mm) film past a lens by a series of sproket holes and 8- or 16-mm movie projectors for sound or silent films. For the most part, however, these types of equipment designed to handle formats used before digitization are more difficult to integrate into your average presentation opportunities.

Document cameras are becoming a more commonplace tool for projecting transparencies because they can also be used to project other formats within the same presentation. Especially when you are planning a multimedia presentation, flexibility of equipment really helps. A document camera will display a transparency just like an overhead projector by turning on a light which projects from the base, sending the image through the lens for projection. What makes document cameras particularly useful for presenters is that, with a flick of a switch, the light in the base can be turned off and the machine used like an opaque projector. Opaque projection means that instead of passing light through a transparent item, the image of a book or magazine page, of the pages of a report, or of a diagram can be projected. In other words, it lets you display material in the detail and color of the original source.

Check out the site of your presentation and the technology available to you and design your presentation accordingly. Knowing some simple details ahead of time is always helpful. Many a high-tech presentation has been foiled because the presenter was left wanting a power strip or an extension cord. Here

A very effective instrument that can greatly enhance your visual presentations is the Elmo Document Camera.

are some questions you might ask ahead of time so that you know your options before limiting yourself or setting yourself up for disappointment.

- Is a PC available?
- Is there presentation software installed on the PC? Check compatibility. For example, if PowerPoint is installed on the PC, you'll need to know which version. Remember, if your presentation is made and saved on a version of Microsoft Software 200X and the machine you use is only equipped with a version of PowerPoint from the 1990s, you'll have a problem reading the files.
- Is a graphic browser installed on the PC and is the PC wired to talk to the Internet?
- How about a VCR for showing videotapes?
- Is there an overhead projector or, better yet, a document camera available?
- What type of projector is available? Is it compatible with the equipment you plan to bring? Do you need any special adaptors or connectors?

CAUTION *Be sure to position your projector so that the image it supplies is clear and your comfortable for your audience. You may be standing behind it or beside it, so be sure that the image is projected high enough so that everyone can view it easily. Take care to place all presentation equipment in a way that is least* *obtrusive for your audience. The tools of technology are just that: tools. Don't give the tools of your trade such a place of prominence that they detract from your presentation instead of adding to it.*

Consider Using Presentation Software

The multimedia capabilities of computers make it easier than ever to include audiovisual materials in your presentation. You don't have to be a wizard of technology to put sound and images into your talk.

Presentation software programs like Microsoft's PowerPoint (see Figure 12.2) include templates that can be easily customized to serve a range of projects. For example, you can create a slide show to display on your computer as a prompt to keep you on track. You can also project those same slides onto a screen or wall to support what you're saying visually for your listeners. If you wish, you can print copies of your slides to use as handouts. This will allow your audience to hear and consider your words while, at the same time, supplying them a place to jot down a few additional ideas from your presentation. Pretty fantastic isn't it? And, we're not through yet.

FIGURE 12.2

PowerPoint Screen Display
You can create, store, and project a slide presentation right from an average PC.

Don't stop at printing some of your slides as handouts. Remember those transparencies we talked so much about earlier in this chapter? PowerPoint gives you templates, designs, colors, and styles that can be adapted to create attention-getting transparencies in black and white or in color. Be original and follow your own preferences and tastes when using software applications. Creators of presentation software know that they are designing for all levels of expertise, so they leave room and opportunity for innovation. If you can take a class to learn how to get all you can from a software package that's great but in the meantime don't be afraid to experiment and take a few risks. This is how you'll learn. You can change the templates, customize your color scheme, insert art and incorporate audio and video files from your personal collection or from the Web. It's amazing what you'll be able to do when you combine a little instruction with a little imagination. *Go for it.*

Remember to pay attention to ownership and intellectual property rights. There are some important tips in Chapter 7 about how to acknowledge and properly cite material you use that belongs to someone else. Copyright law is a very serious matter, and it's your responsibility to know the laws, including changes brought about by the Digital Millennium Act. (The Digital Millennium Copyright Act of 1998 is a complex piece of legislation which made major changes in U.S. copyright law to address the digitally networked environment.)

Don't take any chances that can cast a dark cloud over you and your integrity. Use what you know is yours or what you know is in the public domain. If you have the slightest doubt, ask someone who can advise you responsibly—your librarian, perhaps.

For more creative and adventurous presenters, live, online demonstrations and examples can be produced if there's a telephone or digital line jack within reach of your computer. *Breaking news,* maps and photos, video and audio resources are all there at your fingertips on the World Wide Web via the Internet. Integrating live elements into your talk can bring a spontaneity and immediacy than can help keep your audience attentive and educationally informed and entertained. Just be sure that the material you select and your methods of presentation are appropriate to the topic and that you don't *go overboard.* Sights and sounds are not a substitute for facts, accuracy, and continuity of ideas, but rather are an enhancement to them.

I know I'm repeating myself, but you will do well to keep this in mind: do not fall into the trap of relying too heavily on one tool. Always be prepared with options if the power should go out or a connection can't be established. Have a backup plan in case the file you stored on a floppy disk suddenly can't be retrieved, or a Web server you've connected to goes down without warning. Remember what happened to President Clinton and Chairman Bill Gates. Now go and be as creative as you can be.

Consider Using Recorders and Record Players

Audiotapes, records, and compact discs can add another dimension to your presentation. For example, you might use tapes with a silent film or slides or

---

in other words:
go for it—try it

breaking news—news that is happening as you speak

go overboard—be excessive

A VCR can be a very useful aid. Be sure to position the monitor so that everyone can see it.

use CDs to illustrate a talk on music appreciation. Small cassette tape recorders are convenient to carry and to operate if you plan to interview people, to record statements, or to record sounds to enhance your presentation.

Videocassette Recorder (VCR).   Many how-to videotapes can be rented to enhance your presentation on how to do something like a particular craft, hobby, or trade. Be sure to preview the tape to decide what segment(s) you plan to use. If you want to do your own videotaping, you may be able to borrow equipment from your school.

If you plan to use a VCR, be sure that everyone in the class can see the monitor clearly. If the audience is large, consider setting up monitors on both sides of the room for maximum viewing capability. Again, your school's audio-visual department can probably help you set up the equipment if you make arrangements beforehand. Don't wait until presentation day.

Consider Using Objects

Displaying objects (for example, tools or pieces of equipment) is an excellent way to explain how something operates. If you can't bring in life-sized objects (for example, an auto engine or Stealth Bomber), bring in scale models, but be sure that they are large enough to be seen. Always stand behind or beside the object, never in front of it or between it and the audience. To sustain audience attention, it's a good idea to keep objects out of sight until the point in your presentation at which they're needed. If they're on display at the start of your talk, the audience may be more interested in the objects than in what you're trying to convey. Until you need them, they can be hidden in the recess of the lectern, in a box or bag on a nearby chair, or on the floor. If you're using more than one object, display and discuss them one at a time so that all the attention will be focused on the item under discussion.

Passing objects around the class can be tricky. If all the listeners receive the same objects at the same time, they'll be better able to follow you than if you pass around several different objects at different times. Audiences can become more engrossed in looking at objects in their hands than in what you're saying. After your talk, you might consider displaying the objects on a table so that your audience can inspect them closely.

Consider Using Handouts

in other
words:
follow your talk—proceed along with the speaker

Handouts—maps, charts, tables, photographs, and diagrams—are very effective because everyone in the class gets one, and your listeners can *follow your talk* more closely. Again, if you're planning to pass around several handouts, don't do so all at once because the audience may pay more attention to them than to what you're saying. Hand them out individually at the appropriate time during your talk, and be sure to allow the class enough time to become familiar with the contents before you resume speaking. To save time, several members of the class can assist in distributing the handouts. If you're planning to distribute handouts to be taken home, rather than pass them out during your talk, mention to your audience that they will be available following your presentation.

Preparation of handouts can be considerably simplified if you have access to a computer. Computer graphics now make it possible for the operator to create and print out many unique and imaginative visuals such as line graphs, bar graphs, charts, drawings, and three-dimensional illustrations in both black and white or color. Once you have the finished product, you can easily have copies made for projection or for handouts.

Using more than one type of visual aid is not only acceptable, but can greatly complement your overall presentation. However, if you select too many types, you *run the risk* that they will overpower your message.

run the risk—take the chance

The Demonstration Talk

One type of talk that particularly lends itself to the use of audiovisual aids is the **demonstration** (demo) **talk.** The practical value of using audiovisual aids, particularly in a demo talk, is beautifully expressed in an ancient proverb, a masterpiece in three short lines:

What I hear, I forget.
What I see, I remember.
What I do, I know.

In other words:

> Hearing is good.
> Seeing is better.
> Doing is best.

And now back to the demo talk. The objectives are:

1. To show the class how to do or how to make something, for example,
   - How to make address labels on your computer
   - How to read the label on a bottle of champagne or fine wine
   - How to use a hot-glue gun
   - How to use a scanner or digital camera with your computer
   - How to create a flower arrangement
   - How to make animals from balloons
   - How to create your own basic website.

2. To explain to the class how something operates or functions, for example,
   - How gasoline and electricity can work together in a car to produce incredibly clean emissions and high mileage
   - How solar panels or windmills gather energy
   - What keeps an aircraft from falling out of the sky
   - How to install a home security system
   - The different types of home fire extinguishers
   - The efficacy of a heat pump
   - The differences between an MRI (magnetic resonance imaging) and a CAT (computed axial tomography) scan

Without question, the demonstration talk ranks number one among students. In most cases it truly adds up to a genuine learning experience. A demonstration talk should generally take between ten and twenty minutes. A shorter time will not give you a worthwhile experience in using audiovisual aids, and your audience may just be ***getting warmed up*** to your subject when—poof, it's all over.

Consider Involving Members of the Audience

Whenever you can get a member or members of your class to participate in your demonstration talk, your effort will involve your audience more deeply. For example, if you're to demonstrate how to manicure fingernails, use a volunteer as a model. If your topic is sketching, use a student from the class as your model rather than drawing from a picture or photo. One student showed the Heimlich maneuver for aiding a choking victim. Following the lecture portion of his presentation, he demonstrated the method on a class volunteer. He then had the entire class pair off, and every member performed this life-saving technique on another. The class selected this talk as its favorite. So remember, if possible, involve members of the audience.

in other words:
getting warmed up— starting to become interested

If you're planning to use a volunteer as a part of your demonstration talk, arrange this in advance. Why? Because you want to be sure that you have a volunteer, willing and able, when the time arrives. Incidentally, most professionals who need a volunteer for their presentation "plant" one in the audience.

Consider Yourself as a Visual Aid

Remember, the most effective visual aid can be you. You can add spice and additional interest to your presentation by playing the role. For example, if you plan to show the class how to create a Caesar salad, wear a white apron and a chef's hat. If you plan to show how to set a table professionally, wear a waiter's outfit. To show the class how to take blood pressure, wear a medical uniform. If you're a police officer or firefighter and you plan to talk about some aspect of your job, wear your uniform or fire-fighting gear. With a little imagination, you can significantly enhance your visual presentation by "dressing the part."

How to Select a Topic to Demonstrate

You're probably scratching your head now and wondering, along with many others in the class, what you can demonstrate. This is a common reaction, but from years of experience I've found that those who encounter difficulty in selecting a topic usually end up with a satisfactory one. If you're having a problem, tell your instructor; a five-minute chat may turn up an answer for you.

You can approach this talk from one of two directions. You can either select a topic that you know or one that you know little about but would be interested in researching. If you choose the latter, you'll become involved in a solid learning experience.

A Topic You Know.   The natural choice is a topic you know something about. You should take inventory of your knowledge, experiences, and skills to decide which topic you will present. Did any of your jobs, full-time or part-time, require special skills? Did you receive special training in the service? What about your hobbies? Are you involved in any of the following: rollerblading; collecting CDs, sports cars, matchbook covers, wines, or stamps; cycling; shopping; or aerobics/physical fitness? Do you like to cook or bake? You'll probably be astonished at some of the things you've done or are interested in that would make worthwhile presentations. Don't *sell yourself short.*

The following are some topics that resulted in successful presentations by students whose initial reaction was "There's nothing I can do."

in other words: **sell yourself short**—underestimate your abilities

- A student who had worked in an ice cream parlor demonstrated how to make several types of sundaes.
- A football enthusiast gave an excellent presentation and explanation of the various signals used by referees. He even wore an official black-and-white striped shirt.
- A woman intrigued the class with her talk about—and demonstration of various positions in—yoga.
- A student who was a police officer demonstrated the art of fingerprinting by using classmates for subjects.

Without question, the most memorable demonstration talk was by a student who was a rather good magician. In fact, he was working his way through college by performing at children's birthday parties, bar mitzvahs, and other occasions. Well, while demonstrating his "prestidigitational" skills, he made the class disappear and I never saw them again. (Did I have you going there for a minute?)

A Topic You Know Little About.   If you're ambitious about learning, you may select a topic that you're not too familiar with, conduct research on it, probably receive instruction, and then give the presentation. This approach requires considerable preparation, but it will be rewarding.

NOTICE TO STUDENTS FROM OTHER COUNTRIES *Here's a wonderful opportunity to share with us some of the culture of your native country (customs, traditions, religions, clothing, language, etc.).*

Some Suggested Topics for Demonstration Talks

Here are some topics that you may consider for possible demonstration talks. For further suggestions, see Appendix B.

1. Forecasting the weather
2. Photography
3. Collecting (coins, stamps, figurines, etc.)
4. Performing a cultural dance
5. Showing clothing from your country of origin
6. Framing a picture
7. How to install a light dimmer
8. How to make antipasto
9. How to communicate in sign language
10. Some basic carpentry tools and how to use them
11. How to gift-wrap a package and make bows
12. Applying make-up
13. Performing card tricks
14. Giving first aid to a choking victim (Heimlich maneuver)
15. How to read the stock market page

"Step three in making a pizza is very tricky."

Quick Clicks

Welcome to a "surprise search." To further enhance your research or simply to harvest more information about some of the things you studied in this chapter, just drop in at any of the following addresses. What you'll discover may be serious, educational, bibliographical, surprising, factual, or even downright humorous. But it will definitely be informative.

So, go ahead and give a "Quick Click."

www.historychannel.com/exhibits/index.html
www.altavista.com/cgi-bin/query?mmdo=1&stype=simage
http://ditto.com
http://images.google.com
www.ukans.edu/cwis/units/coms2/vpa/vpa7.htm
www.kumc.edu/SAH/OTEd/jradel/Effective_visuals/VisStrt.html
www.du.edu/~emuhovic/2021visualaids.html

Things to Discuss in Class

1. Visit your audiovisual department and become familiar with its equipment.
2. Tell about a recent talk (presentation) in which audiovisual aids were used—for example, a commercial or a how-to project on TV or a class lecture.
3. Name a profession or occupation in which audiovisual aids play an important role.
4. Select a topic you'd like to talk about and explain which audiovisual aids you'd use and how you'd use them.
5. List a topic that would require the use of audiovisual aids. Explain.
6. Bring three types of graphs to class and explain the differences among them.
7. Watch a news program and weather report on TV and be prepared to discuss the types of visual aids used and their overall effectiveness to the "message."

What Do You Remember from This Chapter?

1. How can the use of visual aids enhance your presentation?
2. Is it permissible to use more than one aid in a presentation? Explain.
3. Explain the impact of pictures.
4. What caution must you exercise when you use handouts?
5. What should you remember if you plan to use a volunteer during your talk?
6. Explain the ancient proverb:
   What I hear, I forget.
   What I see, I remember.
   What I do, I know.
7. Name a common presentation software.
8. What is a PDA and what is its function?
9. No matter what technology you employ, why is it so important for you to maintain your individual style?

10. Explain both "Murphy's law" and "Vasile's law."

11. Why are document cameras becoming more and more popular?

12. Explain the flexibility of PowerPoint.

Vitalize Your Vocabulary

Economic and Financial

Here is a partial list of the most commonly used words you'll find when reading the business and financial sections of your newspaper or news magazine.

acquisition (n.) The purchase of one company by another.

balanced budget (n.) When receipts equal current expenditure.

balance of payments (n.) The difference between all payments made to and from foreign countries over a specific period of time based on imports and exports.

bear market (n.) A market in which prices are falling.

bond (n.) A written promise by an issuer to repay a fixed amount of borrowed money at a specified time.

bull market (n.) A market in which prices are rising.

capital gain or **loss** (n.) A profit or loss from the sale of assets such as stocks, bonds, or real estate.

common stock (n.) Share of ownership in a corporation that entitles you to vote.

conglomerate (n.) A large corporation consisting of many other different companies.

cost of living (n.) What a person or family spends on necessary goods and services such as food, clothing, and rent to maintain a certain standard of living.

deficit spending (n.) Government spending in excess of revenues.

depression (n.) An extended period of economic decline when unemployment is high, prices are low, and there are many business failures.

disposable income (n.) Personal income available to spend after taxes and expenses are paid.

dividend (n.) A sum that is paid by a company to shareholders in the form of cash or shares of stock.

Dow Jones Industrial Average (n.) An index of stock market prices, based on the prices of thirty leading companies on the New York Stock Exchange.

Federal Deposit Insurance Corporation (FDIC) (n.) A U.S. government-sponsored corporation that insures individuals up to $100,000 in any account they may have in a national bank or other financial institution.

full employment (n.) Theoretically, when everyone who wishes to work is gainfully employed.

golden parachute (n.) Provisions in the employment contracts of executives guaranteeing substantial financial benefits if they lose their positions due to a corporate takeover.

gross domestic product (GDP) (n.) The market value of all goods and services that have been bought for final use during a specific period of time. It is a measure of the economy.

individual retirement account (IRA) (n.) A self-funded retirement plan that allows employed individuals to contribute up to a maximum annual amount toward their retirement while deferring taxes until retirement.

inflation (n.) An increase in the level of prices resulting in a loss of currency value.

insider information (n.) Important facts about the condition or plans of a corporation that have not been released to the general public.

interest (n.) What you pay for borrowing money.

junk bonds (n.) Bonds that are issued by companies with low credit ratings and usually pay high interest rates because of their relatively high risk.

leading indicators (n.) A series of eleven indicators from different segments of the economy that the U.S. Commerce Department uses to predict when changes in the level of economic activity will occur.

liquid assets (n.) Assets that include cash or other things of value that can be easily converted to cash.

merger (n.) When two or more companies get together and operate as one.

money supply (n.) All of the currency held by the public, plus checking accounts in commercial banks and savings institutions.

mutual fund (n.) A portfolio of professionally and managed financial assets into which you pool your money along with thousands of other investors.

national debt (n.) The debt of the federal government.

prime interest rate (n.) The rate charged by banks on short-term loans to large commercial customers with the highest credit rating.

recession (n.) A period of economic decline when production, employment, and earnings fall below normal levels; usually lasts from six months to a year.

supply-side economics (n.) The belief that lowering income tax rates will inevitably lead to the increase of economic growth and the revitalization of the economy in general.

takeover (n.) Acquisition of one company by another company or group by sale or merger. When management is agreeable to this action, it is a "friendly takeover." When management is opposed to this action, it is an "unfriendly or hostile takeover."

A more complete listing of economic and financial terms can be found in the current edition of the *World Almanac and Book of Facts*, published by World Almanac Books.

13

Saying a Few
Words . . .
Very Few!

Let thy speech be short, comprehending much in a few words.
—Ecclesiastes 32:8

After reading and understanding this chapter, you should be able to:

- Make an announcement
- Introduce a speaker
- Present an award
- Give a thank-you talk after receiving an award
- Make a nominating speech
- Give an installation speech
- Propose a toast
- Utilize a public address microphone

chapter
preview

Since you probably already belong to or are likely to join some organizations, you may be called on to introduce a speaker, present an award, nominate someone for office, make an announcement, or give a report. You may even be asked to propose a short toast. If you're lucky, you may be elected toastmaster or function chairperson, and in that position you may present some or all of the special types of speeches explained in this chapter. As an active member of your organization, you may also be called on to respond to any of these speech situations.

This chapter briefly touches on these special-occasion talks from the standpoints of the introducer (function chairperson, toastmaster, master of ceremonies) and the person giving the response. Some examples of these talks are included.

Giving a Short Talk

As you mature and start your ascent in the business or social community, the odds are that you will be called on "to say a few words." Industry executives agree that there is no surer way for an employee to earn recognition in the company than to display an ability to communicate effectively before an audience. The same holds true for your fraternal, political, or other social activities. You'll be amazed at the respect and admiration you earn when you can comfortably give a short talk.

No set of rules encompasses all the situations that may surround a **special-occasion talk.** Many factors impinge on the talk: your personality and position, the circumstances of the occasion, the time element, the type of audience, the main speaker, and the reason for the particular talk. All these factors must be considered.

The most important characteristic of these talks is brevity. Usually the talk ranges from one to five minutes except for the toast, which is usually less than a minute. If you're the chairperson, your function is to be an intermediary between the head table and audience. You're not expected to give a ***long-winded*** speech or to poke fun at the guest of honor. Your job is to move the proceedings along quickly and smoothly, with dignity and professionalism.

in other words:
long-winded— a talk that is too long

Regarding brevity, I love the story about "silent" Calvin Coolidge, who is famous for his use of "few" words in conversation, especially before becoming the thirtieth President of the United States. It so happened that Mr. Coolidge was attending a banquet and was seated next to a woman who asked him what he did for a living. He replied, "I'm Lieutenant Governor of Massachusetts." Obviously impressed, she inquired, "Oh, please tell me all about it." His terse retort was, "I just did."

You have the opportunity to "say a few words" and the first thought that ***crosses your mind*** is, "How much could I possibly say in a short time?" Then, carefully consider the following:

crosses your mind—comes to mind

- The Lord's Prayer has 71 words.
- The Ten Commandments have 297.
- The Gettysburg Address has 266.
- General Anthony McAuliffe clearly got his message across during the Battle of the Bulge with one word: "Nuts!"
- A modern record for brevity took place in 1945, when one of President Franklin Roosevelt's wartime speeches lasted only six minutes.
- The all-time record goes to George Washington, whose second inaugural speech contained 135 words and lasted only two minutes.
- In Genesis, the story of the creation of the world is told in 400 words.

For your information (and not necessarily a warning), the longest inaugural speech on record was delivered on a chilly March day in 1841 by William Henry Harrison and lasted 1 hour and 41 minutes. The speech contained 8,445 words. (At the inauguration, President Harrison caught a cold, which developed into pneumonia, and he died precisely one month later.)[1] *So, watch it.*

There are many types of special-occasion talks, ranging from announcements to sales talks, **eulogies,** retirement testimonials, dedications, and after-dinner talks; there are commencement addresses, presenting and accepting awards as well as welcoming speeches, and there are more. However, this chapter focuses on the talks that are most likely to be of immediate concern to you.

How to Make an Announcement

At most organizational meetings, time is set aside to ask for help with a future event and to announce its time and place. **Announcements** should be short and carefully prepared, and they should include all pertinent information.

It's amazing how many announcements exclude an important bit of information—for example, the date or time of the event. Perhaps you can recall attending a meeting in which a committee chairperson announced an upcoming event, only to be asked, "What was that date again?"

How to Get the Facts

If you're responsible for gathering information for an announcement, seek an authoritative source (the president of your organization, the chairperson of a committee, or the member designated by the chairperson). Get the source's phone number so that you can check information or any changes that occur before the announcement has to be made. In preparing your announcement, include as many of the five *W*'s (who, what, when, where, why) as possible and the *H* (how).

When you've prepared the announcement, check it for all details. Ask yourself:

1. What is being planned?
2. When and where will the event be held and what about parking?
3. Do the day and date of the event coincide on the calendar?
4. Will tickets be necessary? If so, how much will they cost?
5. Where will the proceeds go?
6. Is the event open only to members?
7. What is the reason for the event?
8. Who is responsible for the event?
9. Are volunteers needed? If they are, who should be contacted?
10. If there's to be a speaker, what is his or her name?

Gather as much correct information as possible and present only vital information. Most organizations publish newsletters or bulletins that include

---

[1]*Boston Herald,* 18 February 2002, 35.

in other words:
so, watch it—
so, be careful
(like a warning)

additional details. Because of this, your announcement need not give telephone numbers of people to contact.

How to Deliver the Announcement

Delivering your announcement with enthusiasm can bolster interest and positive reaction from your audience. You may conclude your announcement by repeating key facts—for example:

> The Boston College High School Parents' Club will hold its annual May Festival on Saturday, May 18, from 9 A.M. to 4 P.M. on the school grounds. As you know, all proceeds will go toward the scholarship fund.
>
> We can still use some volunteers for an hour or two. Please check in with one of our volunteer coordinators, Mr. Joseph Robert or Ms. Mary Mary, right after this meeting. We would appreciate a little of your time and effort.
>
> Remember, our annual May Festival will be held all day Saturday, May 18, right here on the B.C. High School grounds, and we need more volunteers. Thank you.

How to Introduce a Speaker

The main problem with introducing a speaker is that, all too often, the introducer talks far too long. This situation was highlighted in an anecdote told by President William Howard Taft.

Once he presided at a meeting at which a number of distinguished guests were to give five-minute talks. The young chairman of the event rose to say a few words and rambled on for forty-five minutes. After he sat down, President Taft stood up and said: "I remember once when I was in politics, we had a meeting at which there was to be one of these preliminary addresses. One guest captured and held the platform and when he finally finished, I remarked, 'I will now present Mr. So-and-So, who will give you his address.' Mr. So-and-So arose and stated, with some heat, 'My address is 789A 22nd Street, New York City, where my train goes in fifteen minutes. Good night.' "

In sharp contrast to that angry reply is the humorous response (to a long-winded introduction) made by Alabama Senator Howell Heflin at a meeting of the American Bankruptcy Institute. "I believe," he said, "that was the most comprehensive introduction I have ever received. You omitted one thing—that in 1974 I had a hemorrhoidectomy."[2] (Now, go to your dictionary and learn a new word!)

If you're responsible for introducing a speaker, consider the following guidelines.

---

[2]*Newsweek,* 20 May 1991, 19.

Be Aware of Your Responsibility

Your primary function is to prepare and motivate your audience to listen to the featured speaker. If you can instill such interest, you've done your job.

Be Familiar with the Speaker and the Topic

As soon as you know who the speaker will be, find out as much as possible about his or her background and the subject of the speech. If she is well known, information about her will be available through her press office or in newspapers. If he is not well known, call him for a profile.

If possible, try to meet the speaker before the event to ensure that your information is accurate and current and that you know the speaker's topic. You don't want the speaker to have to correct you during his or her opening remarks. Sometimes the title of the speech will suffice; at other times it may be appropriate to mention the subject matter.

Be Brief

How often have you heard an **MC** (master of ceremonies) say, "Our speaker this evening needs no introduction," and then give a biography from birth to the present? If the speaker needs no more than a short introduction, then give it.

One of the briefest and most humorous introductions was given many years ago by former U.S. Representative Morris "Mo" Udall (D, Arizona). As master of ceremonies at a dinner, he presented Adlai Stevenson (twice governor of Illinois, twice Democratic Presidential nominee in the 1950s, and U.S. ambassador to the United Nations) in one unique sentence: "This man needs no introduction and I'll be damned if I'll give him one."[3]

The length of your introduction should not exceed two or three minutes. No better example of brevity and simplicity exists than the introduction you've heard many times, "Ladies and gentlemen, the President of the United States."

Be Careful Not to Embarrass the Speaker

Sometimes a chairperson can go to extremes in praising the speaker as one of the most brilliant, eloquent, and humorous orators of the day. This is embarrassing for three reasons: (1) the speaker very likely cannot *live up to* such an introduction, (2) the speaker probably *realizes* that, and (3) the chairperson may be preparing the audience for a resounding letdown.

in other words:

live up to—
fulfill the expectations of

---

[3]*The Boston Globe,* 17 February 1988, 29.

Be brief in your introduction.

Be Natural

If you're good at telling anecdotes and jokes or at being humorous, great. Nothing sets an audience more at ease and puts them in a receptive mood than a few laughs. It will benefit you to spice your introductory remarks with humor that directly links the speaker, the subject, and the occasion. However, if you're not a naturally humorous person, *don't try to be.* Humor in the wrong hands can be disastrous. As any professional comedian will tell you, trying to make people laugh is a very serious business.

Be Informative

It's important to know and present a balanced blend of the following pieces of information: the speaker's background, the subject of the message, the specific occasion, and the audience. Ponder each of these items separately and completely when you're preparing your introduction.

Be Careful Not to Make Personal Comments about the Speaker's Subject

This is not the time and place to **editorialize.** When you introduce the speaker's topic to the audience, don't elaborate on the topic. That is the speaker's job. You may mention the importance of the subject, its relationship to the audience, and the speaker's knowledge of it, but leave the contents to the speaker.

Be Sure to Pronounce the Speaker's Name Correctly

The most famous slip of the tongue was uttered by radio announcer Harry Von Zell when he proclaimed to the nation, "Ladies and gentlemen, the President of the United States, Hoobert Heever." Clearly, in his mind, the announcer knew how to pronounce the name; but, at that moment, his tongue thought differently and out came the blooper. There are no sweeter sounds to reach a person's ears than those of her or his name. It's worth getting it right.

If you're not positive about the exact pronunciation of the speaker's name, ask how to pronounce it in advance. If you have to, write it down phonetically.

Present the Speaker to the Audience

If you feel that the speaker is not well known to the audience, you may mention her name several times during the introduction. If she is known to the audience and you want to use a dramatic approach, you may announce her name at the very end of your introduction. After you've presented the speaker, face her and in a warm, welcoming manner, wait until she arrives at the speaker's stand; then return to your seat. (You start the applause.)

The following is an example of a speech of introduction.

> Good evening and welcome to our annual Media Awards Banquet. It is such a pleasure to see so many past recipients of these awards in our audience . . . a special welcome to all of you.
>
> It is, indeed, a rare privilege for me to have the opportunity of introducing our guest speaker for this evening.
>
> Prof. Joan Murray enjoys an international and distinguished reputation as a speaker, educator, writer, and communications consultant. She frequently appears as a guest on the nation's most popular radio and TV interview programs.
>
> During her tenure as chairperson of the Communication Department at Regis College in Weston, Massachusetts, Prof. Murray is responsible for developing media curricula in radio and television, public relations, photography, and motion picture production.
>
> Under her direction and leadership, the college's studio-classrooms, production facilities, and equipment represent the ultimate in state-of-the-art design and operation. Students enjoy individualized as well as small group learning experiences.
>
> Since Prof. Murray's many innovative approaches in media education and curriculum development have attained national prominence, she is a constant recipient of invitations to speak or conduct communication workshops not only in academe but also in private industry. As a matter of fact, she has just returned from a lecture tour in England, Germany, France, and Italy, where she discussed "International Communication," which is also her topic this evening.
>
> We are extremely fortunate to have her here this evening, and I'm delighted to introduce our featured speaker, Prof. Joan Murray.

How to Present an Award

In planning to present an award you should keep in mind the following key points.

Refer to the Award Itself

It is important in your opening remarks to call attention to the award that is about to be presented. What is its significance; when and why was it founded? Who was its first recipient? Is it presented annually or only on special occasions? These are some questions to consider, and you may think of others.

Refer to the Occasion

This will prepare your audience for what is about to take place. You will attract the audience's attention and interest.

Refer to the Recipient

Explain why and how this individual or group was selected. Be sure to point out the achievements that led the recipient to this honor.

Refer to Those Whom You Represent

Mention if the award is being presented on behalf of a lodge, council, club, or company. The source of the award is of vital interest to the recipient and to the audience. The source certainly deserves praise. Express the sincere goodwill of the source and its satisfaction with the person chosen.

Make the Presentation

For the sake of building interest and including an element of mystery, you may wish to mention the name of the recipient last. Then, if the award can be handled easily, hold it up for all to see, read the inscription on it, present it, and congratulate the recipient. Then allow the recipient the opportunity to respond.

The following is an example of a speech used in presenting an award.

> As you know, the highlight of today's annual dinner is the announcement of the CHEF OF THE YEAR. This is the highest honor that a member can receive because the honoree is selected by his or her peers of the Massachusetts Chefs de Cuisine by secret ballot.
>
> This award is presented annually in memory of Peter Berrini, a well-known and respected executive chef and one of the original founders of the American Culinary Federation. It is presented to a member "for years of dedicated and distinguished service and for exemplifying the highest standards of character and unselfish devotion" not only to this organization but to the culinary arts profession as well.

This year's gold medal winner is a very special person. He is a member of the American Academy of Chefs, of which there are only 650 throughout the United States and Puerto Rico, and is a Certified Executive Chef, of which there are only 1500 nationwide. As a past president of the Massachusetts Chefs de Cuisine he has held office for four consecutive years, the longest in the 14-year history of this organization. During his first term as president, he was personally responsible for the largest enrollment of new members of any chapter in the United States, for which he received a special national citation from the prestigious American Culinary Federation.

The eighth recipient of the CHEF OF THE YEAR award is a full professor and is department chairperson of the Culinary Arts and Hotel/Restaurant Management programs at Bunker Hill Community College in Boston for both day and evening divisions. He is a food service consultant, lecturer, and writer. And you may have heard or seen one of his many appearances on radio and television programs.

It's a distinct honor and privilege for me to announce that the members of the Massachusetts Chefs de Cuisine have unanimously voted Walter Bryant as their CHEF OF THE YEAR.

How to Accept an Award

Sometimes when an award is presented, no formal reply is needed or expected. If that's the case, a simple, sincere "thank you" is sufficient. At other times a reply might be appropriate or called for by audience cheers of "Speech, speech." If you're going to a function and there is the slightest possibility that you may be given an award, prepare a thank-you statement. In preparing a speech of acceptance, use the following techniques.

Be Honest

If the award comes as a total surprise, your facial expression may attest to the fact, but don't hesitate to express your surprise orally. The audience will be more delighted. You should have no difficulty expressing your sincere gratitude. Sometimes a heartfelt "thank you very much" will suffice.

Call Attention to the Award

Explain what the award means to you. (You might want to refer to others who have received the award previously and you may want to mention how pleased you are to join their esteemed company.)

Be Generous in Your Praise

If you're accepting an award on behalf of a group or team, be sure to share the honor with them. If it was a singular effort and someone inspired you, don't keep it a secret. If appropriate, mention the future and how this honor may affect your efforts and plans. Don't forget to thank those responsible for presenting you with the award. It may also be appropriate to thank the individual who made the presentation. The following is an example of a speech to accept an award.

> There are two things I will always remember this evening for. One, I'm at a loss for words, and two, I'm deeply moved to receive this plaque naming me the recipient of your "Outstanding Member of the Year Award."
>
> I know what this award represents, because I have actively participated in the voting for our first two recipients. It is indeed a thrill for me to join their elite company.
>
> The honor you have presented me with this evening will always remain very special. I wish to thank the members of the nominating committee and each and every one of you for your most generous expression of recognition.
>
> I will always cherish this award and the precious moments of this evening. Thank you very much.

How to Make a Nominating Speech

As you become more involved in organizations, whether scholastic, business, or political, you may have the opportunity to nominate someone for office. If you belong to an organization, perhaps you recall a meeting when nominations for offices were called for. *Someone from the floor*, after being recognized by the chairperson, may say, "I would like to place in nomination the name of Mrs. Eunice Flagg" or "I would like to nominate Mr. Vincent Shea." What you heard were *names* placed in nomination. Following are some suggestions to use if you want to nominate not just a name, but a person worthy of the office.

Describe the Responsibilities of the Office

Mention the specific requirements attached to the office. Include its duties, importance, and broad responsibilities. (Remember that you want to *build a powerful case* for your nominee.)

Name the Candidate

In a voice so that all can hear *clearly*, announce your candidate and then explain to the gathering why he is the right person for the office. Mention the candidate's background, experience, and other offices held. How long has she been a member and did she serve on any committees? Now's the time to *fire all cannons.*

Place the Name in Nomination

Conclude your nomination talk by formally announcing the full name of your candidate—for example, "Therefore, ladies and gentlemen, it is with a great

Be generous in your praise, but. . . .

deal of pride that I place in nomination for the office of president of local 2259 the name [loud and clear] of Patricia Barbara." At this point your fellow supporters should explode with approval. The following is a sample speech to nominate a candidate.

> I am very proud to place in nomination for president of our alumni association the name of one of our most active members, Mr. Andrew Aloisi.
>
> We all know the demanding responsibilities that this office bears . . . leadership qualities, the talent to select chairpersons of important committees, the ability to look ahead, the gift to motivate, and certainly the love of his alma mater.
>
> Mr. Aloisi possesses all these attributes and more. During the last few years he has *"answered the call"* many times from this organization, and with distinction. As chairman of the membership committee, he was responsible for significantly increasing our active rolls. As program director, he brought many new and interesting events to this organization. Last year he was chairman of the Fund Raising Committee, and our coffers were swelled by the most successful year ever enjoyed by our association. He has also served with credit on our travel committee.
>
> Mr. Aloisi, a successful businessman, has, at the request of this association, generously made himself available to talk and meet with recent graduates and help them in launching their careers.
>
> He is an executive with understanding and compassion and that special talent of being able to get things done. Those of us who have had the good fortune of working with Andrew know only too well his executive ability and devotion to his duties.

in other words:
"answered the call"—
volunteered

This coming year we will be celebrating our 100th anniversary. It is a special occasion that promises to attract renowned educators and political leaders from all parts of the world. This special time warrants special leadership, and with that in mind I take great pleasure to place in nomination for the office of president of our alumni association . . . Mr. Andrew Aloisi.

How to Give an Installation Speech

Congratulations, you've been elected to office. You've worked hard for the victory and you deserve it; however, you must now plan to make your first speech before the group. The following are some helpful ideas.

Express Your Gratitude

The first order of business is to express your sincere thanks for the vote of confidence bestowed on you, particularly by your supporters. You should also assure your nonsupporters that you will represent them fairly.

Accept the Challenge

You may wish to mention what the office is all about and enumerate some significant responsibilities. Explain that you accept all of the challenges the office has to offer and that you look forward to the coming term.

Admit That It's Not a Job for One Person

Tell the group that getting the job done requires more than one person and that you're looking forward to working closely with the other officers and various committees. It's also appropriate (and could win goodwill) to refer to the past president in a complimentary fashion and indicate that you would like to call on him or her occasionally for advice.

Look Ahead

The group will be anxious to hear something about your future plans. You can motivate your audience by outlining some of the steps you plan to take in the coming term. It is not necessary to detail every program, plan of action, or all you hope to accomplish. Brevity is important. You'll have many other opportunities to address the group. The following is an example of an installation speech.

I wish to express my sincere thanks for the honor you have bestowed on me this evening. Our association is well known in the community not only for its active membership, but also for the many acts by its members in and for our community. It is a privilege to have been elected to its highest office.

This organization—and we are all proud of it—achieved many milestones during the past year. It comforts me to know that I will have the full support and cooperation from our now past president, Charlie Flagg, as I begin my new term.

Shortly, I will be calling on you for your assistance—to head committees, to become committee members, and to fulfill other important duties. I know your response will be as generous as it always has been.

This organization, as any organization, is only as effective as the involvement of its members. We have one of the largest memberships of any organization in the state. And we have a record of accomplishments that speaks for itself.

The two major goals I have established for the coming year are to increase our membership and to become more involved in our community. A high-priority item on our agenda will be the establishment of a special fund-raising committee to help us further meet special community needs.

This will be a year of commitment, challenge, and participation. I will furnish that commitment. I will accept that challenge. I now ask for your participation.

Again, I thank you for your vote of confidence and the opportunity to serve you.

NOTE *Be careful not to say anything critical of the preceding year that will reflect unfavorably on your predecessor.*

The Eulogy or Special Tribute Speech

Although giving a eulogy or special tribute speech isn't exactly the type of talk that would most likely be of immediate concern to you, I am including a most eloquent tribute delivered by one of the most outstanding communicators ever to reside in the White House for you to study, analyze, and appreciate.

On January 28, 1986, the Space Shuttle *Challenger* blasted off from Cape Canaveral, Florida, carrying six astronauts and an unusual crew member— Christa McAuliffe, a high school teacher selected to become the first teacher-astronaut to fly into space.

Sixty-three seconds into the flight the space craft exploded before a watching nation, including thousands of horrified schoolchildren.

Instead of delivering his annual State of the Union Address that evening, President Ronald Reagan presented a very moving, emotional, and memorable eulogy to the fallen "heroes."

The impact of this speech was best illustrated by *New York Times* columnist Anthony Lewis, a constant critic of Reagan's policies, when he wrote:

> In a few words, simple and direct, the President gave meaning to the deaths of the seven astronauts. He spoke to their families with consoling respect. He expressed our inchoate feelings. He was touching without being mawkish. He was dignified. Listening to Mr. Reagan, I thought I understood better than ever before the mystery of his enormous popularity as President.[4]

---

[4]Anthony Lewis, "The Dignified Part," *New York Times*, 30 January 1986, p. A21.

Here is Ronald Reagan's Tribute to the *Challenger* astronauts.[5]

1   Ladies and gentlemen, I'd planned to speak to you tonight to report on the State of the Union but the events of earlier today have led me to change those plans. Today is a day for mourning and remembering.

2   Nancy and I are pained to the core by the tragedy of the shuttle *Challenger*. We know we share this pain with all of the people of our country. This is truly a national loss.

3   Nineteen years ago, almost to the day, we lost three astronauts in a terrible accident on the ground. But we've never lost an astronaut in flight; we've never had a tragedy like this. And perhaps we've forgotten the courage it took for the crew of the shuttle; but they, the *Challenger* Seven, were aware of the dangers, but overcame them and did their jobs brilliantly. We mourn seven heroes: Michael Smith, Dick Scobee, Judith Resnik, Ronald McNair, Ellison Onizuka, Gregory Jarvis, and Christa McAuliffe. We mourn their loss as a nation together.

4   For the families of the seven, we cannot bear, as you do, the full impact of this tragedy. But we feel the loss, and we're thinking about you so very much. Your loved ones were daring and brave, and they had that special grace, that special spirit that says, "Give me a challenge and I'll meet it with joy." They had a hunger to explore the universe and discover its truths. They wished to serve, and they did. They served all of us.

5   We've grown used to wonders in this century. It's hard to dazzle us. But for 25 years the United States space program has been doing just that. We've grown used to the idea of space, and perhaps we forget that we've only just begun. We're still pioneers. They, the members of the *Challenger* crew, were pioneers.

6   And I want to say something to the schoolchildren of America who were watching the live coverage of the shuttle's takeoff. I know it is hard to understand, but sometimes painful things like this happen. It's all part of the process of exploration and discovery. It's all part of taking a chance and expanding man's horizons. The future doesn't belong to the fainthearted; it belongs to the brave. The *Challenger* crew was pulling us into the future, and we'll continue to follow them.

7   I've always had great faith in and respect for our space program, and what happened today does nothing to diminish it. We don't hide our space program. We don't keep secrets and cover things up. We do it all up front and in public. That's the way freedom is, and we wouldn't change it for a minute.

[5]Ronald Reagan, Tribute to the *Challenger* Astronauts, White House Address to the Nation, Washington, D.C., 28 January 1986 (*Weekly Compilation of Presidential Documents*, Vol. 22, No. 5, 104–105).

8   We'll continue our quest in space. There will be more shuttle flights and more shuttle crews and, yes, more volunteers, more civilians, more teachers in space. Nothing ends here; our hopes and our journeys continue.

9   I want to add that I wish I could talk to every man and woman who works for NASA or who worked on this mission and tell them: "Your dedication and professionalism have moved and impressed us for decades. And we know of your anguish. We share it."

10   There's a coincidence today. On this day 390 years ago, the great explorer Sir Francis Drake died aboard ship off the coast of Panama. In his lifetime the great frontiers were the oceans, and an historian later said, "He lived by the sea, died on it, and was buried in it." Well, today we can say of the *Challenger* crew: Their dedication was, like Drake's, complete.

11   The crew of the space shuttle *Challenger* honored us by the manner in which they lived their lives. We will never forget them, nor the last time we saw them, this morning, as they prepared for their journey and waved goodbye and "slipped the surly bonds of earth" to "touch the face of God."

How to Propose a Toast

There are many occasions when proposing a toast is appropriate and desirable: births, birthdays, graduations, bar mitzvahs, weddings, anniversaries, promotions, and so on. The occasion could be a large gathering or simply an evening with a companion. No matter what the occasion, the toast should be brief, meaningful, and sincere.

A good exercise is to try to write down as many short toasts for as many situations as possible and keep the list handy for various occasions. Whenever you hear a clever toast, jot it down, perhaps rewording it to fit your own personality.

Another excellent source for getting ideas for "toasts" is from greeting cards. Save them or visit the greeting card section in many stores. The following are examples of toasts for various occasions:

● **Births**

To Kaitlyn Elizabeth
 . . . You're so delicate and beautiful
  From your head to your toes
To your parents, you'll always be
  Their American Beauty Rose. Welcome.

● **Birthdays**

Another candle on your cake
 is really no reason to pout,
Give thanks to God that you have the breath
 To blow the damn thing out. Happy Birthday, Kevin.

"Cheers . . . prost . . . a vôtre santé . . . saluto . . . and . . . here's looking at you, kid. . . ."

● Graduation

May your achievements on campus easily transfer to the world of industry as you matriculate to a new and exciting adventure. We wish you great success . . . and congratulations, Janet.

● Bar Mitzvahs

May the helping hand of God be always near to guide you on your adventurous journey from boyhood to manhood. Shalom.

● Weddings

To Patty and Wally. Two very special people.
   May this day so filled with love, friendship and laughter,
   Be the way of life you both enjoy happily everafter. Saluto.

● Anniversaries

To Barbara and Albie. May the special joy and happiness that you share with us today, intensify with loving abundance in the many years to follow. Congratulations.

● **Job promotions**

Brian, your company has an enviable reputation for making solid business decisions. Like the one they just made—your promotion. Congratulations.

● **Retirement**

May the years that you've spent laboring be doubled as you work on your years in leisure, pleasure and, hopefully, just plain fun. Congratulations Bob, you deserve it.

● **A toast to you**

Here's to the student who's almost completed this course
    I hope you experience no feelings of remorse
But when the opportunity arises for you to get up to speak
    You'll have all my best wishes that you perform at your peak.

Testing . . . 1 . . . 2 . . . 3 . . . 4

Unless you plan a career in radio or TV, the chances are slim that you'll ever appear before a radio microphone (mike) or a television camera to express your views. It's far more likely that you'll appear before a **public address (PA)** microphone at a school, fraternal, or social gathering. Let's discuss some testing and speaking techniques that you may find helpful.

Before you speak, you should test the mike to be sure it's working and at the proper level (volume). To test a mike, *speak* into it. The most common testing phrases are "Testing 1 . . . 2 . . . 3 . . . 4" and "Hello, testing. Can you hear me OK in the back of the hall?"

Above all, never test a mike by slapping it or blowing into it, because it is a very delicate, sensitive instrument. Doing either may damage it and annoy your audience.

Being the right distance from the mike is important. If you're too close, your voice will boom at everyone and your *P*'s and *B*'s (**plosives**) will sound like explosions. However, if you're too far away from the mike, the audience will have to strain to hear you and may then tune you out.

The best way to know the correct distance from the mike is to test it. If the level has been set correctly, your mouth should be 3 to 5 inches away from the mike. If your voice is strong, move back from the mike. If your voice is soft, move closer. It's important to listen to yourself and to look at your audience. You can hear yourself from the loudspeakers in the hall, and you can receive feedback from observing your audience.

When speaking over a PA system, be sure to slow your delivery so that every word can be heard clearly and distinctly. Otherwise, your words may sound jumbled. Because you'll hear yourself over the loudspeakers a split second after you've spoken, you shouldn't speak too rapidly.

Speak directly into the mike and don't move your head from left to right, or the audience will miss half of what you're saying. This guideline applies particularly to MCs who may be introducing head table guests. After you've introduced someone, you may look in his or her direction for a second or two; introduce the next person, speaking directly into the mike; then glance at that person. Face the person you're introducing only if you can speak directly into the mike at the same time.

Above all, speak in your natural voice. For many people, this is the hardest thing to do. It seems that whenever people appear before a microphone, they try to lower their voices, sound dramatic, or start to over-e-n-u-n-c-i-a-t-e. Speak as you always do. Remember, the microphone is like a magnifying glass and will detect and amplify flaws in delivery.

Always treat a microphone with respect and always assume it is "on" (live). Otherwise, you could experience a few humiliating moments.

If you have to sneeze, cough, or blow your nose, be sure to turn your head as far away as possible from the mike. Finally, don't grab or hold onto the mike that you're speaking into. Doing so could produce an annoying hum or static over the loudspeakers.

In Conclusion

Now that you are all experts in the art of small talks, perhaps you will enjoy the following amusing anecdote.

Once upon a time, in the days of the Roman Empire, a mob was gathered in the Colosseum to watch as a Christian was thrown to a hungry lion. The spectators cheered as the wild beast went after its prey. But the Christian quickly whispered something in the lion's ear and the beast backed away with obvious terror on his face. No amount of calling and foot stomping by the audience could get the lion to approach the Christian again. Fearlessly, he walked from the arena.

The Emperor was so amazed at what had happened that he sent for the Christian and offered him his freedom if he would say what he had done to make the ferocious beast cower in fear. The Christian bowed before the Emperor and said, "I merely whispered in the lion's ear: 'After dinner, you'll be required to say a few words.' "[6]

---

[6]S. H. Simmons, *New Speakers' Handbook* (New York: Dial Press, 1972), 22–23.

Quick Clicks

Welcome to a "surprise search." To further enhance your research or simply to harvest more information about some of the things you studied in this chapter, just drop in at any of the following addresses. What you'll discover may be serious, educational, bibliographical, surprising, factual, or even downright humorous. But it will definitely be informative.

So, go ahead and give a "Quick Click."

http://zinnia.umfacad.maine.edu/~donaghue/toasts.html
www.hanksville.org/storytellers
www.eulogywriters.com/famous_eulogies.htm
www.quoteland.com

Things to Discuss in Class

1. Get some news of an upcoming event either from your school newspaper or from the student activities center, and make an announcement of the event to the class.
2. Introduce a classmate who's prepared to give a talk.
3. Prepare and deliver a one- or two-minute talk to present an award.
4. Prepare and deliver a one- or two-minute talk after receiving an award.
5. Make a one- or two-minute nominating speech.
6. Give a one- or two-minute installation speech.
7. Give a short toast for a wedding, birthday, job promotion, bar mitzvah, or christening.
8. From your library research, find a good example of one of the special-occasion talks discussed in this chapter. Read it to the class, and explain the reason for your selection.

What Do You Remember from This Chapter?

1. What information should be included when you make an announcement?

2. Mention two valid sources of information for an announcement.
3. What is a common problem when someone introduces a speaker?
4. When you introduce a speaker, why should you be careful not to overpraise him or her?
5. Why should you try to inject some humor in your comments?
6. Name two elements to include when you present an award.
7. Name two important elements of a speech to nominate.
8. What information should an installation speech contain?
9. When giving an installation speech, what must you be careful of regarding the preceding officers?
10. List two occasions when a toast would be appropriate.
11. How should you test a microphone for operation and level?
12. While speaking into a PA mike, how can you be aware of the right volume?
13. What is the most important characteristic of a special-occasion talk?

Vitalize Your Vocabulary

Health Care

acupuncturist A professional who practices a traditional therapeutic technique whereby the body is punctured with very fine needles in the treatment of certain diseases and pain.

allergist A physician who specializes in the treatment of allergies.

cardiologist A physician who specializes in the diagnosis and treatment of heart disease.

chiropodist A physician specializing in the diagnosis and treatment of hand and foot problems.

chiropractor A doctor who treats specific ailments by performing manipulative adjustments to the spinal column. Chiropractic treatment excludes medicine and drugs.

dentist A doctor involved in the diagnosis, prevention, and treatment of diseases of the teeth.

dermatologist A physician specializing in the treatment of skin problems.

dietitian A professional specializing in the field of diet as it relates to one's health.

geriatrician or **geriatrist** A physician whose practice is devoted to patients of old age.

gynecologist A physician specializing in women's health problems.

immunologist A physician specializing in the study and prevention of certain diseases.

internist A physician specializing in internal medicine but not surgery.

neurologist A physician specializing in the diagnosis and treatment of disorders of the nervous system.

obstetrician A physician whose practice is devoted to the care of women during and after pregnancy.

oncologist A physician specializing in the study and treatment of tumors.

ophthalmologist A physician specializing in the treatment of eye diseases.

optician A professional who makes lenses and eye glasses.

optometrist A professional involved in the examination and treatment of certain visual defects by prescribing corrective lenses.

orthodontist A dentist specializing in correcting misaligned teeth.

orthopedist A physician who performs surgery or manipulative treatment of disorders of the skeletal system.

otolaryngologist A physician who treats diseases of the ear, nose, and throat.

pediatrician A physician specializing in the care of infants and children.

periodontist A dentist who treats problems concerning tissue surrounding the teeth, bone structure, and gums.

pharmacist A professional who prepares and dispenses drugs.

psychiatrist A physician trained in treating mental illnesses.

psychologist A Ph.D. professional who deals with mental and emotional processes and problems.

radiologist A physician trained in radiography or X-ray as a means of diagnosis.

urologist A physician specializing in the treatment of urinary tract problems.

14

Let's Meet and Discuss It

Men are never so likely to settle a question rightly as when they discuss it freely.

—Thomas Babington Macaulay, *Southey's Colloquies*, 1830

After reading and understanding this chapter, you should know:

- Some elements of the Reflective Thinking Process

- Some characteristics of a panel discussion, symposium lecture, round-table discussion, brainstorming session, buzz session meeting, and committee

- Some responsibilities of a panel moderator

- Some responsibilities of a panelist

- Some responsibilities of an audience

- Some responsibilities of a member attending a meeting and of a meeting chairperson

- Some main qualities of a group leader or chairperson

The environment, the consumer movement, health care, and education are just a few areas of public concern in which Americans are demanding and getting a voice. They are serving on more and more committees, participating in forums, on panels, and in symposia. They are interacting in groups to solve problems, to make decisions, and to carry them out.

This chapter explains the Reflective Thinking Process as well as the more common types of group discussion: panel, symposium, lecture, round-table, brainstorming, buzz session, general meeting, and committee. These various groups consist of moderators, chairpeople or leaders, panelists or participants, and sometimes audiences. The significant responsibilities of these people are listed in detail. Also included in this chapter are diagrams of suggested seating arrangements for these major types of group discussions.

Getting Involved

If you're an active member of a business, political, religious, educational, civic, or fraternal organization—congratulations. You're an activist and enjoy getting involved. On the other hand, maybe you would like to participate in an organization but you lack self-confidence. Becoming involved can be a gratifying, rewarding experience and can lead to unexpected opportunities.

Perhaps there's a local group that is *in tune* with your way of thinking; maybe a local issue has you so aroused that you feel compelled to *sound off;* perhaps you would like to volunteer for a worthy cause within your community. If you feel the desire to get involved, go for it.

A trend toward increased activism in the United States began in the 1980s, when the consumer movement, spearheaded by Ralph Nader's Raiders, emerged as a vibrant force in the nation and in our lives. As the 1980s ended, more and more Americans displayed and vented their anger and frustrations over local and national issues by becoming involved in local, statewide, and national affairs. The impact of this voter anger was especially evident during the November 1991 national and state off-year elections, when many insiders were voted out and many outsiders were voted in. And in 1992, dozens of members of Congress, guilty of bouncing checks, quit politics rather than face the likelihood of being *"bounced" out* of office by *teed-off* voters.

These days, average consumers not only are running for political office, but also are being appointed to state and local regulatory boards and commissions. Parents, many from single-parent homes, are participating in advisory councils involving the operations of their children's schools/day care facilities. Concerned and eager citizens are being selected as trustees and advisors to state-supported colleges and universities. No matter how diverse their personal views are, they all have one thing in common—they are all participants in some form of **small-group discussion.** No longer is the average voter a passive one. Many are now ready, willing, and able to "meet and discuss it" with the powers to be.

More than just being present at hearings or large meetings in which they might ask a question or two, citizens are now becoming members of symposia, panels, and committees to communicate, interact, and make decisions. In the business and professional worlds, you may be asked to, or may wish to, participate in a convention, conference, department or committee meeting, seminar, brainstorming or buzz session, or any one of the other types of group communication.

Most small-group communication is either public (open) or private (closed). *Public* discussions take place before an audience, which may or may not be allowed to participate, whereas *private* discussions are open only to group members. (See Figure 14.1.) Federal and state legislation increasingly tends to favor public meetings for government activities.

The group's private or public status depends on certain considerations:

in other
words:

in tune—in agreement

sound off—voice an opinion

"bounced" out—voted out

teed-off—very angry

A Private/Closed Discussion

A Public/Open Discussion

FIGURE 14.1

**Suggested Seating Arrangements for a Private/Closed Group Discussion
and a Public/Open Group Discussion**
M signifies the moderator and P signifies the participants.

- How many group members will participate?
- What is each member's rank and influence?
- What is the subject to be discussed?
- Is the subject confidential?
- How soon must a decision or solution be reached?
- Will the decision affect a small or a large group of people?
- When and where will the meeting be held?

Reflective or Critical Thinking

Among the reasons for the various formations of small-group interactivity are
to inform, to persuade, to gather facts and information, to propose some type of
action, to resolve a problem, or a combination of these.

Finding a solution to an existing problem is a common objective of most
small-group efforts, and how each member of the group approaches that objective can determine the success or failure of that solution. Before a problem-
solving discussion takes place, group members should agree on the approach
that the dialogue should follow. Doing so will ensure a more productive, orderly, intelligent, and time-saving exercise, in which group members stay on
the subject.

"I've already arrived at the consensus that I'm expecting all of you to reach."

One of the most popular approaches is the **Reflective** (or Constructive) **Thinking Process** developed by educational philosopher John Dewey in 1910.[1] Dewey's method consists of five steps:

1. Identify the problem.
2. Analyze the problem.
3. Offer possible solutions to the problem.
4. Evaluate and select the best solution(s).
5. Implement the solution.

Step 1. Identify the Problem

It's critical that all the participants agree not only that a problem *does* exist but also what the actual problem is. The goal to be achieved must be established and clearly understood by all members of the group so that they will know in what direction the discussion is headed. To avoid any misunderstandings, all terms that may come up during the discussion must be clearly defined.

Step 2. Analyze the Problem

The problem must be specifically stated, clearly defined, and completely understood. Once the problem is fully recognized, the members must discuss

---

[1]John Dewey. *How We Think* (Lexington, MA: D.C. Heath, 1910).

such questions as, "How long has the problem existed?" "Have any previous attempts been made to address the problem?" If so, "What were the results?" "Is the problem worth attempting to solve or is it beyond our authority?" "What are the causes of the problem?" Once these and other questions are answered, you're ready to begin the solution process.

Step 3. Offer Possible Solutions to the Problem

Now's your chance to be creative as members of the group offer as many solutions as possible. This stage should focus more on quantity of solutions than on quality. Don't stop to criticize every suggestion made; evaluation comes next. Right now you want to list as many practical solutions as possible so that you'll have a large pool of ideas from which to draw.

Step 4. Evaluate and Select the Best Solution(s)

This step evaluates the ***pros and cons*** of each suggested remedy. Will it work? Would a combination of suggestions be more practical? Is it the most expedient method(s) of producing the desired effect? How difficult is it to implement and receive feedback about its effectiveness? After these important questions are discussed, analyzed, debated, and answered in detail, a solution can be adopted through **consensus.**

in other words:

pros and cons—positions for or against a particular issue

Step 5. Implement the Solution

Your final effort is to decide the best way to implement the course of action in order to solve the problem. An important consideration is that, after the solution(s) is carried out, its effectiveness should be tested, if possible. This testing can be done by telephone inquiry, mail questionnaires to be returned, or by face-to-face polling. If the desired effect is not being attained, you would have to return to one of the previous steps and repeat part(s) of the five-step approach.

Reflective or Critical Thinking is a developing process that progresses from problem identification to a practical solution and its implementation. It is, therefore, paramount that you thoroughly complete each step before going to the next one.

Types of Small-Group Discussion

Some of the more popular types of small-group discussion in which you may likely participate on or off campus include:

- Panel
- Symposium
- Lecture
- Round-table
- Brainstorming session
- Buzz session
- Meeting
- Committee

The Panel Discussion

The **panel** discussion is a popular type of group communication and one that you may become involved in, as either a moderator, a panelist, or a member of the audience. A panel usually consists of four to six members and a moderator seated at a table and facing the audience. Figure 14.2 shows the customary seating arrangement for a panel discussion.

The primary purpose of a panel discussion is for the panelists to explore different aspects of a subject or problem through interaction. The panelists individually express their views on the topic under discussion, interact with each other, and then answer questions from the audience. The interaction among the panelists may result in a spirited, intellectually stimulating discussion. Whenever the audience is allowed to participate, regardless of the type of discussion, it is called a **forum.**

The popularity of panel discussions couldn't be more evident than in the frequency with which many of than appear on TV (regular or cable). And thanks to newly developed sophisticated media technology, it is now possible for viewers to call in questions to specific panelists or the moderator, or just "air" their personal opinions. I strongly suggest that you take advantage of the prolific lineup of Sunday-morning TV talk shows. You'll find them interesting, informative, educational, and an excellent source for possible future class speeches.

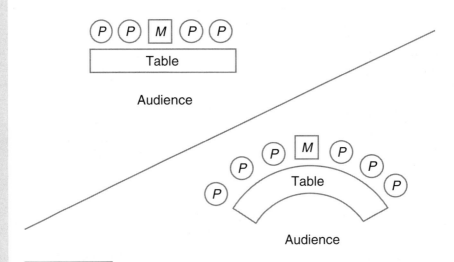

FIGURE 14.2

Two Ways to Set up a Panel Discussion
A semicircular arrangement is preferred so that panelists can easily see each other. M signifies the moderator and P signifies the panelists.

Some Responsibilities of the Panel Moderator

As a panel **moderator,** you have *in your grasp* the power to conduct either a smooth, meaningful discussion or one fraught with chaos.

in other
words:

**in your
grasp**—within
your capability

1. Be sure that the panelists have name cards on the table in front of them so that the audience will know their names. If the room is large, and those in the rear have difficulty reading the names, you might put each panelist's name on the chalkboard directly behind the panel.
2. Greet the audience and introduce yourself.
3. Briefly tell the audience the topic to be discussed.
4. Inform the audience when it may question the panel.
5. Introduce each panel member. You may also mention whether the panelist's position is pro or con.
6. Allow each panelist to make an opening statement of a minute or two.
7. After the opening remarks, allow the panelists to talk and question each other.
8. Be prepared to throw a question or two at the panelists to trigger discussion in case interaction is not immediate.
9. Remain impartial, but be ready to question individual panelists if the discussion starts to lag or veer off course or if an opinion needs clarification.
10. Be sure to give each panelist a chance to express his or her views.
11. When you feel that the discussion has just about run its course, or if a time limit has been established, ask the panelists to summarize their views; allow one to two minutes for each.
12. Present a summary of major ideas or concepts expressed from both viewpoints.
13. Open the discussion to the audience.
14. Call only on those who raise their hands. Again, be aware of time monopolizers.
15. Don't hesitate to declare anyone out of order if the situation warrants.
16. When the time is up, thank the audience and the panel.
17. Be tactful but firm if you have a panelist who's monopolizing the floor. Try to spark some response from the more reticent members.

Being a moderator is an assignment that can be extremely rewarding when the result is a smoothly run interactional experience, followed by a spirited but orderly response from the audience.

Some Responsibilities of the Panelists

As a member of a team, your attitude and participation are vital to the overall success of the discussion.

1. Be informed and prepared to become totally involved in the discussion. In other words, *do your homework.*
2. Keep your opening remarks and summary to a minute or so.

**do your home-
work**—prepare
thoroughly

Be tactful, but firm.

3. If a panelist falters, help out by immediately picking up the discussion and sustaining it. Perhaps the panelist just needs a minute or two to regain composure.
4. Have supporting material with you and be prepared to identify your sources.
5. Don't monopolize the floor; give others a chance to speak.
6. Don't interrupt another speaker.
7. Be tolerant and understanding; don't be overpowering and overbearing.
8. Be brief and to the point; don't ramble.
9. Don't become personal and sarcastic.
10. Always respect the moderator and the other panelists.
11. *Keep cool,* no matter how heated the exchange becomes.

Some Responsibilities of the Audience

Psych yourself for a learning experience and be prepared to jot down questions to ask panelists during the question-and-answer period.

1. Give undivided attention to the discussion and to the participants' views.
2. When you wish to ask a question, raise your hand and wait for recognition by the moderator.
3. *Keep an open mind* until you've heard all of the views. Remember the words of engineer-inventor-author Charles F. Kettering: "Where there is an open mind, there will always be a frontier."
4. You may direct your question to the panel in general or to a specific individual.
5. Keep your question short and to the point; don't make speeches.

in other words:

keep cool— maintain your composure

keep an open mind— avoid prejudice; don't make a decision before you've heard everyone speak

Keep cool, no matter how heated the exchange.

6. Don't question or enter a discussion with another member of the audience.

7. Don't antagonize or embarrass anyone.

8. Remember that you can disagree without being disagreeable. "We owe almost all our knowledge not to those who have agreed, but to those who have differed."[2]

The Symposium

A **symposium** usually consists of three to five members and a moderator. It differs from the panel discussion in that each participant of a symposium covers only one specific phase of the topic being discussed. The remarks should be well planned, prepared, and practiced before the discussion.

The symposium format is very common at large conventions, at business meetings, and in education, where experts are invited to speak on specific phases of a subject, question, or problem. A good example of an educational symposium takes place annually in high school auditoriums across the country as students ponder matriculating to college. (You may have attended one or more such functions yourself and probably never realized that you were present at a symposium.) At such an event several college representatives would discuss his or her expertise in such areas as:

1. A four-year college vs. a two-year college

2. A state-supported college vs. a private college

---

[2]Charles Caleb Colton, *Lacon* (1825), 2.121.

3. The admissions process

4. Applying for financial aid

The moderator introduces the participants and the subject and maintains control over the presentation. He or she informs the audience of the procedure to be followed and whether there will be a forum after the talks. The moderator should also be very much aware of the time element so that the symposium does not interfere with other presentations on the program.

The seating arrangement of a symposium is similar to that of a panel discussion, except that the moderator may sit or stand on one side of the participants instead of in their midst. Figure 14.3 shows the arrangement.

The Lecture

The **lecture** panel is one form of public discussion in which a recognized authority on a specific subject presents a lecture and then is questioned by a panel. A variation is the *lecture panel forum*, in which the audience is allowed to participate once the lecture and questions from the panel are over. Another variation is the *lecture forum*, in which the audience is allowed to ask questions of the lecturer after he or she finishes.

A **chairperson** presides over the lecture and introduces the guest lecturer, subject, and the panel if there is one, and states the format to be followed. Figure 14.4 illustrates the seating arrangement.

FIGURE 14.3

Examples of Symposia Seating Arrangements
M signifies the moderator and P signifies the panelists.

FIGURE 14.4

Example of a Lecture Seating Arrangement
C signifies the chairperson; L, the lecturer; and P, the panelists.

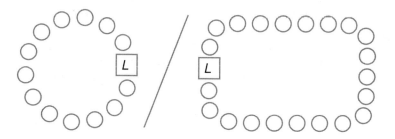

FIGURE 14.5

The Choice of a Seating Arrangement for a Round-Table, or Group, Discussion Depends on the Number of Participants
L signifies the group leader.

The Round-Table Discussion

The **round-table discussion** method is prevalent in classes where discussion and total group interaction are emphasized, as well as in many other settings. The unique feature of this discussion is that there are only participants; there is no audience. Circular seating allows for maximum informality and a sense of closeness.

The leader introduces a subject or question, calls on individuals to present their views, and then invites all members to express themselves freely. This is perhaps the most intimate form of group communication. The seating arrangement for a round-table discussion is shown in Figure 14.5.

The discussion is a learning experience for all participants if they make the effort to prepare and participate, keep an open mind, and are ready to inquire. The words of Joseph Joubert, French moralist and essayist, sum up this topic: "The aim of argument, or of discussion, should not be victory, but progress."[3]

The Brainstorming Session

Brainstorming is a creative, freewheeling, no-holds-barred approach to solving problems. Participants—usually five to ten in the business world and up to twenty in a class—should be given a few minutes of silence to think and unleash their imaginations. They should spout anything and everything that comes to mind, while a recorder lists all the ideas on paper or on a chalkboard. Quantity, not quality, of ideas should be emphasized.

---

[3]Joseph Joubert, *Pensées* (1842), 7.31, tr. Katherine Lyttelton.

The crucial principle behind brainstorming is this: no matter how preposterous an idea may sound, there must be no criticism or evaluation of it or its contributor. Participants must be free to say anything.

This also means that you must control your nonverbal communication, as well, so as not to convey any negative messages such as raising your eyes and head, frowning while spreading your closed lips, or shaking your head. No criticism means nonverbal as well as verbal.

in other words:

screen the ideas—evaluate them

After about fifteen minutes of brainstorming, ***screen the ideas;*** then evaluate, expand, and refine them. Next, sift through the surviving list, focusing on the advantages and disadvantages of each; then reduce the list to the best two or three ideas.

Incidentally, brainstorming can be an excellent way to find speech topics.

The Buzz Session

The **buzz session** is a problem-solving process that demands a knowledgeable discussion leader who is thoroughly familiar with the problem and who can conduct the entire discussion process. He or she explains the discussion format

There should be no criticism of an idea or its volunteer.

and the problem to the audience and divides the audience into clusters of four to six individuals. Each cluster functions independently and may take ten to fifteen minutes to come up with solutions. Someone in each cluster should record them.

At the end of the discussion period, the leader asks each cluster recorder to present a one- to two-minute summary of the cluster's recommendations. The responses are then combined and written on the chalkboard. The results are finally discussed either by a preselected panel or by the entire audience.

Buzz sessions are an outstanding mode of group communication, although some participants tend to ***clam up*** in big groups, everyone usually contributes to a buzz session. These sessions may have various formats depending on the people and problems involved, the time constraints, and the location. Buzz sessions are particularly effective if you have a large audience.

in other words:
clam up—be quiet, do not speak

The Meeting

Two components of any organization are **meetings** and committees. The most popular type of group encounter, which you'll experience even more than the panel discussion, is the meeting. Take a moment or two to reflect on the many meeting situations in which you've participated recently . . . at home, at school, at work, at your health club or day care center. We could consider these types of meetings small and informal. Maybe you were involved in a discussion with your family about a vacation destination; or with fellow students, airing complaints about the school cafeteria or discussing the need for more school funding for women's athletic programs.

At these types of meetings, because of the limited number of participants, you were able to interact either one-on-one or intragroup rather informally . . . like an extended conversation. You could supply input without being officially recognized—that is, you didn't need permission from a group leader to speak. In other words, the type of discussion in which you were participating was unstructured. You were free to ask questions, respond to the statements of others, agree or disagree, as long as you didn't monopolize the time or become disagreeable and personal.

On the other hand, organizations such as labor, civic, fraternal, social, or business-related organizations have large memberships, making it necessary for meetings to be conducted in a stricter and more formal manner to avoid inequities and chaos. As a member, you're entitled to know the organization's constitution and by-laws; its officers; all the working committees and their members; and the time, place, and agenda of each meeting. Of course, you also have the right to speak, to vote, and to run for elective office.

Most large meetings agree to operate by **parliamentary procedure,** which is guided by the authoritative and internationally respected *Robert's Rules of Order* and employ the following **agenda:**

on the other hand—from another point of view

1. *Call to order*—The chairperson calls the meeting to order to officially begin proceedings.
2. *Reading of the minutes*—The secretary reads an accounting of the previous meeting and, if necessary, corrections are made and approved.
3. *Committee reports*—Reports from the various committee chairpersons/officers are presented to the membership.
4. *Action on old or unfinished business*—Unfinished business from the last meeting or from other previous sessions is now acted on.
5. *Action on new business*—Members can now introduce, discuss, and act on new business.
6. *Announcements*—Brief announcements are now made to the membership concerning events and functions related directly to the organization.
7. *Adjournment*—After the motion to adjourn (to conclude the meeting) has been presented and seconded by another member, the chairperson declares the meeting formally adjourned. (At this time you may either go home or continue socializing.)

You've been given a rather basic explanation of how a formal meeting is conducted. For a more complete understanding of parliamentary procedure see Henry M. Robert's, *Robert's Rules of Order.* I'm sure there's a copy in your library.

Some of Your Responsibilities when Attending a Meeting

- *Be on time.* Not only is it rude to be late for a meeting, it can be disruptive. Continual tardiness can weaken your image and effectiveness among your peers.
- *Be prepared.* If you're planning to speak, be sure you've done your homework. Be clear, concise, and correct, and be sure to speak so that everyone can hear you.
- *Be open-minded.* Don't expect everyone to be agreeable or ecstatic about what you have to say. Accept opposing views objectively.
- *Be courteous.* If you disagree with what's being said, don't interrupt the speaker. Wait for your turn to be recognized and don't get personal.
- *Be attentive.* Listen carefully to speakers so you'll understand what's being said. It's embarrassing to respond to or inquire about something that has already been discussed. Also, refrain from talking while someone else ***has the floor.***
- *Be serious.* The temptation to be humorous at times can be overpowering but, generally speaking, keep your remarks sober and pertinent. Most people frown on a constant joker.
- *Be sensitive.* Be aware of other members' needs and anxieties and never try to advance your cause at the expense of others. Hurt feelings can leave deep scars.

in other
words:
has the floor—
is speaking

- *Be responsive.* Offering suggestions and being sympathetic don't get things done. Organizations not only need talkers, they need doers. In order to pursue ideas or implement courses of action, you should be prepared to offer your services. Perhaps you could volunteer to serve on a committee.

The Committee

A **committee** is a small group consisting of five to nine members. (An odd number is usually chosen to avoid tie votes.) It is headed by a chairperson who establishes an agenda and keeps members ***on course.*** The organization's president may name the chairperson, or members of the committee may select their own. Committee members can be appointed or elected, or they may volunteer.

Organizations and action groups may have such committees as:

Entertainment	Health and safety
Fund raising	Building
Scholarship	Retirement
Membership	Student activities
Budget and finance	Taxation
Awards	Education
Political action	Nominations

A member of a committee should exercise the same responsibilities as members attending a meeting and should ideally possess the following qualities.

- *Commitment.* You should be a dedicated individual who can place the group's objectives and best interests above your personal feelings. Your presence and promptness can always be counted on. If you're going to be absent, notify the chairperson well in advance.
- *Intelligence and experience.* You should be an informed individual who knows how to track down information, digest it, and communicate it so that everyone can understand it. You can be depended on to have more than one perspective on the subject and to make positive contributions. If you plan to supply your colleagues with reports, memos, or other types of handouts, do it.
- *Personality.* You should be an even-tempered person who can take as well as give constructive criticism. You can disagree without becoming disagreeable, and your friendliness allows you to get along easily with other committee members. You are quick to compliment and offer support.
- *Integrity.* You should not intentionally belittle or degrade colleagues or their opinions, and you should be mindful of other people's feelings, especially when responding to a questionable viewpoint. You can be relied on for honesty and a high standard of ethics.

in other words:

on course— focused on the subject being discussed

You as the Group Leader

Suppose that you have **made your mark** as an active and responsible participant in your organization, and you have just been selected to play a leadership role. It may be to conduct a large meeting or to chair a committee. For a large gathering (over twenty people), you should prepare and complete a premeeting checklist. (See Figure 14.6.) Nothing can destroy the momentum and effectiveness of a meeting more easily than the lack of proper accommodations, equipment, and supplies. Investing the time to establish and check off such a list will pay dividends.

Also, as an effective leader you should be sensitive to the needs and demands confronting not only the group, but each member as well. You should be able to guide the group and, at the same time, be flexible enough to adapt to changing needs during the meeting. And, finally, you should radiate confidence and authority.

The following are some suggestions for acting as group leader:

- Mention any rules of procedure.
- Announce the topic and goal of discussion.
- Help group members get to know each other (if size permits).
- Encourage maximum participation.
- Allow those with opposing views equal time to speak.
- Encourage, but don't force, a silent member to speak.
- Refer questions back to the group instead of answering them yourself.
- Ask questions to clarify meanings.
- Ask questions that cannot be answered by just a yes or no.

- Keep the discussion **on track.**
- Be impartial, yet question logic and validity.
- Avoid personality clashes.
- Be complimentary whenever possible.
- Don't permit private conversations while a person is speaking.
- Don't allow a speaker to monopolize the floor.
- List important points on the chalkboard if doing so would benefit the group.

- Watch the clock so you won't **run out of time.**
- Take notes so that you can present a salient summary after the discussion ends.
- Make announcements pertaining to a recommended course of action, information regarding next meeting, and so on.
- Accept only one question per person so that as many as possible may speak.
- Thank all participants and praise their contributions.

The position of group leader, or chairperson, is a responsible, challenging one that can also be rewarding and personally gratifying.

FIGURE 14.6

Premeeting Checklist

Reason for Meeting:

Day and Time of Meeting:

Name(s) and telephone number(s) of person(s)
to contact in the event of problems:

Check When Completed	Comments
Room (Name or Number)	
Reserved	
Tables	
Chairs	
Sign designating room	
Name cards	
Lectern	
Seating arrangement	
Refreshments	
Audiovisual Equipment	
Public address system	
Tape recorder	
Presentation tapes	
Microphones	
Chalkboard	
Chalk	
Easel	
Flip chart	
Overhead projector	
Other projectors	
Broad felt-tip pens	
Television monitor(s)	
VCR	
Screen	
Printed Material	
Agenda	
Other handouts (list them)	
Supplies for Participants	
Paper	
Pens or pencils	
Pitchers of ice water and glasses	

Be aware of the time element.

The Correct Form of Address

A common question that I'm frequently asked (by students and nonstudents) is how you should address a person, particularly a woman, who is "chairing" a meeting, committee, panel, or whatever. Quite frankly, and I feel very strongly about this, if a man is chairing an event, he's the "chairman" (is he not?); if a woman is chairing an event, she's the "chairwoman" (is she not?). If you feel compelled to be gender-neutral, use "chairperson" (doesn't that make sense?). I would, however, refrain from referring to a chairperson as simply the "chair." How often have you heard, "The chair says this," "The chair thinks . . . ," "It is the opinion of the chair." I find it repulsive and disrespectful to refer to any individual as a cold, inanimate object, particularly one on which you sit.

Why would anyone find it acceptable to refer to another person as a chair, table, door, or whatever escapes my comprehension. I can't help but recall an excellent response made by Secretary of Defense Donald Rumsfeld at a Pentagon press conference. When asked by a reporter, "Mr. Secretary, today the White House said . . . ," at which point Mr. Rumsfeld abruptly cut off the reporter with, "Stop right there. The White House is a building made up of wood and bricks and doesn't say anything. Now, if you have a question regarding what someone at the White House might have said, I'll be happy to respond."

"The chair has ruled to table; the floor must counter."

Quick Clicks

Welcome to a "surprise search." To further enhance your research or simply to harvest more information about some of the things you studied in this chapter, just drop in at any of the following addresses. What you'll discover may be serious, educational, bibliographical, surprising, factual, or even downright humorous. But it will definitely be informative.

So, go ahead and give a "Quick Click."

www.historychannel.com/discuss/index.html
www.mbcnet.org/debateweb/html/greatdebate/index.htm
www.black-collegian.com/career/archives/leadership300.shtml
www.instituteforstrategicclarity.org
http://parli.com
www.constitution.org/rror/rror--00.htm

Things to Discuss in Class

1. Weigh the advantages and disadvantages of a strong discussion leader.
2. Assume the responsibility for selecting a small group and prepare a fifteen-minute panel discussion. Then, as moderator, present it to the class.
3. List one topic for each of the following:
   a. A panel discussion
   b. A lecture
   c. A symposium
   d. A round-table discussion
   e. A forum
   f. A brainstorming session
4. Assume that you are a panel moderator. Introduce yourself and briefly tell the audience the topic to be discussed. Then introduce each member of the panel and explain the format and ground rules.

What Do You Remember from This Chapter?

1. List two of the more common types of group discussion.
2. Explain the Reflective Thinking Process.
3. How should a panel be set up for maximum impact?
4. Explain two responsibilities of a panel discussion moderator.
5. Explain two responsibilities of a panelist.
6. Explain two responsibilities of an audience.
7. What is a discussion called when the audience is allowed to participate?
8. Briefly explain the symposium.
9. How does the symposium differ from the panel discussion?
10. What is brainstorming?
11. What is a buzz session?
12. Name two qualities that a committee member should have.

Vitalize Your Vocabulary

Common Banking Terms

ATM (n.) Automatic teller machine; a banking machine at which customers may receive cash from their existing accounts by inserting a bank card and entering a special code.

assets (n.) Things of value that are owned and can be turned into cash.

balance (n.) The amount of money that you have in your savings or checking account.

C.D. (n.) Certificate of deposit; a specified amount of money deposited for a certain length of time that cannot be withdrawn earlier without paying a penalty. The interest rate, which remains constant, is higher than for a regular savings or passbook account.

checking account (n.) An account established at a financial institution from which you may withdraw money on demand by writing checks. Some checking accounts earn interest.

collateral (n.) Money or other assets that you pledge as security to protect the interests of the institution that lends you money.

co-sign (v.) When you borrow money, another person may be required to sign along with you; the co-signer would be responsible for the repayment of the loan if you should default.

credit line (n.) A sum of money that a bank makes available to a customer or company from which they may draw as needed.

credit rating (n.) A rating based on a person's history of repaying loans or charges on time.

deposit (v.) Putting money into a savings or checking account.

direct-deposit (n.) An agreement between your employer and your bank that your paycheck will automatically be deposited in your bank account; on payday you receive a statement of the transaction rather than a paycheck.

joint account (n.) A bank account in two peoples names, each of whom may withdraw funds.

loan (n.) Money lent at a certain rate of interest with a written agreement to repay it.

money market account (n.) An account requiring a minimum deposit that may have limited monthly check-writing privileges; the interest rate exceeds that of a regular savings account but fluctuates monthly; withdrawals may be made anytime.

overdraw (v.) Write checks for money that you don't have in your account; these checks are rejected and returned to you for "insufficient funds," and you are charged a penalty.

penalty (n.) An extra charge for any infraction against any of the agreed-on rules or regulations stipulated by the bank.

reconciliation (n.) Balancing your checkbook; a monthly activity you should perform to ensure that the balance in your checkbook is equal to the amount shown on your monthly bank statement.

savings account (n.) An account at a bank in which you have money that earns interest; also known as a passbook account; you may withdraw funds anytime without penalty.

service charge (n.) A fee that banks charge customers for certain services; fee(s) may vary at different banks.

teller (n.) A bank employee who performs various banking services for customers such as cashing checks, selling traveler's checks, accepting deposits, etc.

withdraw (v.) Take money from an account.

What Do You Say after You Say "Hello"?

The art of conversation is the art of hearing as well as of being heard.
—William Hazlett, *The Plain Speaker* (1826)

After reading and understanding this chapter, you should know:

- Some keys to good conversation

- Some preconversational tips

- How to improve your conversational ability

- How to start a conversation

- How to remember names

- How to express sympathy and emotional support

- How to talk on the telephone

chapter preview

Almost all oral communication involves speaking face to face with one or a few persons. It's a daily activity in which you can improve a great deal if you try.

One of the keys to becoming a good conversationalist is to be genuinely interested in people. This interest is reflected by your attitude, eyes, smile, and handshake. Another key is to have many activities or hobbies and to be able to discuss them knowledgeably. Keeping up with the daily news in various fields by means of newspapers, magazines, and radio and TV broadcasts is a third way to help make you a more interesting person to talk with.

You can develop your conversational ability if you practice the suggestions given. For example, you should be sincere and listen attentively; you should not interrupt, monopolize, offend, complain, or pry; and you should not be a know-it-all.

There are also suggestions for initiating a conversation and keeping it moving—for example, how to introduce people and yourself, how to compliment people sincerely, how to discuss politics and religion, how to ask provocative questions, and how to express sympathy.

Since many people have trouble remembering names, we briefly discuss some psychological principles that can be applied to help you remember names.

Lastly, in todays fast-paced world, making contacts is a significant aspect of getting ahead, so there are suggestions that can help you advance your career.

Conversation

So far, our emphasis has been primarily on how to prepare and deliver a talk confidently on a specific topic. Another more common but crucial aspect of communication is one that you engage in daily. It's a skill that you should master—the art of conversation.

You will engage in conversation countless times each day for the rest of your life. As far as making an impact on your daily life, there is perhaps nothing more important than the way you converse with people. At home; at work; at school; at a business, social or community gathering; in dealing with your spouse, your roommate, your children, or your neighbor; in interacting with your bank, utility company, or IRS agent; and in person or over the telephone, conversation plays a vital role in your life.

Conversational skill can be indispensable on the job. Let's look at an incident in the career of Sergeant Paul Crow, a homicide detective with the Daytona Beach (Florida) Police Department. He was investigating a case in which a woman had been stabbed to death. A second woman had been stabbed in a similar manner, but had survived to identify her assailant. Sgt. Crow interviewed the suspect repeatedly, won his confidence and trust, and encouraged him to *"open up."* "Then he would go on and on," said the sergeant, *"to get it off his chest."* I had to talk on his level, laugh at his jokes, talk about things he knew about." In the end, the prisoner confessed to murdering twenty-seven women. He is now serving a life sentence.[1]

Think for a moment. Can you recall social or professional conversations that you wanted to leave (or actually did leave) because you felt the experience was a waste of time? Perhaps the person who spoke the most was boring and conceited and monopolized the conversation, or a tedious know-it-all, or engaged in malicious gossip.

There is no question that interesting conversation is an art that can and should be developed. And that's what this chapter is all about. "Conversation is an art in which a man has all mankind for his competitors, for it is that which all are practicing everyday while they live."[2]

Some Keys to Good Conversation

Some of the most delicious moments of life blossom in conversation. The art of swift and witty response is universally admired and enjoyed. Sarah Bernhardt, who reigned as the queen of the English- and French-speaking theater from about 1880 to 1920, was as skillful at dialogue offstage as on. In her later years,

in other words:

"open up"—freely express himself

to get it off his chest—openly express himself and talk about things that may have bothered him

---

[1]*Boston Sunday Globe*, 24 October 1982, 12–13.
[2]Ralph Waldo Emerson, "Considerations by the Way," *The Conduct of Life* (1860).

she lived high up in an apartment building in Paris. One day an elderly admirer arrived at her door, gasping for air after the long climb. When he recovered his breath, he asked, "Madame, why do you live so high up?"

"My dear," replied the divine Sarah, "it is the only way I can still make the hearts of men beat faster."[3]

You may recall conversations with people who were captivating, people who made you feel that you were part of the action and who listened to you with as much interest as you listened to them. If you're genuinely interested in others, the conversation stands an excellent chance of being absorbing. There's nothing like a stimulating conversation; in fact, a good conversationalist is usually popular and well received. Such people know how to communicate confidently with others. To be well liked, admired, and respected and to feel that you're making a contribution to society, no matter how infinitesimal, is an unequaled experience.

You can become a better conversationalist, a more appealing person, and a more respected and admired individual. You can, that is, if you have the determination to work at it. And what's even better, you're not on a stage or under a magnifying glass, but among friends. Every day you'll have a multitude of opportunities to practice, to experiment, and to evaluate yourself.

If you blunder, so what? In a few moments you'll have another chance. You won't be graded, criticized, or evaluated. You're free to progress as much as you want, at your own pace. You have your friends, even strangers, classrooms, home, work, the beach, social clubs, and meetings for experimentation. The one sure way not to fail at anything is not to try anything. Then, again, you'll never succeed at anything, either. As someone wisely declared, "The greatest risk is not taking one." We all make mistakes. That's a fact of life. There's nothing wrong with that, provided we learn from them and don't repeat them. Remember, the only person who never makes mistakes is the person who never tries anything. What a dull and boring existence. You can and should make your life more interesting, exciting, adventurous, and fulfilling. It's up to you.

Conversation begins even before you speak. As we mentioned in Chapter 2, your physical presence and expression transmit impressions, favorable or unfavorable, to those around you. Before engaging in conversation, consider these four nonverbal elements: your attitude, your eyes, your smile, and your handshake.

Your Attitude

You must look forward to conversation. It can be challenging, rewarding, and informative if you allow it to be. Have an open, unbiased mind and be ready to listen to all. Be eager to see what you can derive from this experience and what you can contribute to it.

---

[3]*The Little, Brown Book of Anecdotes*, ed. Clifton Fadiman (Boston: Little, Brown, 1985), 60.

You're not on a stage or under a magnifying glass.

A burning positive attitude is volatile fuel for the ignition of stimulating conversation. If you're shy, quiet, or reserved, "The important thing is to pull yourself up by your own hair, to turn yourself inside out and see the whole world with fresh eyes."[4] And if you really want some words on which to chew and digest, then savor the following gem from Harvard psychologist William James: "The greatest discovery of my generation is that a human being can alter his life by altering his attitudes of mind." Powerful, powerful words. If you really want to do something then you must believe that you *can* do it. ***Go for it.***

Your Eyes

Your eyes will reflect if you're genuinely interested. "The eyes have one language everywhere,"[5] and it's understood everywhere. Look people in the eye to

---

[4]Peter Weiss, *Marat/Sade* (1964) 1.13, Geoffrey Skelton and Adrian Mitchell.
[5]George Herbert, *Jacula Prudentum* (1651).

communicate your friendliness and sincerity; otherwise you exclude them. This is particularly true when conversing with two or more people. Looking into the eyes of each person present will help bring reciprocity into the discussion. In other words, looking at all present can't help but motivate them to look at you. As far as eye contact and conversation go, remember the old adage, "the eyes have it."

Your Smile

Can you think of a better way to communicate nonverbally with someone than with a sincere smile? Smiling can be contagious. Try it on the next acquaintance you see; you both may be surprised at the results from something that requires so little effort—just spontaneity.

Wilber D. Nesbit put it quite beautifully when he said,

The thing that goes the farthest towards making life worth while,
That costs the least, and does the most, is just a pleasant smile.

Your Handshake

Shake hands with a grip firm enough to convey a meaningful expression. If you're a strong person, don't use your strength for squashing knuckles. By the same token, people turn away from a lifeless, dangling handshake. When you can greet someone with responsive eyes, a friendly smile, and a warm; meaningful handshake, you've mastered the first step in learning to communicate interpersonally with purpose.

Suggestions to Improve Your Conversational Ability

Are there any secrets, special formulas, or rules that can make you a more effective conversationalist? No, but you must have a burning desire and a total commitment to the effort. Let's look at some suggestions that can help you sharpen your conversational ability.

Be Interested

The right attitude is a prerequisite for participating in conversation. Try to be interested not only in all the topics but also in each participant. If you're not interested in the participants, they'll respond in the same way. So, when someone is speaking, focus your entire attention on him or her. Bernard Baruch, a great statesman once said, "You can win more friends in two months by showing interest in others than you can in two years by trying to interest others in you."

Try to avoid the "wet-fish" handshake.

Have Varied Interests

One of the secrets of stimulating talkers is to have varied interests and to be knowledgeable about them. A good conversationalist can discuss (with reasonable confidence) local, state, and national politics and knows something about the economy; sports; and the social, educational, and entertainment world. Relying on information from the daily newspaper, a weekly news magazine, radio talk shows, TV news, movies, and books and magazines, good conversationalists talk with people and *listen critically.* They're generalists.

Read Headlines

You, too, can become a knowledgeable generalist by conducting "personal" daily briefings. How? Read the newspaper daily. Newspapers are composed of various sections such as International, National, State, and Local news; then you have sections on Business/Financial, Education, Arts & Entertainment, and Sports. Your paper may also carry sections on Home & Garden, Real Estate, and Automotive. Every story has a headline (several words in bold type printed above and describing the contents of the story). Skim through all the sections of the newspaper, reading the headlines. (Not just those areas that interest you—Remember, you're trying to broaden your knowledge.) When some story grabs your attention, read the story. You don't have to read every story in detail, but by perusing all the headlines in every, or most, sections of your paper, then being selective for further reading, you'll be amazed at how quickly the level of diversified information will rise to fill your reservoir of knowledge. Try it.

Hobbies, travel experiences, sports, jobs, military service, and people you've met or work with are all possibilities for stimulating topics of conversation. If you make the effort to expand your horizons, you can become more interesting to others.

Be Sincere

In conversation, don't try to ***put on airs*** and don't bluff, lie, or brag. An insincere person usually ends up with no audience. There is no substitute for sincerity. Remember Lincoln's statement: "You may fool all the people some of the time; you can even fool some of the people all the time; but you can't fool all of the people all the time."

in other words:
put on airs—sound phony, conceited

Be a Good Listener

There is no greater compliment to a speaker than a listener's total absorption in what he or she is saying. Listen with your eyes, your ears, your mind—your total self—with intensity. You'll be amazed at how much you can ***get wrapped up in*** an individual and how much information you can acquire, which may ultimately enhance your contribution to the exchange. In the process of communication listening is as important as speaking.

get wrapped up in—become very enthusiastic about

President Franklin D. Roosevelt once received an official visitor who immediately commented on one of the ship models on his desk. FDR took the bait and devoted most of the thirty-minute visit to discussing ships and the Navy. When the visitor left, the Chief Executive said to his secretary, "That man is one of the best conversationalists I have ever met."

You can almost be guaranteed popularity when you can enjoy the reputation of being a good listener.

Don't Interrupt . . . Unless

An easy way to turn people off or to anger them is to interrupt them often while they're speaking. It's a rude thing to do. The guilty person can't wait to finish someone else's story, to correct a speaker, or to announce a punch line prematurely. There are times, however, when interrupting is not only acceptable but, probably, wise. Let's assume that during a conversation, the speaker said something that you didn't understand. It would be wise for you to courteously interrupt the speaker and ask for clarification; otherwise, you run the risk of not understanding most or all of the remaining discussion. You could interrupt by saying something like, "Excuse me, but in other words . . . ?" "You mean . . . ?" or, "Pardon me, but if I heard you correctly, then what you're

On occasion, it's okay to interrupt.

saying is . . . ?" Then restate what you thought you heard. Interrupting for purposes of clarification is acceptable, but constant and "uncontrollable" interruption is not.

If English is not your primary language, it is all the more important for you to politely interrupt a speaker by raising your hand and asking for clarification when you hear something that you don't understand.

A classic example of "uncontrollable" interruption occurred between the two female members of the U.S. Supreme Court, no less. As Justice Sandra Day O'Connor was questioning an attorney during oral argument before the full bench, just-appointed Justice Ruth Bader Ginsburg rudely ***broke in*** with her own question. This brought an immediate acrid stare accompanied by the incisive, "Excuse me! Just let me finish," from an irate O'Connor.[6]

One of the things that the third President of the United States abhorred was being interrupted. As a result, Thomas Jefferson invented the "dumbwaiter," a small mechanical lift that brought food and refreshments from the kitchen to an upstairs dining room and was operated manually by a pulley. Because of this invention, Jefferson no longer was frustrated by the interruptions of servants during important conversations.

As difficult as it may be, at times, try not to interrupt someone until that person finishes speaking. Not only will you be appreciated, you will also gain respect.

---

[6]*Newsweek,* 11 April 1994, 6.

in other words:

broke in— interrupted

Don't Be a Bore

We all know one-track people who discuss the same old topics: job, hobby or sport, house, car, or boat. It might have been interesting the first or second time, but the third time is boring. Family and relatives can be boring topics, especially discussed by a person who can't wait to extract a wallet bursting with children's pictures or to babble incessantly about their offspring at college or about their "prestigious" jobs. Winston Churchill felt that the subject of children was inappropriate for adult conversation. At one particular gathering, an ambassador said to him, "You know, Sir Winston, I've never told you about my grandchildren." The old warrior chomped on his cigar, dragged deeply, and exhaled, "I realize it, my dear fellow, and I can't tell you how grateful I am."

Here's how another international statesman handled boring situations. Prince Otto Bismarck of Prussia had been conversing for rather a long time with the English ambassador when the latter posed the question: "How do you handle insistent visitors who take up so much of your valuable time?" Bismarck answered, "Oh, I have an infallible method. My servant appears and informs me that my wife has something urgent to tell me." At that moment there was a knock at the door and the servant entered with a message from his wife.

Know When to Conclude

Once your turn has come to talk, don't act as though it may be your last chance on earth and go on and on and on. If you have something to say, say it. Then give others the opportunity to express themselves; listen to them, and respond. That's the essence of conversation.

Unfortunately, long-winded speakers have always assailed our ears and taxed our patience. Claude Swanson, a well-known national politician from Virginia at the beginning of the twentieth century, one evening presented a long and rambling speech. Following his talk, an elderly woman approached him to shake his hand. "How did you like my speech?" asked Swanson. "I liked it fine," she replied, "but it seems to me you missed several excellent opportunities." A puzzled Swanson then queried, "Several excellent opportunities for what?" "To quit," she snapped.[7] I once heard someone give some excellent advice: it's okay to hold a conversation, but you should let go of it now and then.

Don't Be Offensive

There are many ways to offend people—for example, by making derogatory remarks about their dress, physical appearance, voice, accent, religion, or politics. These remarks cause two negative results: they anger the recipient and they brand the offender as a person to be avoided. It's far better to say nothing

---

[7] *The Little, Brown Book of Anecdotes*, 530.

in other
          words:
**rub people the
wrong way—**
irritate them

than to **rub people the wrong way.** Remember the words of Darius Lyman: "I have often regretted my speech, never my silence."

Don't Be a Constant Complainer

Everyone has problems and, as a rule, would rather not hear yours. A brief mention of your problem might be acceptable to your listeners, but don't dwell on it for the entire conversation. Some people always complain, no matter what the subject is. Since their negative attitude can be contagious, you'd be wise to avoid them.

Don't Pry

Nobody can be more offensive than one who persists in prying for personal information. Following are some typical questions followed by some apt retorts which may produce some interesting facial expressions. (But be sure you retort with a smile.)

Why don't you have any children?

We don't want any . . . We hate kids. . . . Or: I give up . . . why?

Your drapes are beautiful. They must be expensive; are they?

Thank you. Yes, they are, and very.

And how old might you be, my dear?

I might be 25, 30, 31.

A super reply was once returned by my wife when a busybody asked about the family income. My wife leaned toward the questioner and whispered, "Are you good at keeping secrets?" "Oh yes, certainly," was the reply, to which my wife answered, "So am I."

Don't Be a Know-It-All

Obnoxious people in conversation are experts on everything—politics, labor problems, social problems, religion, family affairs. No matter what the topic of discussion, they have the answers. Being knowledgeable is a tremendous asset when you participate in conversation, but sometimes discretion and good taste are greater virtues.

Don't Be a Gossip

Unfortunately, many people enjoy gossip and rumors. It's very tempting and so easy to say things just for attention and recognition. This activity is not only cruel, it can inflict irreparable damage to another person's character. And, let's face it, no one really trusts or respects a gossip.

As the Greek dramatist Sophocles said in the fifth century B.C.E., "A short saying oft contains much wisdom." Actually, I have two for you, and they're both proverbs that solicit your contemplation:

Whoever gossips to you, will gossip about you.

Spanish proverb

What you don't see with your eyes, don't witness with your mouth.

Jewish proverb

Disagree without Being Disagreeable

Nothing is more stimulating than a conversation sparked with disagreement, provided it remains on a rational, friendly level. There is much to gain from hearing opposing viewpoints, plus the challenge of persuading or being persuaded. Whenever disagreement is introduced into a conversation, everybody's interest perks up. Don't shout or lose your temper if someone gets the better of you. If you feel embarrassed at losing an argument, perhaps you could have been better prepared. There will be a next time. No one likes to lose, but accepting it gracefully could earn respect for you.

A wise old speech professor of mine once said, "It is better to stir up a question without deciding it, than to decide it without stirring it up." Go for it.

Include Everyone

When you're involved in conversation, be sure to direct your remarks to everyone. Look at each person as you make your points. Then they'll be more apt to pay attention to you and to respond. Interest shown by eye contact, a nod of the head, and an occasional gesture toward an individual will do it.

Try to Be More Outgoing

In every conversation there are speakers, listeners, and speaker-listeners. Perhaps you're the kind who'd rather remain in the background and just listen to what's going on. But that's only half the fun. If you tend toward shyness, you belong with the majority of the human race. (This topic is discussed in detail in Chapter 1.)

TV commentator Barbara Walters used to be one of that majority. Some years ago, she and her husband attended a Fourth of July party, where they were introduced to novelist Truman Capote. His book, *In Cold Blood*, had just been published and was zooming to the top of the bestseller list. ". . . I was yearning to talk with him about it," she confessed, "but I couldn't cross the barrier of my own shyness and my fear that Capote must be fed up with people asking about his work."[8]

---

[8]Barbara Walters, *How to Talk with Practically Anybody about Practically Anything* (New York: Dell, 1971), xiii.

If you're a listener or a speaker-listener, you may find that small groups (four or five people) are easier to break into than large groups (ten or more). But you must *want* to engage in conversation. An exercise is to observe good talkers in action and to adopt some of their methods.

In some situations, reluctance to speak up can be dangerous—even fatal. In February 1982, at Washington National Airport, two pilots of a Boeing 737, about to take off, saw snow and ice building up on the wings and engines even after their plane had been de-iced twice. Both pilots were deeply worried—the audiotapes revealed later—but instead of questioning the control tower about the advisability of takeoff, they said nothing. They crashed into the Potomac River, killing seventy-four people aboard and four passing motorists.[9] It pays to speak up, even if you may be ignored or wrong.

As we said earlier, since the whole world is your laboratory, experiment with these techniques. You have a great deal to gain, and when you start to participate more in conversation, it will become easier and will do wonders for your self-confidence. Since improvement depends on active participation, the sooner you start, the better.

How to Start a Conversation

Let's now look at some ways to help you start a conversation and keep it going.

"I'd Like You to Meet. . . ."

Assume that you're being introduced to a small group. Your introducer may mention something about you—your background, experience, or job—and perhaps even tell you some unusual tidbits about individual members of the group you're meeting. During this time you can decide to whom you would like to return for conversation because of a possible common interest.

"Hello, I'm. . . ."

If there's no one to introduce you, you should introduce yourself. Since nearly everyone at a gathering enjoys meeting the other guests, take a deep breath, approach someone, and introduce yourself. In addition to your name, give some information that might be interesting to the person and that might allow him or her to respond in kind. After a handshake, repeat her name aloud. Then you might say something about the host and hostess, your work, your home, sports, or the latest headline news. Then ***toss the ball*** to the other guest and see what happens.

in other
words:

**toss the ball
(to someone)**—
allow the other
person to
respond

---

[9]"We're Going Down, Larry," *Time,* 15 February 1982, 21.

"Excuse Me, but Didn't I Hear You Mention . . . ?"

On occasion you may overhear a topic of interest from someone in a small group. Nothing could be more complimentary, at your first opportunity, than to approach the person with something like, "Excuse me, but I couldn't help hearing you mention. . . . That sounds fascinating. Could I ask you . . . ?" The fact that you're interested in someone enough to pursue his line of conversation will **open the door for you,** and a lively meeting could ensue.

in other words:
open the door for you—allow you the possibility of continuing your conversation

"Say, I Like Your. . . ."

Nothing is easier to accept than a sincere compliment. Perhaps you admire someone's jewelry, shirt, tie, blouse, hairdo, or suit. If you do, say so. Again, since bringing positive attention to someone's abilities or possessions is highly satisfying, you're almost guaranteed an interested listener. Paying a genuine compliment is an excellent springboard for starting a conversation.

"Crummy Weather We're Having, Eh?"

Discussing the weather or natural disasters can serve two purposes: it can fill a silent period between people, and it can be an interesting subject if you're on top of the news. What about the devastation in California caused by the 1998 El Niño, which resulted in pounding rains, mudslides, high winds, record surfs and . . . deaths; or the relentless fires that hungrily consumed hundred of thousands of acres and threatened homes and lives in Florida due to a record drought?

"I Never Discuss Politics and Religion."

Although some people will not discuss politics and religion, these subjects can lead to a stimulating, informative give-and-take. For that to happen, however, the participants must not become hotheaded, irrational, or belligerent. There perhaps has never been a time in our country's history when so much controversy surrounds so many political and religious issues. For that reason alone, we should talk over those subjects more than ever. Exploring them intelligently can be a beneficial experience that could lead to better understanding among people.

These two topics, however, can be very explosive subjects for conversation in some other countries/cultures. We'll discuss this shortly.

Play the Role of Interviewer

Although some people find this technique difficult, it can be most rewarding. It requires discovering someone who has an unusual lifestyle or profession, someone who may be quietly sitting in the background. Get the

"How do you like this weather?"

person to talk. This technique involves asking questions (how? what? why? and when?) and could result in an exhilarating experience for all those present.

A few years ago I attended a large social gathering where I knew only the host and hostess. From talking with the hostess, I learned that one guest—the hostess pointed him out—was a senior design engineer in a company that produced and tested missiles. She added that he was not only brilliant and had a sense of humor, but he could also translate difficult scientific concepts into common language.

At the first chance, I introduced myself to the engineer and started questioning him about his early start in mechanics and electronics, about some design challenges and solutions, about his travel overseas, and so on. As the conversation warmed up, more and more guests began to ask questions and contribute comments. When a lull occurred, I revved up the proceedings with another pertinent question. By the time the conversation ended three hours later, practically all forty guests had participated in this informative and sometimes entertaining experience.

An excellent way to learn this technique is to listen to radio and TV talk shows and to read interviews in the news media. Notice how questions are begun and followed up, how they're developed from answers, and how they're phrased so that they don't elicit one-word responses. Notice how interviewers leave a particular line of questioning and start another and when and how they **_wrap it all up._**

in other words:
wrap it all up—conclude

"I Never Forget a Face . . . but Names?"

How often have you heard that? Some people can remember names but can't match them with faces; others can remember faces but can't recall names. One way to impress people is to remember their names. To most of us, nothing is more important.

Memory can be strengthened if you're willing to work at it. The following are some elements involved in developing your memory for names and faces.

1. *Attention.* Whenever you meet people for the first time, pay strict attention to their appearance, because you want to remember their names. Observe facial features—eyes, hair, ears, dimple, nose—for something striking or peculiar that may make it easier for you to recall the person later.
2. *Association.* Is there any way you can associate the name with the person's features or occupation? Perhaps Ms. Smiley has a beautiful smile. Perhaps Mr. Pearlman is in the jewelry business or his teeth resemble pearls. It's amazing how, with effort and imagination, you can associate a name with a physical feature, occupation, or hobby. Be on the lookout.
3. *Comparison.* Perhaps a person has a name similar to that of a very good friend of yours. Visualize this person in comparison with your friend. Compare their features. Search for a resemblance or vast difference that might make it easier for you to remember your new acquaintance's name. Again, you may be amazed at what you can **come up with.**
4. *Repetition.* When you meet a person for the first time, repeat the person's name as often as possible so that it is firmly implanted in your mind. Be sure that you hear the correct pronunciation of the name. If necessary, have it repeated and spelled; then you repeat it. Repetition is one of the keys to memorizing. But be sure to pay undivided attention to the person and the person's name. I recall a rather embarrassing situation when I was introduced to a gentleman and, due to inattentiveness, I didn't catch his name and replied, "That's an unusual name; how do you spell it?" He obliged with "S-M-I-T-H."

Samuel Johnson put it best when he said, "The true art of memory is the art of attention."

in other words:

come up with—discover

Taboo Topics of Conversation around the World

Although we have discussed a number of ways to initiate a conversation, obviously, not all these suggestions apply to various areas around the world. Each country/culture has its own conversational rules on what should or should not be discussed, especially by visitors from other countries/cultures.

Here is a listing of some countries/cultures where particular topics are not considered appropriate for conversation. This partial submission is from Roger Axtell's extremely interesting and informative book, titled *Do's and Taboos around the World.*[10]

---

[10]Roger Axtell, *Do's and Taboos around the World* (White Plains, NY: John Wiley & Sons, Inc., 1993).

Country/Culture	Avoid in Conversation
England, Scotland, and Wales	Religion, politics, gossip about the monarchy
Algeria	Politics and industrial problems
Egypt	Middle Eastern politics
Libya	Politics and religion
Nigeria	Religion
Israel	U.S. financial aid and religion
Iraq	Religion or Middle Eastern politics
Jordan	Religion, Middle Eastern politics, family, and U.S. financial aid
Saudi Arabia	Middle Eastern politics and international oil politics
The People's Republic of China	Taiwan or Chinese leadership
India	Personal affairs, India's poverty, foreign aid
Japan	World War II
Mexico	Political topics and illegal aliens
The Caribbean	Local politics and religion

How to Make Social and Business Contacts

One of the more pragmatic aspects of life is making business and social contacts. Let's not kid ourselves; the more people we know, the more progress we may make in our careers. You may have friends who were promoted or got jobs because they knew certain people. Others may have received benefits or special treatment because they had contacts.

Getting to know people is very important, but first you have to meet them. An excellent place to do this is at school. Try to get along with as many people as possible by being friendly and helpful and by keeping in touch. You never know who may be able to assist you in the near future or after graduation. If you're in a position to do someone a favor, do it. The day may come when you'll need a favor in return.

If you have a goal to achieve, make it a point to associate with people who can help you. Associate with people you admire and respect; some of their talents may ***rub off on you.*** Whether in your business or social environment, there are always key people, leaders, who get things done. If you can help them in any way, volunteer. Do more than is expected, and that alone will set you apart from the masses. When people in authority can depend on you, you're beginning to build a future for yourself.

in other words:
rub off on you—be transferred to you

How to Express Sympathy and Emotional Support

We all occasionally find ourselves in situations when some comforting words or actions must be expressed. Perhaps a loved one or a friend has died, your spouse was laid off work after fifteen years with the company, a close relative is diagnosed as having a terminal illness, or your closest friend's teenager was arrested for injuring an elderly person while driving under the influence of alcohol.

Perhaps the most difficult situation to be confronted with is someone's death. How often have you heard people ask, "What do you say?" It would be impossible to list all of the appropriate things to say to cover specific situations, but the following suggestions may help make your presence a little more comforting and, at the same time, offer a grieving person some emotional support.

Be an Active Listener

Listening attentively to a bereaved person can be very supportive and therapeutic. If the individual wishes to talk about the situation, listen with all the love and understanding *at your command.* Often, just listening without interrupting or pontificating can provide that person with the needed comfort. If he or she doesn't wish to talk and would rather be alone, respect that decision, but indicate clearly that you'll be available whenever he or she feels like talking.

Empathize

Be sure to communicate that you understand how the person feels by nodding or saying such things as, "I can understand your feelings," "I know what you're going through," "Yes, it is tragic," or "I know what you mean." It's important that the person feels that other people understand, sympathize, and care, even though they might not have actually experienced the same loss. Showing your genuine concern can be therapeutic.

Express Nonverbal Support

At times, just touching is the most eloquent message that you can communicate to a distressed person. A hug, an arm around the shoulder, the squeeze of a hand, or a kiss says it all. If you honestly feel that you are at a complete loss for words, don't attempt any.

Don't Platitudinize

Sayings like "Well, everything happens for the best," "God works in strange ways," or "Think of the good times" are usually not what a grieving person wishes to hear. Your sensitive caring and understanding are far more important

in other words:

at your command—in your power

than your philosophizing. A sincere "If there's anything you need" or "If there's anything I can do, please let me know," or "I'll call you tomorrow" can be very comforting.

Trying to think of just the right words to say to a grieving person can be quite uncomfortable and embarrassing—but it needn't be. You know the situation and the person(s) involved. As long as you are sincere with your expression of understanding, whether verbal or nonverbal, you can feel confident that your presence will be appreciated.

How to Talk on the Telephone

For most people, talking on the phone is an important means of developing and carrying on one-to-one relationships. Talking on the phone is something you do regularly, perhaps many times daily, at home and on the job. The following are some suggestions to help you become more proficient at it.

Courtesy

Always treat telephone callers courteously, not only because it's the right thing to do but because your response colors their impression of both you and your company or organization. If you've had a rough day and your nerves are rubbed raw, don't let your voice and words show it. That's easy to say but hard to do. If you're too pressured to talk at the moment, say so, get the caller's name and number, and call back in fifteen minutes, a half-hour, or whenever you can. But do what you said—call back.

Too many people today answer the phone, "Just a moment, please," and then keep the caller hanging for three or four minutes. It's far more considerate and businesslike to get the caller's name and number and return the call a few minutes later.

This approach especially applies if you have "call waiting," which allows you to answer an incoming call while you're speaking on the phone. If the incoming call is more urgent than your present conversation, politely say so to the first caller and state that you'll call right back. Courtesy and tact on the phone *pay off* in the long run.

in other words:
pay off—eventually bring positive results

Voice

Your voice will come through more warmly if you remember that you're not talking to a piece of office equipment, but to another human being. If you feel what you're saying and visualize the other person (see "Oral Visualization" in Chapter 5), you'll probably even use gestures, such as nodding your head, shrugging your shoulders, and smiling, and your voice will reflect that. As a result, you won't sound mechanical; you'll sound human.

Always treat telephone callers courteously.

For most people, the transmitter, or mouthpiece, should be held 1 or 2 inches away from the mouth and at the same level. If you tend to talk softly, keep the mouthpiece less than 1 inch away; if you blast, 3 or 4 inches would be better.

Pronunciation

Don't chew gum, smoke, or clench a pencil between your teeth. Any of those actions will result in slurred words so that your listener may have to keep asking, "What did you say?" or "Pardon me?" And be sure to speak slowly so that you will be understood. The most common speech problem of telephone users is that they talk too fast.

Brevity of Calls

At work it's a sensible idea to keep most of your calls short, say, five minutes or less. Plan your statement beforehand, and once on the phone, explain the reason for your call and its importance. Then close with a few words on the course of action you or the other person is going to take. Avoid rambling endlessly;

someone else, with an urgent message, may be trying to reach you or the person you're speaking with.

Expressions of Goodwill

Certain expressions "stroke" most people soothingly. Some of these are:

"You have a very pleasant voice."

"Thank you."

"I appreciate that."

"I'm glad to help you."

"If you have any questions, be sure to call me."

When said sincerely, these expressions can build goodwill for you and your company.

Identification

At work, rather than answering with "Hello," you should immediately identify yourself and your department. Not only does this save time, callers will know that they have the right party and, in that case, will most likely identify themselves. Whenever you make a call regarding a serious complaint or problem, be sure to note the date and the other person's name and number for future reference.

Security

Once you pick up the receiver, don't make side remarks to anybody nearby. Even if you cup your hand over the mouthpiece, the callers may hear information through the earpiece that they shouldn't know. In a social sense that could be embarrassing; in the business or professional world, it could be costly to your organization or to your career.

Memory Aids

Always have a pencil and notepad near the phone so you can take messages promptly. Keeping on hand a list of frequently used numbers and emergency numbers can save precious time.

Taking Messages

When you answer for someone who's not in the office, avoid statements like:

"She's having coffee now."

"She's late today."

"She's in the ladies room"

A more tactful approach would be to say, "She's out of the office. May I take your name and number so she can call you when she returns?"

Leaving Messages

When phoning people who don't know you and who are not able to take your call, be sure to give your name and number, including area code and extension, to the person answering. Then repeat that information slowly, because too many of us zip off the phone number before it can be jotted down.

Quick Clicks

Welcome to a "surprise search." To further enhance your research or simply to harvest more information about some of the things you studied in this chapter, just drop in at any of the following addresses. What you'll discover may be serious, educational, bibliographical, surprising, factual, or even downright humorous. But it will definitely be informative.

So, go ahead and give a "Quick Click."

www.pickuplines.org
www.nytimes.com/learning/parents/conversation
www.cyberparent.com/talk/listen.htm
www.cyberparent.com/talk/attend.htm
www.bartleby.com/95/7.html
www.demon.co.uk/mindtool/memory.html

Things to Discuss in Class

1. Before class, in the cafeteria, or at your next social function, select a person you've seen before but never talked with. Introduce yourself and start a conversation. Tell the class of your experience.
2. List a few different sections of a newspaper and tell the class some news items you discovered in each section.
3. Listen to a radio talk program and take notes. Then tell the class about the talk show host and the line of questioning. Was he or she fair? Probing? Interesting? A good listener?
4. Try one or more of the techniques of starting a conversation discussed in this chapter and tell the class about your experience(s).
5. Tell the class how you feel about discussing politics and religion.
6. What methods do you use to remember names and faces? Share your methods with the class.

7. How do you rate yourself as a listener?
   Tell the class how you can become a more
   effective listener.
8. Your closest friend didn't get a much-
   desired job. Tell the class what you
   would say to comfort him or her.
9. List several "prying" questions, and suggest
   some suitable responses to them.
10. You're at a party, conversing with someone
    who doesn't agree with you. Suddenly,
    the other person becomes loud and
    disagreeable. Tell the class what your
    response would be.

What Do You Remember from This Chapter?

1. What are some ways to develop your conversational ability?
2. How can you become a more interesting
   person?
3. List a few good conversational habits.

4. When is it permissible to interrupt
   someone?
5. Comment on this statement: "I never
   discuss politics or religion."
6. Explain several ways to start a conversation.
7. What are some elements involved in
   memory development, especially regarding
   people's names?
8. What is the key to making business and
   social contacts?
9. How can you disagree without being
   disagreeable?
10. When answering a question, should you
    look only at the questioner or at every
    member of the group? Explain.
11. Can you express sympathy nonverbally?
    Explain.
12. When talking on the telephone, how
    far should your mouth be from the
    mouthpiece?

Vitalize Your Vocabulary

Phobias

A phobia is an irrational and exaggerated fear of
an object or situation. The word *phobia* is derived from the Greek word *phobos*, which
means "fear," "terror," or "panic."

Phobia	Fear of
auto or monophobia	being alone
acrophobia	heights
agoraphobia	open or public places
androphobia	men
ailurophobia	cats
anthophobia	flowers
anthropophobia	people
aqua or hydrophobia	water
arachnophobia	spiders
astraphobia	lightning
aviophobia	flying
brontophobia	thunder
claustrophobia	closed or small places
cynophobia	dogs
demonophobia	demons (suffered by some children at Halloween)
electrophobia	electricity (especially from getting a shock)
ergophobia	work
equinophobia	horses
ereuthophobia	blushing
genophobia	sex
graphophobia	writing
gynophobia	women
hemophobia	blood
herpetophobia	lizards or reptiles
hodophobia	traveling
homophobia	homosexuals
hypnophobia	sleep
kakorrhaphiophobia	failure
logophobia or phonophobia	public speaking (The author is sure that this term doesn't apply to anyone taking this course. Not too much!)
microphobia	germs
mysophobia	dirt
numerophobia	numbers
nyctophobia	darkness or night

ochlophobia	crowds
ophidiophobia	snakes
pathophobia	disease
pyrophobia	fire
tachophobia	speed
thanatophobia	death
triskaidekaphobia	the number 13
xenophobia	strangers/foreigners

A Word from the Author

Hi! Since most people experience some type of phobia to some degree, even though they may hesitate to admit it at first, you might consider introducing this subject the next time you encounter a lull in the conversation at your next social engagement. The subject of phobias could also produce a most interesting, revealing, and enlightening class discussion. And don't forget to use the dictionary to learn the correct pronunciations of the words listed above.

A

Speeches to Study

Here are six speeches for you to enjoy, study, and analyze. The first three are not only historical but are, indeed, excellent examples of true oratorical genius. They merit reading and digesting more than once. The fourth, by Mark Twain, is not only classic in its own right, but one with which you should easily be able to associate—the possible apprehension over giving your first talk. The fifth speech, by former First Lady Barbara Bush, appeared in the last edition and because of its very favorable response and "down-to-earth" contents, I've decided to include it again in this ninth edition. And, finally, President George W. Bush's dynamic and memorable 9-11 "War on Terrorism" speech to a joint session of Congress nine days following the terrorist attacks on the World Trade Center and the Pentagon.

To further help you in the study and analysis of these speeches, each one, with the exception of President Bush's address, includes a sentence and topic outline along with its commentary.

General Norman Schwarzkopf

One of the truly great American speeches of this century was delivered by General H. Norman Schwarzkopf in May 1991 to the U.S. Congress. This twenty-minute speech was "interrupted by applause 14 times, often with standing ovations"[1] because it was highly inspirational and emotional, especially when he answered the question "who were we?"—that is, who made up the U.S. Armed Forces. Here is his blockbuster answer to that question: "We were men and we were women . . . Protestants and Catholics and Jews and Moslems and Buddhists . . . black and white and yellow and brown and red, and we noticed that when our blood was shed in the desert, it didn't separate by race."

Without question, this speech "stands by itself on a mountain-top" for several reasons: its inspirational content; its clear, down-to-earth language

---

[1]*Boston Globe*, 9 May 1991, 23.

fortified with parallel structure and repetition; its facts about our Armed Forces; and the general's powerful delivery.

Here is his speech, as recorded in the *Congressional Record.*[2] Because the paragraphs in the *Congressional Record* are overly long, we've altered the paragraphing of the speech according to a nearly illegible copy of the speech received from the general's headquarters in Tampa, Florida. That copy also noted occasions of applause.

■ General Schwarzkopf's Speech to the U.S. Congress

1   (Applause) Mr. Speaker, members of Congress and distinguished guests. It's a great day to be a soldier and it's a great day to be an American. (Applause)

2   I want to thank you for the singular distinction of being allowed to speak to a special session of the Congress of the United States of America. Indeed, I am awed and honored to be standing at the podium where so many notable men and women have stood before me. Unlike them, I don't stand here today for any great deed that I have done. Instead, I stand here because I was granted by our national leadership the great privilege of commanding the magnificent American service men and women who constituted the armed forces of Operation Desert Shield and Desert Storm. (Applause)

3   And before I go any further, I must—through their representatives who are here today—tell each and every one of those extraordinary patriots that I have no idea what the future holds in store for me. But I do know one thing: I will never ever in my entire life receive a greater reward than the inspiration that I received every single day as I watched your dedicated performance, your dedicated sacrifice, your dedicated service to your country. (Applause)

4   Since I was fortunate enough to command these great Americans and since you are the elected representatives of the American people, I would presume today to speak for our service men and women through you to the people of our great nation.

5   First of all, who were we? We were 541,000 soldiers, sailors, airmen, Marines, and Coast Guardsmen. We were the thunder and lightning of Desert Storm. We were the United States military and we're damn proud of it. (Applause)

6   But we were more than that. We were all volunteers. And we were regulars, we were reservists, we were national guardsmen serving side-by-side as we have in every war, because that's what the United States military is. And we were men and we were women, each of us bearing our fair share of the load and none of us quitting because the conditions were too rough or the job was too tough, because that's what your military is. And we were Protestants and Catholics and Jews and Moslems and Buddhists and many other religions

The dramatic opening sentence grabs your attention instantly.

The general is very generous in giving credit to the service men and women who served in Operation Desert Shield and Desert Storm. We Americans admire a public figure who doesn't "hog" the limelight and take all the credit.

The general asked the question: "First of all, who were we?" It's the kind of question that arouses interest. His answer was striking—"We were the thunder and lightning of Desert Storm. We were the United States military and we're damn proud of it."

---

[2]*Congressional Record—House*, 8 May 1991, H2814.

The general portrayed the U.S. military and made his points stick by using repetition. Four times he ended statements with the words, "because that's what your military is."

The general paid respect and recognition to the veterans of the Vietnam War who, when they returned home, were treated much differently. Many of the emotional and psychological wounds and scars of those veterans still fester.

The general thanked God "for the protection He gave us in the deserts of Kuwait and Iraq." This is an especially emotional paragraph.

More thanks, this time to our Commander-in-Chief, Congress, comrades who stayed behind, our families, and the U.S. public. Again, a deeply emotional statement.

fighting for a common and just cause, because that's what your military is. And we were black and white and yellow and brown and red, and we noticed that, when our blood was shed in the desert, it didn't separate by race; it flowed together. (Sustained applause) You see, that's what your military is.

7   And we fought side by side with brothers and sisters at arms who were British and French and Saudi Arabian and Egyptian and Kuwaiti and members of many other Arab and Western nations. And you know what? We noticed the same thing when their blood was shed in the desert. It did not separate according to national origin.

8   We left our homes, our families, and traveled thousands of miles away and fought in places with names we couldn't even pronounce, simply because you asked us to, and therefore it became our duty, because that's what your military does.

9   We now proudly join the ranks of Americans who call themselves veterans. We're proud to share that title with those who went before us. And we feel a particular pride in joining the ranks with that special group who served their country in the mountains and the jungles and the deltas of Vietnam. (Sustained applause) They served just as proudly in Vietnam as we served in the Middle East.

10   And now that we've won a great victory, we dare to ask that, just as we were willing to sacrifice and fight to win the war, you be willing to sacrifice and search to win the peace. (Applause)

11   We would like to offer our thanks. First, we'd like to thank our God for the protection He gave us in the deserts of Kuwait and Iraq. Most of us came home safely. We ask Him to grant a special love to all of our fallen comrades who gave their lives for the cause of freedom, and we ask that He embrace to his bosom not only the 147 of us who were killed in action, but also the 188 of us who gave their lives before the war, during Operation Desert Shield, and since the termination of Desert Storm. They, too, no less than our killed in action, died for the cause of freedom.

12   We also ask that God grant special strength to our comrades who are still in the hospitals with wounds and injuries they received during the war. By their example, we should all remember that the freedoms we enjoy in this great country of ours do not come without a price. They are paid for and protected by the lives, the limbs, and the blood of American service men and women.

13   We would also like to thank our Commander-in-Chief for his wisdom and courage and the confidence he demonstrated in us by allowing us to fight this war in such a way that we were able to minimize our casualties. (Sustained applause) That is the right way to fight a war. (Applause)

14   We'd like to thank the Congress and former administrations for giving us the finest tanks, the finest aircraft, the finest ships, and the finest military equipment in the whole world without question. (Applause) Without question, that is what gave us the confidence necessary to attack into the teeth of our enemy with the sure knowledge that we would prevail. And we would ask that in years to come, as we reduce the quantity of our armed forces, that you never forget that it is the quality of the armed forces that wins wars. (Sustained applause)

15   We want to say a special thanks to our comrades in uniform who stayed behind. You backed us up so we could carry the fight to the enemy. You maintained the peace so that we could win the war. We never could have done our job if you hadn't done yours.

16   We also want to thank the families. It's you who endure the hardships and the separations, simply because you choose to love a soldier, a sailor, an airman, a Marine, or a Coast Guardsman. But it's your love that truly gave us strength in our darkest hours. (Sustained applause) Military families are the wind beneath our wings.

17   Finally, and most importantly, to the great American people. The prophets of doom, the naysayers, the protesters, and the flag burners all said that you wouldn't stick by us. But we knew better. We knew you'd never let us down. By golly, you didn't! (Sustained applause) Since the first hour of Desert Shield until the last minute of Desert Storm, every day and every way, all across America you shouted that you were with us. Millions of elementary school, high school, and college students, millions and millions of families, untold numbers of civic organizations, veterans organizations, countless offices, factories, companies, and work places, millions of senior Americans, and just plain Americans never let us forget that we were in their hearts and you were in our corner. Because of you, when that terrible first day of the war came, we knew we would not fail. We knew we had the strength of the American people behind us, and with that strength, we were able to get the job done, kick the Iraqis out of Kuwait, and get back home. (Sustained applause)

18   So for every soldier, thank you America. For every sailor, thank you America. For every Marine, thank you America. For every airman, thank you America. For every Coast Guardsman, thank you America. From all of us who proudly served in the Middle East and your armed forces, thank you to the great people of the United States of America. (Sustained applause)

> A brief conclusion that is pure dynamite because of parallel construction.

Sentence Outline of General Schwarzkopf's Speech to the U.S. Congress

Introduction

I. It's a great day.

II. Thank you for the privilege of speaking to you.

III. On behalf of the great Americans who fought in Operation Desert Shield and Desert Storm, I speak to the people of our great nation through you.

Body

I. Who were we?

    A. We were 541,000 soldiers, sailors, airmen, Marines and Coast Guardsmen.

    B. We were all volunteers; regulars, reservists, national guardsmen; men and women; members of many religions and races.

C. When our blood was shed in the desert, it didn't separate by race or nationality.

D. That's what your military is.

II. We went to the Persian Gulf because you asked us to.

A. That's what your military does.

III. We proudly join the ranks of American veterans.

IV. Now we ask you to sacrifice and search to win the peace.

V. We would like to offer our thanks—to God; to our Commander-in-Chief; to Congress and former administrations; to our comrades who stayed behind; to our families.

Conclusion

I. But most of all, we offer our thanks to the great American people.

A. You didn't let us down.

B. We derived strength from your support.

II. From all who fought, thank you to the great people of the United States of America.

Topic Outline

Introduction

I. A great day

II. The privilege of speaking to you

III. Congress as representatives of the people

Body

I. Who we were:

A. 541,000 soldiers, sailors, airmen, Marines and Coast Guardsmen.

B. All volunteers:

1. Regulars, reservists, national guardsmen

2. Men and women

3. Members of many religions and races

C. No separation of blood by race or nationality

D. What your military is

E. Response to what you asked of us

F. What your military does

II. American veterans now

III. Admonition to win the peace

IV. Thanks:

A. To God

B. To Commander-in-Chief

C. To Congress and former administrations

D. To comrades who stayed behind

E. To our families

Conclusion

   V. Above all, thanks to the great American people for:
     A. Support
     B. Strength
  VI. Thanks from all who fought to the great people of the United States of America

John F. Kennedy

The following three speeches were also given by men who spoke with eloquence, confidence, and effectiveness. The first speech, delivered by President John F. Kennedy in Berlin in 1963, also ranks among the best of this century. Kennedy had gone to Europe to support democracy and freedom and to strengthen U.S. commitment to Western Europe. He spoke to the people and reached them most effectively. The title won audience goodwill and interest because it is in German. His entire speech—note how short it is—appears below, followed by the outlines.

"Ich Bin ein Berliner"

1   I am proud to come to this city as the guest of your distinguished Mayor, who has symbolized throughout the world the fighting spirit of West Berlin. And I am proud to visit the Federal Republic with your distinguished Chancellor who for so many years has committed Germany to democracy and freedom and progress, and to come here in the company of my fellow American, General Clay, who has been in this city during its great moments of crisis and will come again if ever needed.

2   Two thousand years ago the proudest boast was *"civis Romanus sum."* Today, in the world of freedom, the proudest boast is *"Ich bin ein Berliner."*

3   I appreciate my interpreter translating my German!

4   There are many people in the world who really don't understand, or say they don't, what is the great issue between the free world and the Communist world. Let them come to Berlin. There are some who say that communism is the wave of the future. Let them come to Berlin. And there are some who say in Europe and elsewhere we can work with the Communists. Let them come to Berlin. And there are even a few who say that it is true that communism is an evil system, but it permits us to make economic progress. *Lass' sie nach Berlin kommen.* Let them come to Berlin.

5   Freedom has many difficulties and democracy is not perfect, but we have never had to put a wall up to keep our people in, to prevent them from leaving us. I want to say, on behalf of my countrymen, who live many miles away on the other side of the Atlantic, who are far distant from you, that they take the greatest pride that they have been able to share with you, even from a

JFK's pride in visiting Berlin and his compliments to the Mayor and Chancellor further intensify his hold on audience goodwill and interest. His assurance of U.S. military aid, if necessary, gives his listeners a feeling of security.

His knowledge of history enables him to compare Berlin with Rome. He identifies with his listeners by using their language.

Here is the President of the United States, the most powerful man in the world, poking fun at his German accent and at the same time complimenting the interpreter. Europeans are not used to this kind of humor from heads of state.

The President admits that democracy has its faults, but it does not have to erect walls to keep people as prisoners. Another compliment to West Berlin.

The President builds up powerful emotional impact through repeating "Let them come to Berlin," in German.

Now JFK reaches out emotionally and touches people—husbands and wives, brothers and sisters, families.

Germans have earned the right to be free, to unite their families, and to live in peace. These ideas appeal to West Europeans. Note the transition to the conclusion. "So let me ask you, as I close, . . .". and the emotional buildup using parallel construction, "beyond . . . to. . . ." The President expresses hope for a better tomorrow.

He builds his conclusion on the idea of a better future. Another compliment to Berlin.

An extremely moving conclusion in German words, the title of the speech. Note the conciseness of the last paragraph.

distance, the story of the last 18 years. I know of no town, no city, that has been besieged for 18 years that still lives with the vitality and force, and the hope and the determination of the city of West Berlin. While the wall is the most obvious and vivid demonstration of the failures of the Communist system, for all the world to see, we take no satisfaction in it, for it is, as your Mayor has said, an offense not only against history but an offense against humanity, separating families, dividing husbands and wives and brothers and sisters, and dividing a people who wish to be joined together.

6   What is true of this city is true of Germany—real, lasting peace in Europe can never be assured as long as one German out of four is denied the elementary right of free men, and that is to make a free choice. In 18 years of peace and good faith, this generation of Germans has earned the right to be free, including the right to unite their families and their nation in lasting peace, with good will to all people. You live in a defended island of freedom, but your life is part of the main. So *let me ask you, as I close,* to lift your eyes beyond the dangers of today, to the hopes of tomorrow, beyond the freedom merely of this city of Berlin, or your country of Germany, to the advance of freedom everywhere, beyond the wall to the day of peace with justice, beyond yourselves and ourselves to all mankind.

7   Freedom is indivisible, and when one man is enslaved, all are not free. When all are free, then we can look forward to that day when this city will be joined as one and this country and this great continent of Europe in a peaceful and hopeful globe. When that day finally comes, as it will, the people of West Berlin can take sober satisfaction in the fact that they were in the front lines for almost two decades.

8   All free men, wherever they may live, are citizens of Berlin, and, therefore, as a free man, I take pride in the words *"Ich bin ein Berliner."*

Sentence Outline of John F. Kennedy's "Ich Bin ein Berliner"

Introduction

I. I am proud to be here as the guest of your mayor and to be with the Chancellor and General Clay.
II. "Ich bin ein Berliner."

Body

I. Let those who want to know about the Communists come to Berlin.
II. America's freedom presents a marked contrast to communism.
III. West Berlin remains a city of vitality and force, hope and determination.
IV. The Berlin wall symbolizes the failures of the Communist system and is an offense against humanity.
V. Germany deserves to be free and united.

Conclusion

I. I ask you to lift your eyes to the advance of freedom everywhere.

II. Freedom is indivisible.

III. When this city and country are joined as one, its people can be proud of having been in the front lines for two decades.

IV. "Ich bin ein Berliner."

Topic Outline

Introduction

I. Pride in being here in the company of the Mayor, the Chancellor, and General Clay

II. "Ich bin ein Berliner."

Body

I. Berlin as place to learn about Communism

II. Contrast between Communism and America's freedom

III. Tribute to Berlin's vitality and force, hope and determination

IV. Symbolic significance of Berlin

V. Germany's need to be free and united

Conclusion

I. Anticipation of the advance of freedom

II. Indivisibility of freedom

III. Anticipation of Berlin's pride when the city and country are united

IV. "Ich bin ein Berliner."

Martin Luther King, Jr.

On August 28, 1963, one of the nation's most eloquent voices, on behalf of the Civil Rights Movement, mesmerized and inspired almost a quarter of a million black and white peaceful demonstrators who were gathered at the Lincoln Memorial in Washington, D.C. The purpose of this massive rally was to draw attention to the black demands for equality in employment and civil rights.

The speech, which follows, was delivered by Martin Luther King, Jr., the recognized leader of the nonviolent Civil Rights Movement who, in the same year, was named "Man of the Year" by *Time* magazine and a year later received the Nobel Peace Prize. His speech, "I Have a Dream," also ranks among the finest of this century. Here is the speech and analysis, followed by the outlines.

■ "I Have a Dream"[3]

King opens his speech with references to two historic occasions: the signing of the Emancipation Proclamation and the one hundredth anniversary of that action.

1   Five score years ago, a great American, in whose symbolic shadow we stand today, signed the Emancipation Proclamation. This momentous decree came as a great beacon of light of hope to millions of Negro slaves who had been seared in the flames of withering injustice. It came as a joyous daybreak to end the long night of their captivity.

2   But one hundred years later, the Negro still is not free. One hundred years later, the life of the Negro is still sadly crippled by the manacles of segregation and the chains of discrimination.

3   One hundred years later, the Negro lives on a lonely island of poverty in the midst of a vast ocean of material prosperity. One hundred years later, the Negro is still languished in the corners of American society and finds himself an exile in his own land. So we have come here today to dramatize a shameful condition.

He employs through the next three paragraphs an extended metaphor of cashing a check ("promissory note") and carries it through its bouncing and the bank's being bankrupt.

4   In a sense we have come to our nation's capital to cash a check. When the architects of our republic wrote the magnificent words of the Constitution and the Declaration of Independence, they were signing a promissory note to which every American was to fall heir. This note was a promise that all men, yes, black men as well as white men, would be guaranteed the unalienable rights of life, liberty, and the pursuit of happiness.

5   It is obvious today that America has defaulted on this promissory note insofar as her citizens of color are concerned. Instead of honoring this sacred obligation, America has given the Negro people a bad check, which has come back marked "insufficient funds."

6   But we refuse to believe that the bank of justice is bankrupt. We refuse to believe that there are insufficient funds in the great vaults of opportunity of this nation. So we have come to cash this check—a check that will give us upon demand the riches of freedom and the security of justice.

He establishes a compelling tone of urgency to heighten the force of his demand for Negro equality.

7   We have also come to this hallowed spot to remind America of the fierce urgency of now. This is no time to engage in the luxury of cooling off or to take the tranquilizing drug of gradualism. Now is the time to make real the promise of democracy. Now is the time to rise from the dark and desolate valley of segregation to the sunlit path of racial justice. Now is the time to lift our nation from the quicksands of racial injustice to the solid rock of brotherhood. Now is the time to make justice a reality for all of God's children.

8   It would be fatal for the nation to overlook the urgency of the movement and to underestimate the determination of the Negro. This sweltering summer of the Negro's legitimate discontent will not pass until there is an invigorating autumn of freedom and equality. 1963 is not an end but a beginning. Those who hope that the Negro needed to blow off steam and will now be content will have a rude awakening if the nation returns to business as usual.

[3]Wil A. Linkugel, R. R. Allen, and Richard L. Johannesen, *Contemporary American Speeches*, 3rd ed. (Belmont, CA: Wadsworth, 1972), 289–293.

9   There will be neither rest nor tranquility in America until the Negro is grant-ed his citizenship rights. The whirlwinds of revolt will continue to shake the foun-dations of our nation until the bright day of justice emerges.

10   But there is something that I must say to my people who stand on the warm threshold which leads into the palace of justice. In the process of gaining our rightful place we must not be guilty of wrongful deeds.

11   Let us not seek to satisfy our thirst for freedom by drinking from the cup of bitterness and hatred. We must forever conduct our struggle on the high plane of dignity and discipline. We must not allow our creative protest to degener-ate into physical violence. Again and again we must rise to the majestic heights of meeting physical force with soul force.

12   The marvelous new militancy which has engulfed the Negro community must not lead us to a distrust of all white people, for many of our white broth-ers, as evidenced by their presence here today, have come to realize that their destiny is tied up with our destiny and they have come to realize that their free-dom is inextricably bound to our freedom. This offense we share mounted to storm the battlements of injustice must be carried forth by a bi-racial army. We cannot walk alone.

13   And as we walk, we must make the pledge that we shall always march ahead. We cannot turn back. There are those who are asking the devotees of civil rights, "When will you be satisfied?" We can never be satisfied as long as the Negro is the victim of the unspeakable horrors of police brutality.

14   We can never be satisfied as long as our bodies, heavy with the fatigue of travel, cannot gain lodging in the motels of the highways and the hotels of the cities. We cannot be satisfied as long as the Negro's basic mobility is from a smaller ghetto to a larger one.

15   We can never be satisfied as long as our children are stripped of their self-hood and robbed of their dignity by signs stating "for whites only." We cannot be satisfied as long as a Negro in Mississippi cannot vote and a Negro in New York believes he has nothing for which to vote. No, we are not satisfied, and we will not be satisfied until justice rolls down like waters and righteousness like a mighty stream.

16   I am not unmindful that some of you have come here out of excessive tri-als and tribulation. Some of you have come fresh from narrow jail cells. Some of you have come from areas where your quest for freedom left you battered by the storms of persecution and staggered by the winds of police brutality. You have been the veterans of creative suffering. Continue to work with the faith that unearned suffering is redemptive.

17   Go back to Mississippi; go back to Alabama; go back to South Carolina; go back to Georgia; go back to Louisiana; go back to the slums and ghettos of the Northern cities, knowing that somehow this situation can, and will be changed. Let us not wallow in the valley of despair.

18   So I say to you, my friends, that even though we must face the difficulties of today and tomorrow, I still have a dream. It is a dream deeply rooted in the Amer-ican dream that one day this nation will rise up and live out the true meaning of its creed—we hold these truths to be self evident, that all men are created equal.

He then issues a calming, counter-balancing appeal for restraint—not in the struggle but in the manner in which it is carried out—by denounc-ing "wrongful deeds."

He avoids alienat-ing whites by acknowledging that many of them support the Negro's cause.

Continuing a kind of contrapuntal effect he then arouses the indig-nation of his audi-ence by offering a series of examples of injustice suf-fered by Negroes.

One of the most famous segments of U.S. oratory, the "I have a dream" section of this speech appeals to the audience to share his faith that right will prevail.

19   I have a dream that one day on the red hills of Georgia, sons of former slaves and sons of former slave-owners will be able to sit down together at the table of brotherhood.

20   I have a dream that one day, even the state of Mississippi, a state sweltering with the heat of injustice, sweltering with the heat of oppression, will be transformed into an oasis of freedom and justice.

21   I have a dream my four little children will one day live in a nation where they will not be judged by the color of their skin but by content of their character. I have a dream today!

22   I have a dream that one day, down in Alabama, with its vicious racists, with its governor having his lips dripping with the words of interposition and nullification, that one day, right there in Alabama, little black boys and black girls will be able to join hands with little white boys and white girls as sisters and brothers. I have a dream today!

23   I have a dream that one day every valley shall be exalted, every hill and mountain shall be made low, the rough places shall be made plain, and the crooked places shall be made straight and the glory of the Lord will be revealed and all flesh shall see it together.

24   This is our hope. This is the faith that I go back to the South with.

25   With this faith we will be able to hew out of the mountain of despair a stone of hope. With this faith we will be able to transform the jangling discords of our nation into a beautiful symphony of brotherhood.

26   With this faith we will be able to work together, to pray together, to struggle together, to go to jail together, to stand up for freedom together, knowing that we will be free one day. This will be the day when all of God's children will be able to sing with new meaning—"my country 'tis of thee, sweet land of liberty, of thee I sing; land where my fathers died, land of the pilgrim's pride; from every mountain side, let freedom ring"—and if America is to be a great nation, this must become true.

He then issues a protracted call for action.

27   And so let freedom ring from the prodigious hilltops of New Hampshire.

28   Let freedom ring from the mighty mountains of New York.

29   Let freedom ring from the heightening Alleghenies of Pennsylvania.

30   Let freedom ring from the snow-capped Rockies of Colorado.

31   Let freedom ring from the curvaceous slopes of California.

32   But not only that.

33   Let freedom ring from Stone Mountain of Georgia.

34   Let freedom ring from Lookout Mountain of Tennessee.

35   Let freedom ring from every hill and molehill of Mississippi, from every mountainside, let freedom ring.

He ends on a positive note by predicting victory for "all of God's children."

36   And when this happens, and when we allow freedom to ring, when we let it ring from every village and hamlet, from every state and city, we will be able to speed up that day when all of God's children—black men and white men, Jews and Gentiles, Catholics and Protestants—will be able to join hands and to sing in the words of the old Negro spiritual, "Free at last, free at last; thank God Almighty, we are free at last."

Analysis

To gain the acceptance of his audience, King appeals to quotes or paraphrasing well-known phrases of inspiration: Lincoln's Gettysburg Address ["Five score years ago," "this hallowed spot"], the Declaration of Independence ["We hold these truths to be self-evident . . . "], "America" ["My country 'tis of thee . . . ," "Let freedom ring . . . "], the Bible ["every valley shall be exalted . . . "], and a famous Negro spiritual [Free at last, free at last . . . "].

Throughout the speech, he also uses the technique of chant-like repetition: "One hundred years later," "Now is the time," "we must," "We cannot be satisfied," "Go back to," "I have a dream," and "Let freedom ring from. . . ."

Sentence Outline of Martin Luther King, Jr.'s, "I Have a Dream"

Introduction

I. Cite the Emancipation Proclamation.

II. Describe the lack of freedom of the Negro one hundred years later.

Body

I. Describe the "promissory note" of the founding fathers.

II. Cite America's default on that note.

III. Call upon the nation to make good.

IV. Explain the determination of the Negro.

V. Caution against committing wrongful deeds: bitterness and hatred, physical violence, distrust of all whites.

VI. Exhort Negroes not to turn back from their present militancy.

VII. Acknowledge excessive trials and tribulations of many Negroes.

VIII. Assert faith in the future ["I have a dream"].

IX. Show how that faith can bring about equality and freedom.

Conclusion

Let freedom ring until we are all free at last.

Topic Outline

Introduction

I. Emancipation Proclamation

II. One hundred years later

Body

I. "Promissory note" of founding fathers

II. Default

III. Challenge to make good

Conclusion

Call to action ["Let freedom ring"]

Mark Twain

The following speech was delivered on October 5, 1906, in Norfolk, Connecticut, by Mark Twain (Samuel Longhorn Clemens) to an audience following one of his daughter's singing recitals, her first public appearance. America's greatest humorist, raconteur, and author of such classics as *The Innocents Abroad, The Prince and the Pauper, The Adventures of Tom Sawyer*, and his masterpiece, *Huckleberry Finn*, aptly chose to speak about his first public appearance giving a talk.

You may find it somewhat comforting and, at times, humorous as you read his short talk to know that this literary giant also suffered pangs of stage fright.

Note the brevity of his speech as well as his folksy style, delivery, and language. Here's his speech, "Mark Twain's First Appearance," with analysis and outlines.

◼ "Mark Twain's First Appearance"[4]

He opens with a personal reminiscence, adding a joke about his age [he was actually 70 when he made this speech, not 40].

In a humorous exaggeration, he compares his stage fright to his having been seasick, winning audience sympathy.

1   My heart goes out in sympathy to any one who is making his first appearance before an audience of human beings. By a direct process of memory I go back forty years less one month—for I'm older than I look.

2   I recall the occasion of my first appearance. San Francisco knew me then only as a reporter, and I was to make my bow to San Francisco as a lecturer. I knew that nothing short of compulsion would get me to the theatre. So I bound myself by a hard-and-fast contract so that I could not escape. I got to the theatre forty-five minutes before the hour set for the lecture. My knees were shaking so that I didn't know whether I could stand up. If there is an awful, horrible malady in the world, it is stage-fright—and seasickness. They are a pair. I had stage-fright then for the first and last time. I was only seasick once, too. It was on a little ship on which there were two hundred other passengers. I—was—sick. I was so sick that there wasn't any left for those other two hundred passengers.

---

[4]*Mark Twain's Speeches* (New York: Greystone Press, Mark Twain Company, 1923), 242–243.

3   It was dark and lonely behind the scenes in that theatre, and I peeked through the little peek-holes they have in theatre curtains and looked into the big auditorium. That was dark and empty, too. By-and-by it lighted up, and the audience began to arrive.

4   I had got a number of friends of mine, stalwart men, to sprinkle themselves through the audience armed with big clubs. Every time I said anything they could possibly guess I intended to be funny they were to pound those clubs on the floor. Then there was a kind lady in a box up there, also a good friend of mine, the wife of the Governor. She was to watch me intently, and whenever I glanced toward her she was going to deliver a gubernatorial laugh that would lead the whole audience into applause.

5   At last I began. I had the manuscript tucked under a United States flag in front of me where I could get at it in case of need. But I managed to get started without it. I walked up and down—I was young in those days and needed the exercise—and talked and talked.

6   Right in the middle of the speech I had placed a gem. I had put in a moving, pathetic part which was to get at the hearts and souls of my hearers. When I delivered it they did just what I hoped and expected. Then I happened to glance up at the box where the Governor's wife was—you know what happened.

7   Well, after the first agonizing five minutes, my stage-fright left me, never to return. I know if I was going to be hanged I could get up and make a good showing, and I intended to. But I shall never forget my feelings before the agony left me, and I got up here to thank you for her for helping my daughter, by your kindness, to live through her first appearance. And I want to thank you for your appreciation of her singing, which is, by-the-way, hereditary.

Analysis

Mark Twain's speech is effective because of its simple narrative approach, its conversational tone, and its touches of humor. Twain pokes fun at himself, thus gaining the sympathetic understanding of the audience.

Sentence Outline of "Mark Twain's First Appearance"

Introduction

I empathize with anyone who makes a first appearance before an audience. [Twain's daughter had just made her first public appearance as a singer.]

Body

I. I recall my own first appearance.
   A. I had to force myself by means of an iron-clad contract to go through with it.
   B. I was overcome by stage fright.
II. The dark and emptiness exaggerated my fear.

The details of the darkness and emptiness of the stage and theater heighten the sense of nervousness that he is trying to convey.

His use of people planted in the audience is a technique still widely used by speakers and entertainers to guarantee desired reactions.

He shows how his vanity caused his momentary downfall. He was so proud of having awed the audience that he forgot his own prearranged signals and looked to the governor's wife, presumably in a gesture of self-satisfaction—thereby producing laughter at precisely the wrong time.

After mentioning his subsequent self-confidence, he refers back to his stage fright at the beginning, to tying together the introduction and conclusion of his talk.

He ends with a simple thank you on behalf of his daughter.

   III. I planted people in the audience to make sure there would be laughter.
      A. Several men were to pound the floor with big clubs when I said something funny.
      B. The governor's wife, in a box seat, was to laugh whenever I looked up at her.
   IV. During a moment of touching silence, I ruined the effect by inadvertently looking up at the governor's wife.
    V. In conquering my stage fright, I learned that I had the ability to make a good showing in front of an audience.

Conclusion

Thank you all for helping my daughter to live through her first appearance.

Topic Outline

Introduction

Empathy regarding first appearances

Body

    I. My first appearance
      A. Need to force myself
      B. Stage fright
   II. Confrontation of empty, dark theater
   III. Plants in audience
      A. Men with clubs
      B. Governor's wife
   IV. Looking at governor's wife at the wrong time
    V. Overcoming stage fright and gaining confidence

Conclusion

Thanks on behalf of my daughter

Barbara Bush

The following speech was delivered by Barbara Bush, wife of then-President George Bush, at Wellesley College's commencement in 1990. The speech is extremely effective in persuading the graduates, all women, to make three vital decisions regarding family relationships, volunteer work, and personal growth. Each decision and its benefits to the graduates is explained clearly and fully.

Incidentally, the graduates had previously objected to Barbara Bush as commencement speaker for two reasons. First, they wanted Alice Walker, author of *The Color Purple*, because purple was the 1990 "class color." Second, they asked, "What has Barbara Bush ever accomplished on her own? Her position is a consequence of her marriage to George Bush."

Although Mrs. Bush was the graduates' second choice, she promptly accepted the invitation.

A powerful persuasive tool that highlights the speech is the frequent use of the key words *you* and *your*. They appear over thirty-five times and help to get the audience involved. As you might expect, the speech was such a smashing success that the graduates gave her a standing ovation.

Here is Mrs. Bush's commencement speech.

■ Choices and Change[5]

1   Thank you President Keohane, Mrs. Gorbachev, trustees, faculty, parents, Julie Porer, Christine Bicknell and the Class of 1990. I am thrilled to be with you today, and very excited, as I know you must all be, that Mrs. Gorbachev could join us.

2   More than ten years ago when I was invited here to talk about our experiences in the People's Republic of China, I was struck by both the natural beauty of your campus and the spirit of this place.

3   Wellesley, you see, is not just a place, but an idea, an experiment in excellence in which diversity is not just tolerated, but is embraced.

4   The essence of this spirit was captured in a moving speech about tolerance given last year by the student body president of one of your sister colleges. She related the story by Robert Fulghum about a young pastor who, finding himself in charge of some very energetic children, hit upon a game called "Giants, Wizards and Dwarfs." "You have to decide now" the pastor instructed the children, "which you are . . . a giant, a wizard or a dwarf?" At that, a small girl, tugging on his pants leg, asked, "But where do the mermaids stand?"

5   The pastor told her there are *no* mermaids. "Oh yes there are," she said. "I am a mermaid."

6   This little girl knew what she was and she was not about to give up on either her identity *or* the game. She intended to take her place wherever mermaids fit into the scheme of things. Where *do* the mermaids stand . . . all those who are different, those who do not fit the boxes and the pigeonholes? "Answer that question," wrote Fulghum, "and you can build a school, a nation, or a whole world on it."

7   As that very wise young woman said . . . "Diversity, like anything worth having, requires *effort*." Effort to learn about and respect difference, to be compassionate with one another, and to cherish our own identity, and to accept unconditionally the same in all others.

The First Lady wastes no time in informing the graduates that she has spoken at Wellesley before.

She indirectly acknowledges that her choice as speaker was controversial when she plainly declares that at Wellesley, diversity is not just tolerated, it is embraced. This forthright remark prompted the first of many rounds of applause, and from here on Mrs. Bush captivated her audience.

She tells an interesting anecdote about a child and identity that sets the tone and theme of her address.

---

[5]Barbara Bush, "Choices and Change." Speech delivered at Wellesley College, Wellesley, Massachusetts, 1 June 1990.

8   You should all be very proud that this is the Wellesley spirit. Now I know your first choice for today was Alice Walker, known for *The Color Purple*. Instead you got me—known for the color of my hair! Of course, Alice Walker's book has a special resonance here. At Wellesley, each class is known by a special color, and for four years the class of '90 has worn the color purple. Today you meet on Severance Green to say goodbye to all that, to begin a new and very personal journey, a search for your own true colors.

9   In the world that awaits you beyond the shores of Lake Waban, no one can say what your true colors will be. But this I know: You have a first-class education from a first-class school. And so you need not, probably cannot, live a "paint-by-numbers" life. Decisions are not irrevocable. Choices do come back. As you set off from Wellesley, I hope that many of you will consider making three very special choices.

10   The first is to believe in something larger than yourself, to get involved in some of the big ideas of your time. I chose literacy because I honestly believe that if more people could read, write and comprehend, we would be that much closer to solving so many of the problems plaguing our society.

11   Early on I made another choice which I hope you will make as well. Whether you are talking about education, career or service, you are talking about life, and life must have joy. It's supposed to be fun!

12   One of the reasons I made the most important decision of my life, to marry George Bush, is because he made me laugh. It's true, sometimes we've laughed through our tears, but that shared laughter has been one of our strongest bonds. Find the joy in life, because as Ferris Bueller said on his day off

"Life moves pretty fast. If ya don't stop and look around once in a while, ya gonna miss it!"

13   The third choice that must not be missed is to cherish your human connections: your relationships with friends and family. For several years, you've had impressed upon you the importance to your career of dedication and hard work. This is true, but as important as your obligations as a doctor, lawyer or business leader will be, you are a human being first and those human connections, with spouses, with children, with friends, are the most important investments you will ever make.

14   At the end of your life, you will never regret not having passed one more test, not winning one more verdict or not closing one more deal. You will regret time not spent with a husband, a friend, a child or a parent.

15   We are in a transitional period right now, fascinating and exhilarating times, learning to adjust to the changes and the choices we, men and women, are facing. I remember what a friend said, on hearing her husband lament to his buddies that he had to babysit. Quickly setting him straight, my friend told her husband that when it's your own kids, it's not called babysitting!

16   Maybe we should adjust faster, maybe slower. But whatever the era, whatever the times, one thing will never change: fathers and mothers, if you have children, they must come first. Your success as a family, our success as a soci-

ety, depends *not* on what happens at the White House, but on what happens inside your house.

17   For over 50 years, it was said that the winner of Wellesley's annual hoop race would be the first to get married. Now they say the winner will be the first to become a C.E.O. Both of these stereotypes show too little tolerance for those who want to know where the mermaids stand. So I offer you today a new legend: the winner of the hoop race will be the first to realize her dream, not society's dream, her own personal dream. And who knows? Somewhere out in this audience may even be someone who will one day follow in my footsteps, and preside over the White House as the president's spouse. I wish him well!

18   The controversy ends here. But our conversation is only beginning. And a worthwhile conversation it is. So as you leave Wellesley today, take with you deep thanks for the courtesy and honor you have shared with Mrs. Gorbachev and me. Thank you. God bless you. And may your future be worthy of your dreams.

Mrs. Bush introduces the subject of family by emphasizing the fact that, as time goes on, one thing never changes—fathers and mothers. And if they have children, those children must come first because our success as a society depends on it. This comment leaves no doubt where she stands regarding the responsibilities of parents to their children and the importance of the family in our society.

Analysis

What started out as a negative situation (being turned down as first choice for commencement speaker) was converted into a positive experience by the classy speech of a classy lady.

Here's a sentence outline of the former First Lady's speech:

Sentence Outline of "Choices and Changes"

Purpose

To persuade, inspire, and motivate Wellesley graduates to make their lives personally fulfilling and to suggest guidelines for doing so.

Thesis Statement

To make the most of your life, you must decide on three courses of action: believe in and work for a great cause, have fun, and cherish your family and friends.

Introduction

I. Thank Pres. Keohane, etc., and express excitement that Mrs. Gorbachev can join us today.

II. Wellesley is a place of beauty, an experiment in excellence where diversity is embraced.

    A. Tell story about pastor and children and the game they played called "Giants, Wizards and Dwarfs." Mention the little girl "mermaid" who was different and didn't fit into the usual pigeonhole.

    B. You should be proud that the Wellesley spirit encourages respect for differences among us.

C. Mention author Alice Walker and *The Color Purple,* the color that your class has worn for four years.

Body

III. Today, enriched with your first-class education, you start a new, very personal journey that involves three very special decisions by you:
  A. First, believe in something larger than yourself and become involved in it. I chose literacy because if more people could read, write, and understand, we'd be closer to solving many problems plaguing society.
  B. Whether you're talking about education, a career, or community service, you're talking about life, and life must be joyful. Have fun. One of the reasons I married George is that he made me laugh.
  C. Cherish your relationships with spouses, families, and friends. You're a human being first and your human connections are the most important investment you'll ever make. Families come first and our success as a society depends on what happens inside your homes.

Conclusion

IV. Closing remarks:
  A. For over 50 years Wellesley tradition said that the winner of your annual hoop race would be the first to get married, and lately that she'll be first to become a CEO. Now I offer you a new approach—that she'll be the first to achieve her own personal dream, not society's dream.
  B. "Thank you for the courtesy and honor you have shared with Mrs. Gorbachev and me. God bless you. And may your future be worthy of your dreams."

Topic Outline

Title, Purpose and Thesis Statement,

Same as in the sentence outline

Introduction

  I. Greetings and welcoming remarks
 II. Brief description of Wellesley College where diversity is embraced
  A. Anecdote about "Giants, Wizards and Dwarfs"
  B. Pride of Wellesley
  C. The class color

Body

III. Life's journey involves three decisions
  A. Involvement in a cause larger than yourself

    B. Enjoyment of life

    C. Appreciation of your relationships with family and friends

Conclusion

IV. Closing Remarks:

    A. Traditional Wellesley dream versus your own personal dream

    B. "Thank you. God bless you. And may your future be worthy of your dreams."

President George W. Bush's Speech On Terrorism[6]

On Thursday evening, September 20, 2001, nine days after the infamous 9-11 attacks, President George W. Bush declared "war on terrorism" when he drove from the White House to the Capitol to address a joint session of Congress, the American people and the world.

Although basically an informative speech, it contained elements of persuasion, inspiration, a call to action, a touch of eulogy, and was delicately wrapped in emotion. All questions regarding his lack of eloquence and intellectual capacity were clearly answered when he delivered what columnist Christopher Cox described as "a presidential speech for the ages rating with the best of Abraham Lincoln, Franklin D. Roosevelt, or John F. Kennedy." Tobe Berkovitz, professor of communication at Boston University, said in reference to the speech's text and context, "it was a fabulously written speech, perfectly delivered—and it was the speech America wanted to hear." Here is President Bush's speech for you to study, analyze, read, and reread for practice in delivery, breathing, emphasis, and pacing.

President Bush's Speech on Terrorism

1   Mr. Speaker, Mr. President Pro Tempore, members of Congress, and fellow Americans:

2   In the normal course of events, Presidents come to this chamber to report on the state of the Union. Tonight, no such report is needed. It has already been delivered by the American people.

3   We have seen it in the courage of passengers, who rushed terrorists to save others on the ground—passengers like an exceptional man named Todd Beamer. And would you please help me to welcome his wife, Lisa Beamer, here tonight. (Applause.)

---

[6]President George W. Bush's speech delivered before a joint session of Congress, Washington, D.C., on September 20, 2001.

4   We have seen the state of our Union in the endurance of rescuers, working past exhaustion. We have seen the unfurling of flags, the lighting of candles, the giving of blood, the saying of prayers—in English, Hebrew, and Arabic. We have seen the decency of a loving and giving people who have made the grief of strangers their own.

5   My fellow citizens, for the last nine days, the entire world has seen for itself the state of our Union—and it is strong. (Applause.)

6   Tonight we are a country awakened to danger and called to defend freedom. Our grief has turned to anger, and anger to resolution. Whether we bring our enemies to justice, or bring justice to our enemies, justice will be done. (Applause.)

7   I thank the Congress for its leadership at such an important time. All of America was touched on the evening of the tragedy to see Republicans and Democrats joined together on the steps of this Capitol, singing "God Bless America." And you did more than sing; you acted, by delivering $40 billion to rebuild our communities and meet the needs of our military.

8   Speaker Hastert, Minority Leader Gephardt, Majority Leader Daschle and Senator Lott, I thank you for your friendship, for your leadership and for your service to our country. (Applause.)

9   And on behalf of the American people, I thank the world for its outpouring of support. America will never forget the sounds of our National Anthem playing at Buckingham Palace, on the streets of Paris, and at Berlin's Brandenburg Gate.

10   We will not forget South Korean children gathering to pray outside our embassy in Seoul, or the prayers of sympathy offered at a mosque in Cairo. We will not forget moments of silence and days of mourning in Australia and Africa and Latin America.

11   Nor will we forget the citizens of 80 other nations who died with our own: dozens of Pakistanis; more than 130 Israelis; more than 250 citizens of India; men and women from El Salvador, Iran, Mexico and Japan; and hundreds of British citizens. America has no truer friend than Great Britain. (Applause.) Once again, we are joined together in a great cause—so honored the British Prime Minister has crossed an ocean to show his unity of purpose with America. Thank you for coming, friend. (Applause.)

12   On September the 11th, enemies of freedom committed an act of war against our country. Americans have known wars—but for the past 136 years, they have been wars on foreign soil, except for one Sunday in 1941. Americans have known the casualties of war—but not at the center of a great city on a peaceful morning. Americans have known surprise attacks—but never before on thousands of civilians. All of this was brought upon us in a single day—and night fell on a different world, a world where freedom itself is under attack.

13   Americans have many questions tonight. Americans are asking: Who attacked our country? The evidence we have gathered all points to a collection of loosely affiliated terrorist organizations known as al Qaeda. They are the same murderers indicted for bombing American embassies in Tanzania and Kenya, and responsible for bombing the USS *Cole*.

14   Al Qaeda is to terror what the mafia is to crime. But its goal is not making money; its goal is remaking the world—and imposing its radical beliefs on people everywhere.

15   The terrorists practice a fringe form of Islamic extremism that has been rejected by Muslim scholars and the vast majority of Muslim clerics—a fringe movement that perverts the peaceful teachings of Islam. The terrorists' directive commands them to kill Christians and Jews, to kill all Americans, and make no distinction among military and civilians, including women and children.

16   This group and its leader—a person named Osama bin Laden—are linked to many other organizations In different countries, including the Egyptian Islamic Jihad and the Islamic Movement of Uzbekistan. There are thousands of these terrorists in more than 60 countries. They are recruited from their own nations and neighborhoods and brought to camps in places like Afghanistan, where they are trained in the tactics of terror. They are sent back to their homes or sent to hide in countries around the world to plot evil and destruction.

17   The leadership of al Qaeda has great influence In Afghanistan and supports the Tallban regime in controlling most of that country. In Afghanistan, we see al Qaeda's vision for the world.

18   Afghanistan's people have been brutalized—many are starving and many have fled. Women are not allowed to attend school. You can be jailed for owning a television. Religion can be practiced only as their leaders dictate. A man can be jailed in Afghanistan if his beard is not long enough.

19   The United States respects the people of Afghanistan—after all, we are currently its largest source of humanitarian aid—but we condemn the Taliban regime. (Applause.) It is not only repressing its own people, it is threatening people everywhere try sponsoring and sheltering and supplying terrorists. By aiding and abetting murder, the Taliban regime is committing murder.

20   And tonight, the United States of America makes the following demands on the Taliban: Deliver to United States authorities all the leaders of al Qaeda who hide in your land. (Applause.) Release all foreign nationals, including American citizens, you have unjustly imprisoned. Protect foreign journalists, diplomats and aid workers in your country. Close immediately and permanently every terrorist training camp in Afghanistan, and hand over every terrorist, and every person in their support structure, to appropriate authorities. (Applause.) Give the United States full access to terrorist training camps, so we can make sure they are no longer operating.

21   These demands are not open to negotiation or discussion. (Applause.) The Taliban must act, and act immediately. They will hand over the terrorists, or they will share in their fate.

22   I also want to speak tonight directly to Muslims throughout the world. We respect your faith. It's practiced freely by many millions of Americans, and by millions more in countries that America counts as friends. Its teachings are good and peaceful, and those who commit evil in the name of Allah blaspheme the name of Allah. (Applause.) The terrorists are traitors to their own faith, trying, in effect, to hijack Islam Itself. The enemy of America is not our many Muslim

friends; it is not our many Arab friends. Our enemy is a radical network of terrorists, and every government that supports them. (Applause.)

23   Our war on terror begins with al Qaeda, but it does not end there. It will not end until every terrorist group of global reach has been found, stopped and defeated. (Applause.)

24   Americans are asking, why do they hate us? They hate what we see right here in this chamber—a democratically elected government. Their leaders are self-appointed. They hate our freedoms—our freedom of religion, our freedom of speech, our freedom to vote and assemble and disagree with each other.

25   They want to overthrow existing governments in many Muslim countries, such as Egypt, Saudi Arabia, and Jordan. They want to drive Israel out of the Middle East. They want to drive Christians and Jews out of vast regions of Asia and Africa.

26   These terrorists kill not merely to end lives, but to disrupt and end a way of life. With every atrocity, they hope that America grows fearful, retreating from the world and forsaking our friends. They stand against us, because we stand in their way.

27   We are not deceived by their pretenses to piety. We have seen their kind before. They are the heirs of all the murderous ideologies of the 20th century. By sacrificing human life to serve their radical visions—by abandoning every value except the will to power—they follow in the path of fascism, and Nazism, and totalitarianism. And they will follow that path all the way, to where it ends: in history's unmarked grave of discarded lies. (Applause.)

28   Americans are asking: How will we fight and win this war? We will direct every resource at our command—every means of diplomacy, every tool of intelligence, every instrument of law enforcement, every financial influence, and every necessary weapon of war—to the disruption and to the defeat of the global terror network.

29   This war will not be like the war against Iraq a decade ago, with a decisive liberation of territory and a swift conclusion. It will not look like the air war above Kosovo two years ago, where no ground troops were used and not a single American was lost in combat.

30   Our response involves far more than instant retaliation and isolated strikes. Americans should not expect one battle, but a lengthy campaign, unlike any other we have ever seen. It may include dramatic strikes, visible on TV, and covert operations, secret even in success. We will starve terrorists of funding, turn them one against another, drive them from place to place, until there is no refuge or no rest. And we will pursue nations that provide aid or safe haven to terrorism. Every nation, in every region, now has a decision to make. Either you are with us, or you are with the terrorists. (Applause.) From this day forward, any nation that continues to harbor or support terrorism will be regarded by the United States as a hostile regime.

31   Our nation has been put on notice: We are not immune from attack. We will take defensive measures against terrorism to protect Americans. Today, dozens of federal departments and agencies, as well as state and local govern-

ments, have responsibilities affecting homeland security. These efforts must be coordinated at the highest level. So tonight I announce the creation of a Cabinet-level position reporting directly to me—the Office of Homeland Security.

32   And tonight I also announce a distinguished American to lead this effort, to strengthen American security: a military veteran, an effective governor, a true patriot, a trusted friend—Pennsylvania's Tom Ridge. (Applause.) He will lead, oversee and coordinate a comprehensive national strategy to safeguard our country against terrorism, and respond to any attacks that may come.

33   These measures are essential. But the only way to defeat terrorism as a threat to our way of life is to stop it, eliminate it, and destroy it where it grows. (Applause.)

34   Many will be involved in this effort, from FBI agents to intelligence operatives to the reservists we have called to active duty. All deserve our thanks, and all have our prayers. And tonight, a few miles from the damaged Pentagon, I have a message for our military: Be ready. I've called the Armed Forces to alert, and there is a reason. The hour is coming when America will act, and you will make us proud. (Applause.)

35   This is not, however, just America's fight. And what is at stake is not just America's freedom. This Is the world's fight. This is civilization's fight. This is the fight of all who believe in progress and pluralism, tolerance and freedom.

36   We ask every nation to join us. We will ask, and we will need, the help of police forces, intelligence services, and banking systems around the world. The United States is grateful that many nations and many international organizations have already responded—with sympathy and with support. Nations from Latin America, to Asia, to Africa, to Europe, to the Islamic world. Perhaps the NATO Charter reflects best the attitude of the world: An attack on one is an attack on all.

37   The civilized world is rallying to America's side. They understand that if this terror goes unpunished, their own cities, their own citizens may be next. Terror, unanswered, can not only bring down buildings, it can threaten the stability of legitimate governments. And you know what—we're not going to allow it. (Applause.)

38   Americans are asking: What is expected of us? I ask you to live your lives, and hug your children. I know many citizens have fears tonight, and I ask you to be calm and resolute, even in the face of a continuing threat.

39   I ask you to uphold the values of America, and remember why so many have come here. We are in a fight for our principles, and our first responsibility is to live by them. No one should be singled out for unfair treatment or unkind words because of their ethnic background or religious faith. (Applause.)

40   I ask you to continue to support the victims of this tragedy with your contributions. Those who want to give can go to a central source of information, libertyunites.org, to find the names of groups providing direct help in New York, Pennsylvania, and Virginia.

41   The thousands of FBI agents who are now at work in this investigation may need your cooperation, and I ask you to give it.

42   I ask for your patience, with the delays and Inconveniences that may accompany tighter security; and for your patience in what will be a long struggle.

43   I ask your continued participation and confidence in the American economy. Terrorists attacked a symbol of American prosperity. They did not touch its source. America is successful because of the hard work, and creativity, and enterprise of our people. These were the true strengths of our economy before September 11th, and they are our strengths today. (Applause.)

44   And, finally, please continue praying for the victims of terror and their families, for those in uniform, and for our great country. Prayer has comforted us in sorrow, and will help strengthen us for the journey ahead.

45   Tonight I thank my fellow Americans for what you have already done and for what you will do. And ladies and gentlemen of the Congress, I thank you, their representatives, for what you have already done and for what we will do together.

46   Tonight, we face new and sudden national challenges. We will come together to improve air safety, to dramatically expand the number of air marshals on domestic flights, and take new measures to prevent hijacking. We will come together to promote stability and keep our airlines flying, with direct assistance during this emergency. (Applause.)

47   We will come together to give law enforcement the additional tools it needs to track down terror here at home. (Applause.) We will come together to strengthen our intelligence capabilities to know the plans of terrorists before they act, and find them before they strike. (Applause.)

48   We will come together to take active steps that strengthen America's economy, and put our people back to work.

49   Tonight we welcome two leaders who embody the extraordinary spirit of all New Yorkers: Governor George Pataki, and Mayor Rudolph Giuliani. (Applause.) As a symbol of America's resolve, my administration will work with Congress, and these two leaders, to show the world that we will rebuild New York City. (Applause.)

50   After all that has just passed—all the lives taken, and all the possibilities and hopes that died with them—it is natural to wonder if America's future is one of fear. Some speak of an age of terror. I know there are struggles ahead, and dangers to face. But this country will define our times, not be defined by them. As long as the United States of America is determined and strong, this will not be an age of terror; this will be an age of liberty, here and across the world. (Applause.)

51   Great harm has been done to us. We have suffered great loss. And in our grief and anger we have found our mission and our moment. Freedom and fear are at war. The advance of human freedom—the great achievement of our time, and the great hope of every time—now depends on us. Our nation—this generation—will lift a dark threat of violence from our people and our future. We will rally the world to this cause by our efforts, by our courage. We will not tire, we will not falter, and we will not fail. (Applause.)

52   It is my hope that in the months and years ahead, life will return almost to normal. We'll go back to our lives and routines, and that is good. Even grief recedes with time and grace. But our resolve must not pass. Each of us will remember what happened that day, and to whom it happened. We'll remember the moment the news came—where we were and what we were doing. Some will remember an image of a fire, or a story of rescue. Some will carry memories of a face and a voice gone forever.

53   And I will carry this: It is the police shield of a man named George Howard, who died at the World Trade Center trying to save others. It was given to me by his mom, Arlene, as a proud memorial to her son. This is my reminder of lives that ended, and a task that does not end. (Applause.)

54   I will not forget this wound to our country or those who inflicted it. I will not yield; I will not rest; I will not relent in waging this struggle for freedom and security for the American people.

55   The course of this conflict is not known, yet its outcome is certain. Freedom and fear, justice and cruelty, have always been at war, and we know that God is not neutral between them. (Applause.)

56   Fellow citizens, we'll meet violence with patient justice—assured of the rightness of our cause, and confident of the victories to come. In all that lies before us, may God grant us wisdom, and may He watch over the United States of America.

57   Thank you.

B

Suggested Speech Topics

If you're having difficulty coming up with ideas on what to talk about, here are a number of suggestions to aid you in your selection.

More Topic Suggestions for an Informative Talk

1. The United States Constitution
2. The Bill of Rights
3. The difference between "generic" and "name brand" drugs
4. How to shop at the stock market
5. Getting the most out of the Internet
6. Medical malpractice
7. Home schooling
8. Our Lady of the American Flag (Betsy Ross)
9. The meaning of liberalism/conservatism
10. Watergate
11. December 7, 1941
12. July 4, 1776
13. The high cost of freedom
14. The high cost of attending a sporting event
15. Our civil rights
16. DNA and the death penalty
17. A warning on global warming
18. Becoming a United States citizen
19. Children murdering children
20. How to finance your education
21. Financing a home
22. Buying a used boat/car

23. Energy independence
24. Education—more than a matter of degrees
25. Unscrupulous CEOs
26. Intelligent investing
27. We need more qualified teachers
28. Kids who commit crime
29. Binge drinking
30. Creating a basic website
31. The challenge of being a "caregiver"
32. Windmills as a source of energy
33. Effective contraceptive devices
34. The Holocaust
35. The gas/electric car
36. (Different religions)
37. The Bermuda Triangle
38. Eating healthy
39. Exercise for life
40. What is pornography?
41. How to cite sources from the Internet
42. Smart weapons can do dumb things
43. (Various international holiday/cultural observances)
44. The difference between therapeutic and reproductive cloning
45. Shoplifting
46. How to avoid being ripped off by unscrupulous mechanics or other trades-people
47. You can't pray in public schools but you can get condoms
48. Job prospects through 2025
49. Being a single parent
50. Child abuse/Battered women

More Topic Suggestions for a Persuasive Talk

1. Racial/ethnic profiling should (not) be permitted
2. There is (no) hope for the Middle East
3. Student financial aid should (not) consist only of loans and not grants
4. The federal government should (not) provide more student financial aid
5. Military service should (not) be mandatory for every young man and woman
6. The death penalty should (not) be eliminated
7. Is global warming a lot of hot air?
8. Illegal aliens should (not) be deported
9. Illegal aliens should (not) receive any benefits
10. We must become considerably less dependent on Middle Eastern oil

11. Stem cell research should (not) be federally funded
12. Airlines should (not) be compelled to provide more comfortable passenger seating
13. A drunk driving conviction should (not) mean automatic jail time
14. More stringent restrictions are (not) needed for foreign students
15. Corrupt corporate CEOs should serve jail time
16. Is the FBI still a viable organization?
17. Everyone should (not) be issued a national identification card
18. We should (not) significantly reduce our legal immigration quotas
19. We should (not) build more nuclear power plants
20. We should (not) privatize the U.S. Postal Service
21. Who said, "The customer is always right"?
22. A company should (not) have the authority to forbid employees from selling their company stock
23. Major league sports should (not) be protected from antitrust laws
24. It's time to recognize Cuba
25. Do kids have too much control over parents?
26. You can (not) have a career and be an effective parent at the same time
27. Cameras at traffic lights and other public places are (not) an infringement of our civil rights
28. To be eligible for government assistance, single mothers should (not) be required to name the father
29. Plea bargaining should (not) be eliminated
30. Why you should leave home without your credit and debit cards
31. Residency should be mandatory to receive government assistance
32. We should do away with "Affirmative Action" and hire only the most qualified
33. We should (not) stop sharing our nuclear secrets with other countries
34. Why are members of Congress exempt from certain laws?
35. Gun ownership is a right and not a privilege
36. America should not by playing police officer for the world
37. Presidents should be elected by popular vote
38. The electoral college should take a sabbatical
39. The incredible government waste
40. More student discipline is (not) required in the public schools
41. Plagiarism and cheating should never be acceptable
42. The study of a foreign language should be mandatory in all public schools
43. Gambling/prostitution/drugs should (not) be legalized
44. A candidate's private life should (not) remain private
45. Minors who commit adult crimes should (not) stand trial as adults
46. The Miss America Pageant is (not) sexist
47. Public education should (not) be mandatory
48. Sterilization should (not) be a penalty of certain sex crimes
49. Those convicted of selling drugs to minors should received the death penalty
50. Abortion is a woman's decision, not the government's

More Topic Suggestions
for a Demonstration Talk

1. Reading a weather map
2. How to plot an ocean navigational course
3. The basics of sailing
4. The basics of SCUBA diving
5. How solar panels can make your home more energy efficient
6. Fixing a leaky faucet
7. Installing different shower fixtures
8. Basic household tools and how to use them
9. How to design a basic website
10. How a heat pump functions
11. How to draw cartoons
12. How to perform basic "acupressure"
13. Wok cooking
14. How to eat a lobster
15. The art of "mitering" (carpentry)
16. Very basic wiring
17. Using basic gardening tools
18. The basics of fly fishing
19. How to make your own fishing lures
20. How to wash replacement windows
21. How to install a small goldfish pond or fountain in your garden
22. Reading a label on a fine bottle of wine or champagne
23. Different wines for different foods
24. How to safely and correctly open a bottle of wine or champagne
25. American flag etiquette and how to fold the flag
26. Building a wine refrigerator
27. Making and flying various styles of kites
28. How to give a manicure
29. Effective make-up application
30. Card tricks
31. How to cut a piece of glass
32. How to keep score in bowling, tennis, baseball, etc.
33. How to coordinate outfits and pack a suit case
34. Basic camping gear
35. Basic first aid
36. How to perform the Heimlich maneuver
37. Wrapping presents and making bows
38. How to wallpaper/stencil
39. Exercising
40. How to decorate a cake

41. Basic self-defense
42. Effective contraceptive devices
43. Self breast examination
44. How to make animals from balloons
45. Various types of collections (stamps, coins, dolls, Disney memorabilia, etc.)
46. How to quilt
47. The various ways to set a table
48. Different types of home fire extinguishers
49. Transplanting a plant
50. Police/firefighter's equipment

Common Sexist Words and Phrases and Suggested Nonsexist Alternatives

Instead of Using	Try Using
actress	actor
adventuress	adventurer
alumnae, alumni	graduate(s), alum(s), member(s) of the class of
anchorman	anchor
bag lady	homeless woman
barmaid	cocktail server
bellboy, bellman	bellhop
birth control methods	contraception
busboy, busgirl	waiter's helper, waiter's (or serving) assistant
businessmen	businesspeople
cameraman	camera operator or photographer
chambermaid	hotel worker
cleaning girl/lady/woman	cleaner/domestic/office cleaner
clergymen	clergy, clerics, members of the clergy
coat-check girl	coat checker, coat attendant
co-ed	student
comedienne	comedian

congressman	representative, congressional representative
copy boy, copy girl	copy clerk, runner
cowboy	ranch hand
cowgirl	ranch hand
craftsman	artisan or craftperson
deliveryman	deliverer, delivery clerk, courier, delivery person
doorman	doorkeeper, doorkeep, door attendant
draftsman	drafter
drum majorette	drum major, baton twirler
employed mothers	mothers working outside the home
executrix	executor
family violence	domestic violence
female homosexuality	lesbianism
female homosexuals	lesbians
fireman	firefighter, stoker (ships, trains)
first lady	presidential or governor's spouse
flagman	flagger
flextime	flexible work schedules
forefathers	ancestors, forebears, foremothers and forefathers
forelady, foreman	supervisor, boss, leader, head juror
freshmen	first-year students, yearlings
gay woman	lesbian
gentleman's agreement	unwritten agreement, agreement based on trust
handyman	fixer, jack-of-all-trades
headmaster or headmistress	principal
heiress	heir, inheritor
heroic woman	hero
heroine	hero
homosexual	gay
hooker	prostitute
hostess	host
househusband	homemaker
housewife	homemaker

household violence	domestic violence
lady	woman
laymen	laypeople, laity,
longshoreman	longshore worker
lumberman	lumber cutter
maiden name	birth name
maid	household worker
mailman	mail carrier, letter carrier, postal worker
male nurse	nurse
man, mankind	the human species (*Homo sapiens*), humans
man (meaning person)	person, one, individual, you, I
man (as verb)	operate, work, staff, serve at (or *on* or *in*)
man-hours	work-hours, labor time
man-made	handmade, hand-built, human made, synthetic, manufacturered,
man of letters	literary person, writer, author, pundit
man of the year	newsmaker of the year
manpower	personnel, staff, human resources, labor, people power, muscle power, labor force
man-to-man	one-to-one, one-on-one, person-to-person
matron	married woman, supervisor, prison guard
meter maid	meter attendant, meter tender, meter reader
middleman	contact, go-between, intermediary, agent
minorities	ethnic groups, people of color
minority women	ethnic women
mistress	lover
mistress of ceremonies	master of ceremonies, host, emcee
motherhood	mothers or parenthood
newsman, newswoman	newsperson, reporter, journalist
number one man	head, chief, number one
number two man	second in command, chief aide
office boy, office girl	office helper, office assistant, clerk
one man, one vote	one person, one vote
one-man show	one-person show, solo show, one-artist show
patroness	patron, benefactor, sponsor, mentor
pitchman	hawker, promoter

poetess	poet
policeman, policewoman	police officer
repairman	repairer
rewrite man	rewriter
right-hand man	chief assistant
salesman, saleswoman saleslady, salesgirl	salesclerk, salespersons, sales agent, sales representative (or rep)
sculptress	sculptor
seaman	sailor, mariner, seafarer
seamstress	tailor, needleworker
seductress	seducer
servant	household worker
sex role identification	sexual identity
sexual practices	sexual behavior
signalman	signal operator, signaler
spaceman	astronaut, spacefarer, space traveler
sportsman	sports enthusiast
sportsmanship	fair play, fairness,
state policeman	state trooper, trooper
statesmen	diplomats, political leaders
stewardess	steward (ship, union shop), flight attendant (aircraft)
test-tube babies	in vitro fertilization
the pill	oral contraceptives
trashman	trash collector
tribesman	tribe/tribal member, member of a tribe
triggerman	professional/armed killer, hired gun, assassin
unborn child	fetus
union man	union member, labor/trade unionist, member of a union
unman	unnerve, disarm, weaken, incapacitate, undermine
unmarried father	single father
unmarried man	single man
unmarried mother	single mother
unmarried women	single women
VD or venereal disease	sexually transmitted disease

waitress	waiter, server
watchman	night guard, guard, security guard, caretaker, custodian
weathergirl/weatherman	weathercaster, meteorologist (not all weather people are meteorologists), weather reporter, forecaster
water boy	water carrier
welfare mother	welfare client/recipient
widow/widower	surviving spouse
women's lib	feminism, women's movement
working girl/working man	worker, employee, wage earner, job holder
working men/working women	workers, employees, wage earners, job holders
working mother	mothers working outside the home, wage earning/job holding/ salaried woman/ mother
working wives	wives working outside the home.
workman	worker, wage earner
workmen's compensation	workers' compensation
yachtsman	yacht owner/captain, yachter

More extensive listings of meanings of words and phrases with nonsexist alternatives can be found where these words were researched:

Mary Ellen S. Capek, ed., *A Women Thesaurus: An Index of Language Used to Describe and Locate Information by and about Women,* a project of the National Council for Research on Women and the Business and Professional Women's Foundation (New York: Harper & Row, 1988).

Rosalie Maggio, *The Bias-Free Word Finder, a Dictionary of Nondiscriminatory Language* (Boston: Beacon Press, 1992).

Some Commonly Mispronounced Words

For further practice in pronunciation, here is a list of some of the more commonly mispronounced words. The mispronunciations may be due to substituting one sound for another, an omission of one or more sounds, adding sounds, transposing sounds, or misplacing accents. The accented syllable(s) is underlined.

1. abdomen (<u>ab</u>-do-men)
2. absolve (ab-<u>solve</u>)
3. absorb (ab-<u>sorb</u>)
4. absurd (ab-<u>surd</u>)
5. accompaniment (ac-<u>com</u>-pa-ni-ment)
6. accompanist (ac-<u>com</u>-pa-nist)
7. accurate (<u>ac</u>-cu-rate)
8. admirable (<u>ad</u>-mi-ra-ble)
9. adult (a-<u>dult</u>)
10. almond (<u>al</u>-mond)
11. amicable (<u>am</u>-i-ca-ble)
12. analogous (a-<u>nal</u>-o-gous)
13. antidote (<u>an</u>-ti-<u>dote</u>)
14. antithesis (an-<u>tith</u>-e-sis)
15. applicable (<u>ap</u>-pli-ca-ble)
16. archipelago (<u>ar</u>-chi-<u>pel</u>-a-<u>go</u>)
17. arctic (<u>arc</u>-tic)
18. aria (<u>a</u>-ri-a)
19. auxiliary (aux-<u>il</u>-ia-ry)
20. aviator (<u>a</u>-vi-<u>a</u>-tor)
21. behemoth (be-<u>he</u>-moth)
22. beige (<u>beige</u>)
23. beneficiary (<u>ben</u>-e-<u>fi</u>-ci-ar-y)
24. berserk (ber-<u>serk</u>)
25. bilingual (bi-<u>lin</u>-gual)
26. blasé (<u>bla</u>-sé)
27. blatant (<u>bla</u>-tant)
28. bouquet (bou-<u>quet</u>)
29. bravado (bra-<u>va</u>-do)
30. buffet (buf-<u>fet</u>)
31. buoy (<u>bu</u>-oy)
32. cache (<u>cache</u>)
33. candidate (<u>can</u>-di-date)
34. cashmere (<u>cash</u>-mere)
35. casualty (<u>cas</u>-u-al-ty)
36. center (<u>cen</u>-ter)
37. cerebral (ce-<u>re</u>-bral)
38. chagrin (cha-<u>grin</u>)
39. chasm (<u>chasm</u>)
40. chimney (<u>chim</u>-ney)

41. coiffure (coif-<u>fure</u>)
42. comparable (<u>com</u>-pa-ra-ble)
43. corsage (cor-<u>sage</u>)
44. cuisine (cui-<u>sine</u>)
45. cumulus (<u>cum</u>-u-lus)
46. cupola (<u>cu</u>-po-la)
47. curriculum (cur-<u>ric</u>-u-lum)
48. debauched (de-<u>bauched</u>)
49. deluge (<u>de</u>-luge)
50. demise (de-<u>mise</u>)
51. despicable (des-<u>pi</u>-ca-ble)
52. diphthong (<u>diph</u>-thong)
53. dirigible (<u>di</u>-ri-gi-ble)
54. disparate (dis-<u>pa</u>-rate)
55. drama (<u>dra</u>-ma)
56. ecstatic (ec-<u>sta</u>-tic)
57. environment (en-<u>vir</u>-on-ment)
58. etiquette (<u>et</u>-i-quette)
59. exquisite (ex-<u>quis</u>-ite)
60. extraordinary (ex-<u>traor</u>-di-nar-y)
61. familiar (fa-<u>mi</u>-li-ar)
62. formidable (<u>for</u>-mi-da-ble)
63. genuine (<u>gen</u>-u-ine)
64. gondola (<u>gon</u>-do-la)
65. homage (<u>hom</u>-age)
66. human (<u>hu</u>-man)
67. hygienic (hi-gi-<u>en</u>-ic)
68. incomparable (in-<u>com</u>-pa-ra-ble)
69. interesting (<u>in</u>-ter-est-ing)
70. irreparable (ir-<u>rep</u>-a-ra-ble)
71. kindergarten (<u>kin</u>-der-<u>gar</u>ten)
72. laboratory (<u>lab</u>-o-ra-<u>tory</u>)
73. lamentable (la-<u>men</u>-ta-ble)
74. library (<u>li</u>-bra-ry)
75. massage (mas-<u>sage</u>)
76. medieval (<u>me</u>-di-<u>e</u>-val)
77. mischievous (<u>mis</u>-chie-vous)
78. ominpotent (om-<u>nip</u>-o-tent)
79. particular (par-<u>tic</u>-u-lar)
80. peculiarly (pe-<u>cu</u>-liar-ly)
81. plethora (<u>pleth</u>-o-ra)
82. poem (<u>po</u>-em)
83. poinsettia (poin-<u>set</u>-ti-a)
84. prerogative (pre-<u>rog</u>-a-tive)
85. pronunciation (pro-<u>nun</u>-ci-<u>a</u>-tion)
86. radiator (<u>ra</u>-di-a-tor)
87. reptile (<u>rep</u>-tile)
88. reputable (<u>re</u>-pu-ta-ble)
89. sandwich (<u>sand</u>-wich)
90. schism (<u>schism</u>)
91. secretary (<u>sec</u>-re-tar-y)
92. sentence (<u>sen</u>-tence)
93. similar (<u>sim</u>-i-lar)
94. statistics (sta-<u>tis</u>-tics)
95. strength (st<u>rength</u>)
96. superfluous (su-<u>per</u>-flu-ous)
97. theater (<u>the</u>-a-ter)
98. tremendous (tre-<u>men</u>-dous)
99. Wednesday (<u>Wednes</u>-day)
100. zealous (<u>zeal</u>-ous)

While going over these words, it might be wise . . . no, it *would* be wise to have a dictionary handy.

Abstract words Words that derive their meaning from personal interpretation and opinion; the opposite of concrete words. (Ch. 6)

Actuate To convince people to take a form of action. (Ch. 11)

Agenda Matters to be discussed, acted or voted upon during a meeting. (Ch. 14)

Aggressive Being offensive. Trying to force your views/opinions on others. (Ch. 1)

Analogic reasoning Predicting that, because two things or situations are similar in several important respects, they will be similar in other respects and will therefore produce similar results. (Ch. 11)

Announcement A short statement of an event including all pertinent information. (Ch. 13)

Argument Persuading through evidence and reasoning. (Ch. 11)

Articulation Movements of lips, tongue, jaw, and soft palate that convert vocal sounds into speech. The most common faults among college students are running words together and omitting word endings. (Ch. 5)

Artifact Objects in our possession—clothes, jewelry, furniture, autos—that transmit messages about us, our education, status in the community, etc. (Ch. 3)

Assertive Able to express true feelings and opinions honestly and comfortably, and able to say no without feeling guilty. (Ch. 1)

Audience analysis Finding out as much as possible about the make-up of an audience. The more you know about the members of the audience, the more effectively you'll be able to communicate with them. (Ch. 6)

Audiovisual aids Material that helps a speaker clarify and reinforce his or her message; photographs, cartoons, objects, videotape, and so on. (Ch. 12)

Bibliography A listing of authors and sources of information on a particular subject. (Ch. 7)

Body (of speech) The central part of a speech, which contains the key information, ideas, or emotions to be communicated by a speaker to the audience. (Ch. 8)

Body language See *nonverbal communication.* (Ch. 2, 3)

Brainstorming A stimulating exercise using the imagination for the purpose of generating as many ideas as possible. (Ch. 14)

Browser A client application that enables a user to view the markup language used for documents on the Web and then perform certain applications. (Ch. 7)

Buzz sessions Small groups of people who gather to try to solve a common problem. All of the participating groups collectively present their proposed solutions. (Ch. 14)

Card catalog A file of cards listing all books in a library by author's name, title, and subject and indicating where they may be found. (Ch. 7)

Causal reasoning Establishing a relationship between causes and effects. (Ch. 11)

CD-ROM (Compact Disk—Read Only Memory) The term applied to a variety of storage formats by which audio, text, and graphics are retrieved from the disk by laser beam. (Ch. 7)

Chairperson One who presides over a meeting, panel, forum, round-table discussion, or symposium; a moderator or discussion leader. (Ch. 14)

Chromatics The study and application of color as a mode of nonverbal communication. (Ch. 3)

Chronemics The study of time as a mode of communication. (Ch. 3)

Cite To quote from a book, a speech, a magazine article or some other source. (Ch. 7)

Clichés Expressions that have been around and used for so long that they have become virtually meaningless. (Ch. 6)

Codes Messages or methods of communication. (Ch. 3)

Committee A small group of people delegated to investigate, consider, report, or act on a matter. (Ch. 14)

Communication In this book, the interpersonal exchange of ideas and feelings between speaker and listeners. (throughout text)

Conclusion (of speech) The ending of a speech, which often sums up the main points or stresses the major idea. A conclusion should contain no new material. (Ch. 8)

Concrete words Words that pertain to objects you can perceive through the senses; tangible things. (Ch. 6)

Consensus Unanimous agreement from all group members on a decision or solution. (Ch. 14)

Consonant A speech sound produced by a partial or total stoppage of the air stream— for example, the letters *t, k, f, b, p*. (Ch. 5)

Converging technologies The joining of two or more disparate technologies. For example, a multimedia presentation can include text, photos, a video clip, and sound coming together using a graphic-based computer software application delivered via telecommunications technology. (Ch. 12)

Credibility The degree to which a speaker and/or his or her message is considered believable. (Ch. 3, 11)

Database A large collection of information stored in a well-organized format that can be retrieved by specific software. (Ch. 7)

Deductive reasoning Making deductions or drawing conclusions. It involves moving from a general principle to a specific principle. (Ch. 11)

Delivery The way a speech is given; it can be read, memorized, or spoken extemporaneously (with or without notes after preparation beforehand). Delivery may also refer to the use of the voice. (Ch. 9)

Demonstration talk A talk intended to show how to do or how to make something or to explain how something functions with the use of audiovisual aids. (Ch. 12)

Diction Pronunciation and enunciation of words: clarity, intelligibility, and distinctness are essential in public speaking. (Ch. 5)

Digitization To translate into digital form—for example, scan a photograph and save it to a floppy disk for viewing through a graphic interface. (Ch. 12)

Download To transmit data from a central to a remote computer, from a file server to a workstation, or from a computer to a floppy disk. (Ch. 7)

Duration Length of time that vowel sounds are held. (Ch. 5)

Easel An upright three-legged frame on which to display something. (Ch. 12)

Editorialize To offer one's opinion, as opposed to a factual account. (Ch. 13)

E-mail Electronic mail. Tool for sending messages over the Internet. (Ch. 7)

Empathy The ability to experience another person's feelings; "putting yourself in the other person's shoes." (Ch. 9)

Enthusiasm Interest, animation, emphasis, and excitement conveyed while speaking. (Ch. 9)

Enunciate To pronounce every syllable of a word clearly and distinctly; to articulate. (Ch. 5)

Ethics The branch of philosophy dealing with values relating to human conduct. Doing the right thing. (Ch. 1)

Ethnocentrism Believing that your own ethnic group, nationality, or culture is superior to others. (Ch. 6)

Ethos Speaker credibility. (Ch. 11)

Eulogy Also referred to as a speech of tribute. A speech given to honor the deceased. (Ch. 13)

Evaluative listening Questioning the validity of the speaker's message and credibility. (Ch. 4)

Evidence Facts and/or expert testimony to support a person's position or statements. (Ch. 11)

Expert opinion Testimony by a recognized authority in his or her field. Such testimony is admissible in a court of law. (Ch. 11)

Extemporaneous Researched, thought about, outlined, rehearsed, and then delivered with or without notes. (Ch. 9)

Eye contact A communicative two-way relationship in which a speaker constantly looks at the listeners and reacts to their feedback (cheers, boos, facial expressions, gestures). (Ch. 2, 3)

Fact Any information which can be substantiated and is documented. (Ch. 11)

Feedback The audience's verbal or nonverbal reaction to your message. (Ch. 3)

Field One of many sections that come together to constitute an electronic record. (Ch. 7)

Forum A public speaking situation in which members of the audience are allowed to participate by asking questions or making comments. (Ch. 14)

General meeting A gathering of all active members of an organization. (Ch. 14)

Gestures Movements by hands, arms, head, shoulders, or body to emphasize or clarify spoken thoughts and emotions. (Ch. 2)

Gobbledygook Language that is hard to understand because of its wordy jargon. A master of this type of verbosity is the government. (Ch. 6)

Group discussion The verbal and nonverbal interaction among five to twenty people who are engaged in a discussion with a specific purpose and objective. (Ch. 14)

Handout Printed information distributed to members of the audience. (Ch. 10)

Haptics The study of touch as a mode of communication. (Ch. 3)

Hypertext A section of web-page text that responds to a user command by establishing a connection to a file of information. (Ch. 1)

Identification with audience Associating oneself with the ideas, opinions, and feelings of listeners, usually in an attempt to persuade them. (Ch. 11)

Impromptu talk A talk given on the spur of the moment, without prior notice or time for preparation. (Ch. 9)

Inductive reasoning The reverse of deductive reasoning; starts with specific examples or cases and ends with a general conclusion based on the examples or cases. (Ch. 11)

Inferences Drawing a conclusion or generalization based on observation, experience, and/or logic. (Ch. 11)

Inflection A change, up or down, in vocal tone or pitch. (Ch. 3, 5)

Informative talks Communication in which the chief aim is to share knowledge and understanding with the audience. (Ch. 10)

Internet An electronic network linking computers together, originally called ARPANET, the Advanced Research Projects Agency of the U.S. Department of Defense. (Ch. 7)

Interpersonal communication A verbal or nonverbal exchange of ideas, knowledge, and feelings between two or more people. (throughout text)

Introduction (of speech) The part of a speech in which the speaker usually explains the purpose and scope of the speech and, at the same time, tries to win audience interest and goodwill. (Ch. 8)

ISP Internet Service Provider. Establishes connections between computers and the Internet. (Ch. 7)

Kinesics The study of body movements, such as posture, facial expressions, arm movement, and so on. (Ch. 3)

Laser pointer An instrument the size of a fountain pen that emits a beam that produces a small red dot on any surface. (Ch. 12)

LCD (liquid crystal display) panel Device positioned between a computer monitor and a projector to display a computer screen image on a screen or wall. (Ch. 12)

Lectern A speaker's stand with a slanted top that supports the notes (if any) of a speaker; a lectern may rest on a table or floor. See *podium*. (Ch. 2)

Lecture An exposition of a given subject to a group for the purpose of disseminating information. (Ch. 14)

Link A hypertext screen section, usually underlined words or a framed graphic, that responds to a user's command to move from one file of information to another on a web page or to another web site. (Ch. 7)

Liquid crystal display See *LCD*. (Ch. 7)

Listening Making an effort to hear and understand a speaker's statement. (Ch. 4)

Loaded words Words concerning race, religion, politics, or personal character that can produce overpowering, negative reactions. (Ch. 6)

Manuscript Copy that is written out word for word. (Ch. 9)

MC Master of ceremonies. (Ch. 8, 13)

Meeting A gathering of people to discuss topics of mutual concern and perhaps to make decisions on them. (Ch. 14)

Moderator A group leader whose basic responsibilities include introducing the members of a panel and its subject, presiding over a smooth and fair discussion, bringing the discussion to a close, and allowing questions from the audience. (Ch. 14)

Modes of communication Certain elements that communicate messages, often non-verbally—for example, facial expressions, eye contact, gestures, objects, space, time, touch, and paralanguage. (Ch. 3)

Monorate The tendency to speak each syllable, word, phrase, and sentence at the same rate of speed. (Ch. 5)

Monotone The tendency of a voice not to move up and down the tone scale, thus resulting in very little expression. The voice sounds flat, dull, and boring. (Ch. 5)

Motivation An inner drive, impulse, or incentive that causes a person to do something or to act in a certain way. (Ch. 11)

Nervousness An emotional state characterized by tension or fear. (Ch. 2)

Nonverbal communication The transmission and reception of messages, knowingly or unknowingly, other than by spoken words: through facial expressions; eye contact; posture; and gestures by hands, arms, head, shoulders, and body. Also known as body language, silent language, and soundless speech. (Ch. 2, 3)

Note cards 3-inch-by-5-inch or 5-inch-by-7-inch cards on which key ideas are written or printed to aid a speaker's memory. (Ch. 7)

Online Connected to the Internet. (Ch. 7)

Opinion One's personal beliefs or thoughts, not necessarily based on facts. (Ch. 11)

Oral visualization Conveying a message by feeling, experiencing, or reliving the ideas and emotions one wishes to communicate. (Ch. 5)

Outline A plan of a talk that lists the topics and subtopics, plus their major and minor backup points. (Ch. 8)

Pacing Creating an interesting rate and variety of delivery that will hold your listeners' interest. For example, you may slow down or speed up your delivery, or you may use pauses. (Ch. 5)

Panels Discussion groups of three to six or more people, led by a moderator or chair, who explore a subject. The purpose is to inquire, deliberate, and enlighten, not to argue and persuade. Audiences usually ask questions after the panelists have spoken. (Ch. 14)

Paralanguage How you say it as opposed to what you say. Some elements of paralanguage, or vocalics, are the quality of the voice, its pitch, rate of delivery, inflection, emphasis, and pauses. (Ch. 3)

Parallel construction The repeated use of the same words, phrases, or clauses in a sentence or paragraph to achieve greater impact. (Ch. 6)

Paraphrase Rewriting material in your own style and in about the same number of words as the original. (Ch. 7)

Parliamentary procedure A strict set of rules to follow during a meeting so as to maintain order and ensure fairness to to all participants. (Ch. 14)

Pauses Momentary silences in speaking. They can stress a point, separate ideas, and give a speaker time to organize his or her thoughts. (Ch. 3)

PDA (Personal Digital Assistant) A handheld device that combines computing, telephone/fax, and networking features; also called a palmtop, handheld computer, or a pocket computer. (Ch. 7)

Persuasive speaking Speaking that tries, by logical reasoning and emotional appeals, to convince listeners to change their opinions, to hold fast to them, or to perform an action recommended by the speaker. (Ch. 11)

Pitch The highness or lowness of a voice. Normal pitch should allow a speaker to comfortably raise or lower his or her voice for varied expression. (Ch. 5)

Plagiarism The act of taking ideas and opinions, or actual wording, from another and passing them off as one's own. (Ch. 1, 7)

Plosives Initial sounds produced by the sudden release of breath, such as *k*, *p*, and *t*. (Ch. 13)

Podium An elevated platform or stage, not to be confused with lectern or speaker's stand. (Ch. 2)

Prolongation Extension of the duration of a vowel sound. (Ch. 5)

Proxemics The study of space as a mode of communication. (Ch. 3)

Public address (PA) system An electronic amplification system used in halls or auditoriums so that speakers can be heard by a large audience. (Ch. 13)

Purpose What you want your audience to get from your speech. (Ch. 8)

Question-and-answer period A portion of time, after a talk, when the speaker answers questions from the audience. (Ch. 2)

Rate of speaking The average number of words spoken in one minute. The average person speaks between 130 and 160 words a minute. (Ch. 5)

Reasoning The forming of conclusions based on known or assumed facts; the use of reason. (Ch. 11)

Reflective Thinking Process A method of thinking involving five steps that was developed by educational philosopher John Dewey. (Ch. 14)

Round-table discussion A meeting in which several people sit at a table and, under a moderator or chair, discuss a given topic. See *forum, panel discussion*, and *symposium*. (Ch. 14)

Search engine A World Wide Web tool designed to look for and display information in response to a user's query. (Ch. 7)

Self-image What and how one thinks of oneself. (Ch. 3)

Silent language See *nonverbal communication*. (Ch. 2)

Slang Informal language that doesn't conform to standard usage. (Ch. 6)

Sloppy speech Careless speech habits such as poor pronunciation, diction, and articulation; not sounding all the syllables within words or word endings. (Ch. 5)

Small-group discussion A discussion in which as few as five or as many as twenty people may participate. There are many types of small-group discussion. (Ch. 14)

Soundless speech See *nonverbal communication*. (Ch. 2)

Space The distance between a speaker and listeners. Space may affect the quality of communication. (Ch. 3)

Speaker's stand See *lectern*. (Ch. 2)

Speaking apprehension See *nervousness*. (Ch. 2)

Special-occasion talks Speeches given under special circumstances and for a particular reason: presenting or accepting an award, nominating a candidate for office, making an announcement, and so on. (Ch. 13)

Speech tension See *nervousness*. (Ch. 2)

Stage fright Nervousness felt by the vast majority of speakers, both before and during speaking. (Ch. 2)

Summary The essence of a work, for example, the essence of an important paragraph in a few sentences. (Ch. 7)

Symposium A panel in which participants speak on specific phases of the same question. Then the participants answer questions from the audience. (Ch. 14)

Talk radio A radio program presided over by a host who encourages opinions and questions, by phone, from the general public. (Ch. 1)

Thesaurus A book of synonyms and antonyms. (Ch. 9)

Thesis statement A sentence that states the main purpose of a talk. (Ch. 7, 8)

Title A name, phrase, or sentence of a speech, book, chapter, poem, play, movie, etc., briefly depicting the content of the subject and/or to pique the audience's or reader's interest in the subject. (Ch. 8)

Touch In the context of this book, communication with a person with one's fingers or hands to express a meaning or emotion. (Ch. 3)

Transitions Words, phrases, or sentences that smoothly connect parts of a talk. (Ch. 8)

Transparency A positive film or slide with an image that is visible when light shines through it; usually projected onto a screen. (Ch. 12)

Videocassette recorder (VCR) A magnetic tape instrument that records audio and video signals; the recording can be played back any number of times. (Ch. 7)

Vocal pitch The level of tone—low, medium, high—of a voice. (Ch. 3)

Vocal volume The loudness or softness of a speaker's voice. (Ch. 5)

Vocalics See *paralanguage*. (Ch. 3)

Vocalized pause A distracting hesitation filled with vocal "static" such as *ah, er, like, right, you know,* and so on. It is caused by habit, nervousness, or both and can be cured by conscious effort. (Ch. 5, 6)

Vowel The strongest sound in most syllables; the letters *a, e, i, o, u,* and occasionally *y.* (Ch. 5)

World Wide Web An international collection of information searchable using text or graphic browsers. (Ch. 7)

Credits

Photo

Page 1: Bob Daemmrich/Stock Boston; 22: Photo courtesy of Debee Tlumacki Photos/The Patriot Ledger; 48: AP/Wide World Photos; 73: Republished with permission of Globe Newspaper Company, Inc; 91: AP/Wide World Photos; 111: Ben Nighthorse Campbell, by Glenn Asakawa/Rocky Mountain News, 1993. Reprinted with permission of the Rocky Mountain News; 142: Index Stock Photography; 168: Uniphoto; 196: AP/Wide World Photos; 217: South Light/Gamma-Liaison; 239: Reuters/Gary Cameron/Archives Photos; 275: AP/Wide World Photos; 300: Reuters/NASA/Archive Photos; 322: David Young-Wolff/PhotoEdit; 344: Jim Whitmer Photography

Text

Page 65: From *Silent Language* by Edward T. Hall, copyright © 1959, 1981 by Edward T. Hall. Used by permission of Doubleday, a division of Random House, Inc.

Page 69: From *How to Read a Person Like a Book* by Gerard I. Nierenberg and Henry H. Calero, copyright © 1971 by Gerard I. Nierenberg and Henry H. Calero. Used by permission of Dutton, a division of Penguin Group (USA) Inc.

Page 375: Reprinted by arrangement with the Estate of Martin Luther King Jr., c/o Writers House as agent for the proprietor, New York, NY. Copyright © 1963 Dr. Martin Luther King, Jr., copyright renewed 1991 by Coretta Scott King.